LINKING CITIZENS TO GOVERNMENT

LINKING CITIZENS TO GOVERNMENT

INTEREST GROUP POLITICS
AT COMMON CAUSE

LAWRENCE S. ROTHENBERG
University of Rochester

CAMBRIDGE
UNIVERSITY PRESS

Published by the Press Syndicate of the University of Cambridge
The Pitt Building, Trumpington Street, Cambridge CB2 1RP
40 West 20th Street, New York, NY 10011-4211, USA
10 Stamford Road, Oakleigh, Victoria 3166, Australia

First published 1992

Printed in the United States of America

Library of Congress Cataloging-in-Publication Data
Rothenberg, Lawrence S. Linking citizens to government: interest group politics at
Common Cause
/ Lawrence S. Rothenberg.
p. cm.
Includes bibliographical references and index.
ISBN 0-521-41560-8 (hardback). – ISBN 0-521-42577-8 (paperback)
1. Common Cause (U.S.) 2. Pressure groups – United States.
3. Lobbying – United States. I. Title.
JK1118.R68 1992 91–31621
324′.4′0973 – dc20 CIP

A catalog record for this book is available from the British Library.

ISBN 0-521-41560-8 hardback
ISBN 0-521-42577-8 paperback

To Barbara

Contents

List of figures   *page* xi
List of tables   xii
Preface   xv

1 Organized groups and the political system   1
   Understanding organized groups: The lack of consensus   1
   Moving ahead   4
   The focus of analysis: Common Cause   7
   Some caveats   12
   Structure of the analysis   13

2 A unified framework for understanding citizens' decision
   making: A theory of experiential search   15
   Toward a unified view   15
   General analytic approaches to citizens' decision making   15
   Members' decision making   17
   A theory of experiential search   21
   Common Cause and experiential search   24
   Conclusions: Experiential search as a unified framework   28

3 Who contributes?   29
   Common Cause members: Painting a portrait   29
   Common Cause members and the national citizenry   30
     Sociodemographic differences   31
     Political attitudes   36
     Participatory activities   41
     Summary   42
   The Common Cause membership: Activists versus rank
   and file   43
     Sociodemographic differences   44
     Political attitudes   47
     Participatory activities   54
     Summary   56

Conclusions: Group members – external and internal
comparisons   56
Appendix 3.1. Question wording of Common Cause and
National Election Study questions   58
   General political attitudes   58
   Specific political attitudes   59
   Participatory activities   62

4 Why do citizens join groups?   63
   Joining – the first step   63
   Studying the membership choice   64
   Why members think they joined   66
   The determinants of membership: An individual-level
   analysis   69
     Measurement   75
     Estimation   77
     Results   78
   An aggregate-level replication   82
   Choosing among public interest groups   86
   Conclusions: The determinants of membership   93
   Appendix 4.1. Critique of Kau and Rubin   95
   Appendix 4.2. Formal presentation of WESML estimator 99

5 The internal politics of organizations I: Learning and
  retention   100
   Life in the organization   100
   Do members learn?   102
   Exploring the retention process   108
     Measurement   110
     Understanding retention   111
   A validity check   120
   Conclusions: Learning, the retention choice, and
   experiential search   123
   Appendix 5.1. Testing the retention model   124

6 The internal politics of organizations II: Activism   127
   Separating the activists from the rank and file   127
   Checkbook versus temporal activism   128
   Checkbook activism and its determinants   130
   Temporal activism: An introduction   134
   Alternative scenarios   136
   The costs and benefits of Common Cause activism   137
   An empirical test: Activism and Common Cause   139
     Measurement and estimation   140
     Results   144

Activism: A validity test 151
A final note: Activism and retention as a joint commitment
decision 152
Conclusions: Moving up 156

7 The internal politics of organizations III: Leadership
behavior and the determinants of group goals 158
Moving from the "demand" to the "supply" side 158
Democratic processes at Common Cause 160
Members' attitudes toward representation 166
Shifting the issue agenda 169
The MX missile debate 171
A strange match: Common Cause versus MX 173
Theoretical perspectives on organizational goals 176
Common Cause, goal formation, and the MX missile 180
Making sense of it all: The politics of organizational goals 186
Conclusions: Leadership behavior and goal formation 187

8 Does group activity make a difference? The case of the
MX missile 190
The policy linkage 190
Lobbying strategy and voting behavior 194
Setting the stage: The battle for the Peacekeeper 196
The role of the MX's opponents 202
Does lobbying make a difference? 203
Measurement and estimation 205
Results 209
The structural determinants of lobbying 215
Conclusions: Voting, lobbying, and public policy 221

9 Does group activity make a difference? The politics of
campaign finance 223
Returning to course 223
Campaign finance, the MX, and Common Cause 224
Charting the divisions 229
Events of 1985–1991 234
The entrepreneurs: Boren and Byrd 235
The first offensive: The push for PAC reform 237
The second offensive: Byrd joins the fray 241
Life after Byrd 244
Common Cause and campaign finance reform 247
Conclusions: Coalition formation and group influence 252

10 Conclusions: Citizens' preferences, internal politics, and
public policy 255

Interest groups and representation   255
Individual choice, internal politics, and systemic
influence   256
   Individual choice behavior   257
   Internal politics and goal formation   259
   Systemic impact   260
The big picture   262
   Linking citizens to policy   262
   Viewing organizations   265
Some final thoughts   266

Notes   267
References   293
Index   303

Figures

1.1 Groups and the political system: A schematic   *page* 5
1.2 Common Cause membership over time   11
2.1 Organizational membership as experiential search   25
3.1 Geographic distribution of Common Cause membership
     (membership/voting age population)   35
4.1 A model of contribution behavior   76
5.1 Retention predictions and organizational experience   118
6.1 Probability of activism and organizational experience   150
8.1 Determinants of congressional vote choice   197
8.2 Lobbying and fence straddling   219
9.1 Possible campaign finance reform strategies   235
9.2 Support for the Boren initiative   240

Tables

3.1 Common Cause members and the national electorate: Selected sociodemographic characteristics *page* 32

3.2 Common Cause members and the national electorate: General policy preferences 37

3.3 Common Cause members and the national electorate: Participatory activity 42

3.4 Comparing rank and file and activists: Selected sociodemographic characteristics 44

3.5 Comparing rank and file and activists: General policy preferences 48

3.6 Comparing rank and file and activists: Policy preferences on nongroup issues 49

3.7 Comparing rank and file and activists: Policy preferences on group issues 52

3.8 Comparing rank and file and activists: Participatory activity 55

4.1 Members' proclaimed reasons for joining Common Cause 67

4.2 Sources of initial information about Common Cause 72

4.3 Determinants of group membership (WESML estimates) 79

4.4 Determinants of aggregate membership (group logit estimates) 85

4.5 Determinants of initial membership choice, nonprioritized model (WESML estimates comparing groups to League of Women Voters) 89

4.6 Determinants of initial membership choice, prioritized model (WESML estimates comparing groups to League of Women Voters) 91

4.7 Classification of initial decisions by group (column/row percentages) 93

4.8 Tests of Kau and Rubin model (WESML estimates) 97

5.1 Organizational experience and knowledge about group 103

5.2a Organizational experience and group issue opinions (percentage of Common Cause members without opinions) 105

5.2b Organizational experience and personal issue opinions (percentage of Common Cause members without opinions) 106

5.3   Determinants of retention decisions   112
5.4   Cost sensitivity and income level   114
5.5   Retention decisions of newcomers and veterans   119
5.6   Determinants of retention: Four-group study (probit estimates
      with standard errors in parentheses)   122
6.1   Determinants of checkbook activism (logit estimates)   132
6.2   How contributors became Common Cause activists   141
6.3   Determinants of activism (WESML estimates)   143
6.4   Probability of activism   146
6.5   Determinants of activism: Four-group study (probit estimates
      with standard errors in parentheses)   153
6.6   Joint determinants of activism and retention: Four-group
      study (probit estimates with standard errors in parentheses)   155
7.1   Results of issue polls on the appropriate role of Common
      Cause: 1987–1991   163
7.2   Members' attitudes about internal politics   167
7.3   Members' attitudes toward increased defense spending   183
8.1   MX House votes analyzed   207
8.2   Determinants of anti-MX voting (HR5167), 1984 (probit
      estimates with standard errors in parentheses)   210
8.3   Determinants of anti-MX voting (SJRES71 & HR1872), 1985
      (probit estimates with standard errors in parentheses)   211
8.4   Effects of anti-MX lobbying on vote outcomes (estimates of
      number of anti-MX votes for those lobbied)   214
8.5   Determinants of anti-MX lobbying (HR5167), 1984 (probit
      estimates with standard errors in parentheses)   216
8.6   Determinants of anti-MX lobbying (SJRES71 & HR1872), 1985
      (probit estimates with standard errors in parentheses)   217

Preface

While many studies have peculiar odysseys, that of the present work certainly qualifies as idiosyncratic. In early 1987, in my first year of teaching, I confronted a handful (three) of undergraduate students at the California Institute of Technology. As a group, they were bright, scientific, lacked any interest in making a long-term commitment to social science, and had no idea (but they knew that they were skeptical) of what research outside the hard sciences looks like.

Rather than force the class to take a standard walk through textbooks and watered down versions of social scientific theories and findings, I decided to concentrate on the real thing by emphasizing the actual practice of research. I thought it would be more interesting both for these scientists and engineers and for me if they developed a real understanding of how the other half lived.

Thus, in order to allow my students to gain a taste of what it meant to do social science research, I asked Jonathon Siegel, an old graduate student friend, to send a data set that he had collected but had never quite got around to analyzing and he, collegially, agreed. Out of fairness to the students, I announced that I too would do a project and present it to the class just as they would present their own research.

Needless to say, I got engrossed. My class project turned into an *American Political Science Review* article and I was off to the races. A break from transforming my dissertation into published work – a three-week commitment – became an on-and-off project for five years, involving considerable data collection, a number of trips to Washington, and all else that conducting a major research project entails.

Along the way, I have encountered a host of people to thank. Parts of this project have been presented in seminars at the California Institute of Technology, the University of California at Berkeley, the University of Rochester, and Stanford University, and at the American, Midwest, Southern, and Western Political Science Association meetings. Thanks to all those who gave such valuable feedback during these encounters. I would also like to single out David Austen-Smith, Larry Bartels, Richard Fenno, Mark Hansen, Bruce Jacobs, Rod Kiewiet, Morgan Kousser, Keith Krehbiel, James Lindsay,

Terry Moe, Jonathan Nagler, David Weimer, and John Wright. Thanks also to Linda Donnelly, Jeffrey Flynt, Brian Mau, and Phyllis Pugh, for research and typing assistance.

Among those who deserve special mention for service beyond the call of duty are Jon Siegel; Bruce Cain, who provided special encouragement during the project's early stages; Tom Gilligan, who furnished similar encouragement; David Grether, who made funds available as Chairman of the Division of Humanities and Social Sciences at Cal Tech during the early stages of the project; Jeffrey Dubin, for skilled econometric assistance; Fred Wertheimer, who was generous with his time and interceded on my behalf even though he had never met me; and Bing Powell, who fought for needed funds when I moved to the University of Rochester. The University, through a Summer Research Grant and the Public Policy Analysis Program, also deserves thanks for underwriting some of my forays to Washington. A special note of gratitude goes to Andrew McFarland who, rather than viewing me as intruding on his turf, supplied valuable comments on the entire manuscript and generally was helpful in all conceivable respects.

Thanks also to Emily Loose of Cambridge University Press, who provided the impetus for me to take the plunge and commit to writing a book. Her guiding of the manuscript through the various publication stages is greatly appreciated.

A special mention also must go to my wife, Barbara, who made life eventful and painstakingly edited every page of this manuscript. Not many marital units could put up with one spouse systematically tearing apart the carefully crafted words of the other – especially when the latter's response varied with the mood swing of the day.

1

Organized groups and the political system

Organized groups are a pervasive element in the American political land-scape. Over time, the interest group system itself has exploded in numbers and diversity (e.g., Walker 1983). Not surprisingly, the study of organized interests has traditionally constituted one of the hallmarks of social scientists' quest to understand the American political system. For the better part of a century, scholars – sociologists, economists, and especially political scientists – have proposed theoretical alternatives (e.g., Bentley 1908; Truman 1951; Latham 1952; Olson 1965), conducted detailed case studies (e.g., Garceau 1941; McConnell 1953; Bauer et al. 1963), and generated propositions about the role that organizations play in the larger political system (e.g., Dahl 1961; Lindblom 1977; Lowi 1979).

Through their efforts, social scientists have made considerable headway on any number of fronts. Yet, at the same time, those assessing overall progress have exhibited a certain frustration about the pace at which gains have been made in the past quarter century (Arnold 1982; Cigler 1989).

Perhaps most notably, there remains little consensus about the importance of associations in determining how the political system operates. This dis-agreement is pervasive: It encompasses both the extent to which groups are believed to have an influence on public policy and how they function as organizations as well. It is reflected not only in the discourse of scholars, but in the commentaries of popular critics and even in the statements of group participants themselves.

For example, although much of the news media focuses on the efforts of formal political leaders – legislators, presidents, cabinet secretaries, and members of the judiciary – a core of modern-day progressives exists who are ardent critics of most organizations and their allegedly undue influence (e.g., Jackson 1988; Stern 1988). These critics lament how special interests control politics; frequently they claim that these collectivities consist of an oligarchic leadership that directs politicians through the leverage provided by honoraria, campaign contributions, the offer of future employment, nefarious lobby-

ing techniques, or sundry other means at their disposal. More mainstream observers may note examples of ethical transgressions or instances where it is believed that mobilized interests play a major role, but such commentators rarely imply that associations and the resources they wield are the guiding forces in American politics.

Analogously, organizational participants in the political process often exhibit a self-serving schizophrenia when it comes to assessing their importance. When the inference is that interest groups are corrupting the political process, participants are "strategically modest" (Pertschuk and Schaetzel 1989, p. 9) and maintain that they play only a limited, indeed a beneficial, role. Alternately, in promoting their own associations, "institutional and ego needs" (ibid.) motivate a party line that frequently centers on claims about the considerable impact that the organization has on the political status quo. While such posturing is not surprising, little can be inferred from it about the effectiveness of organized interests in the political system.

Most important, this ambivalence about organizations and politics carries over into the social scientific world. Indeed, in the academic sphere the disagreement about the role of interest groups is evidenced on two levels: how collectivities are conceptualized as part of the political process and what inferences are drawn about organizational influence.

On the first level – how groups should be theoretically conceptualized vis-à-vis the larger political system – the principal divide among social scientists (now largely disciplinary in nature) is whether organizations are considered to be the fundamental building blocks of politics or simply constituent components that may or may not have an influence on the outputs of government. During the first half of this century, the former perspective was in vogue among political scientists. They tended to place collectivities at the center of political analysis in proposing group theories of politics (Bentley 1908; Truman 1951; Latham 1952). Attempts to fashion a theory of politics around the role of groups have long been discredited among the vast preponderance of contemporary political scientists; they have concentrated instead on identifying where groups fit into the political system.

To the extent that the traditional political science viewpoint continues to exist in the world of social science, it is embodied in the work of "Chicago school" economists such as George Stigler (1971), Sam Peltzman (1976, 1984), and Gary Becker (1983, 1985), and their followers (for recent reviews, see Mitchell 1990 and Mitchell and Munger 1991).[1] These scholars concentrate on deriving mathematical approximations of the political process in which formal institutions tend to be, more or less, black boxes through which groups operate, and the driving force in the political environment is the "influence" created by group demands.

However, few outside the Chicago school subscribe to this vision of group dominance. The Chicago approach is criticized by most other scholars as being too vague in its description of what makes groups influential, very

difficult to falsify because few definitive hypotheses can be derived from the models, and too simplistic in placing formal institutions in a black box. Most social scientists working within other research traditions reject the assumption that organizations are the essential component of the political system. For them, the germane issue is determining whether, and to what extent, associations are important.

Among those with intellectual roots that extend beyond the reaches of Chicago economics, there is considerable disagreement about the importance of associations. Some argue that such collectivities are a consequential part of the political decision-making process through their application of technical and political expertise, their mobilization of constituent pressure through the grassroots, and their strategic utilization of campaign contributions and that they therefore require careful monitoring. Others, while not necessarily dismissing organizations as completely ineffectual, maintain that group influence is largely ephemeral; they focus instead on the pertinence of formal institutions and the preferences of the electorate. For example, efforts to establish the efficacy of political action committee (PAC) contributions have proven highly problematic (e.g., Wright 1985). Organizations, in the words of one notable scholar, "come to Washington [to a large extent] out of need and dependence rather than because they have influence" (Salisbury 1990, p. 229).

Why is there such variance among scholars about the effect of groups? To answer this question requires citing at least three interrelated factors.

1. *The difficulty of doing research.* There are many admirable efforts, but conducting precise quantitative analysis in this field is notoriously difficult. The econometric problems faced in analyzing interest groups' role in the political system are legion: the pitfalls of gathering good data on a host of group characteristics (e.g., budgets, expenditures, membership); the frustrations of trying to disentangle the simultaneous effects of organizations on different sides of political issues, even when the available information appears at first blush to be of high quality (e.g., with reports on political contributions)[2]; and the problems of developing data on a control group, when those are needed (for instance, to study who joins these organizations). When scholars are forced to rely heavily on either quantitative results derived from imperfect data or qualitative information (which is not plentiful either), findings – if they exist at all – tend to be contradictory and heavily disputed.

2. *As part of a larger discipline, the study of organized groups has tended to get lost in the shuffle.* Given the difficulties of analyzing organizations and the aforementioned movement away from group-centered theories of politics, the study of associations in American politics has become sporadic. The low watermark for organizational analysis commenced in the mid-1960s after the publication of two seminal works that cast doubt on the need to

pay attention to groups. In *American Business and Public Policy* (1963) Bauer, Poole, and Dexter suggested that the effect of group lobbying was far smaller than many had previously thought. Olson argued in *The Logic of Collective Action* (1965) that groups are very difficult to form and that political concerns generally do not constitute the basis of organizational formation and maintenance. While a number of notable works followed in the next quarter century (a few examples are Salisbury 1969, Lowi 1979, and Moe 1980a), it has become widely accepted that the analysis of interest groups is an undertilled area of political science (Arnold 1982; Cigler 1989).

3. *The fragmentation of current research.* A final reason for the present confusion in understanding organized entities is that the analysis of interest groups is fragmented. Many of the reasons have already been discussed. Research is difficult and groups are frequently not considered to be at the core of political analysis. Scholars who consider themselves experts in other substantive areas – Congress, the bureaucracy, elections, political participation – analyze interest groups only because these entities happen to impinge on their areas of concern. Consequently, research, much of it of very high quality, tends to focus only on small pieces of the whole. Social scientists study the decision to join groups, the role of money in influencing roll call votes, or the efforts of a set of interests to affect a given governmental decision. As Allan Cigler puts it, "Interest group politics is a 'catch all' subfield ... [whose scope] will continue to broaden" (1989, pp. 48–9). Rarely outside of textbooks is any effort made to draw the linkages necessary for understanding the role that associations play.

Thus, while interest groups have been on the rise empirically, their traditionally central role in the study of politics has waned. Of course, important work has been carried out from a variety of perspectives and much has been learned in the process; nonetheless, few would deny that organized interests have been given low priority in the academic division of labor.

Perhaps the biggest price attached to the combination of related factors noted – the difficulty of doing research, the low priority given for many years to understanding groups, and the fragmentation of research on organizations – is the previously mentioned failure of students of politics to develop a consensus about the role that organizations play. Notably, because organizations are so frequently viewed somewhat peripherally, the bottom line is that there is no integrated perspective on groups. This translates into disagreements about exactly where organizations fit into the political scheme of things.

MOVING AHEAD

Thus, while much has been accomplished with respect to understanding organized interests, more remains to be done. But what exactly should scholars be doing to further their understanding of associations?

The answer advanced in this analysis, but certainly not the only one that is reasonable, is to focus on developing and applying an *integrated perspective on organizations*. Rather than selecting one small piece of the larger whole and examining it in isolation, an effort must be made to analyze interest groups in broad perspective. To understand a part of the political environment such as organized interests requires drawing together the various elements that are important for determining group success qua organization and as a political force in the external environment.

This, it should be emphasized, is neither a call for a new group theory of politics nor an endorsement of the Chicago school of thought. Rather, it is a recommendation for bringing interest groups fully back into the picture as a constituent unit in the study of politics.

One purpose of the present study is to make the case, in a modest fashion, for an integrated perspective about organized interests by demonstrating what it might look like and then applying it in practice. The research strategy adopted in this analysis follows the organizational process from the "ground up" – from leaders' decisions about how to structure a group, to the initial choice of citizens to join, to the resulting members' decisions about the nature and extent of their contributions, through the internal organizational processes that lead to decisions about organizational goals, and up to the

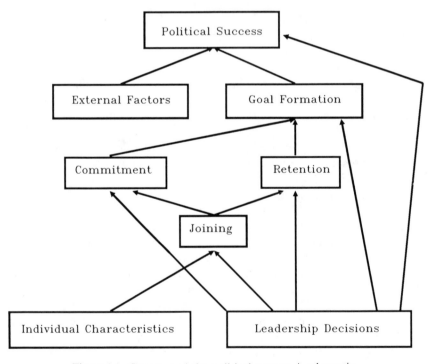

Figure 1.1. Groups and the political system: A schematic.

effects of the group's efforts on the larger political system. This entails more than examining a whole host of questions separately. Rather, the more grandiose intent is to try to see how the various pieces fit together into an interlocking whole and to focus on what impact this perspective has on understanding the political system.

Put another way, the focus of this enterprise is to draw as many of the crucial linkages in the group process as possible. In a rather simplistic manner, these connections are sketched for membership groups in the schematic presented as Figure 1.1.

The first questions about a group that readily spring to mind focus principally upon citizens' decision making – with the acknowledgment that leadership choices shape the organization and the decisions that individuals must make.[3] Thus, for example, an intuitive question about any membership organization is Who are its supporters? Why do these people, rather than another group of individuals in the larger population, join this particular association? Once they join, why do some stay in the organization while others depart? And why are some contributors active and others inert?

Answering these questions inevitably directs attention away from a primary focus on individuals and toward leaders and, ultimately, the larger political system. Perhaps an even more fundamental question for political analysis is Does joining, activism, or the threat of departure have an impact on the behavior of group leaders in determining organizational goals? And – probably the ultimate question for a political scientist: Does the organization, in turn, actually structure the decisions made in the larger political environment, whether it be Congress, the bureaucracy, the White House, or the judicial branch?

To make matters more complicated, Figure 1.1 is a simplified version of the world in two respects. One is that while the sequence of questions posed seems to imply that influence is unidirectional, this is unlikely to be the case. Feedback mechanisms undoubtedly operate within this system of relationships. For example, does what goes on in the larger political world actually have an impact on the association's health (i.e., joining, commitment, and retention) and leadership behavior?

This figure also oversimplifies the world by subsuming the complex role of outside forces that might influence political success under the term "external factors." This is shorthand for the myriad of features that might condition how successful a group is in achieving its political goals – assuming that it has any and is not simply interested in perpetuating itself. It includes all of the institutional features of the political world that are frequently characterized by the much trumpeted "new institutionalism" (for an excellent general discussion, see Krehbiel 1991; see also Shepsle 1979; March and Olsen 1984, 1989). It also encompasses noninstitutional factors such as the preferences of the unorganized (e.g., Denzau and Munger 1986), the presence of other organizations and the building and maintenance of coalitions with them

(Salisbury et al. 1987), and simply exogenous systemic shocks created by economic changes or political disruptions (e.g., Kingdon 1984). In addition, these outside forces may also feed back by determining an association's success in soliciting membership donations and by shaping the behavior of the leadership. Thus, the integrated perspective elaborated here may be criticized, undoubtedly justifiably, for not including all of the conceivable factors that might be relevant. Nonetheless, while recognizing the trade-offs that have been made in the name of parsimony over comprehensiveness, the general point to emphasize is that the effort in the present analysis to bring together key organizational features should allow a more accurate assessment of where associations fit into the political system.

The upshot of the foregoing discussion is that answering accurately and completely as many questions like the ones stated as possible requires under-standing an organization and its role in the political system in totality; examining specific aspects one at a time is not sufficient. For example, it is not feasible to ascertain the importance of joining or activist behavior without knowing whether leaders are responsive to their members and, if so, whether they are more sensitive to some contributors than others. Furthermore, only by investigating whether the political system is influenced by group efforts can the true relevance of organizational democracy (or the lack thereof) be gauged. To bring the story back full circle, the assessments of whether group leaders and the political system are responsive to members will be conditioned by both whether the membership is motivated by political concerns and how the group actually behaves. In short, both positive and normative con-clusions regarding organizations and politics hinge crucially on how strongly interrelated are the critical decisions made by those in and dealing with groups.

THE FOCUS OF ANALYSIS: COMMON CAUSE

Because this is a large endeavor for any one researcher to tackle, certain limiting choices had to be made. The most important was that the spotlight is principally on one organization, Common Cause, which is routinely classified under the rubric of public interest group. Ideally, a truly compara-tive study of a larger set of associations would be undertaken; the analysis presented in this book may be thought of as a pilot study of sorts. Whenever possible, Common Cause will be compared to other organizations that vary along specific attributes of theoretical interest.

Why public interest groups? Why Common Cause? With respect to the first question, public interest groups are an especially fascinating topic of study because the variance of opinion among students of the political process regarding the role of such associations is even more extreme than is generally the case when it comes to interest groups. Remarkably sweeping claims have been made that these public-regarding organizations have reshaped the

American political environment with their boom in the late 1960s and early 1970s (e.g., Hayes 1981; Wilson 1981; Walker 1983). For example, David Vogel writes that the public interest group movement effectively "transformed both the nature of the political agenda and the way in which administrative decisions ... were made" (1989, p. 112). By contrast, others believe that these groups are quite ineffectual and little more than symbolic – either because the leadership or the membership does not care about being effective or because these organizations simply lack the requisite resources, financial and otherwise, that it takes to shape the operations of government. Thus, for instance, a frequently heard critique of public interest groups (which a number of interviewees voiced regarding Common Cause) is that they are exclusively mail-order operations that exist to aggrandize and perpetuate themselves rather than for the pursuit of political goals (e.g., Hayes 1983).

However, while sweeping claims have been offered about public interest groups, these entities have only sporadically been studied (but see, e.g., McFarland 1976, 1984; Berry 1977). In addition, now that the groups created during the 1960s and 1970s have been in existence for a number of years, a series of new issues have arisen on which scholars must reflect. Possibly of greatest interest, myriad public interest groups have now entered middle age. How do they function as institutionalized entities rather than as part of a fashionable new social movement? Do they maintain effectiveness, assuming that they had it originally, and have they preserved their commitment to the same issues? As the political world around them changes, how do they both keep the membership committed and have an impact on the political system?

As for why Common Cause was chosen, the explanation is twofold. Some bases for selecting it are admittedly idiosyncratic to the research process, but there are a variety of strong theoretical arguments for picking this organization.

One convenient reason for concentrating on this organization is that a data set was available for analysis. In the fall of 1981, over 1,200 responded to a mail survey of Common Cause members.[4] All interviewees were queried about a wide variety of issues – membership and its benefits, personal attitudes, previous history in Common Cause, level of commitment to the organization, and future intentions, to name a few. A stratified design oversampled Common Cause–designated activists, who were defined as steering committee coordinators in congressional districts (the basic unit of Common Cause organization) or activators of telephone networks.[5] These data furnish a rare opportunity to explore a host of questions about why people participate in political organizations despite all the obstacles to collective action.

A more theoretical impetus for focusing on Common Cause is its importance in the realm of public interest groups. The organization is routinely characterized as the quintessential public interest group (e.g., McFarland 1984).[6] It is widely considered to be quite effective in achieving what it sets

out to do – although as research conducted for this project makes clear, this sentiment is not unanimous.

Of course, because it is the quintessential public interest group, Common Cause is not the *average* symbolic organization. Given the initial vision behind the creation of the organization and its large membership, the leadership has focused on grassroots lobbying, particularly in combination with efforts by Washington lobbyists. Consistent with such a strategy, it tries to focus much of its attention on Congress and comparatively less than some other public interest groups on the courts or the executive branch. (This emphasis on Congress does have the benefit of making the analysis of influence somewhat more straightforward.) However, if one is trying to develop a general framework for understanding organizational issues and is able to study only one association, selecting the most notable group – while keeping in mind that it is generic processes that are of concern – certainly seems the logical solution.

Common Cause is also especially interesting because the organization has faced some of the crises of middle age alluded to here. The group's core issues have alternately been at the heart of the national political agenda and virtually dropped from sight; over the years, membership has also had rather dramatic peaks and troughs.

The group was founded in 1970 as a so-called People's Lobby when John Gardner, a former secretary of Health, Education, and Welfare in the Johnson administration, put an advertisement in the *New York Times* requesting memberships and donations. "It was my notion that the chief mission of Common Cause should be to hold government accountable," recounts Gardner (pers. commun., 1990), a concept that the group's current president, Fred Wertheimer, continues to endorse vigorously. Within six months 70,000 people had signed on.[7] While the organization soon after developed a relationship with the anti–Vietnam War movement, it quickly reoriented its focus during the Watergate period to classic progressive concerns, which around Common Cause are known as "structure and process" issues. Although it became involved in some substantive issues beginning in the late 1970s, its identity appears to continue to revolve around these earlier concerns. Such matters include ethics laws, "sunshine" legislation (laws requiring that government agencies hold formal meetings that are open to the public), and campaign finance reform. As Wertheimer puts it, "Our area is government. That's our thing … no matter what else we may be doing, that has to be the central issue."

The association and its leadership has most notably gained a reputation for its activities with respect to campaign finance. Common Cause was quite active during the debates leading to enactment of the Federal Election Campaign Act (FECA) amendments of 1974. (The resulting legislation, with some court-induced modifications, forms the basis of the present campaign finance system.) It is the group in Washington that mines data from the public

files of the Federal Election Commission (FEC) and puts out a blizzard of press releases intended for media consumption about electoral spending generally and the actions of PACs and elected officials specifically. The hope is that generating easy-to-digest documents will foster media publicity about what, according to Common Cause, is the inherently corrupt nature of the current electoral system; the group can then collect a listing of Common Cause–generated editorials for reform as evidence of support for its cause. Keeping the public eye on the system is a top priority, even when it may cause certain turbulence with the organization's efforts to navigate the waters of Washington.

The organization's preoccupation (at least currenlty) with campaign finance is tangible. Its efforts to recruit new members since the mid-1980s have focused almost exclusively on electoral reform. Much of *Common Cause Magazine* is devoted to stories on the subject and the magazine typically includes an "alert" designed to inspire members to contact legislators on the subject. In polls, members invariably place at the top of their list of priorities group involvement in reforming elections. In addition to the considerable effort devoted to money and elections by the Common Cause staff responsible for political issues generally, the organization assigns two staff members (a director and a research assistant) to monitor campaign finance exclusively. This is the only issue accorded a separate place in the formal organizational structure. Not surprisingly, Common Cause is the group that the popular press contacts when it needs commentary on a breaking scandal involving campaign abuses or on political proposals to amend the way elections are regulated.[8]

This focus on progressive issues has led to some problems for the association's leadership. Most important, the group's principal concerns largely fell off the national political agenda in the late 1970s and through at least the first half of the 1980s. Reasons for this transformation include the economic difficulties that began to plague the country in the 1970s, the election of Ronald Reagan and numerous other conservative Republicans in the 1980s, and the lack of desire by those who would seem to be the group's natural political allies to tackle the issues that concern Common Cause after changes opening up government and regulating campaign finance were implemented in the early 1970s.

The leadership has made some fairly dramatic adjustments in its political agenda. As will be discussed, for a time they moved somewhat away from structure and process issues and turned to defense issues. In the second half of the 1980s, however, they refocused with a vengeance on issues of good government, especially campaign finance reform.

Membership has also waxed and waned during this difficult period (Figure 1.2). Like many public interest groups, Common Cause is highly dependent on voluntary contributions; unlike some, it relies little upon foundation support or large gifts. At some times (as in 1982) the number of

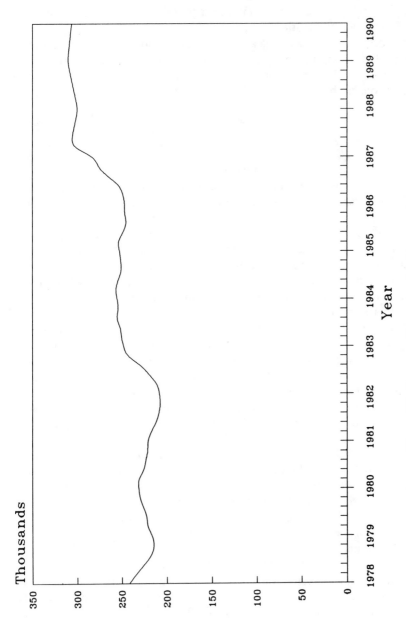

Figure 1.2. Common Cause membership over time.
Source: Common Cause and Encyclopedia of Associations

contributors dwindled to under 200,000, while at others (as in 1987) it rose to well over 300,000.[9] Although the exact relationship between the problems that the group faced with respect to its traditional issue agenda and these membership fluctuations is not immediately evident, it is clearly an issue that deserves scholarly attention.

In short, Common Cause is an obvious choice for analysis because of its high profile among interest groups. Beyond that, it is a particularly appropriate case for the evaluation of the internal politics of organizations and the relationship between such politics and both group survival and political success.[10]

SOME CAVEATS

When a single group is being studied, caveats are always in order. An analysis of Common Cause will not answer all of the questions regarding organizations or even all public interest groups, despite the fact that every effort will be made to deal with more general concerns that occupy students of American political processes. Nevertheless, this analysis is designed not for those necessarily fascinated with Common Cause per se, but rather for those concerned with understanding general issues about citizens, organizations, and the political system. Indeed, "validity checks" are employed whenever possible to show that Common Cause is not sui generis.

Furthermore, it is important to acknowledge that the approach taken here is fairly explicitly "political economy" in orientation. That is, it represents an effort to apply economic ways of thinking to political problems to see if they shed light on these issues. Since interest group analysis has been conducted over the years from a variety of perspectives, including sociological (e.g., Knoke 1990) and psychological (e.g., Uhlaner 1986, 1989b), as well as economic, it is important to keep in mind that this analysis is coming from a certain direction. Inevitably, the literature cited and the ideas relied upon tend to draw fairly heavily from a political economy tradition: This is meant neither to belittle other approaches nor to minimize the contributions of work inspired by them. However, building upon a political economy approach provides a view of organizations that is not only parsimonious but makes much about them intuitive and explicable.

Finally, as already foreshadowed, this investigation focuses centrally on only some of the issues that interest group scholars have studied over the years. In particular, the emphasis is on interest *groups* and not on the interest group *system*. Thus, the following analysis pays close attention to issues regarding membership, the conversion of contributors' preferences into goals, and the subsequent translation of goals into policy. The purpose, to reiterate, is to develop a vantage point for understanding interest groups. By contrast, systemic issues such as the impact of the rise of patrons on the political system (Walker 1983; Salisbury 1984), the structure of group lobbying (e.g.,

Salisbury et al. 1987), the nature of conflict (e.g., Schattschneider 1960), the domination of privileged interests (e.g., Lindblom 1977; Lowi 1979), or macro-economic performance (e.g., Olson 1986) are not central to this research. It is hoped, however, that the results of this analysis will have something significant to say about general issues of representation that concern those who think about the group system.

Despite all these caveats, the present analysis should be of interest to scholars. Drawing together a host of issues that social scientists normally deal with separately can provide insights into the underlying generic processes at work.

Finally, a few words about the methodology and data that will be employed. Despite the initial impetus provided by the existence of the mail survey, it became increasingly clear that the Common Cause data were insufficient for satisfactorily answering even a subset of the questions of interest. To further the investigation, a variety of other quantitative data sources are also used: the 1980 National Election Study (NES), the General Social Surveys (GSS) conducted annually since 1970, a 1982 mail survey of Common Cause members and those from three other public interest groups (the League of Women Voters, the American Civil Liberties Union, and the Conservative Caucus),[11] the *Vanderbilt Television News Abstracts* (summaries of national news broadcasts), and a miscellany of data provided by Common Cause and other sources, to furnish an incomplete list.

While this analysis relies heavily on quantitative research it became clear that richer, qualitative source materials were needed as well. Hence the results of the quantitative analyses presented in this book are balanced with inferences culled from interviews with those involved with Common Cause and from descriptive source materials.[12] This is particularly true in the later chapters, where attention moves from citizens' decision making to public policy. Although admittedly far from perfect, this mixture of results furnishes a richer, more accurate study than either strategy could provide by itself.

STRUCTURE OF THE ANALYSIS

This analysis is organized roughly as the schematic presented in Figure 1.1 would suggest. To begin, a unified framework for understanding citizen decision making – conditioned, of course, by leadership choices – that recognizes the interrelationships among individual decisions is introduced in Chapter 2. While this unified framework will have implications for the entire analysis, it is principally oriented toward Chapters 3 through 6, which primarily examine citizens' and contributors' behavior. In Chapter 7 this unified view on citizens' behavior is built into a theory of organizational goal formation; this, in turn, is linked to a theoretical discussion, in Chapter 8, of how interest groups might have a policy impact. Although each theoretical approach is tested separately, they are informed and the results are made comprehensible

by one another. Taken together, these theoretical discussions essentially constitute what is meant operationally as the development of an integrated perspective on organized groups.

As for the empirical side, Chapter 3 provides a descriptive picture of Common Cause members as a starting point for understanding citizens' choices regarding interest groups. This is followed by an examination in Chapter 4 of why people join. Chapters 5 and 6 explore the internal politics of organizations by delving into how citizens behave once they get into the group, initially, by examining why members stay in the organization once they join and, subsequently, by investigating the motivations for some contributors to take a more active role in the group. Chapter 7 looks at internal politics from the slightly different vantage point of how the leadership mediates between the membership and the larger political system in arriving at organizational goals. The focus then turns more squarely toward the world of public policy. Chapter 8 presents an analysis of whether Common Cause has had an impact on decisions concerning the production and the deployment of the MX missile, while Chapter 9 examines whether the organization has been able to structure the regulation of elections. Finally, in Chapter 10 the focus returns to the issues discussed in the present chapter and to drawing some conclusions once groups have been viewed from the ground up.

2

A unified framework for understanding citizens' decision making: A theory of experiential search

The previous chapter introduced a number of key questions about citizens' behavior toward organized groups: Why do people join? How do potential contributors choose one association over other possibilities? Why do some elect to remain in the group while others decide to depart? Of those remaining, why do a subset volunteer to be activists and give more of themselves than others who remain within the rank and file? Satisfactorily responding to these queries about membership and commitment is fundamental for understanding not only formation and maintenance of interest groups but goal formation, and, ultimately, such groups' success in the political arena.

Before the questions posed can be answered, two prerequisites must be satisfied. First, a theoretical framework must be developed from which to understand this host of decisions and the interrelationships among them. To reiterate, this constitutes only part of what is meant by an integrated perspective. Second, data have to be gathered to determine if this framework is reasonable.

The present chapter consists of four parts: (1) a broad discussion of alternative approaches to understanding citizens' behavior vis-à-vis organizations; (2) a survey of the literature on members' decision making to identify the alternative specifications that have been employed by scholars; (3) a section outlining and developing an *experiential search* theory; and (4) a presentation of the specific implications of the experiential search framework and a comparison to the inferences stemming from the previously proffered theories. This will be followed by some brief conclusions about experiential search and its implications for the study of organizations.

GENERAL ANALYTIC APPROACHES TO CITIZENS' DECISION MAKING

The distinguishing feature of the analytic approach to conceptualizing citizens' decision making presented in this chapter is not that it highlights different variables of interest or proposes new relationships among them.

Rather, what sets it apart is the proposition that the series of decisions individuals make regarding groups are fundamentally intertwined.

A principal premise of this viewpoint is that this series of alternatives cannot be understood in isolation from one another. Each decision is viewed as part of a larger process that determines a set of individual choices. Thus, understanding the host of citizens' decisions delineated at the beginning of this chapter demands a unified framework for understanding choice – just as the overall manner in which organizations must be conceptualized requires integration. This approach is intuitively sensible and is consistent with the way in which social scientists generally study either political or economic choice behavior.

Such a viewpoint stands in contrast to the approach commonly adopted by contemporary scholars of organizational decision making. As mentioned briefly, social scientists studying contributors' behavior often view given decisions without regard to the other choices individuals make either simultaneously or sequentially. They adopt whichever theoretical framework they perceive is appropriate for the question at hand. While in many respects this is a quite reasonable strategy, one potential drawback is that incorrect, or at least incomplete, inferences might be drawn.

A game theoretic analogy can be drawn that relates the viewpoint advanced in the current analysis with that commonly employed. The approach proposed here is completely consistent with the game theoretic logic of making decisions when there are multiple stages to the process (for a concise review of game theory and its applications to political science, see Ordeshook 1986). Even in a game against nature – which is frequently the situation that is being analyzed here – this logic is compelling.

The traditional framework can be characterized as the equivalent of not applying backward induction when confronted with a game tree. In simplest terms, this means that those making choices do not look ahead; it is well understood that such an approach can lead to grave mistakes because decision makers may select less preferred alternatives if they do not consider what comes next. Put another way, the problem with the alternative viewpoint is that under a wide variety of conditions, not "looking up the game tree" can have extremely damaging consequences. Decision makers have strong incentives to anticipate future choices.[1]

However, whether this traditional myopia has negative consequences for understanding the behavior of either contributors or leaders is an empirical question. As will be elaborated later, the impact may depend on citizens' level of knowledge or on their ability to incorporate new information into their decision calculus.

Testing whether previous approaches can be built upon requires developing an alternate, unified framework for citizens' decisions regarding interest groups that yields testable propositions. In other words, the propositions generated from an explicitly unified framework can then be compared to

those derived from more traditional approaches. If such comparisons seem to suggest that a unified framework is more appropriate, attention can then be turned to whether such a viewpoint can help shed light on the goal formation and policy processes.

An example that will be developed in more detail later in this analysis serves to illustrate how this research strategy might be useful. Consider the question of which members will decide to remain in an organization. Although this choice would seem to be crucial for a number of reasons, approaches to citizens' decisions with respect to organizations have largely ignored it and have focused almost exclusively on the initial choice to sign up.

Standard models seem to imply that members should remain in a group forever once they sign up in the first place. Because there is no mechanism for contributors to anticipate that they will learn and subsequently accrue knowledge about an organization, they will join the association and remain in it based on a straightforward evaluation of whether the benefits exceed the costs.[2] By contrast, the experiential search approach that is developed in this analysis assumes a sophisticated anticipation of future events. Thus, the decision to join should be linked to the choice of whether or not to stay in the organization – that is, knowing that one has the option of quitting should influence whether or not one signs up in the first place. People may have incomplete information about a group or they may find it difficult to evaluate all of the data that come their way; but they generally know that they will have the opportunity to quit later on, when they will have a better idea about the nature of the group. It is anticipated that some individuals will quit, and these departures ought to be explicable. Thus, the traditional models provide one testable prediction about members' behavior (departures should be for idiosyncratic reasons), and the approach presented here furnishes another (departures will occur because individuals join, update their beliefs after acquiring additional information, and realize they have made a bad match).

In the remainder of this chapter, a framework that more fully incorporates the host of organizational decisions is developed. This approach, labeled experiential search, is thought both to be intuitively plausible and to constitute a preliminary effort to devise a unified theory on citizen decision making regarding interest groups.

MEMBERS' DECISION MAKING

Despite frequent assertions in the literature that the study of organizational membership is theory rich and data poor (e.g., Arnold 1982; Shaiko 1986; Cigler 1989), it will be suggested here that the available models, which represent important contributions and have considerable merits, can benefit from further development. Although this larger study looks at a host of decisions by citizens, the initial reason for joining is the logical place to start.

In the first place, virtually all of the available theoretical research focuses on the original membership calculus; in the second, an analysis of the initial choice furnishes a vantage point to consider subsequent behavior.

Rather than reviewing all of the literature on organizational membership (for such reviews, see Moe 1980a; Schlozman and Tierney 1986; Berry 1989), the emphasis here is on works directly relevant for the present study.[3] Such research has focused on how the assumption of individual rationality bears on the choices that citizens make regarding organized groups specifically and participation generally. Research within this tradition has dominated discussions on member behavior for the past several decades.

The starting point of most analyses of how choices are made is some form of a Downsian (1957) cost/benefit calculus in which it is proposed that individuals participate if their expected benefits are greater than their expected costs.[4] The feature that is generally highlighted is the well-known collective action problem associated with the probability of actually having an impact on the desired outcome. Enjoying benefits may not be enough to motivate behavior; having a nontrivial impact on the level produced may be relevant as well.

However, moving from this starting point to a richer framework for understanding organizational decision making is no simple matter. Such an endeavor requires definition of both the incentives – what goes into assessments of probabilities, benefits, and costs – and the underlying process that structures the decision-making process. The former appears reasonably straightforward, while the latter seems considerably more difficult.

With respect to incentives, most theorists working in the research tradition drawn upon here (e.g., Clark and Wilson 1961; Salisbury 1969; Wilson 1973; Moe 1980a) typically identify a number of incentive or benefit types: selective, solidary, and purposive. *Selective* benefits are tangible returns that have monetary values and are derived from contributions. They either may be *divisible*, private rewards or may emanate from members' impacts on the level of *collective* goods provided to everyone. *Solidary* benefits stem from associational interactions, while *purposive* benefits are intangible rewards garnered from contributing to the group because of its stated goals.[5] Costs are not given very much attention; implicitly they are assumed to be monetary (the importance of examining costs in more depth will be discussed shortly). These theorists then examine which of these benefit types are important and specify the process underlying the cost/benefit calculi by which some individuals decide to become members and others refrain.

The best known of these efforts regarding groups is Olson's (1965). As discussed, he revolutionized perceptions about why citizens join organized groups and spurred the movement away from those developed by scholars such as Arthur Bentley (1908), Earl Latham (1952), and David Truman (1951). His seminal contribution details the difficulties associated with collective action. Individuals join large groups, he argues, because the value of the available selective benefits exceeds the costs of membership.

Olson's work, however, rests on a trio of very strong assumptions: (1) that individuals have full information, (2) that they are only interested in economic rewards, and (3) that they maximize without error. In large groups – where individuals' impact on the production of collective goods is sufficiently small that the collective benefits accruing to them are less than the costs – this implies that only dues levels and divisible selective benefits will be relevant. Political activity is a by-product of narrowly self-interested behavior.

These assumptions have a number of implications (which have not been generally recognized) if they are extrapolated to other choices about member-ship and commitment. As mentioned in the previous section, one is that members' decision whether to sign up for another period of membership should follow the identical cost/benefit analysis that governed their decision to join. Since, in general, not much will change from one contribution period to the next, particularly given the assumption of perfect information, little explicable organizational attrition is possible. The expectation is once a member, always a member.

Two other implications involve the willingness of contributors to commit additional time or money to the organization as activists. The first is that only those who can derive private economic rewards from activism will be receptive to making this additional commitment. In all likelihood, this will involve a very small percentage of contributors in many organizations, unless leaders offer lucrative incentives to attract activists. For example, group appeals for additional funds directed at current members should yield nothing unless the association offers something in return besides a pledge to pursue collective goals. Similar results should meet attempts to lure contributors into giving time as well as money.

The other implication is that – like signing up in the first place – perfectly informed members should separate themselves into the rank and file and activists immediately upon joining. Barring dramatic exogenous events, this level of commitment should remain steady throughout one's tenure in the organization.

Those challenging Olson's theory (but still adopting the same general framework) have taken two principal tacks. Some (e.g., Clark and Wilson 1961; Wilson 1973; Moe 1980a) emphasize that purposive and solidary incentives are important, along with selective returns, in the decision calculus.

Individuals who possess perfect information and maximize without error but are not satisfied by selective incentives alone may join because the potential purposive and solidary payoffs push them over the threshold where benefits exceed costs. People derive consumption benefits from interpersonal interactions and the purposive statements their contributions make.

A multiplicity of incentives can be easily incorporated into the Olsonian framework. This argument is intuitively reasonable; Olson himself recognizes the potential importance of nonmonetary returns but ignores them for reasons of parsimony. However, the same inference about the conditional membership decision (that is, the choice by existing contributors to stay in

the association) still holds. So too does the implication that members will only make further contributions if additional rewards are proffered – although these potential rewards, like those for joining, retention (the decision whether or not to stay in the association), and activism, may now be more varied. The inference that the commitment level is determined jointly with the decision to join also remains unchanged.

Another critique of the Olsonian framework focuses less on the breadth of incentives than on the assumption of perfect information. Moe (1980a; see also 1980b, 1981) maintains that potential group members do not possess perfect information. Consequently, some decision makers have ex ante expectations about their own contribution to the provision of collective goods and hence overestimate the level of selective incentives the group offers. A subset of the population mistakenly think of themselves as highly influential. They incorporate into their membership calculi their allegedly substantial contributions to the provision of collective goods (which perfectly informed contributors in large groups will recognize to be zero). Individuals whose perceptions of their efficacy put them at the upper end of the population distribution join in disproportionate numbers. The assumption seems to be that once these contributors overestimate their impact, they repeat the same mistake over and over.

Again, organizational membership ought to be quite stable. There should be little explicable attrition or change in commitment (but see Salisbury 1969). While there may be some exogenous forces prompting a few individuals to change their behavior, almost all outcomes ought to be the same under the three models surveyed. Interestingly, then, despite different assumptions about incentives and information that lead to varying predictions about who joins, these models yield identical predictions about who stays.

The relaxation of the perfect-information assumption – as well as the incorporation of a multiplicity of incentives – is eminently reasonable and clearly significant. But precisely how imperfect information affects contributions needs to be rethought.[6] It ought to influence more than simply individuals' initial estimates of the benefits they derive from contributing to collective goods.[7] The conclusion that many members join organizations only because they make mistakes is unsettling. This is especially disquieting because educated individuals tend to join in greater proportions: For example, an astounding 55 percent of respondents to the Common Cause survey reported having some postgraduate education.

Even more difficult to believe is the logical implication that imperfectly informed members never learn. The assumption seems to be that those making errors keep contributing for years without revising (even incorrectly) their prior beliefs. Members keep opening their wallets, and perhaps committing their time, without reevaluating their opinions.

A more reasonable supposition, consistent with the general analytic approach presented here, is that the decision to join makes sense as a strategy

by individuals who recognize their lack of knowledge. Members join groups to learn about them, and as they acquire knowledge, some can be expected to leave. The politics of experiential search offers such a framework for understanding individuals' decisions vis-à-vis groups.

A THEORY OF EXPERIENTIAL SEARCH

Organizational membership can be conceptualized as a search process. Citizens lack complete information about all of the alternative groups they might join and the associated costs and benefits. They presumably would like to discover an organization(s) that will give them enough returns relative to costs – regardless of the types of benefits they seek – that they will be content to remain at a given commitment level.

Experiential search is distinct from sequential search, which is the principal subject of discussion in the economics literature (for an excellent review, see Mortensen 1986). In sequential search, individuals, either workers or consumers, typically search until they meet their reservation wage or price, where the expected marginal cost of an additional iteration equals the expected marginal return. In these models, decision makers gather information before taking a job or purchasing a product.

Some models (e.g., Burdett 1978; Wilde 1979) permit on-the-job or experiential learning by workers within a sequential search framework. These approaches are much closer in spirit to the experiential search theory propounded here, but there are still important differences. For example, by and large, workers *must* search for a job, while there is no similar compulsion to join a public interest group. In other words, while the search process is analogous and in both cases certain characteristics can best be learned by experience, other factors, especially the free rider problem, also come into play when the focus is on public interest groups.

In looking for an organization to fill their needs, individual decision makers with fixed preferences have three options: (1) They can conclude that given the problems of obtaining information and the costs of membership, they should give up. (2) They can search over alternative associations without contributing. Or (3) they can join an organization to learn whether membership is worthwhile. This final option, learning through exposure, can have a number of facets – developing an understanding about how a group functions, whether it is effective in achieving its goals, and whether its outputs are in line with one's preferences, to name a few. Given the many opportunities to sign up and the low monetary cost of joining numerous voluntary associations (presumably at least partially a function of leaders' own recognition of the possibility of experiential search), particularly public interest groups, many should opt for experiential learning because it is an efficient information-gathering technique.[8]

A factor predisposing searchers to join an organization is that many

attributes of membership are observable only by participation.[9] These are *specific characteristics*, while those that can be observed without joining are *general characteristics*. These two types can be thought of as opposite poles on a continuum that reflects the difficulty of acquiring information without making a commitment; most informational traits combine elements of both.

Almost every factor incorporated into the organizational decision calculus can be described, at least partially, as a specific characteristic. The only purely general feature of membership is the dues level. (Even here some joiners may not realize that the organization that they are signing up for may have a higher rate for renewal.) If the remaining factors were ranked from more to less general, they might roughly be ordered as follows: costs other than dues levels, purposive benefits, divisible benefits, solidary benefits, and collective benefits.

When the costs of evaluating specific qualities are relatively low, prospective contributors will tend, ceteris paribus, to join, usually at a low commitment level; accumulate knowledge; and then decide what level of commitment, if any, to give to the organization. This has a number of obvious implications. One is that, since a reasonable inference is that one accumulates knowledge more and more slowly over time, the expected rate of dropping out should diminish temporally. Another is that the average commitment levels should increase over time but at a diminishing rate. More veteran contributors are expected to be more likely to contribute more than the basic dues level, but the marginal effects of experience should decrease with time. Specific characteristics should also be more important for veterans than for newcomers in settling upon a commitment level or in deciding whether or not to remain a member.

In the organizational context, first-time joiners will have imperfect information about costs other than dues. How can the costs of phone calls asking for assistance – writing legislators, contacting other members, and so forth – or written appeals for monetary contributions in excess of dues be established without error ex ante? How will those who might be willing to assume a high commitment level know the implicit opportunity costs of participating: the time involved or the costs of being active compared to estimates about similar involvement in substitute organizations, for example? As contributors spend time in the group, they will develop a growing awareness of the true price of membership and behave accordingly.

Along these same lines, the value of purposive benefits will be increasingly evident with experience. Although members will probably have some initial idea about what the group stands for, they will gradually learn whether it represents those things that provide them with consumption benefits.

Before they join, potential members will also lack complete information about the quality of the divisible benefits furnished to participants. While not commonly noted in the literature, private returns may be either direct products that the group provides to its contributors or by-products that

represent the opportunities that membership in the group can facilitate, such as contacts that are useful for career advancement. Accurately assessing the full value of such offerings without consuming them regularly is all but impossible; membership supplies an opportunity to learn about their utility firsthand. Full information about both the direct divisible benefits that are provided by the group and the indirect benefits of membership is likely to be acquired through experience.

The inference that fully appreciating divisible benefits requires experience has an important implication. Suppose that as in Olson's model, only divisible rewards matter: Before engaging in experiential search, small contributors deduce that their donations will have no impact on the level of collective goods provided; and they do not value purposive and solidary incentives. Even in this extreme case where lack of knowledge is irrelevant for an individual's valuation of collective, purposive, or solidary benefits, imperfect information *still* ought to be a major factor in members' decision calculi.

If contributors are motivated by solidary returns, however, it is unlikely that they will have a full idea of the value of these benefits either. They may not even know, for example, whether interactions are primarily face-to-face or indirect through telephone calls or letters. Only immersion in day-to-day organizational operations will permit members to gauge whether the interpersonal interactions are sufficiently rewarding.

Experiential search should be especially germane for learning about collective goods. Educating members should have several elements. Contributors ought to become more cognizant of what collective benefits their organization actually proffers. However, even with the improved information gained through time, members' judgments of how effective an association actually is may sometimes be inaccurate because of the difficulties associated with measuring political influence.[10] Nevertheless, many of those who initially believe that their contributions to the provision of collective goods are nontrivial can be expected to learn about the value of these goods and the insignificance of their contributions. Members who donate resources to have an impact on the magnitude of public goods provided – and not because they gain purposive rewards from contributing to collective goods – probably leave the group over time, ceteris paribus.

To reiterate: Citizens with perfect information (or those who have imperfect information but never learn) will join those organizations that have the highest net benefit for them. While changes in exogenous conditions might lead some to change their behavior, the strong presumption is that once a commitment level is established, it will remain constant.[11] But when the assumption of imperfect information is embedded within the experiential search framework, changes in behavior become comprehensible as citizens update their expectations about net benefits. Interestingly, then, at any given time it is predicted that citizens will join groups that they would not have if they possessed perfect information (and many of them will eventually quit).

while others who "should" join will not. The implications for Olson's free rider problem cut two ways and the net effect will depend, to a large degree, on how effectively leaders structure their organization.

Thus, group membership might usefully be conceptualized as a decision theoretic process in which members join an organization, decide upon an initial level of commitment, and then reevaluate their decision as they learn about the costs and benefits of participating (see Figure 2.1). Each membership renewal period might be thought of as another stage in this process of choice; and each time, the contributor has better information. Learning about specific characteristics continues indefinitely, but the amount of additional information accumulated through experiential search diminishes over time. Members weed themselves out, especially during their first few years in an organization. Updating beliefs with better information can reinforce a propensity to remain in the group for another contribution period, to be actively involved or to remain in the rank and file, or to conclude that membership is less valuable than forgone opportunities. Those abdicating membership either become politically inactive or continue to search for an alternative that makes participation worthwhile. For those who stay in the organization, over time learning should become a less and less salient factor in their decision calculi.

COMMON CAUSE AND EXPERIENTIAL SEARCH

Common Cause is a prime candidate for citizens to employ experiential search. Leaders, the other side of the citizens' decision-making equation, have quite consciously kept down the initial cost of joining and have made it easy to join – reducing costs in a different sense – by extensively using direct mail to recruit new members. Organizational dues are predictably moderate: $20 per year (there are reduced student and family rates) for first-time joiners and $30 for renewals. This higher renewal rate was not in place when the Common Cause survey was conducted. Members are fairly well off – their median family income in 1980 fell in the $25,000 to $35,000 range, which is about 50 percent higher than the national average. A tenable assumption is that relatively well-heeled contributors can learn about Common Cause or other moderately priced organizations through experiential search. What, then, will they learn about the costs and benefits that are associated with contributing to Common Cause?

Members should discover that there are additional costs to participation besides paying their dues. Leaders routinely solicit them as part of the organization's mailings to give more financial support, and many comply. In fact, 63 percent of those surveyed report contributing more than the required $20.[12] Despite this generosity, Common Cause, with a staff of approximately eighty, lacks the financial resources to compete on an even footing with private interest groups. "There's just no question ... we have

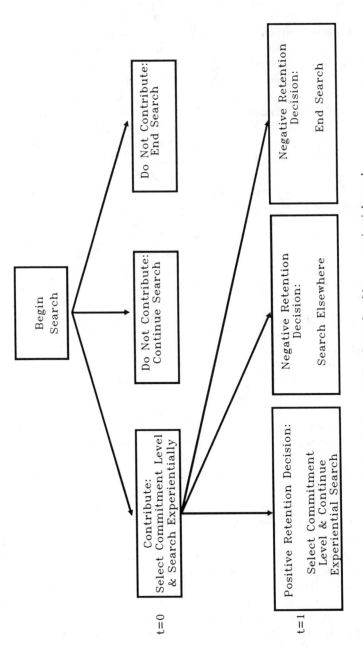

Figure 2.1. Organizational membership as experiential search.

far more tasks, far more responsibility, far more to do than resources," is the way Wertheimer puts it. Thus, Common Cause, like public interest associations generally, employs other instruments to make up for these shortfalls. One critical resource is energizing contributors to give of their time and become part of Common Cause's core of activists. Given that John Gardner's vision of creating a People's Lobby resulted in a large membership, it was virtually predetermined that the leadership would attempt to take advantage of this resource. Contributors are encouraged, principally by phone calls made by volunteers, to immerse themselves in the association's sophisticated, congressionally based, grassroots network, as well as in state and local organizations. As mentioned earlier, roughly 4 percent of group members are designated by Common Cause as activists; about another 11 percent of all members involve themselves in what can be labeled activist behavior.

It is difficult to be simply a passive contributor. Those preferring only to write checks will find themselves the targets of periodic mobilization efforts when battles over issues pinpointed by the leadership come to a head. Forty-three percent of all members in the Common Cause survey (32 percent of the rank and file, and 68 percent of the members designated as activists by the group) said they had been contacted by the association in the past year and asked to write to Congress about some issue.

Contributors also have opportunities to learn about the complete gamut of organizational benefits. Although the stereotypical individual who joins Common Cause is characterized as a liberal do-gooder, the leadership obviously believes that divisible benefits are necessary to keep members happy. A bimonthly magazine is distributed to association members as an enticement to contribute; perhaps the consumption of this and the other political information provided is sufficient to elicit at least a minimal annual contribution.[13]

As mentioned in the discussion of divisible benefits, some may perceive another private return from participation, namely, career advancement. Suggesting self-promotion as a motivation is antithetical to the high moral ground that Common Cause tries to occupy, but it is consistent with Olson's theory that political activity is only a by-product of members' quest for divisible, private rewards. An unexpectedly high proportion of respondents, 23 percent, reply that they have political aspirations. Thirty-five percent of those surveyed state that they either have political aspirations or had at some time sought a party position, elected office, or appointed office. (When broken down between the rank and file and activists, the percentages are 32 and 45, respectively.) This discovery suggests that the participation of many allegedly altruistic liberals may be at least partially motivated by the search for a springboard onto the political opportunity structure (Schlesinger 1966), or perhaps by a desire to gain politically relevant information. If it does the trick, membership may be renewed and perhaps additional money and time

will be donated; if not, the aspirant moves on and continues to search. Members will also learn about Common Cause's struggles to generate collective goods. What they learn is necessarily conditioned by the group's leaders' decisions. The organization has taken part in many celebrated battles, generally associated with "good government" issues designed to provide a host of nonexclusive collective goods. In the 1980s, the group curiously shifted its agenda to include more substantive, especially defense-related, concerns. As will be discussed later, the leadership selects its policy areas carefully to maintain membership loyalty. The staff employs polls and other less formal mechanisms to gather data on constituents' preferences regarding Common Cause's political agenda.

This decision-making strategy has several interesting implications. It implies a belief among leaders that members either think they have an impact on the provision of collective goods or get considerable value from the purposive statement that their participation in Common Cause makes to the world. Assuming that the leadership's inference is correct, this conflict-minimizing strategy should also mitigate the impact on future decisions of contributors' satisfaction or dissatisfaction over the association's political actions. In other words, if those in charge selected issues exclusively on other criteria such as their own personal preferences, for example, if they mistakenly viewed political action as a by-product that has no weight in participants' decision calculi, then contributors would be more likely to learn that they disagree with Common Cause's political efforts. As a consequence, these assessments would be more germane for their choices because there would be greater variability among member opinions.

Members will also learn about the opportunities for interpersonal inter-actions that the group provides. Common Cause's decentralized structure provides a variety of vehicles for such solidary returns (see also McFarland 1984). Although much of this is a product of organizational weakness – lack of funds forces the staff to rely heavily upon its other major resource, an energetic membership – it may also be a strength when it comes to keeping contributors in the organization and highly committed to it.

However, many interested in interpersonal interactions may also learn that Common Cause is not the place for them. In particular, they will discover that the group offers limited opportunities for face-to-face contact among members. Rather, relationships are largely through the telephone or, to a lesser extent, via letter writing. Members desiring more direct interactions may withdraw from the group altogether or elect to remain in the organization but not to engage in activist behavior.

In summary: Individuals interested in Common Cause have much to learn. For $20, citizens can sign up and find out about the organization. They might immediately do this as an activist (indeed, the "welcome package" received by new contributors allows for them to indicate such a willingness, but the response is, predictably, low) or, more likely, as a member of the rank

and file, since the latter is a far less expensive proposition. With time, they will learn about the group and make better informed decisions. They will approach the informational ideals of previous models not at the point of joining but only after a considerable commitment of time.

Standard conceptualizations of group members' decision making have focused on the initial decision to join an organization. While these analyses have represented important contributions to the understanding of citizens' behavior, it is also the case that once the fuller gamut of individual choices is examined, the implications of these traditional approaches for citizens' decisions seem somewhat counterintuitive. Thus, the present analysis provides an alternative approach – experiential search – that builds on previous research but, it is hoped, is more intuitively reasonable.[14]

Experiential search is notable for the predictions that emanate from its combination of assumptions that citizens are imperfectly informed and can learn. The forecasts derived from considering the learning process through which rational decision makers address deficiencies in knowledge is what makes this framework stand out.

The resulting comparisons of experiential search and alternative viewpoints yield testable hypotheses. The former implies that individuals will join a group relatively uninformed about it but learn over time at a gradually diminishing rate. (This assumes, of course, that leaders recognize this logic and keep the costs of joining low.) They will stay as members if they find that it suits them; otherwise, they can be expected to depart. Few will enter the association intent on being activists. Rather, this decision will also be structured by a process of learning whether the organization is a good match.

All of these assertions clash with the implications of previous models in which members join, choose a commitment level, and then maintain the status quo indefinitely. The immediate issue to be addressed, then, is Which viewpoint it more empirically accurate? This is the subject of the next four chapters. The results shed light on goal formation and, ultimately, political success or failure.

3

Who contributes?

Without empirical testing, the effort to analyze the linkage of citizens' opinions to public policy via organizational processes represents a rather barren exercise. Whatever may be said about assertions regarding the need to take an integrated approach to the analysis of organizations generally and a unified view on citizens' choices specifically, the acid test – as it is for all theoretical ideas – is validation through attempts at falsification.

Nonetheless, before jumping immediately into the fray by assessing relevant hypotheses, it is instructive to step back and acquire an initial empirical base. At least three reasons make developing such a firm, if descriptive, grounding a desirable exercise. One is merely that the subsequent analysis becomes more intuitively interesting: Contextual information eliminates much of the abstract quality that might permeate such an enterprise. Second, when conducting a single case study, it is important to have an idea of how the case under consideration compares to the rest of the population about which generalizations are being postulated. While groups such as Common Cause are alleged to have arisen in order to represent the public interest, how closely does its membership really correspond to this assertion by mirroring the general public? Third, and probably most important for this analysis, is determining whether those at various junctures in the group hierarchy differ from one another. Particularly given the argument in the previous chapter that a variety of individuals may decide to sample an organization, such a judgment may be relevant for understanding an organization's creation and subsequent maintenance, how its internal politics operates, and, ultimately, its attempts to mold public policy.

Thus, the present chapter is geared toward providing an initial vantage point from which to examine Common Cause contributors by furnishing an overview of the membership. Comparisons center broadly on two sets of differences: those between participants and the national citizenry, and those between organizational activists and rank-and-file contributors.[1]

While the population at large might seem to be the wrong control group for many traditional economic associations, when it comes to so-called public

interest groups it is the obvious one. Although membership in the former may be restricted to subsets of the citizenry, all who wish to sign up for the latter are allowed to do so. In other words, for an organization such as Common Cause whose membership is not restricted to those with either certain ascribed (e.g., race, creed, or age) or achieved (e.g., professional or occupational) characteristics, the adult population of Americans is the logical baseline for assessing contributors. Interestingly, because of the obvious difficulties in producing the relevant data, most descriptions of group participants involve making implicit judgments about how they correspond to the larger population – whatever the appropriate comparison. Developing an idea of who belongs to Common Cause might be illuminating regardless; however, it should be more insightful if explicit information is available to demonstrate how contributors vary from the national populace.

By contrast, few analyses have been able to detail generally more subtle intraorganizational differences (once again, for reasons of understandable data deficiencies). As already discussed, in most membership groups a hierarchy exists among those who contribute based on their commitment level. Some are rank-and-file members who donate the basic dues and little else, while others are activists who contribute more of themselves personally or of their financial resources. Indeed, when it comes to Common Cause, the leadership is very definite about who are the roughly 4 percent of all contributors whom they consider activists.[2]

Happily, details on what would appear to be the germane intraorganizational differences can be garnered from the stratified sample design producing the Common Cause data. The resulting information on the group's structural complexity should provide some important insights. Assuming that members can learn, any dissimilarities between activists and the rank and file are of interest – especially if political goals and objectives are relevant for membership choices.

Thus, the main body of this chapter compares Common Cause members initially to the national citizenry and, subsequently, with one another according to their location in the group hierarchy. In each instance, three types of characteristics are highlighted: (1) sociodemographic, (2) attitudinal, and (3) behavioral. It will then be possible to assess the hypotheses in future chapters with a clear understanding of who actually is the focus of the analysis.

COMMON CAUSE MEMBERS AND THE NATIONAL CITIZENRY

Common Cause's image as a middle class, good government group yields strong expectations that there are considerable differences between those who do and do not participate. In particular, it is anticipated that contributors should be more upper class socially, liberal attitudinally, and (especially) active politically than the average American.

To judge how contributors differ from the larger universe, three principal information sources were employed: the 1981 mail survey of Common Cause members, the 1980 National Election Study (NES) survey of the national population, and (for data on nonelectoral participation) the annual General Social Surveys (GSS) studies.[3] While the joint utilization of different data sources dictates that there are some limits to the amount of material that can be brought to bear, the ensuing results provide a reasonably comprehensive picture of how Common Cause members differ from the national constituency.[4]

Sociodemographic differences

Very much according to expectations, there are rather dramatic sociodemographic differences between Common Cause members and the national citizenry. Common Cause participants might be euphemistically dubbed "aging yuppies" (Table 3.1). They possess all the requisite "yuppie" achievements – an urban life style, financial well-being, educational attainment, and professional standing – but they are also considerably older than the average American (or, by definition, the average young, upwardly mobile, urban professional). By and large, this description also conforms to the conventional wisdom about the correlates of participation (e.g., Verba and Nie 1972; Milbrath and Goel 1977; Wolfinger and Rosenstone 1980; Bennett 1986).

For example, while the average citizen lives in a metropolitan area, the Common Cause member resides in a region that is almost 7 percent more urbanized. This is reflected when data on the geographic distribution of Common Cause's membership are explored: The propensity of the association's contributors to come from urban areas is evidenced by a pronounced concentration of members in the more urban Northeast and Far West (Figure 3.1). Although the likelihood that a member of the voting-age population in these areas belongs to Common Cause is about 1 in 100, the probability in other areas shrinks to roughly 1 in 500.

Returning to the data in Table 3.1, differences between members and nonmembers are even starker when it comes to income. Common Cause contributors are almost five times less likely than the average citizen to have had 1980 family incomes under $10,000, and are almost four times more apt to have had earnings over $50,000. This conforms roughly with the beliefs of direct marketers that about 30 percent of all families have the requisite discretionary income to join political organizations (Rothenberg 1991).

As dramatic as these discrepancies appear for income, they pale relative to those for education. Common Cause members are an incredibly well-schooled bunch. A phenomenal 93.6 percent of participants report having been to college, compared to 36.8 percent of the national electorate. Even more striking is that 54.9 percent of group members – ten times more than the average citizenry – have received postgraduate education. Not surprisingly

Table 3.1. *Common Cause members and the national electorate: Selected sociodemographic characteristics*

	Category (percentage)	
Characteristic	Common Cause	National electorate
Urbanization		
Congressional district	78.1	71.4
Family income		
Less than $10,000	5.0	23.1
$10,000—$20,000	17.0	23.3
$20,000—$25,000	14.8	16.7
$25,000—$35,000	19.5	15.3
$35,000—$50,000	22.4	16.0
More than $50,000	21.4	5.5
Education		
Some grade school	0.0	3.4
Grade school	0.7	1.5
Some high school	1.0	21.0
High school	4.7	37.4
Some college	14.1	20.6
College	24.6	10.7
Postgraduate	54.9	5.5
Work status		
White collar	90.9	45.9
Self—employed	15.7	6.9

Table 3.1 (*continued*)

Characteristic	Category (percentage)	
	Common Cause	National electorate
Work for others	39.7	51.0
Retired	31.3	13.9
Housewife	9.6	16.0
Student	1.2	3.9
Looking for work	0.7	3.3
Other	1.7	5.0
Marital status		
Married	68.9	61.7
Race		
White	98.5	87.3
Religion		
Protestant, general	3.7	5.1
Protestant, Reformation era	22.3	16.1
Protestant, pietistic	13.6	21.5
Protestant, neofundamentalist	0.4	17.8
Neotraditional Christian	11.5	3.0
Catholic	12.3	23.2
Jewish	16.3	3.4
Greek Catholic/Eastern Orthodox	0.2	0.3
Other non-Christians	5.2	1.6
None	14.6	8.1

Table 3.1 (*continued*)

Characteristic	Category (percentage)	
	Common Cause	National electorate
Gender		
Male	56.6	43.3
Age		
18—25	2.0	16.4
25—30	3.9	12.5
31—40	12.8	20.3
41—50	12.2	12.7
51—60	21.5	15.3
61—65	14.1	6.8
66—70	11.7	5.8
70—older	21.7	10.3

Source: 1981 Common Cause survey, 1980 National Election Studies, and
Congressional District Data Book.

given this wide gulf, the group's contributors are also far more prone to occupy white collar jobs. Over 90 percent of (employed) Common Cause members are white collar workers. Group contributors are also more apt to be either retired or self-employed and are somewhat more likely to be married.

Those signing up also differ markedly from the national citizenry on other characteristics that correlate with an upper class status. Common Cause is a notably white group. While 12.7 percent of those in the NES survey are nonwhite, a meager 1.5 percent of those in Common Cause qualify. Clearly, this is an organization that has scant appeal to minorities, perhaps because as a collectivity it has not generally concerned itself with the everyday struggles of economic survival.[5] They are also far more likely to be "high church" Reformation-era Protestants, so-called neotraditional Christians

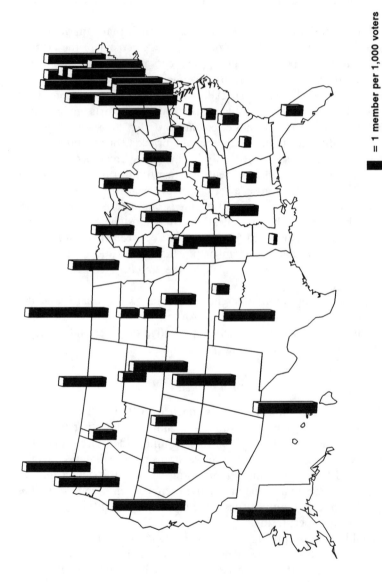

Figure 3.1. Geographic distribution of Common Cause membership (membership/voting age population). *Source*: Common Cause.

■ = 1 member per 1,000 voters

(mostly, confirming their popular image, Unitarians), Jewish, believers in alternative religions, or not religious. Participants are less prone to be "low church" (pietistic and especially neofundamentalist) Protestants or Catholics.[6] They are additionally, in line with conventional wisdom about participation (e.g., Verba and Nie 1972), considerably more likely to be male than female.

As mentioned, perhaps the one exceptional finding is that Common Cause members are much older: Although only about 22 percent of the citizenry are over 60, almost 50 percent of group members qualify. This discrepancy between the national and organizational age distributions becomes less pronounced when the 51–60 and especially the 41–50 brackets are considered, and becomes dramatically reversed when the younger cohorts are examined. While 16.4 percent of the national electorate is under 26, a mere 2 percent of association contributors falls into this age bracket. Surprisingly – given that Common Cause was founded only in the 1970s – members are of the Franklin Roosevelt and Adlai Stevenson generations rather than of the George McGovern and Jimmy Carter era. Moreover, the Common Cause data reveal, and staff members confirm, this is characteristic of both their group and other comparable organizations, that most new organizational contributors have consistently fallen somewhere between their mid-40s and mid-60s. Rather than having a membership that grows old over time, the group has from its inception appealed to the middle-aged reader of the *New York Times*.[7]

In short, sociodemographic differences exist across the board, and they generally point in predictable directions. Although Common Cause contributors might not self-select themselves perfectly, they certainly seem to conform to the organization's broad public image.[8]

Political attitudes

Do Common Cause members differ as much from the national citizenry when it comes to their political attitudes? Despite the fact that the survey data are perhaps less rich on this topic than they are concerning sociodemographic characteristics, the answer appears to be that discrepancies exist but that they are not quite as uniform.[9] There are significant gaps between group members and the national citizenry when it comes to a host of attitudes. Although many of these findings are again intuitive, some of the results are more perplexing.

The available data on preferences can be roughly divided into two types: those that measure broad assessments of politics and political institutions and those that deal with specific issues. For each, substantial differences between members' attitudes and those of the national population are evident.

Much of the information employed as indicators of general political evaluations revolves around attitudes toward political parties (Table 3.2). This is not inappropriate for assessing Common Cause members, since the

Table 3.2. *Common Cause members and the national electorate: General policy preferences*

Characteristic	Category (percentage)	
	Common Cause	National electorate
Ideology		
Extremely liberal	6.2	2.5
Liberal	41.3	9.3
Slightly liberal	21.8	13.5
Middle of road	14.4	30.6
Slightly conservative	10.3	21.0
Conservative	5.4	19.8
Extremely conservative	0.6	3.3
Party identification[a]		
Strong Democrat	15.8	18.1
Weak Democrat	12.7	23.6
Leaning Democrat	40.4	11.7
Pure independent	14.3	13.2
Leaning Republican	10.2	10.5
Weak Republican	4.3	14.3
Strong Republican	2.3	8.7
Performance rating: Political parties		
Very poor	8.8	5.7
Poor	32.8	31.7
Fair	50.6	52.2
Good	7.3	8.9
Very good	0.4	1.4

Table 3.2 (*continued*)

Characteristic	Category (percentage)	
	Common Cause	National electorate
Performance rating: Federal government		
Very poor	10.8	6.9
Poor	28.0	31.5
Fair	49.6	52.7
Good	10.9	8.5
Very good	0.7	0.5
Performance rating: Congress		
Very poor	10.0	6.9
Poor	33.0	35.8
Fair	48.3	46.0
Good	10.0	8.4
Very good	1.4	0.3
Performance rating: Supreme Court		
Very poor	2.2	8.3
Poor	7.3	23.3
Fair	38.4	41.9
Good	43.0	23.2
Very good	9.1	3.4

Source: 1981 Common Cause survey and 1980 National Election Studies.

"Independents are divided into leaning Democrat, pure independent, and leaning Republican.

group expends so much of its political efforts trying to undermine parties as institutions. Most notably, the association's efforts on behalf of campaign finance reforms have frequently constituted attacks on political parties as well as on special interests. For example, the group has been a vocal critic of parties' use of so-called soft money – electoral resources used for party building rather than for a particular candidate's campaign (about $25 million in the 1989–90 election cycle).

Therefore, it is not shocking to discover that Common Cause contributors are also less likely to favor parties as institutions. In their "running tally of retrospective evaluations" (Fiorina 1981, p. 84), two differences come through. Despite the fact that Common Cause as an organization is avowedly nonpartisan, which is also reflected in a propensity to identify oneself as a liberal, group members are considerably more Democratic if persons who identify themselves as leaning toward the Democratic party are included (68.9 percent compared to 53.4 percent). However, this discrepancy in the numbers identifying with each party is the product of group members' propensity to be leaning Democrats rather than to claim to be party identifiers. While there are far fewer Republican contributors in an absolute sense, the proportion of those favoring the GOP who are leaning partisans is roughly the same as Democrats.

Curiously, however, Common Cause contributors are only slightly more apt to give parties negative performance ratings overall. They have a strong propensity to rate the job performed by parties (and other political institutions) as fair. Group members are also no more likely to agree with the traditional NES statement designed to measure external political efficacy, that "Parties are interested in people's votes but not their opinions." One explanation may be that members perceive higher levels of efficacy but have less regard for political parties, and these two effects roughly balance each other.

Along the same lines, similar results are uncovered with respect to the performance rating of the federal government – members and nonmembers are statistically undifferentiable. Furthermore, there is barely any difference in their assessment of Congress. Again, it is possible to speculate that confounding effects are behind the similarities between citizens and contributors. Perhaps beliefs by Common Cause members (roughly consistent with the organization's public stance) that these institutions are not sufficiently open and fair in a procedural sense are counterbalanced by a liberal, Democratic faith that government should take an active role.[10]

The association's members actually respond more favorably than the average citizen when it comes to the Supreme Court. This makes a certain intuitive sense; those who are most committed to changing partisan institutions are most impressed with nonpartisan politics.[11] Yet, this is also somewhat ironic since the Common Cause leadership has largely eschewed the

strategy of heavy reliance on litigation that so many other public interest groups have adopted.

A number of specific policy items from the NES and Common Cause surveys can also be employed to compare group members with the national electorate. However, an important caveat is in order. The wording and coding of survey questions is significantly different from one interview instrument to the next (see Appendix 3.1 at the end of this chapter). Therefore, the results must be viewed especially cautiously.

Nevertheless, Common Cause members can be broadly characterized as more progressive on social and defense issues than the average citizen.[12] However, when it comes to economic concerns, group contributors are as, or more, hard nosed as the modal person.

Thus, organizational participants were more supportive of the Equal Rights Amendment (ERA), which Common Cause endorsed, than others in the electorate. For example, a considerable majority (66 percent) of Common Cause respondents claimed that they were "strongly [in] favor" of the ERA, and a total of 83 percent gave some sort of favorable reply. By contrast, only 31 and 61 percent, respectively, of those interviewed in the NES claimed to be strongly in favor of the amendment or gave a favorable reply.

Or consider the issue of abortion. Over 86 percent of Common Cause contributors agreed that abortion should not be forbidden, since one should not require a woman to have a child she doesn't want; compare this to the 27 percent in the NES study who selected the same statement (out of 4 alternatives). While the nature of the alternative question formats might somewhat exaggerate this huge discrepancy, there is undoubtedly a real difference in the aggregate. Along the same lines, although the majority of Common Cause members were opposed to busing, the 38 percent who replied that it should be used to achieve racial balance is considerably greater than the 10 percent of NES respondents arguing that busing should be used to achieve integration.

Similarly, as best as can be discerned, there are tremendous differences among the two groups on defense issues. A whopping 75 percent of Common Cause contributors thought that defense spending should not be greatly increased. By contrast, only 11 percent of citizens made similar claims. While, once again, timing and question wording might be responsible for some of this enormous gulf, it is unlikely to explain all of it.

But on economic issues, the progressiveness of group members is far less clear-cut; indeed, there is evidence that Common Cause members are more conservative when it comes to pocketbook issues. While slightly more favorably disposed toward a guaranteed income (42 percent agree compared to 31 percent in the NES), contributors are more likely to prefer spending reductions at the expense of governmental services (47 percent versus 34 percent) and to choose the Republican solution of inducing unemployment if it diminishes inflation (50 percent as compared to 35 percent). That there

are not consistent differences, particularly in a progressive direction, over economic policies makes sense. Common Cause has never been a traditional liberal group based on the cleavages associated with the Democratic New Deal coalition. Rather, its foundations lie in the social cleavages that emerged as this coalition showed signs of wear and tear; it is an organization that was formed during a period of rising social unrest by those who espoused a particular vision of procedural fairness and freedom.

In summary, Common Cause members seem neither wildly enthusiastic about the state of government nor extremely pessimistic. To the degree it is possible to measure these differences, existing distinctions generally pertain to attitudes toward partisan institutions and social issues. However, when the subject is economics, the limited data suggest that members are not more progressive across the board than the average American. Rather, the pronounced liberal attitudes of Common Cause members probably reflect underlying social rather than economic cleavages.

Participatory activities

Given the fact that they already belong to one association, it would certainly be expected, a priori, that Common Cause contributors would be more participatory than the average citizen (besides their donations to and activities with respect to the group). This would be predicted whether the spotlight were on electoral participation or involvement in other collectivities.

When the focus is on electoral activities, the data from the Common Cause and NES surveys are straightforward. While information on the voting participation rate of Common Cause members per se is not available (although it is undoubtedly far higher than for the population as a whole), contributors are a dozen times more likely to report that they contributed money to the 1980 campaign and six times more apt to recount that they did political work in the campaign (Table 3.3).

Strong results for nonelectoral participation are also uncovered. Consider the data – although often not directly comparable – from the Common Cause poll and the GSS:

1. While 16 percent of Common Cause participants say that they belong to service clubs, only 10 percent of the citizenry claim the same.
2. While more than 62 percent of group contributors respond that they are members of a "church, synagogue or other religious groups," less than 37 percent of GSS respondents identify as being in "church-affiliated groups."
3. While 38 percent of Common Cause members are in "school and school related groups," only 14 percent of the general population are in "school service groups."
4. While 53 percent of Common Cause members are in "professional or occupational groups," 14 percent of the GSS respondents say that they are in "professional or academic societies."

Table 3.3. *Common Cause members and the national electorate:*
Participatory activity

Characteristic	Category (percentage)	
	Common Cause	National electorate
Electoral activity		
Did political work in campaign	20.2	3.6
Contributed money in 1980	72.2	5.9

Source: 1981 Common Cause survey and 1980 National Election Studies.

Additionally, consider that a full 25 percent of Common Cause members are also members of the League of Women Voters, compared to the roughly 1 in 1,200 likelihood, based on the League's aggregate membership of about 125,000, that a member of the citizenry is a League member. Or consider that, while Mitchell (1979) estimates that about one million persons belonged to environmental groups in the late 1970s, 52 percent of Common Cause respondents claim membership. Moreover, although general numbers are not readily available for the likelihood that a member of the general population belongs to "feminist groups" or "consumer groups," enough is known about these types of organizations to recognize that they are much lower than the 37 and 25 percent that Common Cause contributors report.[13]

Summary: Common Cause members and the national citizenry

Clearly, the differences between Common Cause members and the national citizenry are considerable and range across a wide array of characteristics. Sociodemographically, they comprise a relatively narrow subset of the American population. In terms of political attitudes, they seem to embody beliefs that are associated with a social consciousness. Finally, an analysis of their activities demonstrates that they are true participators.

Whatever influence Common Cause might have on policy, to claim that it is a public interest group (or a People's Lobby for that matter) requires a

careful definition of the term. If such organizations are thought of as entities that pursue the production of collective goods that do not selectively and materially provide benefits to the entities', then Common Cause would seem to satisfy many of the relevant criteria. If, by contrast, these groups are supposed to be somehow representative of the citizenry as a whole, then the group (not surprisingly) does not qualify. In representational terms, those who join the association do not look, think, or behave like the average citizen in society.

THE COMMON CAUSE MEMBERSHIP: ACTIVISTS VERSUS RANK AND FILE

From the outside, collectivities like Common Cause frequently appear as if they are composed of one large, homogeneous mass of persons. Indeed, the data contrasting its membership with the national citizenry demonstrate that on any number of attributes, the variance across all contributors appears to be rather low. Certainly, the association's members are more homogeneous than the national citizenry as a whole.

To reiterate, the structure of the Common Cause mail survey actually makes contrasting different types of contributors to the organization far easier than comparing them to the national citizenry. The 4 percent of those whom the association formally defines as activists are the individuals who form the backbone of the group, who contribute the volunteer labor essential for the association's political endeavors given its limited resources. Consequently, their oversampling in the Common Cause survey furnishes a rare opportunity to compare the average contributor with the participant who represents the workhorse of an organization.

Given the group's apparent homogeneity, it might seem surprising at first that the association could be structured so that one class of contributors appears distinct from another. Yet, while certainly there are no expectations that the group's members will vary as dramatically from one another as they do from the populace as a whole, there are valid reasons to believe that evidence of real intraorganizational differences should be uncovered. Furthermore, any discrepancies should be in fairly obvious directions.

The basis of beliefs about where activists and rank-and-file members might go their separate ways rests with the enormous differences in commitment that are entailed. This would lead to presumptions that activists might possess more of the sociodemographic characteristics associated with participation and more of those features that would make donations of time less costly. In addition, activists might appear to reflect a better attitudinal match with Common Cause, because members might initially self-select themselves. Those in the rank and file who like what they learn might shift to the activist level, or activists who discover that there is not a close match might reduce their commitment by moving to the rank and file or quitting altogether.

Finally, and most obviously, there ought to be differences in members'
levels of participation generally, since there are presumably some citizens
who perpetually throw themselves into the fray while others are innately
checkwriters.

Sociodemographic differences

Interestingly, while there are some real sociodemographic discrepancies as
well as similarities between the two classes of Common Cause contributors,
these differences do not necessarily pertain to those characteristics that
might initially be expected from the literature on political participation
(Table 3.4).[14] In a broad sense, what seems to distinguish activists most is that

Table 3.4. *Comparing rank and file and activists: Selected sociodemographic
characteristics*

	Category (percentage)	
Characteristic	Rank and file	Activist
Age		
18—25	2.1	1.4
25—30	3.7	4.6
31—40	13.7	9.2
41—50	11.7	13.4
51—60	20.6	25.4
61—65	13.3	16.5
66—70	11.4	13.0
70—older	23.4	16.5
Marital status		
Single	16.4	10.6
Married	67.5	73.5
Separated, widowed, divorced	16.1	15.9
Urbanization		
Congressional district	80.2	71.1

Table 3.4 (*continued*)

Characteristic	Category (percentage)	
	Rank and file	Activist
Rural town/farm	9.4	10.7
Town/small city	26.9	40 9
Medium-sized city	20.5	18.9
Large city	21.2	12.5
Suburb	21.9	17.1
Religion		
Protestant, general	4.1	2.6
Protestant, Reformation era	22.3	22.0
Protestant, pietistic	13.0	15.7
Protestant, neofundamentalist	0.6	0.0
Neotraditional Christian	9.9	16.4
Catholic	12.0	13.1
Jewish	18.3	9.7
Greek Catholic/Eastern Orthodox	0.1	0.4
Other non-Christians	5.1	5.2
None	14.5	14.9
Race		
White	98.5	98.6
Education		
Grade school	0.8	0.4
Some high school	1.2	0.4
High school	4.7	4.9
Some college	14.7	12.4
College	24.3	23.8
Postgraduate	54.4	56.2

Table 3.4 (*continued*)

Characteristic	Category (percentage)	
	Rank and file	Activist
Gender		
Male	57.3	53.7
Family income		
Less than $10,000	4.6	6.1
$10,000—$20,000	15.8	21.2
$20,000—$25,000	14.8	14.7
$25,000—$35,000	18.9	21.9
$35,000—$50,000	22.2	20.9
$50,000—$75,000	12.3	9.4
$75,000—$100,000	5.1	3.2
More than $100,000	5.8	2.5
Work status		
White collar	92.1	86.8
Self-employed	19.8	15.4
Work for others	43.4	44.2
Not employed	1.6	1.9
Retired	25.7	29.8
Housewife	8.5	8.7
Other	1.0	0.0

Source: 1981 Common Cause survey and *Congressional District Data Book*.

they lead quite stable lives. They are generally a bit older than rank-and-file members – over forty as a rule – although they are somewhat less likely to be over seventy. They are more apt to be married and less prone to be single. There is also a greater likelihood that they are from small town America, which is reflected in the lesser degree of urbanization of activists' congressional districts. The only religious difference is the tendency of activists to be neotraditional Christians, which is a product of 11 percent of all activists being Unitarians.

By contrast, there are no significant differences between rank-and-file members and activists on the qualities most associated with political participation: race, education, and gender.[15] Of course, the lack of any racial distinction between the composition of the activist cadre and the rank and file is not surprising since the organization is extremely homogeneous racially. The absence of any statistical differentials in terms of educational achievements or gender might come as more of a surprise, especially given all the discrepancies concerning other sociodemographic features.

Political attitudes

The data on political attitudes are considerably richer than those employed in comparing Common Cause members to the national citizenry. As a means of presenting these data, they can be divided into three parts: (1) broad outlooks on politics, parties, and personalities; (2) attitudes toward general political issues; and (3) opinions regarding Common Cause–specific issues.[16]

The general picture that emerges from exploring these three types of attitudes is that real differences exist between the beliefs of members of the rank and file and activists. Basically the former are somewhat more conservative than the latter on all three dimensions.[17]

Consider the first type of data regarding general, not issue-specific, matters. Interestingly, when it comes to overarching measures of political preferences, activists are somewhat more Democratic than rank-and-file contributors, particularly as strong partisans, but they are no more liberal (Table 3.5).[18] Along the same lines, activists were also slightly more pro–Jimmy Carter and anti-Ronald Reagan. Thus, even within Common Cause, there are discrepancies among members in their broad outlook on parties and personalities, if not in their general liberal or conservative orientation.

Given these general differences, it is perhaps not terribly surprising to discover systematic variations between rank-and-file and activist contributors when they were asked about a series of issues that were not part of Common Cause's issue agenda at the time (Table 3.6).[19] Although statistically significant contrasts between the two classes of members across types of contributors are not evident for every concern, where they do exist they consistently demonstrate that activists are more liberal than their rank-and-file counterparts (despite their self-assessments, which reveal no difference). Furthermore,

Table 3.5. *Comparing rank and file and activists: General policy preferences*

Preference	Category (percentage)	
	Rank and file	Activist
Ideology		
Extremely liberal	6.3	6.3
Liberal	40.7	48.1
Slightly liberal	22.8	20.4
Middle of road	12.7	11.1
Slightly conservative	10.9	9.6
Conservative	6.0	4.1
Extremely conservative	0.7	8.4
Party identification[a]		
Strong Democrat	14.3	21.5
Weak Democrat	13.2	11.5
Leaning Democrat	40.3	42.7
Pure independent	13.6	12.2
Leaning Republican	11.8	5.7
Weak Republican	4.2	4.7
Strong Republican	2.6	1.8
Feelings toward Jimmy Carter		
Very favorable	10.0	8.0
Somewhat favorable	43.7	51.1
Somewhat unfavorable	31.0	29.2
Very unfavorable	15.3	11.7
Feelings toward Ronald Reagan		
Very favorable	11.8	6.6

Table 3.5 (*continued*)

| | Category (percentage) | |
Preference	Rank and file	Activist
Somewhat favorable	19.1	20.1
Somewhat unfavorable	22.0	17.9
Very unfavorable	47.1	55.5

Source: 1981 Common Cause survey and 1980 National Election Studies.

*a*Independents are divided into leaning Democrat, pure independent, and leaning Republican.

Table 3.6. *Comparing rank and file and activists: Policy preferences on nongroup issues*

| | Category (percentage) | |
Preference	Rank and file	Activist
Defense spending		
Strongly agree	4.6	2.1
Agree somewhat	14.0	12.4
Not sure	7.5	6.7
Disagree somewhat	19.5	15.2
Strongly disagree	54.4	63.6
Equal opportunities for blacks		
Strongly agree	18.5	17.7
Agree somewhat	27.5	33.0

Table 3.6 (*continued*)

Preference	Category (percentage)	
	Rank and file	Activist
Not sure	14.9	13.8
Disagree somewhat	26.8	27.3
Strongly disagree	12.3	8.2
Services/spending trade-off		
Strongly agree	20.0	22.0
Agree somewhat	23.0	30.7
Not sure	7.6	8.3
Disagree somewhat	33.5	25.6
Strongly disagree	15.9	13.4
Soviets taking advantage		
Strongly agree	14.2	11.3
Agree somewhat	16.1	14.1
Not sure	29.4	31.8
Disagree somewhat	24.3	25.4
Strongly disagree	16.0	17.3
Inflation/unemployment trade-off		
Strongly agree	17.5	11.4
Agree somewhat	34.8	32.5
Not sure	18.6	19.6
Disagree somewhat	16.4	22.5
Strongly disagree	12.7	13.9
Permit abortion		
Strongly agree	76.6	73.5
Agree somewhat	9.8	12.0

Table 3.6 (*continued*)

Preference	Category (percentage)	
	Rank and file	Activist
Not sure	3.1	3.9
Disagree somewhat	4.4	4.9
Strongly disagree	6.0	5.7
Guarantee minimum income		
Strongly agree	17.7	20.8
Agree somewhat	23.1	23.3
Not sure	14.4	18.3
Disagree somewhat	18.9	18.3
Strongly disagree	25.8	19.4
No busing for integration		
Strongly agree	28.9	17.4
Agree somewhat	20.9	23.1
Not sure	14.1	12.5
Disagree somewhat	22.6	29.2
Strongly disagree	13.5	17.8
Increase nuclear plants		
Strongly agree	9.3	6.0
Agree somewhat	11.7	7.8
Not sure	13.7	10.6
Disagree somewhat	12.1	13.1
Strongly disagree	53.1	62.4

Source: 1981 Common Cause survey.

this breakdown includes at least one economic measure; the absolute gulf between social and economic issues that existed in the previous analysis is not present here. Thus, activists are more likely to be against defense spending, for social services, opposed to inducing additional unemployment, for school busing, and against nuclear energy.

Perhaps even more striking is the fact that these differences in issue preferences are evident when the subject is concerns specific to Common Cause (Table 3.7). On four of six issues – constitutional amendments to require a balanced budget, "sunset" legislation (laws fixing termination dates on programs and agencies), campaign finance regulation, and reapportionment – the variations are statistically significant and, again, activists' preferences are more liberal or, at least, more pro–Common Cause. For the two issues where there are no discrepancies (the ERA and lobby disclosure), responses are extremely skewed.

Table 3.7. *Comparing rank and file and activists: Policy preferences on group issues*

Preference	Category (percentage)	
	Rank and file	Activist
Balanced Budget Amendment		
1. Strongly favor	15.6	11.8
2.	12.8	3.2
3.	14.8	8.2
4.	9.1	6.8
5.	8.5	9.3
6.	11.5	15.0
7. Strongly oppose	21.8	30.7
8. Can't say	6.0	5.0
Sunset legislation		
1. Strongly favor	47.5	61.9
2.	18.7	19.2
3.	13.2	8.2
4.	5.9	2.5

Table 3.7 (*continued*)

	Category (percentage)	
Preference	Rank and file	Activist
5.	4.3	2.1
6.	2.6	1.8
7. Strongly oppose	4.5	3.2
8. Can't say	3.3	1.1
Campaign finance legislation		
1. Strongly favor	51.6	67.0
2.	19.2	14.7
3.	11.4	7.0
4.	5.8	3.9
5.	3.4	2.1
6.	2.2	1.4
7. Strongly oppose	3.6	1.4
8. Can't say	2.8	2.5
Equal Rights Amendment		
1. Strongly favor	63.2	71.1
2.	10.5	8.1
3.	6.2	5.3
4.	4.8	5.3
5.	4.0	2.8
6.	3.1	3.5
7. Strongly oppose	6.0	2.5
8. Can't say	2.0	1.4
Lobby disclosure		
1. Strongly favor	87.3	89.9
2.	7.1	7.3

Table 3.7 (*continued*)

Preference	Category (percentage)	
	Rank and file	Activist
3.	2.3	1.4
4.	0.8	0.7
5.	0.8	0.3
6.	0.3	0.3
7. Strongly oppose	0.0	0.8
8. Can't say	0.0	0.8
Who should reapportion		
congressional districts		
1. State legislature	5.3	5.9
2. Bipartisan commission	79.7	86.0
3. Does not matter	5.4	3.5
4. Can't say/not sure	9.4	3.8

Source: 1981 Common Cause survey.

Thus, even when it comes to political attitudes, activists and rank-and-file contributors are far from identical. Quite simply put, the former are slightly more extreme in their opinions than the latter. This distinction is reflected in how they think about politics broadly, issues generally, and Common Cause specifically.

Participatory activities

As mentioned, if there exists any area where differences between rank-and-file members and activists should be expected, it has to do with participation. Especially when the subject is high-cost, nonmonetary forms of participation that are analogous to activist behavior, it is highly likely that the two types of contributors will differ markedly.[20]

Table 3.8. *Comparing rank and file and activists: Participatory activity*

	Category (percentage)	
Preference	Rank and file	Activist
Electoral activity		
Contributed money in 1980	70.6	76.7
Did political work in campaign	16.2	33.3
Gave a candidate advice	7.9	18.8
Gave a public endorsement	18.9	28.1
Asked others to contribute	23.5	34.5
Asked an organization to support a candidate	7.4	10.1
Sought party, elected, or appointed office	20.1	31.9
Group membership and activism		
Environmental groups		
Not active	33.2	28.4
Active	18.8	21.5
Feminist groups		
Not active	17.9	18.1
Active	6.5	9.8
Consumer groups		
Not active	28.3	25.9
Active	8.5	12.6
League of Women Voters		
Not active	16.5	16.1
Active	6.5	15.1

Source: 1981 Common Cause survey.

Indeed, this is the case (Table 3.8). The picture that emerges from these data is that activists are more willing to get involved in those activities that require considerable expenditures of time and energy. For example, when it comes to electoral activities, activists are only slightly more liable to have given money to a candidate in 1980.[21] However, they are roughly 50 percent more apt to have given a public endorsement that might influence others or asked friends and associates to participate, and twice as likely to have done political work in campaign organizations or to have given a candidate advice on campaign strategy. Only with respect to the comparatively rare act of asking an organization to support a candidate was there no statistically significant difference whatsoever.

Similar results emerge when it comes to other forms of participation. For example, the likelihood that activists had sought political party positions, public elective office, or public appointive office in the past was more than 50 percent greater than that for rank-and-file contributors. But the probability of membership in organizations that might be alternatives to Common Cause – environmental groups, feminist groups, consumer groups, or the League of Women Voters – differed only with respect to the League. This one discrepancy makes sense in that the League is a group for which, probably more than any other of its kind, making contributions of time forms an intimate part of membership. By contrast, Common Cause activists were about 50 percent more prone to report that they were members in at least one of these four organizations. Once again, acts that seem to require only money and modest effort show small differences, if any, between those occupying different places in the organizational hierarchy; by contrast, those behaviors that dictate that contributors give heavily of their own time and effort are characterized by wide variations.

Summary: Membership variations

Obviously, Common Cause activists and rank-and-file contributors are not quite birds of the same feather. While the group is homogeneous relative to the rest of the outside world, there is a structured heterogeneity. Activists lead more stable lives, have more liberal attitudes, and are not merely satisfied with being Common Cause volunteers but engage in analogous behavior elsewhere.

Thus, there is something more to the organization than simply a collection of individuals who are all alike. As will be discussed later, this has important implications not merely for understanding what motivates activists, but for how organizational goals are formulated and, ultimately, for group influence.

CONCLUSIONS: GROUP MEMBERS – EXTERNAL AND INTERNAL COMPARISONS

In many respects, the analysis of Common Cause members conducted here seems to offer a contradictory message. On the one hand, relative to other

members of society, Common Cause contributors appear qualitatively, indeed dramatically, different and quite homogeneous. Not only do participants vary considerably in socioeconomic background, but their conception of the public interest diverges as well. On the other hand, when the contrast is between those who contribute greatly of their time (as well as their income) and the larger mass of members, the picture is one of considerable heterogeneity among types of members. Since contributors are not identical, it leaves open the possibility that variations in characteristics among contributors (rather than mere idiosyncratic factors) may help to explain why some members stay and others quit, and why some become activists and others stay in the rank and file; it also suggests that whether or not one class of participants is more influential than another within the organization could have a huge impact on the group goals that are pursued and, ultimately, on the association's impact on public policy.

More specifically, there are a number of interesting contrasts as the analysis moves from the organization/citizen to the rank and file/activist dichotomy. For example, when the sociodemographic differences between citizens and contributors are examined, many of the relevant discrepancies concern those factors that are most associated with participation. By comparison, when it comes to intraorganizational comparisons, variations principally revolve around other elements. With regard to political preferences, Common Cause contributors are not necessarily more liberal across the board than the electorate-at-large – for instance with respect to economic issues. However, activists are consistently more liberal than their rank-and-file counterparts. Concerning all types of participation, members are far more energetic than the national citizenry. Activists tend to be more involved than other members with respect to those behaviors that principally require a commitment of time.

In short, Common Cause contributors are, not surprisingly, representative of a very specialized segment of society. Differences between them and the national citizenry can be painted with broad strokes. By contrast, distinctions between contributors require a finer brush but are very real nonetheless. Whether these statistical distinctions reflect germane differences on who decides to join and experience an organization, on subsequent contributor choices, on how the association is run, on what objectives it pursues, and on what impact it has remains to be seen. But as preliminary findings, they suggest that the process by which (or whether) citizen attitudes are linked to the political system may exhibit subtleties that make analysis worthwhile.

Having offered all these comments, this chapter should end the way it began: with a caution that nothing definitive can be concluded from the preceding data about why some individuals join and stay in symbolic organizations such as Common Cause and others abstain, why some are activists and others are not, how the group functions qua organization, or how this relates to political influence. These tasks necessitate developing and testing the implications of the perspective developed earlier on citizen

decisions, and then relating the results to goal formation and public policy. It is to these assignments that attention is now directed.

Appendix 3.1. Question wording of Common Cause and National Election Study questions

For many of the sociodemographic questions – on age, sex, income, race, etc. – question wording is not problematic and is not presented here. The possibility that wording nuances will make a difference is more germane for attitudinal questions, particularly with regard to specific issues. There is also some possibility that differences in wording will be relevant for the two behavioral measures that use NES indicators. In general, the questions in the NES instrument were somewhat longer and, particularly with respect to specific issues, usually provided alternative responses that were more specifically geared to the question (rather than just a generic pro or con). These differences undoubtedly reflect the fact that NES is an in-person interview rather than a mail questionnaire such as the survey instrument identified here as CC, used by Common Cause.

GENERAL POLITICAL ATTITUDES

Party identification

(CC) "We hear a lot of talk about liberals and conservatives. Below is a scale on which the political views that people might hold are arranged from extremely liberal to extremely conservative. Where would you place yourself on this scale?" (This possible alternative responses are shown in Table 3.5.)

(NES) "Generally speaking, do you usually think of yourself as a Republican, a Democrat, an Independent, or what?"

To those identifying a partisan preference: "Would you call yourself a strong Republican (Democrat) or a not very strong Republican (Democrat)?"

To those calling themselves Independents: "Do you think of yourself as closer to the Republican or to the Democratic party?"

Liberalism–conservatism

(CC) "We hear a lot of talk these days about liberals and conservatives. Here is a seven-point scale on which the political views that people might hold are arranged from extremely liberal to extremely conservative. Where would you place yourself on this scale?" (Again, the possible alternative responses are shown in Table 3.5.)

(NES) Same wording, except the phrase "or haven't you thought much about this" is appended to the question.

Performance rating questions

In both surveys, performance ratings were requested for the federal government in Washington, the presidency, Congress – specifically defined as the U.S. Senate and the House of Representatives – the Supreme Court, and the political parties. For the NES, respondents are coded on a nine-point scale with points labeled very poor job (0), poor job (2), fair job (4), good job (6), and very good job (8); the Common Cause respondents had these five options without intermediate options. The introductory statements were slightly different:

(CC) "Now we'd like to know how good a job you feel some of the parts of our government are doing for the country as a whole. Do you feel that each of the following parts of government is doing a very poor job, a poor job, a fair job, a good job, or a very good job?"

(NES) "Now we'd like to ask you how good a job you feel some of the parts of our government are doing. As I read, please give me the number that describes how good a job you feel that part of government is doing for the country as a whole."

Political efficacy and attitudes toward parties

The NES and CC studies ask one nearly identical question designed to tap political efficacy and attitudes toward parties: The NES version states that "Parties are only interested in people's votes but not in their opinions." The CC question omits the word "only." In the NES, respondents are asked whether they agree or disagree; in the CC study, respondents may check strongly agree, agree somewhat, not sure, disagree somewhat, or strongly disagree.

SPECIFIC POLITICAL ATTITUDES

All of the Common Cause survey indicators employed to measure specific political preferences, except for that concerning the Equal Rights Amendment, gave respondents five choices: (1) strongly agree; (2) agree somewhat; (3) not sure; (4) disagree somewhat; and (5) strongly disagree. For the ERA, they were provided with a seven-point scale, anchored by "strongly favor" and "strongly oppose" on each end, with "can't say" as an eighth option.

Equal Rights Amendment

(CC) "There has been a good deal of discussion about the Equal Rights Amendment to the United States Constitution (the E.R.A.). Where would you place yourself on the Equal Rights Amendment?"

(NES) "Do you approve or disapprove of the proposed Equal Rights

Amendment to the Constitution, sometimes called the ERA Amendment?"
"Do you approve (disapprove) strongly or not strongly?"

Abortion

(CC) "Abortion should *not* be forbidden, since one should not require a woman to have a child she doesn't want." The possible alternative responses are shown in Table 3.6.

(NES) "There has been some discussion about abortion during recent years. Which one of the opinions on this page best agrees with your view? You can just tell me the number of the opinion you choose." Opinions include: (1) Abortion should never be permitted. (2) Abortion should be permitted only if the life and health of the woman is in danger. (3) Abortion should be permitted if, due to personal reasons, the woman would have difficulty in caring for the child. And (4) abortion should never be forbidden, since one should not require a woman to have a child she doesn't want. A small number of respondents specified other opinions or said that they did not know.

Busing

(CC) "School children should *not* be bused to achieve racial balance in schools."

(NES) "There is much discussion about the best way to deal with racial problems. Some people think achieving racial integration of schools is so important that it justifies busing children to schools out of their own neighborhoods. Others think letting children go to their neighborhood schools is so important that they oppose busing. Where would you place yourself on this scale or haven't you thought much about this?" Respondents were given a seven-point scale, with (1) representing the statement "Bus to achieve integration" and (7) the statement "Keep children in neighborhood schools." Those choosing (1) to (3) were considered probusing.

Defense spending

(CC) "Defense spending should be greatly increased."

(NES) "Some people believe that we should spend much less money for defense. Others feel that defense spending should be greatly increased. Where would you place yourself on this scale, or haven't you thought much about this?" Respondents were given a seven-point scale, with (1) representing the statement "Greatly decrease defense spending" and (7) representing the statement "Greatly increase defense spending." Those choosing (1) through (3) were considered against defense spending.

Guaranteed income

(CC) "The federal government should guarantee that all Americans are provided with a minimum income."

(NES) "Some people feel the government in Washington should see to it that every person has a job and a good standard of living. Others think the government should just let each person get ahead on his own. Where would you place yourself on this scale, or haven't you thought much about it?" Respondents were given a seven-point scale, with (1) representing the statement "Government see to a job and good standard of living" and (7) representing the statement "Government let each person get ahead on own." Those choosing (1) through (3) were considered to favor a guaranteed income.

Trade-off between services and spending

(CC) "The government should continue the social services it now provides even if it means no reduction in spending."

(NES) "Some people think the government should provide fewer services, even in areas such as health and education, in order to reduce spending. Other people feel it is important for the government to continue the services it now provides even if it means no reduction in spending. Where would you place yourself on this scale, or haven't you thought much about it?" Respondents were given a seven-point scale, with (1) representing the statement "Government should provide many fewer services; reduce spending a lot" and (7) representing the statement "Government should continue to provide services; no reduction in spending." Those choosing (1) through (3) were considered to favor reducing government spending.

Trade-off between inflation and unemployment

(CC) "The Federal government should take action to reduce inflation even if this means unemployment will go up."

(NES) "Some people feel the federal government should take action to reduce the inflation rate, even if it means that unemployment would go up a lot. Others feel the government should take action to reduce the rate of unemployment, even if it means that inflation would go up a lot. Where would you place yourself on this scale, or haven't you thought much about it?" Respondents were given a seven-point scale, with (1) representing the statement "Reduce inflation even if unemployment goes up a lot" and (7) representing the statement "Reduce unemployment even if inflation goes up a lot." Those choosing (1) through (3) were considered to favor inducing unemployment.

Two questions tapped the same political activities in the 1980 election.

(CC) "Did you do *any* of these activities on behalf of a candidate in the 1980 election?"
   "Contributed money to a political campaign?"
   "Did political work in a campaign organization?"

(NES) "What about other contributions? Did you give any money this year to a candidate running for public office?"
   "Did you do any work for one of the parties or candidates (during the campaign)?"

4

Why do citizens join groups?

The results of the previous analysis specify the nature and extent of differences among Common Cause members and between them and the general public. Findings that contributors are a skewed sample of the national population but that there are discernible differences between them are consistent with the unified view of citizens' behavior presented earlier. But, by definition, such patterns do not explain what motivates people to behave the way they do. Put another way, this descriptive portrait cannot furnish any semblance of an explanation about *why* citizens join groups.

Yet, it is important to know why people join if an understanding of the linkages between citizens' choices, goal formation, and the policy process is to be developed. Joining has potentially quite considerable organizational and systemic ramifications. Organizationally, members are the sine qua non for organizational survival if the collectivity is not bankrolled via the largess of foundations or governments (on the phenomenon of institutional backing of associations, see Hayes 1983; Walker 1983, 1990; Salisbury 1984). Although the initial choice to sign up may be only one determinant of how many members an organization has (the rate of member retention being the other crucial component) or the aggregate amount of contributions (commitment and retention levels are the other primary elements), it is certainly a key for each. In addition, why people join should be a crucial conditioning element for retention and activism decisions and for how leaders behave in deciding which goals to pursue.

Systemically – and in conjunction with retention, activism, and goal formation – the initial decision is relevant if groups are to have a policy impact. For example, in discussing roll call voting, Kingdon argues that "In particular, interest groups appear to have slight influence on congressmen's voting decisions unless the groups are connected with their constituencies in some fashion" (1989, p. 174).[1] Of course, for other mechanisms of influence such as litigation, grassroots representation is likely to be far less important. In other words, for many reasons, attracting a substantial membership is seen as an important facilitator in being influential.

STUDYING THE MEMBERSHIP CHOICE

Given all these reasons for studying the membership choice, it should not be surprising that, as discussed previously, the vast preponderance of theoretical analysis of interest group members has focused on joining. Yet, as a form of political behavior, why individuals participate at all has long been a puzzle (Brody 1978). Understanding why citizens would contribute to an association in the first place, particularly one that fails to offer extensive private rewards, is of considerable inherent interest. Yet, it is generally acknowledged that there is relatively little in the empirical literature that actually succeeds in *explaining* why people join. Although there are any number of models and theories, empirically there is a "conventional wisdom" about the sociodemographic correlates of participation.

To reiterate, the reason for this dearth of causal analysis is understandable and straightforward: Studying joining is difficult because, as evidenced by the efforts to develop comparative data, it is problematic to develop a representative sample. More specifically, group contributors are so rare that surveys of the general population, which are not principally designed to explain why people join, yield numbers of members that are too small by themselves for meaningful analysis. Alternatively, surveys of those belonging to an organization, while furnishing illuminating information about the groups themselves, lack control groups providing a basis of comparison with the national citizenry. Aggregate analyses (e.g., Kau and Rubin 1979, 1982; Hansen 1985) solve the problem of being able to contrast the group population with the national citizenry at the obvious expense of the detailed information that is available from microlevel studies. By definition, individual-level inferences must be made from aggregate-level data. Generally, authors of such analyses acknowledge that they have not provided the key that explains why people contribute.[2]

The ideal means to study joining would be to (1) design a questionnaire that could be administered to both members and nonmembers of an association(s) with little alteration; (2) survey a stratified sample in which group members are overrepresented; and (3) use econometric weighting techniques to analyze the data. However, it is very costly to collect this kind of information, and there are a number of practical obstacles as well. The alternative strategy, which will be employed in this examination, is to exploit the available evidence – some of which was presented earlier – in new ways to shed light on the relevant issues. The means of analysis employed here should advance current research in at least two respects.

The first is that information is drawn from the available data sources in a manner that permits hypothesis testing. To estimate econometrically defensible results, statistical weighting techniques designed to deal with samples stratified on the dependent variables are utilized to test why people are members of political groups. The present investigation represents one of

the first attempts to assemble data in a manner that permits the formulation and execution of tests about why people are members of political groups.

In addition, the present research does not rely on any single source for evidence, each of which has its own imperfections. Instead, it employs a variety of different kinds of data and examines several distinct levels of analysis to compile a more complete picture of the membership process. Taken together, this mixture of approaches provides a more coherent picture of why group members choose to sign up than any single approach; this, in turn, represents a first step toward testing the experiential search framework.

This framework suggests a number of hypotheses that may be tested more or less directly with the available data. Basically, it implies that citizens probably join organizations – assuming that the leadership has set dues at a relatively inexpensive level and that membership makes learning significantly easier – with little group-specific knowledge and for general rather than specific reasons. The key to signing up should therefore be a general belief that the citizen and group may be well matched and, particularly, a strong enough interest in the organization that sampling is deemed worthwhile. In choosing among groups, contributors do not necessarily select the collectivity that is the best fit for them, because they possess imperfect information and factor in their opportunity to learn.

This outlook is considerably different from Olson's perfect-information scenario. In the latter, it would be expected that perfectly informed citizens would base their choices on a great deal of organization-specific knowledge and a strong fit between group positions and individual preferences. In short, very precise reasons would structure joining. Similarly, while the argument that individuals are imperfectly informed but never learn is more difficult to differentiate empirically from the experiential search perspective in an unambiguous fashion, it might be expected to be relatively similar to the Olsonian scenario. Individuals who sign up would possess higher levels of knowledge than those who anticipate learning and would believe (even if incorrectly) that there is a tight fit between their personal preferences and group policies. In other words, while not a decisive test for the viewpoint that members learn (this will be dealt with in subsequent chapters), it stands to reason that members with incomplete information who are incapable of updating should also rely upon very precise data in their joining decisions. Simply possessing a great deal of interest ought not to suffice.

The structure of the remainder of this chapter is to attack the issue of why people join from four angles. The first is an examination (albeit descriptive) of Common Cause members' beliefs about why they joined. This is followed by an individual-level analysis that builds on the comparison with the national citizenry presented in the preceding chapter. Data from the NES survey and the Common Cause mail questionnaire are combined using econometric weighting techniques to construct a representative sample. The

next section replicates this examination using a more conventional aggregate-level research design. Finally, a different tack on citizens' choices about associational membership is taken. The techniques of the individual-level analysis are applied to the issue of how people choose among organizations using a sample of four public interest groups.

WHY MEMBERS THINK THEY JOINED

Like comparisons with the national citizenry, information on members' professed reasons for joining Common Cause cannot explain why people belong. This requires data on those electing not to sign up as well as on those who are part of the group. However, contributors' beliefs about why they originally made a commitment do furnish a vantage point from which to understand both analyses of joining and subsequent decisions.

To reiterate, the implication of the experiential search theory is that members in a group such as Common Cause where the leaders have made it easy to join generally ought to believe that they joined for broad reasons. It should also be possible to reconcile participants' decisions after they join with their assessments of why they initially contributed – a point that will be taken up in later chapters. By contrast, those with perfect information should have far more specific reasons for signing up. Subsequent choices about whether to remain in the organization should also be based on the same factors as their decisions to enlist.

In the mail survey, respondents were asked the following question: "As you know, people may belong to Common Cause for many reasons. What would you say is the *principal* reason you belong to Common Cause?" The roughly 100 different responses were coded and condensed according to the type of benefits – purposive, selective (collective or divisible), and solidary, as defined already – that members seem to value. The most intriguing result is that the vast majority of contributors believe that they got involved for broad, purposive reasons (Table 4.1). Even employing a generous definition of selective benefits, 72 percent of respondents must be classified as professing that purposive concerns stimulated them to sign up.

These data are consistent with the experiential search argument that members know little about the specific costs and benefits of belonging when they initially join. General reformist tendencies were especially evident among those with a purposive impetus. Even many whose initial participation allegedly reflects the quest for selective benefits exhibit a broad participatory impulse. They claim they chose Common Cause to be politically effective or mobilized and generally not because their participation would further specific issues or other detailed benefits.

If a preponderance of these individuals had extremely broad and general reasons for joining, what prompted them to sign up in the first place? While it is clear that Common Cause members are descriptively different from

Table 4.1. *Members' proclaimed reasons for joining Common Cause*

Reason for joining	Number of respondents	Percentage
Purposive benefits		
Supports general goals, issues, efforts	169	14.7
Keeps government honest and fair	162	14.1
Reforms, improves government; makes government more responsive	132	11.5
Combats special interests, lobbyists, PACs, corporations, big business	79	6.9
Supports public interest and the common good	71	6.2
Is a watchdog-investigatory group	53	4.6
Is a nonpartisan group	26	2.3
Protests political power and corruption	21	1.8
Supports group in general (no issue content)	20	1.7
Is concerned about democracy	18	1.6
Is antigovernment or anti— political party	17	1.5
Appeals to sense of civic duty	13	1.1
Addresses problems in society, government policies	11	1.0
Maintains checks and balances	10	0.9
Is unique and important	9	0.8
Needs financial support	8	0.7

Table 4.1 (*continued*)

Reason for joining	Number of respondents	Percentage
Is a liberal and anticonservative group	6	0.5
Subtotal	825	71.9
Selective benefits		
(collective or divisible)		
Makes members effective	65	5.7
Provides political information	53	4.6
Addresses specific issue(s)	35	3.0
Offers a chance for personal political activity	32	2.8
Provides collective action necessary for change	28	2.4
Supplies leadership	26	2.3
Provides representation	18	1.6
Informs citizens and encourages participatory democracy	12	1.0
Offers a chance to be mobilized on issues	11	1.0
Is effective	9	0.8
Is an activist organization	5	0.4
Subtotal	294	25.6

Table 4.1 (*continued*)

Reason for joining	Number of respondents	Percentage
Solidary benefits		
Family or friends belong	11	1.0
Joining is part of life-style—		
social reasons	3	0.3
Subtotal	14	1.3
Miscellaneous	16	1.4
Total	1,149	100.2

others in the population of potential contributors (Godwin 1988), which, if any, of these factors can explain why some individuals join and others decline?

THE DETERMINANTS OF MEMBERSHIP:
AN INDIVIDUAL-LEVEL ANALYSIS

Before getting directly to answering this question, a note on the general context of citizens' decision making is in order. Unfortunately, like so much about analyzing group participation, examining why some imperfectly informed citizens sign up and others defer is more complicated than the preceding discussion might lead one to believe. Put in the simplest terms, the root of this complexity revolves around leadership decisions. Associations routinely make it easier for some individuals to join than it is for others. Organizational behavior itself has an influence upon the cost and benefit estimates made by potential contributors.

These obstacles make empirical examination of the decision-making process more problematic than might be thought at first blush. Usually estimating a cost/benefit participation calculus at one point in time entails identifying which participant characteristics make a difference at the aggregate equilibrium observed: That is, at a given price, what is the probability

that an individual will get involved? This assumes that leaders choose to offer a given set of benefits at a particular cost to everyone in a particular population. Given this supply, possible contributors will sort themselves out depending upon their level of demand. However, analyzing who becomes a group member is more intricate because organizational leaders also vary the cost of joining across individuals.

This difference can be illustrated with a comparison to the voting participation decision. Assume that the choice whether or not to cast a ballot follows the conventional Downsian calculation where citizens go to the polls when benefits exceed costs. In this scenario, individuals assess the benefits that accrue to them from voting. Political decision makers, in turn, may dictate how costly it is for any citizen (all are treated equally) to cast a ballot by defining the registration rules and other criteria that must be fulfilled. Subsequently, each citizen resolves whether to go to the polls depending upon whether these costs exceed the perceived benefits.

By contrast, in the group membership process, citizens are differentially requested to participate. Organizations vigorously contact some persons and ask them to join, in the belief that this will raise their probability of doing so. This makes sense if one cost of membership is initially finding out about a group and getting the necessary meterials to join. But because it is not feasible to contact the entire electorate, organizations focus on some individuals and ignore others (see, e.g., Rothenberg 1991). In other words, associations functionally vary the cost of membership from individual to individual.[3]

As a result, there are two extreme scenarios that could, in theory, produce exactly the same set of members. One is a world in which citizens who are contacted join randomly – anyone who is canvassed has precisely the same probability of signing up – and all that matters is whom the organization chooses to solicit. In this case, individual characteristics are germane only to the extent that they may determine whom the association approaches. Alternatively, it is conceivable that advertising has no effect and that the joining process is completely driven by potential members' preferences.

It is almost certain that reality is more complicated than either of these extremes. Both citizen and leadership decision making are almost sure to matter. The problem is disentangling the two.

This dual process can be illustrated by distinguishing between *organizational* and *citizen* attributes. Two organizational characteristics are potentially germane for an association such as Common Cause: the level at which annual dues are set and decisions about which citizens to solicit to join. The organization exercises no price discrimination for first-time joiners, making everyone pay the same amount for membership (with the exception of entire families or students). Therefore dues levels are relevant for predicting supply only temporally, not cross-sectionally.

As mentioned, contact is likely to be an important determinant of

membership because it essentially lowers the cost of being in the organization for poorly informed contributors. In principle, then, data would be desirable on (1) whom Common Cause contacted and whether they joined or not, and (2) citizens who were never contacted and whether they joined or not. This information could be combined to estimate an initial equation on whom the group contacted and a subsequent equation on who actually joined. The results would estimate the relative importance of various factors for contact and for joining net of contact.[4]

However, information on which individuals Common Cause got in touch with before they made their decision not to contribute is unavailable; a second-best alternative that is adopted in this analysis is to employ data that are linked to the probability of being contacted to estimate a reduced-form equation of who joins.[5] Such specifications produce estimates that have desirable statistical properties. The only drawback is that the derived effect of a given factor on joining reflects the linear combination of the impact of that factor on whom the organization contacts and on who joins, controlling for contact. Thus, it is impossible to measure separately the effects of each factor on the probability of being contacted and on joining.

For Common Cause, the likelihood of being asked to join is virtually tantamount to whether one receives a mail solicitation:

While television and other methods of membership recruitment are being explored, direct mail remains the only means of recruiting members in sufficiently large numbers to maintain and expand our membership levels. Direct mail is initially expensive. In all but one year of Common Cause's history it has cost more to recruit new members than we have received from those new members in first year dues and contributions. (*Common Cause 1984 Budget* 1983, p. B5)

An inkling of the importance of Common Cause mail solicitations can be uncovered in the responses to a series of questions about where members initially heard about Common Cause (Table 4.2).[6] Mail from the group is secondary only to media coverage on the organization as a source of pre-membership information about the association. Furthermore, while the association values media coverage (undoubtedly correctly), such attention rarely provides much data to prospective members about how one actually goes about joining. The same can be said about conversations with those not in the group; mail and, to a secondary extent, conversations with members are likely to be the contacts that provide the requisite instructions on how to sign up.

However, given the considerable expense of advertising through the mail, it is imperative that the organization recruit members in a cost-effective manner. Common Cause consequently contacts only those citizens who it believes are most likely to join, to stay in the group, and to contribute more than the minimum dues. The probability of being solicited is therefore a function of an estimated earnings stream, that is, a discounted assessment of how much individuals will contribute – either monetarily or through

Table 4.2. *Sources of initial information about Common Cause*

Source of information	Percentage of Common Cause membership
Mail from Common Cause	
Very important	35.3
Somewhat important	30.2
Not sure	9.0
Not very important	9.9
Not at all important	15.6
Advertisements in newspapers, radio, or television by Common Cause	
Very important	10.4
Somewhat important	20.0
Not sure	14.4
Not very important	21.8
Not at all important	33.4
News coverage of Common Cause	
Very important	43.0
Somewhat important	28.8
Not sure	9.0
Not very important	7.5
Not at all important	11.7
Conversations with a Common Cause member	
Very important	24.0
Somewhat important	15.6
Not sure	7.9

Table 4.2 (*continued*)

Source of information	Percentage of Common Cause membership
Not very important	10.4
Not at all important	42.1
Conversations with friends, relatives, or	
co-workers about Common Cause	
Very important	19.3
Somewhat important	21.7
Not sure	8.2
Not very important	10.6
Not at all important	40.2

Source: 1981 Common Cause survey.

donations of time – during their years in the organization. Common Cause and its direct mail consultant Roger Craver (a former organization employee) use any number of surrogates for this kind of information, such as the groups to which an individual already belongs. Other methods, for example, identifying readers of upscale magazines, have been largely dropped after they have been found to be inefficient.

Which attributes, then, structure the probability of a person's joining and contributing, and presumably the likelihood of a person's being contacted, for symbolic groups such as Common Cause? The two characteristics that stand out are the ability to purchase membership and having the taste for it.

A maintained hypothesis in this analysis is that belonging to Common Cause is a normal good; that is, it is the type of good that consumers buy more of (or purchase at all) as they become richer.[7] The ability to purchase membership should reduce the relative costs of being a Common Cause contributor. However, a caveat that has already been foreshadowed in the discussion of experiential search ought to be added: Given leaders' desire to get citizens to sample a group and their awareness of the collective action problems that plague symbolic groups, they are likely to try to keep the

costs of joining low. Citizens either willing to pay more when they initially sign up or who subsequently discover that they are so satisfied that they are disposed to make an added contribution will undoubtedly be asked for additional donations. As already mentioned, about 60 percent of Common Cause members contribute more than their dues at some point.

Put another way, group leaders have an incentive to act in the same way that business executives behave in trying to get consumers to sample their product and decide whether they like it.[8] A low introductory price – perhaps a free sample, a coupon, a reduced price for first-time purchasers, or a lower price than will be posted in the future – is offered with the hope that potential customers will respond favorably to the product and will be willing to pay more later on. The major difference is that leaders of symbolic groups can (and do) ask for additional donations as well as the initial dues, while those selling consumer products cannot. In each instance, however, the end result will be the sampling of the good by those with lower income levels (or lower expectations generally) who would otherwise choose to abstain.

Demand should also differ across individuals because of variations in tastes. Differences in tastes, in turn, should be a function of two factors: policy preferences and political interest.

Common Cause will be more attractive to those individuals with a positive view of what the organization represents. As a nonpartisan, liberal group, it should be more alluring to independents and Democrats than to Republicans – as the descriptive information presented previously certainly suggests.[9] It should be remembered that partisanship is a general indicator of policy preferences. Independents should find the organization desirable because it has frequently campaigned against political parties and partisan institutions. Democrats should view it favorably because its political activities have led to the forging of alliances with that party considerably more frequently than with the Republicans, and its efforts have been far more in tune with the former's policy positions.

Those who are interested in politics will be more likely to receive benefits from contributing, ceteris paribus. It is not exclusively whether an organization's issue stance corresponds to citizens' personal preferences that is important, but also how much weight these individuals place on political matters (and presumably their sense of efficacy vis-à-vis these issues).

Thus, high levels of political interest and policy preferences that are roughly consistent with Common Cause's stances will drive up the probability of agreeing to be an association member. The expected benefits of joining are based on very rough estimates not only of the returns from the collective goods the organization allegedly furnishes, but also of the interactions and the selective benefits – notably its magazine but also political information and potential contacts for self-promotion – that the group may provide (these specific benefits are explored in more depth in the subsequent studies of retention and activism). Those running the association will seek out individuals with a high probability of joining, which will in turn lower the costs to

these individuals and make them more aware of the benefits of giving. To summarize: Organizational recruitment is a two-stage process (Figure 4.1). This system can be expressed as follows:

$$p_{\text{CONTACT}} = f(\text{INTEREST, PREFERENCES, ABILITY TO PAY, } u^1) \tag{1}$$

$$p_{\text{JOIN}} = f(\text{CONTACT, INTEREST, PREFERENCES, ABILITY TO PAY, } u^2), \tag{2}$$

where p_{CONTACT} represents the probability of being contacted; P_{JOIN}, the probability of joining; INTEREST, the level of political interest; PREFERENCES, the relevant political preferences; ABILITY TO PAY, the ability to purchase membership; CONTACT, whether the citizen has actually been contacted; and u^1 and u^2 are the corresponding error terms. In reduced form, this translates into the equation

$$p_{\text{JOIN}} = f(\text{INTEREST, PREFERENCES, ABILITY TO PAY, } u^3), \tag{3}$$

where u^3 represents the error term for forces outside the model. The estimated coefficients from equation (3) will be linear combinations of (1) and (2); however, the available data make it impossible to determine the relative contributions of the two sets of coefficients.

Measurement

The previous discussion makes it clear that it is necessary to measure four underlying concepts: membership, the ability to purchase it, political interest, and policy preferences. All of these can be measured – with varying degrees of difficulty – using data from the NES and Common Cause surveys presented in the last chapter. With the proper econometric estimation (to be discussed shortly), such data can be profitably employed to gain insights into the joining decision.

Membership, the dependent variable, can be measured straightforwardly. The 57 percent of respondents who were interviewed as part of the NES sample are scored 0, and the remaining 43 percent who were part of the Common Cause sample are scored 1.

The three factors specified to predict membership are measured as follows:

1. The *ability to pay* for membership is measured using 1980 family income.[10]
2. *Political interest* cannot be directly measured in the Common Cause/NES data set, but its sociodemographic determinants (Bennett 1986) can be employed as surrogates. In other words, factors that are known to raise political interest are substituted for a direct measure. By far the most important of these components is education; age and gender, however, both matter as well. Interest is therefore tapped by a series of dummy variables: one measuring educational achievement, in which those who have not been to college are scored 0; a group that categorizes respondents according to their age (those who are less than twenty-five years old are excluded); and another dummy variable in which males are scored 1.

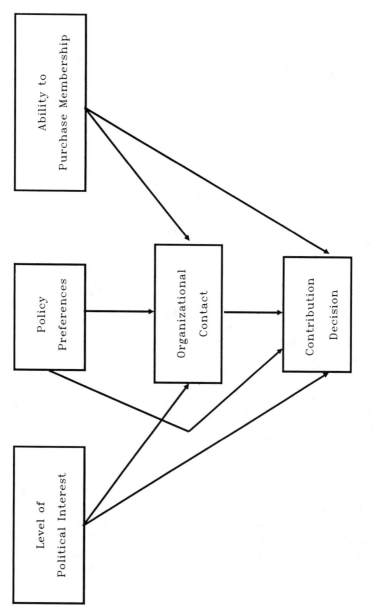

Figure 4.1. A model of contribution behavior.

3. *Policy preferences* are gauged with a series of six dummy variables measuring party identification, where strong Republicans are the group omitted. (Using dummy variables rather than an ordinal measure guards against the possibility that identification's impact may not be linear.) Additionally, a dummy variable in which whites are scored 1 is incorporated based on the assumption that Common Cause has been active on procedural issues and not on the economic and social agenda that especially concerns nonwhites.[11]

Expectations for the impact of each factor are straightforward. A greater ability to pay will encourage membership; that is, wealthier individuals should be more willing (or as willing) to purchase membership. A higher level of political interest will also be a positive determinant of contributory behavior. Specifically, male, educated, and older respondents will all be more prone to join. It is possible, however, that extremely aged respondents may be somewhat less likely to sign up (although simply joining Common Cause is not a very strenuous activity) than those who are slightly younger (see, e.g., Milbrath and Goel 1977), but the effect of age relative to the very young should still be positive. It is also posited that Democrats and independents will be more likely to join than strong Republicans, although the effect of party identification may not increase monotonically.

Estimation: Dealing with endogenous·sampling designs

This model cannot be estimated with standard econometric techniques (probit or logit, in this case) because of the problem of *sampling endogeneity*: The determinant of who gets sampled is the action – joining – that is being explained. The NES sample would contain, on average, two Common Cause members. The magnitude in the combined data set exceeds 40 percent; that is, this sample is stratified on the choice that is under investigation. Any model that is estimated without adjusting for this fact will produce inconsistent estimates.

The solution to this problem lies in the use of choice-based probability models (for surveys, see Madalla 1983; Amemiya 1985; Ben-Akiva and Lerman 1985). The weighted exogenous sample maximum likelihood function (WESML) proposed by Manski and Lerman (1977) in particular is appropriate because the actual probability that an individual belongs to Common Cause is known.

The intuition behind the Manski–Lerman solution is straightforward. In instances like the present where both the real-world proportions of the groups in the sample $[Q(i)]$ and the sample proportions $[H(i)]$ are known, the sample can be treated as if it were exogenously selected, except that each observation must be weighted by $Q(i)/H(i)$. Besides this weighting, the maximization of the WESML function is identical to that of an exogenously chosen sample. In a random sample $Q(i)/H(i)$ is 1; in others, underrepresented choices are more heavily weighted. Derived coefficients are not generally asymptotically

efficient, but they are consistent; this makes WESML a quite satisfactory solution in reasonably large samples (Appendix 4.2 contains a more formal presentation of WESML).

Results: Separating Common Cause contributors from the national citizenry

The WESML estimates for the total sample demonstrate that contributory behavior is explicable (Table 4.3). Given the overwhelming probability that a citizen will not join Common Cause, any properly estimated model will still predict that no one will be a member; nevertheless, the structural model specified in this analysis permits the categorization of respondents by the likelihood of joining.

This can be illustrated by examining two extreme cases. The results show that the probability of joining for a black woman who is under twenty-five years of age, does not have any college education, earns less than $10,000 per year, and is a strong Republican is an astronomical 1 in 20,000,000. Contrast this with the 1 in 9 likelihood – ninety times greater than for the average citizen – that a white male who has been to college, earns over $50,000 yearly, is over seventy, and is an independent Democrat will sign up for Common Cause.[12]

More specifically, both political interest (especially) and policy preferences influence the contribution decision in a highly predictable manner. However, the ability to purchase membership is apparently irrelevant; clearly, drawing inferences only from the descriptive data is a risky exercise.

By contrast, the results for political interest can be dramatic. Although females are as prone to sign up as males (despite the significant descriptive differences in the number of males in the group), older citizens are more likely to join than their younger counterparts. (Nor is there an obvious diminution of participation even among the oldest group – perhaps reflecting the fact that it requires little effort to write a check once a year to maintain membership status, so political interest is not mitigated by the physical effects of aging?) But, similar to studies of voting participation (e.g., Wolfinger and Rosenstone 1980), it is education that has the strongest impact on decision making. Better schooled citizens have a greater interest in politics, increasing considerably their propensity to sign up for a symbolic organization.

While having the "correct" policy preferences also raises the probability of being a member, it is not nearly as important. Democrats and independents are both more likely to join Common Cause. Those identifying with the Republican party are indistinguishable whether they claim that they are weak or strong partisans. The effect of party identification is not monotonic: The quintessential associational contributor is a Democratically leaning independent.

Table 4.3. *Determinants of group membership (WESML estimates)*

Variable	Results
Constant	—15.919***
	(2.420)
Ability to purchase membership	
Family income	0.221
	(0.324)
Political interest	
Gender (male)	0.226
	(0.994)
Age	
25—30	0.573*
	(0.435)
31—40	1.485***
	(0.480)
41—50	2.160***
	(0.834)
51—60	2.624***
	(0.829)
61—65	3.384**
	(1.657)
66—70	3.059***
	(1.095)
70—older	3.914**
	(1.814)
Education	3.273***
	(0.635)

Table 4.3 (*continued*)

Variable	Results
Policy preferences	
Party identification	
Strong Democrat	2.337***
	(1.005)
Weak Democrat	1.516**
	(0.686)
Leaning Democrat	3.268**
	(1.716)
Pure independent	2.455***
	(0.858)
Leaning Republican	1.724*
	(1.089)
Weak Republican	0.475
	(0.654)
Race (white)	1.786***
	(0.750)
Number of cases	2,545
—2×log-likelihood function	36

Note: Each coefficient represents the maximum likelihood estimate; standard errors are in parentheses. Weights are [.9987/.5462] and [.0013/.4538] for nonmembers and members, respectively.

*p ≤ .10   **p ≤ .05   ***p ≤ .01

These relative effects can be well illustrated by taking, for purposes of comparison, the average citizen to be a white female, lacking a college education, with a family income in the $20,000 to $25,000 range, between the ages of forty-one and fifty, who identifies herself as a weak Republican. The probability that she will be in Common Cause is about 6 in 100,000. If another person possessed all of the same attributes except that she was twenty years older and had a college education – and hence, was presumably more politically interested – she would have a roughly 500 in 100,000 likelihood of being in the association. The second citizen would be more than *eighty times* more likely than the first to be in Common Cause simply as a consequence of being more interested in politics.

Now, compare this first citizen to someone with identical characteristics except that he or she is a leaning Democrat rather than a weak Republican. While the former would have a 6 in 100,000 chance of being in the organization, the latter would have a probability of 30 in 100,000 (the jump would be from 1 in 100,000 if a strong Republican were being compared rather than a weak Republican). If the base of comparison is a black rather than a white leaning Democrat, the probability of being in Common Cause shrinks to 1 in 100,000; that is, a change in policy preferences (party identification and race) produces only a sixfold shift in the probability of being a member. In short, the magnitude of differentials in policy preferences, while undeniably significant, is overshadowed by those for political interest when considering the likelihood of joining Common Cause.[13]

Thus, in the spirit of experiential search, interested if somewhat uninformed citizens sample Common Cause and decide if they like being members. By contrast, ability to pay is irrelevant for joining. Assuming that family income accurately measures relative membership costs – and despite the previously demonstrated dramatic differences in the income levels of members and nonmembers – this result implies that the price of belonging is unimportant for membership in a symbolic group. There is no support for the hypothesis that membership is a normal good. Nor is it a Giffen good that people purchase in larger quantities as they become poorer. What explains these curious findings?

One possibility is that income has been misspecified. Yet, no matter how the variable is respecified, the findings are negative.[14]

The answer that is most convincing has already been foreshadowed in the previous discussions. Organizational leaders recognize the problems of collective action and have an incentive to keep the monetary cost of membership so low that the ability to pay is irrelevant and that citizens will sample the organization. If contributors are willing to spend more on membership, which should be particularly true over time for those learning that the group is a good match, they can be assured that they will get requests for additional donations.

Those running Common Cause seem to have learned that it pays to keep dues low: They have consciously allowed the real cost of joining the association to decline by more than 50 percent over the years. "We want to make Common Cause membership as available to as wide a spectrum as we can," is the way Randy Huwa, the group's vice president for membership, puts it. The original $15 membership rate was increased to $20 in 1980 and has remained stable ever since (although renewal is now $30), despite the fact that prices have more than tripled since the group's founding. (Indeed, Common Cause found that when they experimented with a $25 initial dues level they were no better off financially because of the fall off in the contribution rate.) These leaders have simultaneously tried to make up for this revenue erosion by "a steady intensification of fund raising to supplement dues" (Common Cause Expenditure Review 1984, p. 7) and by improvements in production processes (e.g., computerization and changes in the recruitment package employed) to lower Common Cause's costs. Put another way, by keeping costs of membership low, leaders can winnow down their original undifferentiated mailing list to include only those with a fairly high probability of contributing additional sums and remaining in the association for a long time.

AN AGGREGATE-LEVEL REPLICATION

Many might find the preceding results suspect. They are based on complicated econometric methods and the combination of two data sources collected at different times and through different means. There is the (very minor) possibility of incorrect attribution of NES respondents as nonmembers and of distortions created by slight alterations in question wording. The contention that income is inconsequential for membership as a consequence of leadership decisions might provoke skepticism.

Are the findings of the individual-level analysis artifactual or real? To shed some light on this question, another tack is taken on the membership issue: the use of ecological data to test hypotheses about membership levels.

Aggregate analysis comes with its own set of econometric pitfalls. However, it is also widely acknowledged that with sensitivity to ecological fallacies it can be a profitable mode of analysis (the classic work on this topic is Robinson 1950; see also Hanushek, Jackson, and Kain 1974; Kramer 1983). Indeed, as mentioned earlier, aggregate investigations have been about the only way that scholars have tested hypotheses about why people join groups, although the results have been, by and large, indeterminate.

Besides econometric difficulties, another often unavoidable problem with aggregate research is that the number of cases is frequently small – data are available only at high levels of aggregation (such as cross-sectionally by state or temporally by year at the national level). (The difficulty in making individual-level inferences from such highly aggregated data may help to explain why previous findings from research of this kind are frequently

ambiguous.) Luckily, Common Cause's dispersed structure and grassroots mobilization efforts obviate this problem: The availability (through the organization's generosity) of geographically distributed data on the congressional district level means that a fairly large number of cases can be employed.

As touched upon in the last chapter (where these data were presented by state for convenience), the group's organizational strength varies considerably. At the district level, membership ranges from just under 5,000 to 0, with a standard deviation of 684 participants and an average of 650. There are almost 1,000 members per congressional district in the Northeast, Mid-Atlantic, and Far West states (0.26 percent of the voting-age population) and slightly under 450 persons per district (0.11 percent) throughout the rest of the country.

These data make it possible to measure the probability that a citizen will belong to Common Cause. This is done using the *log-odds ratio of membership*, $\log(p_{ic}/1 - p_{ic})$, as the dependent variable, where p_{ic} is the probability that an individual, i, who is part of the voting-age population of a congressional district, c, belongs to Common Cause.

To replicate the individual-level model, district-level data generated from the census were also collected on all of the previously specified determinants of membership except for gender – the distribution of which varies little across districts and is not readily available at this level of aggregation. The explanatory variables are measured in the following manner:

1. The *ability to purchase membership* is measured as the 1980 median family income for the district (in hundreds of dollars).
2. *Political interest* is tapped by the median age of those in the district and by the percentage of individuals having four or more years of college.
3. *Policy preferences* are gauged by a three-election moving average of the percentage of the two-party vote that the Democrats garnered in the district (such an approach has been profitably used as a surrogate for underlying partisanship in the past, for example in Rothenberg and Brody 1988); the interaction of this measure with a dummy variable measuring whether or not the congressional district lies within a southern state, because of the more conservative nature of southern Democrats; and the percentage of whites in the district (divided by 10 for convenience).

When the log-odds ratio, also known as group logit, is used, ordinary least squares (OLS) can be applied for estimation (e.g., Hanushek and Jackson 1977). The one correction that is needed to estimate this model properly is to weight the data by the reciprocal of the square root of the variance $(1/p_{ic}n_{ic}(1 - p_{ic}))$, where n_{ic} is the number of members of Common Cause in congressional district c. This addresses the possibility of heteroskedasticity. Finally, before estimating the model, a singular value decomposition (SVD) on the independent variables was performed to check for multicollinearity.[15] The results showed that despite the use of aggregate data, which increases

the likelihood of multicollinearity, there is little evidence of a problem (SVD = 42).

The ecological regressions themselves were run in two steps. The first included all cases except the two congressional districts with no Common Cause members (the log of zero is, of course, indeterminate). The second excluded outliers as indicated by an examination of studentized residuals from the first estimates, as advocated by Belsley, Kuh, and Welsch (1980).[16]

The results in either case are strong and generally confirm the individual-level analysis (Table 4.4). Once again, political interest is especially relevant. Older people are far more likely to join Common Cause. A ten-year increase in the median age of those residing in a congressional district translates into roughly 497 more members, which, considering the average number of members per district, is a substantial change (average age in congressional districts ranges from twenty-two to forty-seven years).[17] Education again stands out as particularly essential: A 10 percent hike in the proportion of college-educated constituents in a congressional district (actual levels vary between 4 and 43 percent) will roughly double the number of Common Cause members.

Policy preferences are once more significant but less crucial than previously estimated in the individual-level analysis. Democratic districts are more likely to produce Common Cause members, but an increase of one standard deviation – a 16.7 percent jump in the Democratic vote – will result in only thirty-four more contributors, ceteris paribus. Southern Democratic districts are less likely to have association members within their boundaries. A 16.7 percent increase in partisans will still result in sixty-eight fewer Common Cause members than found outside the region. Race is inconsequential, after other factors are controlled. Once again, then, there is evidence that while preferences are important, an interest in politics is the most fundamental determinant of joining.

The findings for income are certainly intriguing. In the individual-level analysis the results concerning income are simply insignificant; but at the aggregate level, they are actually *negative* once other related factors are controlled. The estimates suggest that a $5,000 increase in median income (which fluctuates between $8,000 and $33,000), for example, results in a decrease of roughly 164 members per congressional district. While too much stock should not be put in the finding that poverty drives membership, this result should be taken as confirmation that income is not what counts for attracting Common Cause contributors.

Overall, then, these aggregate results buttress the general findings of the individual-level data. The ability to pay for Common Cause membership is not a positive determinant of why people join: Consumption of a group affiliation is not a conventional, normal good. The association's membership price is made inexpensive enough that anyone can join. Those who are greatly interested in politics and who possess liberal democratic policy preferences have a propensity to sign up. Concern with politics is crucial, a reasonable

Table 4.4. *Determinants of aggregate membership (group logit estimates)*

Variable	Model I	Model II
Constant	—9.053***	—9.411***
Ability to purchase membership		
Median family income	—0.003***	—0.005***
Political interest		
Median age	0.067***	0.076***
College education	0.083***	0.100***
Policy preferences		
Party identification		
Democrat	0.002*	0.003***
Southern Democrat	—0.008***	—0.009***
Race	—0.004	—0.008
Number of cases	433	405
Adjusted R^2	.94	.96

Note: Model I includes all congressional districts with Common Cause
     members (two have no members); Model II drops cases where the
     absolute value of the studentized residuals from model I exceeds
     1.96.

$*p \leq .10$ $***p \leq .01$

policy match is important, but income level is irrelevant. If not unambiguously confirming experiential search, these results are certainly explicable from this perspective.

CHOOSING AMONG PUBLIC INTEREST GROUPS

The preceding analyses contain the implicit assumption that citizens decide whether or not to join a single organization. In reality, such choices may be considerably more complex. Potential contributors may decide upon abstaining from membership completely, belonging to a single group, or signing up for a number of organizations.

The issue, then, is whether incorporating a more realistic assumption would lead to different inferences about how citizens decide upon joining a group. Thus, besides being of interest in its own right, an analysis incorporating a multiplicity of associations represents a validity test of the conclusions drawn in the examination specific to Common Cause.

Although data limitations prevent capturing the entire richness of this decision process, it is possible to look at how citizens choose among associations that might seem to be substitutes for one another at least on some qualities. The data employed are from a 1982 mail survey that includes members of the League of Women Voters of the United States, the Conservative Caucus, and the American Civil Liberties Union in addition to Common Cause.[18] These data, despite imperfections, provide the opportunity to explore what factors motivate individuals to select one group over another. In other words, this section examines what happens if citizens have the option of searching elsewhere rather than joining Common Cause.

Each of these four associations can broadly be classified as a public interest group. The League of Women Voters, formed in 1920, lists its principal purpose as the promotion of political responsibility through informed and active participation in politics and action on selected governmental issues. It endorses no candidates or political parties and is especially noteworthy for its over 1,300 local groups, which foster interaction among its 125,000 members. The Conservative Caucus stands a bit apart from the other three organizations because it was founded (in 1974) as an explicitly conservative group with the avowed purpose of building a grassroots "new majority" lobbying coalition in every congressional district to aid the conservative effort. It is the largest of the four associations studied here, with roughly 400,000 members. The American Civil Liberties Union, also begun in 1920, has approximately 250,000 members. As is well known, it – in conjunction with its tax-deductible arm, the American Civil Liberties Union Foundation – presents itself as a protector of individual rights and is heavily reliant on working through the legal process. (These descriptions are principally drawn from Akey 1983; see also Donohue 1985 on the ACLU, Wittenberg and Wittenberg 1989 on the Conservative Caucus, and Young and Young 1989 on the League of Women Voters.[19])

The four-group study can be used to determine what precipitates the choice to sign up, conditional on choosing one of these organizations.[20] In other words, it is possible to identify both the combination of rewards that new members think their chosen alternative will supply best and the types of individuals for whom the organization is most attractive. It is again assumed that cost/benefit calculations are clouded by imperfect information and that decisions are made with the intention to learn through experience. If individuals are completely knowledgeable, they will pick the organization that gives them the highest benefits relative to costs; if not, they will sort themselves out according to which of these groups seems to provide the best potential match.

Whether individuals perceive alternative groups as fulfilling different needs can be examined by looking at members' choice mechanisms across the four public interest groups in the sample. Those surveyed were asked which of the following were important to them: (1) efficacy; (2) civic duty; (3) ideology; (4) information; (5) political experience; (6) political interactions; and (7) other motivations.[21] The first three motivations roughly measure purposive and collective rewards; the next gauges divisible, selective benefits; and the fifth and sixth, solidary returns.

The multiplicity of benefits were measured in two ways: Each contributor was initially asked if the reward in question was important in an absolute sense and then was requested to select from the seven the most valuable alternatives. Consequently, two models are specified and estimated, one version incorporating the unranked motivations (the *nonprioritized* model) and another utilizing the rankings (the *prioritized* model).

For these two models, dummy variables are created to correspond to each of the benefit types. An affirmative response is scored 1 and a negative response, 0. Political experience and political interactions are combined (only six respondents chose experience in the prioritized version). In addition, the trio of sociodemographic characteristics – gender, age, and education – which are used above as surrogates of political interest are again included in each model. Gender is measured by a dummy variable scored 1 for male; age, by a six-point scale; and education, by a five-point scale. Data on League of Women Voters members are omitted in both models so that the League serves as the basis of comparison. The choice "other motivations" is also dropped in the second specification so that this selection can be the basis for comparison for the prioritized version of motivations for joining.

Although making a priori, pairwise (between groups) predictions of the relative attractiveness of each factor is impossible, some general expectations can be sketched. The Conservative Caucus, the American Civil Liberties Union, and Common Cause all place greater emphasis than the League of Women Voters on a substantive agenda; therefore efficacy should be less germane for the latter. As principally a service organization, the League might be especially useful for fulfilling a sense of citizen duty. The American Civil Liberties Union and the Conservative Caucus are the more ideological

of the four; the League's lack of a strong substantive agenda and Common Cause's explicitly nonpartisan stance with its emphasis on structure and process should mitigate their ability to satisfy the ideologically motivated. The League of Women Voters, in contrast, should be especially good at offering information and political experience and personal interactions.

While there were clear expectations about the impact of the sociodemographic determinants of political interests when the universe was all citizens and the decision was whether or not to join Common Cause, this is not the case when the focus shifts to which group to choose. In fact, only two strong expectations stand out for the group member sample. One is quite trivial: The League, although allowing male group members, has traditionally been dominated by women. The other is that given its conservative stance and the propensity of the well-educated to favor liberal causes (e.g., Miller, Miller, and Schneider 1980), the Conservative Caucus will probably have less-educated contributors.

Estimation is again less straightforward than it might seem at first glance. The standard technique for estimating a selection model where the decision involves choosing among a limited number of unordered alternatives is multinomial logit. However, conventional strategies are inappropriate because a choice-based sample, stratified this time on the decision to join a given organization, is again being employed. The WESML method provides a solution once more.

The results of the two models are shown, respectively, in Tables 4.5 and 4.6. Both sets of findings are roughly congruent with expectations, although those for the prioritized version are slightly weaker. The results from the non-prioritized model demonstrate that all three groups are more attractive than the League of Women Voters for those seeking to be efficacious, and the coefficient for Common Cause is the largest. There are no statistically significant results with respect to civic duty, although the coefficients for the American Civil Liberties Union and Common Cause are negative and approach levels of significance. The findings for ideology and miscellaneous benefits are also insignificant. In accordance with expectations, selective and solidary returns are perceived by contributors as the province of the League of Women Voters.

In a few instances when the principal reason individuals join is substituted for the nonprioritized information – efficacy with respect to the American Civil Liberties Union, divisible benefits with regard to the Conservative Caucus, and solidary rewards concerning the Conservative Caucus and the American Civil Liberties Union – the results are now insignificant.[22] This may reflect the difficulties people have in choosing priorities. One somewhat surprising finding is that members of the League of Women Voters are apparently more motivated by ideological concerns than contributors to Common Cause, contrary to the expectation that neither group should be particularly attractive to the ideologically committed. Nevertheless, the basic

Table 4.5. *Determinants of initial membership choice, nonprioritized model (WESML estimates comparing groups to League of Women Voters)*

Variable	TCC	ACLU	CC
Constant	1.011	—2.326***	—1.958***
	(1.440)	(1.186)	(1.202)
Motivations for joining			
(not prioritized)			
Efficacy	1.241**	0.939**	2.268***
	(0.615)	(0.420)	(0.482)
Civic duty	—0.120	—0.560	—0.621
	(0.524)	(0.379)	(0.391)
Ideological commitment	0.181	0.334	—0.443
	(0.499)	(0.374)	(0.379)
Information	—1.063**	—0.855**	—0.007
	(0.509)	(0.381)	(0.408)
Experience/interactions	—2.531***	—2.105***	—2.700
	(0.695)	(0.402)	(0.453)
Other	—9.935	—0.173	—0.922
	(145.142)	(0.770)	(0.934)
Political interest			
Gender (male)	4.292***	3.204***	3.187***
	(0.571)	(0.428)	(0.448)

Table 4.5 (*continued*)

Variable	TCC	ACLU	CC
Age	0.469***	—0.036	0.293***
	(0.160)	(0.110)	(0.116)
Education	—0.726***	0.655***	0.098
	(0.262)	(0.218)	(0.212)
Number of cases		538	
—2xlog likelihood function		956	

Note: Each coefficient represents the maximum likelihood estimate;
standard errors are in parentheses. Weights are [.13158/.25090],
[.42105/.21190], [.21053/.26950], and [.23684/.26770] for the
League of Women Voters, the Conservative Caucus (TCC), the
American Civil Liberties Union (ACLU), and Common Cause (CC),
respectively.

*$p \leq$ .10   **$p \leq$ .05   ***$p \leq$ .01

inferences drawn from the results of the prioritized model are consistent with those derived from the nonprioritized version.

Together, the findings for these two models demonstrate that contributors discriminate between organizations. Individual decision makers distinguish among these groups in ways that are largely consistent with the organizations' political agenda and public appeals. Yet, it is hard to paint an absolutely clear picture of why individuals select one interest group over another, since some sign up for reasons other than those for which the association seems to have a comparative advantage. This finding lends additional credence to the argument that citizens join groups without full knowledge about them.

That many initially contribute for curious reasons can be seen more clearly if individuals' principal motivations for joining are classified

Table 4.6. *Determinants of initial membership choice, prioritized model
(WESML estimates comparing groups to League of Women Voters)*

Variable	TCC	ACLU	CC
Constant	—0.217	—2.203*	—0.940
	(1.855)	(1.186)	(1.202)
Motivations for joining			
(prioritized)			
Efficacy	2.985**	1.101	1.832***
	(1.388)	(0.733)	(0.776)
Civic duty	0.677	—1.085	—1.109
	(1.408)	(0.729)	(0.785)
Ideological commitment	0.706	—0.203	—1.525*
	(1.411)	(0.706)	(0.790)
Information	—0.043	—2.051***	—0.733
	(1.631)	(0.864)	(0.833)
Experience/interactions	—9.793	—11.866	—2.943*
	(195.662)	(86.528)	(1.539)
Political interest			
Gender (male)	4.598***	3.169***	3.301***
	(0.575)	(0.363)	(0.397)
Age	0.395***	—0.074	0.245**
	(0.163)	(0.108)	(0.112)

Table 4.6 (*continued*)

Variable	TCC	ACLU	CC
Education	—0.777***	0.587***	0.028
	(0.265)	(0.205)	(0.201)
Number of cases		518	
—2xlog-likelihood function		941	

Note: Each coefficient represents the maximum likelihood estimate;
standard errors are in parentheses. Weights are [.13158/.25090],
[.42105/.21190], [.21053/.26950], and [.23684/.26770] for the
League of Women Voters, the Conservative Caucus (TCC), the
American Civil Liberties Union (ACLU), and Common Cause (CC),
respectively.

*p ≤ .10   **p ≤ .05   ***p ≤ .01

according to whether they are "correct" or "incorrect" (Table 4.7). Exactly half of all respondents joined for what is labeled the wrong reason. It must be emphasized that this classification is rough and makes sense only if individuals are imperfectly informed but are capable of learning. If contributors are either perfectly informed or incapable of learning, there is no such thing as a potentially rectifiable mistake.[23]

The League of Women Voters has the highest percentage of people in the correct group, and the Conservative Caucus has the largest proportion of misfits. If not an artifact of the coding scheme, this distribution across groups may reflect how well they are known by citizens before joining and variations in the real cost of membership. The League of Women Voters' sponsorship of public forums such as televised presidential debates gives it a visibility that the other organizations in this analysis probably cannot match. By contrast, it is likely that the Conservative Caucus is the least known of the

Table 4.7. *Classification of initial decisions by group (column/row percentages)*

Organization	"Incorrect" choice	"Correct" choice	Number of cases
League of Women Voters	18.5/38.1	30.2/62.0	137
Conservative Caucus	27.8/61.9	17.1/38.1	126
American Civil Liberties Union	27.8/53.4	24.2/46.6	146
Common Cause	26.0/47.7	28.5/52.3	153
Number of cases	281	281	562

four organizations, which may partially explain why its members are most likely to make a mistake. The League's emphasis on members' participation may also make the real price of joining much higher than for the other associations. This has two consequences for potential contributors. It provides an incentive to invest in learning about the group before joining, in much the same way that consumers invest more heavily in acquiring information before making a major purchase than before buying something inexpensive. It also furnishes an inducement for members who think they might have made a mistake to leave quickly rather than to stay and learn more. Both of these processes should lead to the empirical observation that the League of Women Voters seems to match its members well.

It is possible to debate whether or not it is reasonable to classify a given decision as correct. There is only one ultimate test of this scheme's utility: whether this dichotomy explains subsequent behavior. This will be one of the subjects of the next chapters.

CONCLUSIONS: THE DETERMINANTS OF MEMBERSHIP

Having shown that there are differences between members and the citizenry, the next step has been to show which, if any, of these variations make a

behavioral difference for the joining decision. Building upon the conventional wisdom about participation produces some rather interesting findings. These results, while far from conclusive, provide preliminary support for the utility of the experiential search theory specifically and the importance of developing an integrated approach to organizations generally.

As would be expected from the experiential search framework, political interest is especially important for making the initial contribution choice. Better educated and older citizens are far more interested in politics. These are the people who are willing to sample a group and learn about it. Moderate jumps in interest levels result in dramatic differences in the likelihood of joining.

Changes in general policy orientations also count but are less important. Democrats, independents, and whites (although the latter finding does not hold up in an aggregate replication) all have preferences that coincide with Common Cause and prompt them to join. Yet the impact of these factors on signing up pales in comparison to political interest.

In all likelihood, the factors precipitating membership funnel into the participation calculus in a number of ways that cannot be disentangled with a reduced-form estimation. Probably two underlying processes are key.

First, high levels of interest and policy preferences that match an organization's reputation raise the probability of being contacted by the group and consequently reduce the cost of membership. It may be that surrogates for political interest are far better (or more accessible) indicators of who will join than any analogous measures of preferences that the organization may have at its disposal.

Second, policy orientations and especially political interest increase the expected value to citizens of the benefits the organization offers and make these individuals more likely to sign up. To reiterate, the benefits of membership not only may derive from the association's stated goals but also may emanate from rough estimates concerning the value of whatever private inducements or opportunities for interaction are furnished. Given the descriptive findings presented, it also seems clear that interested citizens are more likely to know others in the association and are more prone to be among the few who seek out membership opportunities.

The findings for the four-group study add to this picture by suggesting that not every joiner gets things right. Individuals may join an association that simply seems wrong for them. Again, this may reflect two related factors: An organization may contact the wrong people, or "misfits" may simply choose to join. If contributors are truly engaging in sampling behavior, those who have made the wrong choice should tend to correct their mistakes and leave the organization.

By contrast, the monetary cost of joining is not germane. Common Cause membership is a very unusual type of good. Organizational leaders keep the price so low that income does not represent a barrier to joining. This allows

imperfectly informed citizens to join and sample the organization and learn whether what it offers is consistent with their preferences and worth continued contributions.

To summarize: Politically interested individuals whose broad policy preferences are most likely to be a good match for Common Cause will join in greater proportions because their estimated costs are lower and their expected benefits are higher. This attraction can reflect not only their own behavior but the actions of organizational leaders.[24]

These findings do not square well with the Olsonian full-information scenario. Contributors' behavior is far more consistent with how individuals normally act when confronted with imperfect knowledge. They initially behave as if they are prepared to learn about the organization firsthand. Over time, those who join should become more knowledgeable about the real costs and benefits of membership and make better informed decisions about both whether to stay in the group and what level of monetary and nonmonetary contributions is appropriate for them. This, of course, also does not fit easily with the assertion that individuals join with imperfect knowledge but do not update their beliefs once they become more informed.

Such results set the stage for the analysis of internal organizational politics. In particular, does the assertion that political interest is key provide any leverage for understanding what goes on within the group? It is to this and other related concerns that attention can now be turned.

Appendix 4.1. Critique of Kau and Rubin

In their analysis, Kau and Rubin (1979, 1982) take an important first step in attempting to explain state membership levels in Common Cause and Ralph Nader's Public Citizen through cross-sectional analysis with a considerably different specification than that employed in the present research. They claim that membership ought to be a function of five factors: (1) communication costs, measured by urbanization; (2) ability to pay, tapped by income; (3) education, measured by the percentage of the population with a college education; (4) race, gauged by the percentage of the population that was black in 1970; and (5) other forms of participation that might serve as substitutes for membership, measured by turnout levels in the 1972 presidential election. However, their results are, as they acknowledge, disappointing. Only education was relevant for Common Cause membership; for Public Citizen, urbanization was also weakly significant, contrary to the expectation that it should be germane for Common Cause rather than for Nader's group. While exponents of Olsonian models and others might predict that any model based on rudimentary characteristics ought to produce few positive findings, the results (e.g., Table 4.4) stemming from the current research dispute such a contention. Thus, the issue becomes whether Kau and Rubin's contradictory

findings (compared to those presented in this chapter) are a consequence of the highly aggregated level of their data, problems with their theoretical specification, or some other idiosyncratic reason.

With respect to possible model specification problems, a number of difficulties stand out. One is that it is frankly somewhat perplexing how the use of mail service would systematically reduce the cost for urban citizens of being recruited as well as of communicating with each other and with the Washington organization for lobbying purposes (which was the argument they made regarding communication costs). Besides the fact that it is unclear whether urban members are necessarily better off than rural contributors, the implicit assumption that potential contributors are aware of these differences in communication costs before they join up is rather heroic if the informational assumptions of the present analysis are reasonable.

A second problem is that Kau and Rubin maintain that forms of participation ought to be substitutes for one another. Yet, a long-accepted empirical fact is that participation levels are positively correlated with one another (e.g., Verba and Nie 1972). Indeed, as demonstrated earlier, Common Cause members are far more likely than the average citizen to be involved in other activities. Rather than one causing the other, electoral participation and organizational joining undoubtedly have many of the same determinants.

A final difficulty, which should be obvious from the earlier analysis in this chapter, has to deal with omission: As the previous individual-level and aggregate analyses suggest, it is likely that Kau and Rubin left out a number of meaningful determinants of contributing that are associated with both political interest and policy preferences. These exclusions may lead to serious mistakes when drawing inferences.

To begin to determine if any of these contentions is correct, a slightly modified individual-level version of the Kau and Rubin model – which excludes whether citizens substitute one form of participation for another – was estimated. The reason for the absence of participation is econometric. As implied in the preceding discussion, the measures of such behavior in the joint Common Cause/NES sample (see Table 3.3) are endogenous to membership. Among other sources of endogeneity, the actions in question occurred after almost all of the group members surveyed joined. Unfortunately, there are no obvious indicators that can be used to create instruments. However, if any misspecification is likely, it will almost undoubtedly be in favor of the Kau and Rubin model, since Common Cause contributors are so prone to engage in other participatory behavior.

When the modified Kau–Rubin specification is estimated using the WESML technique, communication costs (measured as urbanization in congressional districts), income, race, and education are all statistically significant (Table 4.8, model I). This demonstrates that Kau and Rubin's negative results, given their model, were a function of data limitations.

However, because communication costs were not included in the previous analysis and income was earlier found to be insignificant, the obvious next

Table 4.8. *Tests of Kau and Rubin model (WESML estimates)*

Variable	Model I	Model II
Constant	—11.746***	16.463***
	(0.402)	(3.487)
Ability to purchase membership		
Family income	0.194***	0.209
	(0.055)	(0.332)
Communication costs		
Urbanization (congressional district)	0.708***	0.524
	(0.335)	(1.986)
Political interest		
Gender (male)		0.273
		(1.017)
Age		
25—30		0.630*
		(0.465)
31—40		1.481***
		(0.493)
41—50		2.191***
		(0.872)
51—60		2.667***
		(0.855)
61—65		3.416**
		(1.740)
66—70		3.074***
		(1.125)
70—older		3.946***
		(2.180)
Education	2.834***	3.230***
	(0.090)	(0.662)

Table 4.8 (*continued*)

Variable	Model I	Model II
Policy preferences		
Party identification		
Strong Democrat		2.311**
		(1.090)
Weak Democrat		1.490**
		(0.718)
Leaning Democrat		3.257**
		(1.794)
Pure independent		2.391***
		(0.869)
Leaning Republican		1.695*
		(1.139)
Weak Republican		0.496
		(0.712)
Race (white)	1.957***	1.985**
	(0.190)	(0.871)
Number of cases	2,579	2,522
—*2xlog-likelihood function*	46	39

Note: Each coefficient represents the maximum likelihood estimate; standard errors are in parentheses. Weights are [.9987/.5502] and [.0013/.4498] for model I and [.9987/.5508] and [.0013/.4492] for model II for nonmembers and members, respectively.

$*p \leq .10$ $**p \leq .05$ $***p \leq .01$

step is to examine whether these contradictory results are artifactual or real. Thus, communications costs are incorporated into the model estimated earlier in this chapter (Table 4.3). The results (Table 4.8, model II) demonstrate that the positive findings in model I regarding communication costs and income are artifactual. Ironically, in this sense, Kau and Rubin's findings about these two factors – that they were insignificant – were correct for the wrong reason. Given the factors they examined, only their finding for race was incorrect. However, more important, their larger conclusion that the decision process is essentially inexplicable was a function of the fact that they did not have disaggregated data to estimate a more general model of participation.

Appendix 4.2. Formal presentation of WESML estimator

The formal presentation of the WESML estimator is straightforward. For each $i \in C$, where C is the choice set, it is possible to define the function $w(i)$ by $w(i) = Q(i)/H(i)$. Assuming that $Q(i)$ is known and $H(i)$ can be calculated directly from the data, $w(i)$ is known. Consider then the weighted exogenous sampling likelihood function

$$W_N(y, \boldsymbol{\theta}) = \sum_{n-1}^{N} w(i_n) \log P(i_n, z_n, \boldsymbol{\theta}) + \sum_{n-1}^{N} w(i_n) \log g(z_n), \qquad (1)$$

where z_n is a vector of attributes, $\boldsymbol{\theta}$ is a parameter vector, and $y = (i_n, z_n)$. It is possible (although complicated) to show that (1) yields coefficients that are strongly consistent and asymptotically normal. The resulting covariance matrix is

$$V = \Omega^{-1} \Delta \Omega^{-1}, \qquad (2)$$

where

$$\Omega = \left[-E \left[\frac{\partial^2 w_i \log P(i, z, \boldsymbol{\theta})}{\partial \boldsymbol{\theta} \partial \boldsymbol{\theta}'} \right]_{\theta'} \right]$$

$$\Delta = \left[E \left[\frac{\partial w_i \log P(i, z, \boldsymbol{\theta})}{\partial \boldsymbol{\theta}} \right]_{\theta'} \left[\frac{\partial w_i \log P(i, z, \boldsymbol{\theta})}{\partial \boldsymbol{\theta}'} \right]_{\theta'} \right]$$

and the expectation E operates over i and z with respect to the distribution given by $\delta_c(z/i)H(i)$, where $\delta_c(z/i)$ is the likelihood of drawing z conditional on drawing a decision maker who has selected i.

5

The internal politics of organizations I: Learning and retention

If group leaders successfully attract a significant membership, what happens once these citizens sign up? In particular, in collectivities such as Common Cause, how does a politically interested, somewhat heterogeneous clientele attracted by low costs and intense recruitment react to life in the organization? How do their actions, in turn, reflect leadership behavior and structure goal formation? These are the issues that motivate the next three chapters.

Curiously, life inside political organizations has rarely received much attention from contemporary social scientists. (This is true even though traditional scholars, especially those working in the case study tradition, have certainly been aware of the internal workings of organizations; for example, see Garceau's 1941 discussion of the American Medical Association and its active minority.) The reasons individuals join groups have been debated; similarly, associations' efforts to influence public policy have received at least sporadic notice. By contrast, the politics of membership organizations have largely been ignored by social scientists.

Why this lack of emphasis on the internal politics of organizations? One possible explanation is that the intricacies of conducting research on how interest groups function, which takes a great deal of time, combined with the lack of an integrating theoretical perspective from which to understand such behavior, discourage investigators. Although this explanation surely has merit, it is also true that other topics that are difficult to explore and that might be claimed to lack theoretical grounding have received much more attention.

Two other reasons for the neglect of internal politics might also be cited; they are essentially the flip sides of the same coin. One might be labeled the residual of pluralism, and the other, the aftermath of the Olsonian logic.

Remember that pluralist scholars typically believe that organizations exist because members share a common interest. If this is true, there is little pressing need to investigate an association's inner workings. Members, from the rank and file through the leadership, are assumed to be pursuing the same goals. Consequently, there is every reason to presume that no subgroup advances

its own interests at another's expense. Although pluralism's popularity as a means of understanding collectivities has waned considerably, the residual effect may be to discourage work on intraorganizational politics.[1]

The lesson that it is acceptable to ignore internal group politics may also be reinforced by those subscribing to the Olsonian viewpoint that only private economic rewards matter for perfectly informed contributors. If this assertion is correct, then internal politics largely reflect the will of the leaders. By logical definition, those running the organization have satisfied the economic desires of perfectly informed members if they have been successful at getting individuals to sign up in the first place; that is, the implication that once a contributor, always a contributor, directs attention away from internal politics.[2] Although there is now basis for believing that the Olsonian perspective is not quite accurate even as a stylized description, the aftereffect of its popularity may be to inhibit research on internal organizational politics.

By contrast, if the experiential search framework specifically and the integrated perspective generally are appropriate for viewing individual decision making and organizations, then understanding intraorganizational dynamics is crucial. If members can learn, group survival and policy success will be predicated not only on getting people to sign up, but on keeping them in the association and inducing at least a subset of them to contribute additional time and effort to the cause. Such choices should be related to one another and ought to be linked not only to who joins and why they do so but to the goal formation and policy processes as well. Intraorganizational politics represent the key intermediate step in linking citizen preferences to the political system.

The next three chapters explore what happens once a citizen signs up at Common Cause and examine whether this is consistent with experiential search and the idea of an integrated perspective more generally. In particular, taken together, these analyses represent perhaps the key test of the former as a model of member behavior. Specifically, two questions will be examined in this initial chapter: (1) Do citizens learn about the group? (2) Assuming that citizens learn, does this accrual of knowledge induce some members to leave and others to stay according to some systematic pattern? The next chapter, which focuses on member activism, also emphasizes two issues: (1) Is it possible to separate out a priori those who are active in an organization from those who are not, even in an association as homogeneous as Common Cause? (2) If it is possible, does this also reflect a learning process by group contributors? Finally, the subsequent chapter asks the question, Is there a link between what has been established about citizens' decision making and the leadership's formulation of political goals at Common Cause?

The first two of these chapters relies largely on data from the Common Cause survey. In addition, the four-group study will be employed for purposes of validation. Together, these two sources provide an excellent opportunity to examine individual behavior and learning. In the latter chapter, qualitative

information, such as that derived from in-depth interviews, will be employed more heavily.

DO MEMBERS LEARN?

As mentioned many times throughout this analysis, an assumption under-pinning the experiential search framework is that members learn about the costs and benefits of participating once they join. Without evidence of a positive relationship between relevant knowledge and length of organiza-tional membership, the validity of this entire research enterprise must be questioned. Fortunately, it is possible to demonstrate that contributors learn through exposure to the organization.

In Common Cause, individuals with many years of associational experience are no different sociodemographically than newcomers. They are indis-tinguishable in terms of education or income, for example; therefore any variation must emanate from other sources.[3] Findings that long-term contri-butors know more about the organization would demonstrate that members learn and would provide important side evidence that experiential search is fundamental for association membership.[4]

Indeed, several straightforward tests clearly show that new arrivals and long-time contributors are only distinguishable as a result of their organi-zational exposure. The only reasonable explanation for these findings is that members learn.

Consider knowledge about how Common Cause formally operates as an organization. Those surveyed answered a battery of four basic questions about their organizational acumen. The four statements and the correct answers, to which members could reply true, false, or don't know, are these:

1. Members of Common Cause elect the governing board. [true]
2. Members of Common Cause elect the Common Cause chairman. [false]
3. Common Cause is a federation of state and local organizations. [false]
4. Common Cause state organizations determine their own issue agendas. [true][5]

To put it bluntly, these are not questions of extraordinary difficulty. Yet, when respondents' knowledge is sorted by length of membership, the experiential search framework receives strong support. Long-time contri-butors know a great deal more than newcomers (Table 5.1). Roughly one-third of the one- or two-year members missed all four of these questions: a quite remarkable finding, since if respondents simply guessed true or false (eschewing the "don't know" option) only about 6 percent would be expected to miss all four.[6] By contrast, less than 5 percent of the members who have been in the group for more than ten years missed all four.

Also, as expected given the theory outlined earlier, the mean level of knowledge from one cohort to the next shows a clear pattern of diminishing marginal returns with organizational experience. A year has roughly four times as much impact for newcomers as for long-time members.

Table 5.1. *Organizational experience and knowledge about group*

Years in group	Percentage correct					Mean percentage correct
	0	25	50	75	100	
1	34.1	31.7	26.8	4.9	2.4	27.5
2	34.9	23.3	30.2	8.1	3.5	30.5
3	20.4	18.4	28.6	25.5	7.1	45.2
4	9.6	19.3	22.9	42.2	6.0	53.9
5	7.3	15.9	35.4	30.5	11.0	55.5
6	12.1	13.6	28.8	30.3	15.2	55.7
7	5.4	14.7	28.7	31.0	20.2	61.4
8	2.5	13.6	25.9	42.0	16.0	63.9
9	4.9	10.7	29.1	32.0	23.3	64.6
10	3.4	11.2	16.9	47.2	21.3	70.0
11	2.8	8.4	25.2	28.0	35.5	71.3
12	5.3	5.3	23.7	39.5	26.3	69.1

Table 5.1 (*continued*)

Years in group	Percentage correct					Mean percentage correct
	0	25	50	75	100	
Number of cases	116	159	307	368	205	1,115

Note: $X^2 = 254$, $df = 44$. Each cell gives the percentage of members who have been in the group for x years (row) who get the designated percentage (column) of the answers correct.

These results about knowledge are also confirmed if examined in a multivariate context. Even if controls are incorporated for factors that might condition knowledge and learning about Common Cause – education, activism, and readership of *Common Cause Magazine*, all of which are significant determinants – experience is relevant in the predicted manner (results not shown). For example, a rank-and-file member with a postcollege education who reads the magazine carefully would be expected to answer one question right in the first year of membership, two by the second, and three by the fifth year; by the twelfth year of membership the probability of getting either 75 or 100 percent of the questions correct would be roughly 65 percent.

Next, consider knowledge about the collective goods (what were earlier labeled group issues) that Common Cause tries to furnish: limits on government spending, sunset legislation, campaign finance, the ERA, and lobby disclosure. In four of five instances, new members are substantially more likely to reply that they do not know the Common Cause position on these policies (Table 5.2a).[7] But when members were queried about their own positions on either these issues or other items not on the Common Cause agenda at the time – defense spending, equality of opportunity, social service spending, inflation, abortion, minimum guaranteed income, school busing, nuclear energy, and Soviet relations, differences between older and newer members were nonexistent, with one slight exception (Table 5.2b).[8]

While recent members are as opinionated about the public agenda as long-time contributors, they are less well versed in the organization's stances. These results – again not shown – are also confirmed in a multivariate context.

Table 5.2a. *Organizational experience and group issue opinions (percentage of Common Cause members without opinions)*

Issue	Organizational experience (Years in group)												Mean %	No. cases	X²
	1	2	3	4	5	6	7	8	9	10	11	12			
Limit government spending	58	38	37	31	40	37	33	39	51	45	51	43	41	1,155	22**
Sunset legislation	40	23	20	21	11	13	9	11	6	8	14	10	14	1,164	54***
Campaign finance	24	24	11	10	6	7	5	1	2	1	7	3	7	1,167	74***
Equal Rights Amendment	28	30	26	19	24	19	13	18	17	12	15	13	18	1,162	25***
Lobby disclosure	20	20	14	8	5	9	5	1	3	1	11	4	7	1,174	56***

**$p \leq .05$ ***$p \leq .01$

A substantial percentage of new members could not have been motivated to join the group by its overall issue positions, since they did not know them. This finding supports the belief (already discussed) that general, largely purposive benefits lie at the heart of the initial decision to join. Returns from specific collective goods will be important only for choices that take place

Table 5.2b. *Organizational experience and personal issue opinions (percentage of Common Cause members without opinions)*

	Organizational experience (Years in group)												Mean %	No. cases	X^2
Issue	1	2	3	4	5	6	7	8	9	10	11	12			
Limit government spending	5	8	7	7	6	9	3	2	8	5	3	6	6	1,173	9
Sunset legislation	2	3	9	2	1	6	2	1	1	3	1	3	3	1,183	21**
Campaign finance	2	1	6	6	2	4	2	1	0	1	2	4	3	1,181	15
Equal Rights Amendment	0	3	6	1	1	1	1	2	2	1	2	2	2	1,182	13
Lobby disclosure	0	1	2	1	0	0	0	0	0	0	0	1	1	1,186	11
Defense spending	10	10	4	11	12	9	6	3	5	5	5	10	7	1,180	15
Equality of opportunity	3	16	19	12	17	6	18	10	17	17	19	12	15	1,179	18

Table 5.2b (*continued*)

| | Organizational experience (Years in group) | | | | | | | | | | | | Mean | No. | |
Issue	1	2	3	4	5	6	7	8	9	10	11	12	%	cases	X^2
Social service spending	5	11	6	10	1	14	6	6	10	8	8	8	8	1,167	13
Inflation	13	22	16	22	20	18	11	16	21	21	24	19	19	1,167	11
Abortion	10	1	7	5	2	4	2	4	2	1	3	3	3	1,178	16
Minimum guaranteed income	13	8	16	14	17	14	12	18	16	16	20	17	15	1,172	7
School busing	8	15	10	14	11	6	15	15	16	17	20	13	14	1,176	12
Nuclear energy	8	10	10	14	20	11	15	11	13	11	8	17	13	1,180	13
Soviet relations	33	39	25	20	32	34	32	27	29	31	29	30	30	1,180	10

**$p \le .05$

after members gain organizational experience, such as decisions about activism and retention.

Thus, examination of the learning process provides strong evidence that members become educated about the group once they sign up. Consistent with the analysis of joining, many contributors are quite ignorant when they first enlist; in time, they become better and better informed. However, the findings provide only initial side evidence that experiential search is a fundamental component of organizational membership. Members learn by acquiring information, but does updating of beliefs actually influence their behavior?

EXPLORING THE RETENTION PROCESS

The obvious place to start analyzing the impact of organizational learning is the decision to remain in the group. The reason for this is straightforward. Organizational maintenance is a fact of life all group leaders confront. For the majority of interest group entrepreneurs, who depend on constituent giving as a prime funding source, maintenance dictates the need to keep members contributing (but see Walker 1983).[9] Even seemingly small drops in numbers – 10 or 20 percent net of replacements – are viewed with great alarm; and the loss of long-time contributors is perceived as a threat to the entity's survival. The key to creating a successful organization can be summarized simply: Entice potential members to join, keep attrition below the rate at which replacements can be found, and establish a core membership.

This translates into a true dilemma for interest group entrepreneurs. How do they retain members for whom leaving may be an attractive option?[10] Producing the selective incentives that the membership wants is one answer. Not antagonizing constituents in ways that will lead them to cease contributing is another. In other words, leaders structure and operate the interest group so as to facilitate contributions (Moe 1980a). How else, for example (and to foreshadow later discussion), can one explain the elaborate lengths to which many leaders go to ensure the appearance of rank-and-file participation in their organization's decision making?

In the political arena, the retention problem should hit home hardest for public interest groups such as Common Cause. Their leaders lack the occupational or industrial basis that underlies so many private associations. They cannot draw on a "natural" membership, among whom either selective incentives are easily generated or coercion induces contributions. That people sign up for public interest groups in the first place in light of the collective action dilemma, no less retain their organizational allegiance, is a phenomenon that has generated considerable scholarly interest (e.g., McFarland 1976; Berry 1977; Smith 1985). But joining is not enough: As mentioned, if members are solicited, sample once, and then drop out, the group may actually be worse off than if they were never contacted in the first place. It

is not surprising that among all types of political organizations public interest groups are the most likely to fail.

Why, then, do members of an association, especially a public interest group, choose to remain? Is this process indistinguishable from the original decision to join? How are the two connected, if at all?

Not only are these inherently interesting empirical questions but – as discussed already – quitting is an important implication of experiential search. This framework requires that some members leave as they update their assessments of the association's costs and benefits, but the likelihood of exit (Hirschman 1970) should diminish with experience. In other words, retention is not a function of beliefs about costs and benefits per se, but rather how they have *changed* with experience.

The factors going into the assessments of the costs and benefits of retention should remain much the same as for Common Cause membership. The major difference ought to be knowledge. As was demonstrated in the previous chapter, those who join typically know very little about the organization, despite their generally high levels of political interest; they simply write a check for $20. The preceding section illustrates that they subsequently become more knowledgeable about the association. The experiential search framework implies that this learning should be reflected in the utilization of more precise data in making a retention choice than in the original participation calculus.

Consequently, this conceptual framework implies that withdrawal is a rational response by imperfectly informed decision makers. Unlike predictions emanating from perfect information models or imperfect information frameworks where contributors never learn, under this formulation members' precise cost/benefit calculations should change substantially over time.

Moreover, in contrast to the somewhat rudimentary examination of why people join allowed by the data, the 1981 Common Cause survey provides information that can be employed to test these ideas in considerable detail. The major limitation is that only expectations that can be tested with cross-sectional data on Common Cause members can be investigated.[11] Specifically, the experiential search framework has three such implications: (1) A model of the conditional membership decision should uncover fairly strong relationships between costs and benefits (many of which were elaborated earlier), even for those individuals who have previously elected to join; (2) the longer contributors have been in the organization, the less likely they ought to be to leave, because the probable increment in knowledge declines over time; and (3) the impact of those factors specified to guide the retention calculus, particularly highly specific characteristics, ought to be stronger for relative newcomers.

To test this, four nested models inspired by the earlier theoretical discussion are operationalized: (I) an Olsonian model in which divisible benefits are assumed to exceed costs, (II) the same model with organizational experience

incorporated, (III) this second specification with collective benefits added, and (IV) a complete formulation that also takes into account purposive and solidary returns. Estimation of these alternatives permits the determination of both whether organizational search is involved and what specific factors drive Common Cause participants to retain or revoke their membership.

Measurement

The underlying concepts that form these four models can be measured without complication using the Common Cause data. The *likelihood of membership retention* in the next contribution period – the dependent variable – is operationalized using a seven-point scale. Scores range from 1, for those certain to quit, to 7, for those certain to renew. Roughly consistent with Common Cause's 78 percent renewal rate, 54 percent of all members queried responded that they were certain to renew (it should be remembered that the sample is weighted toward activists; only 49 percent of the rank and file expressed certainty). The other 46 percent expressed different levels of uncertainty (scored from 6 to 1): 26 percent called renewal very likely, 12 percent said it was likely, 3 percent suggested that they were not sure, and another 6 percent claimed that they were not very likely to, were unlikely to, or definitely would not renew their membership. Half of the organization was up for grabs to one degree or another, and a nontrivial minority was relatively certain of leaving Common Cause.[12]

The factors posited to structure this choice are operationalized in the following manner:

1. *Costs of membership* are measured as the ability to pay (family income) and the respondent's sensitivity to costs.[13]
2. The relevance of three *divisible benefits* are incorporated: (a) the importance of publications and whether contributions would cease without them; (b) the perceived value of political information; and (c) whether or not a member has political aspirations.[14]
3. The lure of *collective benefits* is gauged by whether (a) individuals agree with the positions of Common Cause on key issues; (b) they consider the leadership effective in providing collective goods; (c) they are active in the group (assuming that such behavior yields collective benefits – a point that will be followed up in the next chapter); and (d) they believe that they are efficacious in the production of collective goods.[15]
4. *Learning* is measured by experience in the organization, operationalized to capture the hypothesis of diminishing marginal returns with both a logarithmic and a linear term of the number of years in the organization. Incorporating linear and logarithmic terms is a standard means of measuring diminishing marginal returns (e.g., Madalla 1977).
5. *Purposive benefits* are tapped by whether respondents feel an obligation as good citizens to participate and whether they care about the group.[16]

6. *Solidary benefits* are measured by whether the members value the interpersonal interactions Common Cause provides and a dummy variable on whether they have friends and colleagues within the organization.[17]

Given these indicators, many expectations are straightforward. Others are not as clear as they might seem and will be contingent on how well Common Cause provides benefits – for example, the degree to which the organization satisfies members who want to promote their political careers or seek rewarding interpersonal relationships.

One clear, important expectation is that the sign for the logarithmic version of organizational experience ought to be positive (but there is no expectation for the linear term); this would reflect the diminishing marginal impact of experiential learning. Organizational experience acts as a surrogate for the respondents' level of information and their certainty about a host of factors that are correlated with time. As the previous empirical analyses demonstrate, members gradually learn about how a group functions and slowly develop an understanding of its positions. They should also become more certain about their subjective valuation of the host of benefits that the association offers. A big advantage in employing years in the organization is that it is a continuous measure, which makes it feasible to test the hypothesis of diminishing marginal returns.[18]

It is possible to debate whether some of the other indicators measure one factor or another: Some ambiguities are inevitable, since benefit types are not empirically orthogonal to one another, and particularly in the case of collective or purposive rewards (to be discussed shortly), imperfectly informed individuals are likely to confound one benefit with another. On the whole, however, the indicators in this analysis gauge what has traditionally been meant by divisible, collective, purposive, and solidary benefits, as well as the costs of membership.

Understanding retention

The results make it clear that retention is an explicable phenomenon. They also strongly demonstrate that a specification incorporating various kinds of returns and learning does a job superior to more limited alternatives (Table 5.3).[19] A series of tests comparing each model with its more restricted predecessor clearly identify model IV as the best specification.[20] Looking at selective incentives generated via divisible benefits is not enough; collective, solidary, and purposive benefits, as well as organizational learning, also affect the decision calculus.

The gamut of costs and benefits goes into the retention decision.[21] The price of membership is an important consideration, although ability to pay per se is not. While all members know the monetary cost of joining, some are especially sensitive to it. (Remember that when Common Cause experimented with a $5 higher dues level for first-time joiners, they found that the number of new members fell off appreciably.) Those finding that membership is

Table 5.3. *Determinants of retention decisions*

Variable	Model I	Model II	Model III	Model IV
Constant	6.253**	5.381**	2.547**	0.611**
Costs				
Ability to pay	0.049	—0.006	0.026	0.028
Low sensitivity to costs	1.107**	1.037**	0.826**	0.777**
Moderate sensitivity to costs	0.511**	0.516**	0.453**	0.416**
Divisible benefits				
Value of political information	0.007*	0.006	0.026	0.028
Publications' value	0.150**	0.149**	0.091**	0.075**
Low sensitivity to provision				
of publications	0.289**	0.199**	0.124	0.075
Moderate sensitivity to provision				
of publications	0.243**	0.210**	0.117	0.057
Political aspirations	—0.150**	—0.190**	—0.180**	—0.108
Learning				
Organizational experience		—0.026	—0.019	—0.019
Natural log of organizational				
experience		0.599**	0.380**	0.385**
Collective benefits				
Agreement with group's positions			0.012**	0.011**
Assessment of leadership's				
effectiveness			0.302**	0.267**
Activism in group			0.076**	0.104**
Feeling of personal efficacy				
regarding group			0.051**	0.051**

Table 5.3 (*continued*)

Variable	Model I	Model II	Model III	Model IV
Purposive benefits				
Care about group				0.039**
Sense of civic duty				0.071**
Solidary benefits				
Value interaction				0.115**
Friends or colleagues are members				0.097**
Number of cases	1,114	1,085	986	930
Adjusted R²		.18	.23	.35	.37

*p ≤ .10   **p ≤ .05

not worth the opportunity costs – of forgoing participation in another organization, for instance – depart and either search elsewhere or become inactive.[22]

Again, this does not mean that income is insignificant, only that leaders have structured the organization to neutralize its importance for the equilibrium that is observed. Consider the relationship between income and sensitivity to costs (Table 5.4).[23] When asked if they would stay in Common Cause if dues were doubled, only 9 of the 117 contributors (less than 8 percent) with 1980 family incomes over $75,000 responded negatively; by contrast, 101 of 257 members (over 39 percent) with income under $20,000 answered that a doubling of dues would precipitate their departure. As will be detailed in greater depth later in the analysis, many of those with low cost sensitivity end up giving additional contributions to the organization above the dues level. Dues are kept at a sufficiently minimal level that membership is not income sensitive. Some members may decide that the benefits are not worth the costs, but this calculation is not heavily influenced by income levels.

The salience of divisible benefits is more nebulous. When the Olsonian model is operationalized, the group's publications, the political information it provides, and the opportunities it furnishes to political aspirants all appear important. When other benefits are fully integrated into the decision framework, however, everything but the value of Common Cause publications is insignificant, and even the estimate of its impact is halved.

Table 5.4. *Cost sensitivity and income level*

	Degree of cost sensitivity (percentage)		
Income level	Low	Moderate	High
Less than $10,000	24.1	32.8	43.1
$10,000—$20,000	31.7	30.2	38.2
$20,000—$25,000	35.6	33.9	30.5
$25,000—$35,000	39.5	33.8	26.8
$35,000—$50,000	43.2	33.7	23.1
$50,000—$75,000	47.4	36.5	16.1
$75,000—$100,000	51.9	38.9	9.3
More than $100,000	66.1	27.4	6.5

Source: 1981 Common Cause survey.

The utility of the Olsonian framework as a predictive model for retention decisions in public interest groups is questionable; as an explanatory framework, it is even less convincing. This is far from a direct indictment of a model designed to explain initial joining in economic groups. However, it does provide some additional reason to doubt the general utility of this decision-making model.

The effect of political aspirations, although insignificant in the final model ($t = 1.3$), is nevertheless intriguing. As mentioned earlier, one would presume that joining Common Cause is generally an inefficient means for the politically ambitious to get ahead. Indeed, individuals with such aspirations appear less likely to remain in Common Cause than other contributors. Once they learn about the true nature of the organization – its antagonistic stance toward political parties, for example – they may decide that it is the wrong place for them and move on. Even if the politically ambitious are more likely than others to join the association (remember that a third of the association's members had either previously sought a position or had future political aspirations), they can still be more prone to quit. Conversely, the relationship between future aspirations and retention should be positive in organizations that are good mechanisms for building political careers.

To foreshadow a point to be developed later in this analysis, another reason for this weak relationship may be that retention is a necessary but

insufficient condition to using an organization to foster upward mobility. Simply contributing money to an entity is unlikely to further a career: One must be active as well. To test whether this is the case, model IV was rerun, except this time an interaction term for aspirations and activism was included. The results (not shown) suggest that activism is indeed necessary for aspirations to make a difference (the coefficients for the other factors in the model are essentially unchanged). Individuals who are both politically ambitious and activists are more likely to stay in the group, while those who are rank-and-file aspirants are less likely to do so than the average member. Presumably, the former are satisfied with Common Cause as a means for advancement, while the latter are disenchanted.

Collective benefits appear to be an important element in the conditional joining calculus. These findings refute the assertion that members never learn about collective goods; if the latter were the case, these estimates would be insignificant. Despite the fact that few members cited such returns as the principal reason for initially joining, they seem to be the most relevant factor for the retention choice.[24] Assessment of the leadership, level of activism, and feelings of efficacy all have an impact. So too does agreement with Common Cause's positions. Of particular salience are those good government issues – sunset legislation, campaign finance, and regulation of lobbyists – that the organization has traditionally emphasized.[25]

An explanation for this tension between the apparent insignificance of collective benefits in joining decisions and their critical role for retention calculi centers on experiential search. Many people are ignorant about the organization when they first sign on but gradually learn upon joining. All they might know initially is that Common Cause is a group that deals with good government issues and for which experiential search comes cheaply. After contributing, they discover more specifically what the organization does and how much it accomplishes. These data are employed in calculating whether or not to stay in the group. Members move away from a concern about seemingly purposive benefits toward an interest in more specific collective returns.

The results imply that the standard dichotomy between purposive and collective benefits – the former representing an adherence to the group's stated goals and the latter reflecting members' beliefs about their impact on the production of collective goods – reflects a false distinction. In the Olsonian world collective goods (or usually the inability to influence their production) are a key ingredient in an individual's decision whether or not to contribute, while purposive rewards are incidental. Yet, in the present analysis, the difference between these two types of rewards is overwhelmed, at least as it is tapped by survey instruments in the public interest group context, by the conditioning effect of information on the estimated policy benefits derived from membership. Those with little knowledge tend to give vague responses that suggest that purposive benefits structure these decisions;

those with experience often provide more precise reasons that seem to imply that they are motivated by collective benefits.

Put another way, what is being interpreted as collective benefits may really be specific statements about purposive returns (this has previously been implied in Hardin 1982). Contributors' responses may reflect their perception of the group's, and not their personal, impact on the provision of collective benefits. Their assessment of the association's leadership and policies is important for deciding whether to exit, because they think the organization can have an impact on the production of public goods. They learn about the group's efficacy and how their policy preferences correspond to the organization's and then either stay or depart accordingly. Thus, education integrates initial and conditional membership. Broad motivations are replaced by more specific ones. Group leaders have an incentive to foster the confusion between individual and associational efficacy. To the extent that they control the information contributors employ to update their cost/benefit calculi, elites will add to the confusion by telling members that they make a difference by acting collectively. Certainly, Common Cause literature freely interchanges terms connoting individual efficacy ("You can help make certain") with those implying group efficacy ("We can win this fight").

Explicitly purposive benefits are still germane. Common Cause is a good place for people who really care about such returns and want to be good citizens. Even broad policy attachments to the group may make participation satisfying. Consequently, contributors who have an abiding interest in being good citizens or who develop a strong identification with Common Cause tend to keep on giving.

To summarize: These findings about collective and purposive rewards support the proposition that members go from general to specific reasons for staying or leaving as they become more knowledgeable. This explanation is consistent with the side evidence about learning. All that is additionally required is the assumption that individuals recognize their informational shortfalls before joining and employ experiential search to remedy them partially. This strategy leads politically interested individuals to offer vaguely purposive reasons for joining and more specific concerns about collective goods for staying or leaving.

Similarly, solidary benefits are rarely mentioned as a major reason for joining. Yet they too are significant factors in the retention choice. For those seeking such interactions, the organization delivers the goods. Others may discover that a by-product of search for purposive and collective benefits is a rewarding associational involvement. Again, the tension between initial and subsequent conditional membership choices stems from the fact that contributors learn over time. Those who find rewarding interpersonal interactions stay in Common Cause; those who decide that the organization does not provide the solidary benefits they come to desire, depart.

The findings regarding learning offer a second test of the experiential search

theory and, once again, provide validation. Specifically, they lend credence to the hypothesis that experiential learning yields diminishing marginal returns. Each year has a positive, yet declining, impact on the probability that members will remain committed even after all the standard costs and benefits of joining are incorporated into the model. Ceteris paribus, a newcomer scores three-quarters of a point lower on the seven-point retention scale than the most veteran contributors. In other words, there is considerable vacillation among new members about their future intentions, but this uncertainty dissipates over time. By and large, departing contributors are recent converts who, upon learning about the group, become disenchanted rather than long-term participants who grow bored with Common Cause.[26]

The overall predictions from the full experiential search model (model IV) also lend credence to the hypothesis that the probability of staying increases temporally but at a diminishing rate (Figure 5.1). The impact of the early years is roughly five times greater than the effect of the later years; and, as discussed previously, there are no obvious sociodemographic differences between long-term members and newcomers that might render this relationship artifactual. The only possible inference is that individuals learn and update their beliefs. After revising their evaluations, those liking what they see stay, and the rest search elsewhere. This conclusion is consistent with Common Cause's own troubles in holding on to new members. Only about 55 percent of first-year members contribute the following year, while roughly 90 percent of long-time members remain.

Finally, consider what happens when the sample is split between relative newcomers – those contributing six years or less – and comparative veterans, who have been involved for more than six years, and a revised version of model IV is estimated (Table 5.5).[27] Most strikingly, but predictably from an experiential search viewpoint, the model does a superior job of explaining why newcomers come and go compared to veterans. Longer term members more closely approximate the full-information ideal and are prone to depart for idiosyncratic reasons. Also as predicted, specific characteristics loom larger in newcomers' retention decisions.

While there is no appreciable difference between the two samples in the findings for purposive benefits (no coefficient is significant), there are variations in the effects of solidary benefits and especially collective returns. In all but one instance (efficacy) where there is a significant relationship, the impact of these factors is stronger for newcomers than for veterans. Not only is learning about specific characteristics crucial, it is especially salient for those who are new to the organization.[28]

All three tests of experiential search support its validity as a superior framework for conceptualizing the retention choice. Members make their decisions in a systematic, comprehensible fashion. The decision to remain in the organization reflects their discovery that the group provides the benefits for which they are searching. Learning is an important component of

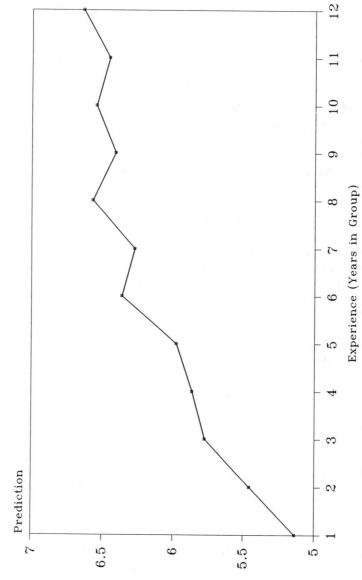

Figure 5.1. Retention predictions and organizational experience. Predictions are based on the seven-point scale used to measure a respondent's probability of retention.

Table 5.5. *Retention decisions of newcomers and veterans*

Variable	Newcomers	Veterans
Constant	—0.233	2.058**
Costs		
Ability to pay	0.044	0.014
Low sensitivity to costs	1.115**	0.555**
Moderate sensitivity to costs	0.583**	0.234**
Divisible benefits		
Value of political information	—0.005	0.058
Publications' value	0.119*	0.069*
Low sensitivity to provision of		
publications	0.290*	0.102
Moderate sensitivity to provision		
of publications	0.094	—0.032
Political aspirations	—0.188	—0.098
Learning		
Organizational experience	0.101**	0.038*
Collective benefits		
Agreement with group's positions	0.013**	0.010**
Assessment of leadership's		
effectiveness	0.281**	0.235**
Activism in group	0.155**	0.082*
Feeling of personal efficacy		
regarding group	0.022	0.055*

Table 5.5 (*continued*)

Variable	Newcomers	Veterans
Purposive benefits		
Care about group	0.046	0.035
Sense of civic duty	0.103	0.037
Solidary benefits		
Value interaction	—0.043	0.126
Friends or colleagues are members	0.198**	0.059
Number of cases	370	560
Adjusted R^2	.40	.24

$*p \leq .10$ $**p \leq .05$

understanding how conditional membership choices are made. Overall predictions about the probability of remaining in the organization reflect the diminishing marginal returns to be expected if individuals garner information through experiential search. An individual's first years in the organization are especially important, particularly for learning about highly specific characteristics.

A VALIDITY CHECK

The four-group survey data can again be used to validate the findings specific to Common Cause. To reiterate: While these data are not as rich as those from the Common Cause survey, the experiential search framework still generates the following three testable expectations: (1) The retention decision is explicable; (2) those who have been in an association for a considerable time should tend to remain; and (3) contributors choosing the "right" organization should be more likely to update their beliefs positively and therefore remain in the association. The first two tests are essentially replications of the preceding analysis, while the third is an extension.

Specifically, the data make it possible to gauge whether members think that their participation can have an impact, whether they are activists, and

whether they have been in the group for a considerable time. They also permit the measurement of whether individuals have made the right choice of organization. Finally, as a precaution given the data limitations, respondents' level of political interest (or, at least, the surrogate for it used in the analysis of joining) is also included in a second estimated model (model VI).

The perception that members are efficacious is tapped by a series of dummy variables comparing those who believe that decisions in the group are made by the members or by interactions between the members and the leadership or staff, or who do not know how they are made, with those who think that the leadership and staff are in control. Whether contributors are activists is measured using a dummy variable, while organizational experience is gauged by two dummy variables tapping whether the contributor has been in the organization for two to five years or for more than five years. The reasonableness of the member–association match is measured using a dummy variable, which indicates whether individuals made the right choice of an organization, as reported in Table 4.7.

The likelihood of membership retention is measured trichotomously. Those claiming that they will renew their membership in the next contribution period – about 83 percent of all respondents – scored a 2; those stating they don't know if they will stay or go were assigned a 1; and those saying that they are planning to quit were given a 0. League of Women Voters contributors were most prone to claim that they will remain in their organization (90 percent), presumably for the same cost-based reasons (remember that being in the League often entails a significant time commitment) that they were most likely to be well suited to their association, although members of the American Civil Liberties Union were not far behind (87 percent); 80 percent of Common Cause contributors and only 67 percent of the Conservative Caucus respondents answered affirmatively.[29]

Given the ordinal nature of the dependent variable, ordered probit is the obvious estimation technique. Intercorrelations demonstrate little problem with multicollinearity, and a pooling test suggests that it is possible to combine the responses of the four groups' members.

The results strongly confirm the findings specific to Common Cause (Table 5.6).[30] Once again, retention is explicable, and the ability to learn is key. Members selecting the right organization are more likely to renew membership in the next period, and those learning they made a mistake try to rectify it. Activists, who have presumably learned about the group and decided it is worthwhile, also exhibit a much greater tendency to remain. The learning process explains why those who have been in the organization a long time are more likely to stay as well – they approach the full-information ideal.

By contrast, assessments of who makes organizational decisions are unimportant. Individuals do not weight these judgments heavily in their retention calculus. They are probably content, given the small costs of being

Table 5.6. *Determinants of retention: Four-group study (probit estimates with standard errors in parentheses)*

Variable	Model V	Model VI
Constant	0.692***	0.058
	(0.196)	(0.433)
Predisposition toward activism	0.694***	0.703***
	(0.247)	(0.250)
"Correct" choice	0.264**	0.240***
	(0.141)	(0.143)
Organizational responsiveness		
Members decide	0.036	0.031
	(0.275)	(0.285)
Interaction with leaders	0.185	0.176
	(0.179)	(0.182)
Don't know how operates	0.074	0.124
	(0.185)	(0.193)
Organizational experience		
Two to five years in group	0.650***	0.684***
	(0.172)	(0.178)
More than five years in group	1.240***	1.224***
	(0.189)	(0.198)
Political interest		
Gender (male)		—0.052
		(0.151)
Age		0.036

Table 5.6 (*continued*)

Variable	Model V	Model VI
		(0.047)
Education		0.131*
		(0.071)
Number of cases	507	502
—2x*log-likelihood function*	489	474

*p ≤ .10   **p ≤ .05   ***p ≤ .01

an associational member, to make a purposive or policy statement that is in accord with their own beliefs. Of the three sociodemographic surrogates for political interest included in model VI, only education is relevant: The weakness of the findings regarding interest is not surprising, given that only group members are being examined. Other findings are substantially the same whether either model V or model VI is considered.

To summarize: These results once again support the supposition that members are imperfectly informed but learn over time. Even an extremely truncated sample of society like the one examined here yields evidence buttressing this viewpoint. Besides validating the Common Cause–specific results, what is especially noteworthy is that contributors who join the wrong organization eventually realize it and attempt to rectify the situation. Those sampling a group and finding that it is wrong for them tend either to stay in the rank and file or to quit altogether – presumably to try another association or return to private life.

CONCLUSIONS: LEARNING, THE RETENTION CHOICE,
AND EXPERIENTIAL SEARCH

When it comes to learning and retention, Common Cause members behave very much in the manner predicted by experiential search. The following picture of the average contributor emerges from this analysis: Induced by the ease and low cost of signing up that leaders offer, a somewhat hetero-geneous number of individuals join an inexpensive organization about which they are largely uninformed. These citizens have a rough idea about what

the group stands for, but they lack the detailed knowledge needed to decide whether this is the best association for them. They are as informed about politics, as educated, and as wealthy as long-time members; but they lack organization-specific information, which is best gained experientially.

Consequently, the retention process is explicable by specifying a model that reflects the accrual of information and the resulting updating of beliefs. Among other things, the findings make clear that early on, when the incremental informational gains are greatest, there is a higher probability that revising prior beliefs will precipitate departures. As time progresses and the additional impact of another period diminishes, so too does the likelihood of dropping out. The accumulation of knowledge about the organization also leads members to rely upon more specific criteria in making their conditional membership decisions than they claim motivated their initial contributions. Examining the model's overall predictions about future membership behavior simply buttresses the experiential search story further. So too does the contrast between what the model reveals about newcomers versus veterans.

Specifically, the results provide strong confirmation for the experiential search framework as a unified viewpoint on the initial joining decision and subsequent membership choices. Citizens do join groups intent on learning more about them – in particular, presumably ·those associations that the leadership has structured to encourage such behavior. Some inevitably choose the wrong organization for them, but many remedy their mistakes by quitting. Those who find out that it is the right organization for them become more and more loyal over the years.

More generally, these findings show why an integrated approach to organizations is desirable. Only by understanding how the leadership structures the association to make it appealing to large numbers to join and sample it is it possible to comprehend why diverse individuals who do not know much about the organization sign up. And only by understanding that such a process is at work can the underlying processes that determine the retention decision be fully appreciated.

Appendix 5.1. Testing the retention model

Despite the fact that temporal inferences are being drawn from cross-sectional data, the attrition of members (who are therefore unavailable to interview) should not have an impact on the estimates of the retention model presented in this chapter (e.g., Table 5.3). As long as quitting is related to exogenous factors – unhappiness with the group, evaluations of the leadership, and so on – and these factors are controlled for, the ensuing estimates are unbiased. None of the difficulties associated with choice-based sampling, such as those encountered in Chapter 4, are relevant in this case.

However, there are a number of characteristics of the Common Cause

membership and the retention decision that raise important econometric issues about the analysis specific to Common Cause: the reasonableness of pooling activists and rank-and-file members, the specification of the dependent variable, and the potential for multicollinearity.

Pooling members: To ensure that it is acceptable to pool the Common Cause–designated activists with rank-and-file members, a Chow test (Chow 1960) was conducted. The results of the test proved to be insignificant, thus permitting the pooling.

Endogeneity: Hausman tests (Hausman 1978) were used to ascertain whether any of the independent variables is endogenously determined (the logarithmic and linear organizational experience terms were tested jointly): None is.

Specification of dependent variable: Additional tests were undertaken to investigate whether the standard sevenfold specification of the dependent variable is correct. A Hausman test for determining whether the slopes for a seven-ordered probit are identical to those for a threefold analog (*no, can't say, yes*) led to the rejection of the null hypothesis that $B_7 = B_3$ ($\chi^2 = 35$, $df = 19$). This finding implies that the seven-category operationalization is subject to specification error of some sort, although the ramifications are uncertain. This discovery precipitated a further investigation to uncover whether a better specification is available. The obvious alternative is a two-stage conditional structure that breaks the retention decision first into a direction (*no, can't say, yes*) and then into a strength (*certain, very likely, likely*) choice. When the log-likelihood ratios of the conditional and unconditional processes are compared (see Vuong 1989), however, the latter model is far superior. Given this strong finding, the unconditional, sevenfold specification was adopted with the caveat that there might be some superior alternative.[31]

Multicollinearity: Examination of a correlation matrix reveals that multicollinearity is not a major problem in these models. The linear and logarithmic learning terms are highly correlated. This intercorrelation is to be expected, but as mentioned, a logarithmic and a linear term were employed to tap for diminishing marginal returns (see, for example, Madalla 1977). If one of the two terms is excluded, the other findings do not change substantially. On examining the intercorrelations between the independent variables, only two other pairs of correlations are above the 0.30 level: the valuation of political information and publications (.59) and the two dummy variables on cost sensitivity ($-.60$). Combining the information and publication variables results in a poorer-fitting model. The resulting variable is insignificant (whereas the value of publications is significant in Table 5.4),

and no other substantive results change. There is also no appreciable change if the variable measuring moderate sensitivity to costs is dropped, except that the coefficient for high sensitivity increases in magnitude.

To explore more systematically the potential for multicollinearity, an SVD was performed for model IV. As mentioned earlier, SVD is a technique designed to ensure that least-squares estimation is identified. Interestingly, the SVD for the full model shows a moderate level of multicollinearity (SVD = 60). However, a major cause of this multicollinearity is the relationship between the intercept term and other variables: This result is common when using dummy variables but does not harm the estimates. If the intercept and the logarithmic learning terms are dropped, the SVD is cut in half, to a level where experimental work shows the multicollinearity is quite small (SVD = 30). Again, the findings are robust with respect to multicollinearity.

Summary: The foregoing findings suggest that the estimates of the retention model found in this chapter should be quite reasonable. The most obvious potential methodological objections can be dismissed.

6

The internal politics of organizations II: Activism

SEPARATING THE ACTIVISTS FROM THE RANK AND FILE

Those members who remain in the group face another decision besides whether or not to stay: what level of commitment to make. Contributors can elect to write their dues check and stay in the rank and file, or they can choose a higher level of involvement in the organization.

Up to this point in the analysis, when considering activists, the empirical investigation has focused only on those designated by Common Cause. However, activism, more broadly construed, may take one of two forms. For some group members, the choice may be to donate additional money. Just as many joiners have been labeled checkbook participants (e.g., Hayes 1983), contributors of additional financial resources can be called *checkbook activists*. Alternatively, members, some of whom will be Common Cause–designated activists, can supplement their mode of participation by actually volunteering time. For lack of a better term, such contributors can be labeled *temporal activists*.[1]

Yet, as foreshadowed in the last chapter's introduction to the study of internal organizational politics generally, there is virtually *no* contemporary empirical analysis of activism and interest groups. There are data on the correlates of activism for members of political parties – with largely inconclusive results (for a survey, see Eldersveld 1982; see also Carmines and Stimson 1989) – but information on its interest group determinants is extremely sparse.

It is unnecessary to speculate again on why there has been a void in analyzing a topic that most social scientists would agree is important. The more consequential point to reiterate is that it is assumed that studying contributors' commitment levels requires a unified framework from which joining (the initial commitment), quitting (the abandonment of commitment), and activism (the choice for additional commitment beyond mere membership) are made comprehensible within the larger context of organizational activity. Another obvious point to emphasize is that studying activism necessitates procuring information on a substantial number of activists and utilizing techniques to overcome the inherent methodological obstacles involved.

As will be shown in more detail later, while both checkbook and temporal activism entail a higher commitment level than rank-and-file status, in many other ways they are quite different from each other; the explanations for each ought to vary in predictable ways as a consequence. In a broad sense, the factors structuring the decision to be a checkbook activist should be relatively similar to those for retention, while those for temporal activism might appear sui generis. Still, in each case members should follow a discernible pattern of experiential search if this framework is a viable, unifying theory of contributors' behavior.

CHECKBOOK VERSUS TEMPORAL ACTIVISM

Specifically, checkbook and temporal activism should differ from each other on at least four broad dimensions. They are the importance of costs, income, selective benefits, and solidary rewards. Taken together, these potential differences lead to the expectation that checkbook and temporal activists are qualitatively different from one another.

1. *Costs.* The relative costs of temporal activism should, on average, be far greater than writing a check if a reasonable valuation of the time that is sacrificed is employed. In other words, even a few hours per month of the modal (highly paid) Common Cause member's time will be a relatively expensive pledge if translated into dollars. Not surprisingly, contributors to the group are roughly seven and a half times more likely to be checkbook activists than temporal activists. (Also, not surprisingly, the group uses mail as the principal means of soliciting checkbook contributions but uses phone calls as its major vehicle to request members' time.) As the logic of collective action suggests, and in understandable contrast to the finding that income does not matter for joining or retention because of the way that the leadership sets up the organization, the supply of contributions goes down as the price goes up – even for so-called do-gooders such as the stereotypical Common Cause member.

2. *Income.* A related distinction to that concerning costs involves the role of income. Level of income should be a positive determinant of checkbook giving, at least for the level of money contributed, but not necessarily of temporal activism. While the leadership has a desire to keep the dues low and induce people from different societal strata to sample the group, they then have a motivation to extract as much as possible from those who decide to stay. Ceteris paribus, such appeals ought to be most successful with those who have more cash in their pockets. By contrast, given that temporal commitments involve time and not money, expectations for the relationship between income and these in-kind donations are reversed: Despite the conventional wisdom that income is positively correlated with participation, when contributions of time rather than money are involved it is likely that relatively poorer persons will donate more because their opportunity costs are lower.[2]

3. *Selective benefits.* A third difference between checkbook and temporal activism is the potential relevance of selective rewards. Only a few specific scenarios might be constructed in which selective rewards would stimulate additional financial donations. One is if the leadership makes a conscious decision to furnish a separate set of benefits to the organization's larger contributors. This is a tactic, for example, that universities and arts organizations frequently adopt; Common Cause, not surprisingly given its egalitarian, progressive image, does not. Another possibility is that a contributor might believe that a sufficiently large gift will facilitate upward mobility – however, this is undoubtedly a very rare occurrence. Finally, contributors who highly value selective benefits might conclude that giving additional sums ensures or expands their supply. But given the collective action problems involved, such scenarios are probably quite uncommon; that is, the impact of any contribution on the aggregate supply of selective benefits is likely to be small.

By contrast, temporal activism might be expected to produce selective returns. While too much should not be made of the private benefits likely to be generated from temporal contributions in an organization like Common Cause, the possibility is greater than that associated with simply writing a larger check. This statement should be especially true for political aspirants who may consider involvement in organizational activity as a means of making contacts and gaining valuable private information.

4. *Solidary rewards.* Finally, because checkbook participation involves few personal interactions, it is likely that it will not be strongly driven by solidary rewards. For exactly the same reasons, such benefits should be a significant impetus for temporal activism. If members want interpersonal contacts, they must give of their time, not of their wallet. About the only logical means by which solidary benefits might spur checkbook activism is analogous to the story told above regarding selective returns: It is possible that contributions are made to ensure the continued supply of opportunities for interaction. However, once again, such motivations are unlikely to carry much weight. By comparison, solidary rewards should be important for temporal activism for obvious reasons (despite some Common Cause–specific caveats that will be mentioned shortly). In other words, by its very definition such activism involves interpersonal inter-actions, and members are likely to self-select according to whether they enjoy such activities.

Thus, the factors motivating different types of activism can be compared to each other. It should be immediately clear that the determinants of check-book activism should be very similar to those spurring retention, except that there should be less emphasis on selective and solidary rewards and more on the participant's ability to pay. The forces driving temporal contributions, on the other hand, should be quite different because the costs are considerably higher and qualitatively more demanding and because the benefits vary substantially as well. Indeed, reflecting this, at Common Cause the task of

soliciting financial contributions is largely assigned to the same individuals in charge of member recruitment and renewal; by contrast, the recruiting of, and the caring for, temporal activists is largely the province of others.

Given the similarities to the previous analysis of retention and the weakness of the available data (to be discussed shortly), checkbook activism will be examined only briefly. Because the determinants of temporal contributions should be substantially different from those motivating either retention or the donation of additional monies and because the available data are quite rich, much of this chapter will focus on such behavior. The costs and benefits of temporal activism will be elaborated, and specific hypotheses will be derived from the experiential search framework and subsequently tested. The analysis of Common Cause–specific activism will also be supplemented with an examination of the four-group study. The latter data will be employed for two purposes: first, as a validity check of the single group findings, and second, to investigate more rigorously the relationship between the two decisions members make that have been examined as part of the analysis of internal organizational politics – retention and activism.

CHECKBOOK ACTIVISM AND ITS DETERMINANTS

Checkbook activism provides an important source of additional income for organizations such as public interest groups. As mentioned in the discussion of joining, Common Cause is conscious of the need to extract from its members as much as they are willing to give. New Common Cause members are also immediately encouraged to establish a pattern of giving; even those with a history of not giving additional contributions will be asked two or three times a year to contribute more. In a given year, nondues contributions account for about one-quarter of the organization's budget.

As the discussion in the previous section made clear, giving additional funds requires only a modicum of effort on the member's part. In many ways the benefits associated with making such contributions should mirror those stemming from the choice to renew membership, with certain modifications regarding solidary and selective rewards. Once again, experience in the organization should also matter, and those who have been in the association for a long time should be more likely to give money than newer members. With respect to the individual contributor's costs, the major sacrifice is financial. All else that is required is the few moments it takes to fill our a check.

Having said all this, it must be admitted that the measure provided in the Common Cause survey is far from ideal for the analysis at hand. The information that would be most useful is how *much* money, if any, an individual supplies within a given membership period, say one year. The question respondents were asked, by contrast, reads, "Have you ever contributed money to Common Cause in addition to your annual membership dues?" This means that a member who contributed *any* additional funds during their *entire* time in the group could respond affirmatively. As

mentioned several times previously, almost 63 percent of those surveyed (just under 60 percent of the Common Cause population given oversampling) answered that they had indeed donated additional funds. Also, given this wording, the probability of responding positively would be partially a function of years in the group; that is, the issue of concern – whether some members are more likely than others to give money to the group at any given time – is obscured.

Despite the obvious caveats implied by measurement shortfalls, it is still possible to test the aforementioned hypotheses regarding checkbook activism. The retention model specified earlier can be rerun with several changes. The dependent variable, temporal activism, now is generated from the question cited above regarding whether or not a member had given additional dues. The 63 percent who replied yes are scored a 1, and the remainder, 0. As for independent variables, the activism and sensitivity to dues measures are dropped for the obvious reasons that the former is to a large degree measuring the same thing as the dependent variable and the latter is irrelevant. Also, after a specification test revealed that organizational experience is endo-genous to checkbook activism (not surprisingly, given how the dependent variable is measured) an instrument that includes a variety of factors, such as age, region, income, and other demographic features was inserted to replace the original experience measures. Once again, the stratified sample neces-sitated no exceptional econometric analysis.

The logit results are largely consistent with expectations (Table 6.1). As hypothesized, solidary rewards are relatively unimportant, since checkbook activism offers few such returns. While such returns are likely to facilitate retention and temporal activism, they do not enter into the equation when the decision is to adjust contribution levels. Somewhat surprisingly, however, divisible rewards, in particular with respect to publications, are significant; an average contributor who claimed that publications were very important rather than somewhat important is 4 percent more likely to contribute and a member who would quit the group if publications were not provided is 7 percent more likely to give extra funds. Individuals who place greater value on these perks are, indeed, willing to pay more.

Also as anticipated, collective benefits – at least as tapped by leadership assessments and efficacy – are significant, with increases in the probability of an average member engaging in checkbook activism ranging from 4 to 6 percent (assuming a change of one standard deviation). Rather than focusing on broad purposive rewards, those who contribute additional funds are motivated by a more specific belief that they or the group have an impact on policy. In addition, organizational experience is once again a determinant: While caveats must be added, those who have been in the group a long time and know more about it are more likely to dig deeper into their pockets. Indeed, the difference in probability between a seven- and ten-year veteran making additional contributions is a substantial 14 percent. In addition, both the impact of the learning term and the total model predictions exhibit

Table 6.1. *Determinants of checkbook activism (logit estimates)*

Variable	Estimate
Constant	—4.648***
Costs	
Ability to pay	0.001
Divisible benefits	
Value of political information	—0.136
Publications' value	0.126*
Low sensitivity to provision	
of publications	0.304*
Moderate sensitivity to provision	
of publications	0.252*
Political aspirations	—0.021
Learning	
Organizational experience (instrument)	—0.019
Natural log of organizational	
experience (instrument)	1.582*
Collective benefits	
Agreement with group's positions	0.007
Assessment of leadership's	
effectiveness	0.139**
Feeling of personal efficacy	
regarding group	0.124***

Table 6.1 (*continued*)

Variable	Estimate
Purposive benefits	
Care about group	0.052
Sense of civic duty	0.052
Solidary benefits	
Value interaction	0.151
Friends or colleagues are members	—0.109
Number of cases	766
—2xlog-likelihood function	891

$*p \leq .10$ $**p \leq .05$ $***p \leq .01$

the expected pattern of diminishing marginal returns. Thus, to the extent that these data can be employed to test the experiential search model, they substantiate it.

But perhaps the biggest surprise in this set of findings is that income is *not* a determinant of checkbook activism. Analogous to the findings for joining and retention, the expectation that income is a significant determinant of participation, implied by the traditional correlation between the two, is not borne out when a causal model is estimated. Whether this result is artifactual or real is open to question.[3] To repeat, the dependent variable's considerable shortcomings might obscure a relationship between members' ability to pay and their generosity. It is quite likely that income is relevant for how *much* contributors give to the group annually, even if not for *whether* they contribute. Nevertheless, using the measure provided, the relationship between ability to pay and checkbook participation is nonexistent; even the bivariate association between the two is statistically insignificant ($\chi^2 = 2.7$, $df = 7$). Another possible explanation of these results is that, consistent with the interpretations advanced concerning joining and retention, in an organization with a membership as sociodemographically homogeneous as that of Common Cause, money does not matter when the cost is small relative to the ability to pay.

In summary: The decision to dig deeper into one's pockets than necessary

is determined by factors very similar to those underlying retention, with some generally explicable exceptions. Leaders have structured the organization so that members join the group for very little money, learn about it, and if they think what is going on is especially worthwhile, they give some more. Surprisingly, since checkbook activism was supposed to differ from joining and retention in this respect, income continues to be irrelevant as a positive determinant of group behavior. Although it is possible that this particular finding is artifactual, the fact that earnings are consistently unrelated in any positive sense to members' choices is – to say the least – suggestive.

TEMPORAL ACTIVISM: AN INTRODUCTION

Temporal activism is a key to an organization's political success, and survival, for a myriad of interest groups.[4] It is especially vital for associations lacking a large financial base, like the vast majority of public interest groups. Even in entities like Common Cause, where so many members provide extra financial support (above an admittedly very low dues level), the leadership is very conscious of being strapped for resources relative to the group's needs. Almost all leaders of membership groups who wish to sustain their associations or have a policy impact must pay attention to the decision-making calculus motivating those who might be willing to give time as well as money.

In particular, activists frequently perform two vital functions. *Internally*, they provide free services for which leaders would otherwise have to pay and forgo other opportunities. Given the problem of eliciting contributions to political organizations, this makes volunteers crucial for associational maintenance. *Externally*, they often furnish the representational linkage in the hinterlands that is thought to be a key element in determining a group's influence over public policy: As mentioned and as will be examined in more depth shortly, it is commonly believed that no matter how sophisticated a Washington lobbying operation is, without a base of support in congressional districts an organization is likely to be frustrated in achieving its policy goals.

When it comes to Common Cause, activists play both internal and external roles. The organization actively solicits volunteers to help with routine operations; it also frequently calls alerts to those in its grassroots networks to mobilize. In each instance, contributors who get involved perform tasks that are generally oriented toward the organization's policy initiatives. Overall, Common Cause activists play a vital role when it comes to the group's policy forays; they are less central for efforts that are focused primarily on the association's maintenance.[5]

Why rely on volunteers for pushing the associational policy agenda? The reason is actually very simple. Given all of the problems of collective action, just keeping an organization's body and soul together – recruiting and retaining members, fund raising, producing publications, overseeing state and local organizations, developing issue positions, performing a host of administrative

duties, and fighting political battles – places great demands on a group. Common Cause's small, professional staff of around eighty cannot manage all of the functions necessary to keep this 300,000 member association operating and hope to have a substantial policy impact without the assistance of volunteers. The leadership has to make choices about which areas will get large amounts of staff attention and which will have to rely more on volunteer collaboration.

At Common Cause, the decision has been made to structure the organization so that about one-third of the staff has a policy-related responsibility. They are expected to develop Common Cause issues and positions, lobby on Capitol Hill, act as liaisons with the state organizations, and coordinate grassroots lobbying (Wertheimer 1986). Obviously, this is an enormous set of responsibilities for such a small number of staff members. They must inevitably turn to activists if they wish to achieve some success. Common Cause consequently relies on implementing an insider–outsider lobbying strategy by employing professional Washington representatives in conjunction with voluntary networks in over 300 congressional districts.[6] It is largely activists' responsibility to mobilize members to transmit the direction and intensity of the rank and file's preferences to political decision makers, usually by writing letters. The organization's intricate, congressional district-based, grassroots lobbying network is arguably its most valuable resource in influencing public policy. Political success hinges on the efforts of unpaid personnel.

This process, examined in more depth in later chapters, works as follows: Roughly sixty headquarters' volunteers ("the Washington Connection"), sometimes supplemented with interns and guided by three Common Cause organizers each assigned a region of the country, regularly maintain telephone contact with congressional district coordinators and others involved with the local organizations. Several times a year, all district coordinators are asked to mobilize the participants in the complete local telephone chains; many other times, subsets of the association, networks in specific congressional districts, or all activists, for example, are asked to mobilize. As mentioned previously, the professional staff coordinates grassroots mobilization with its efforts in Washington.

In addition, these volunteers help solicit new activists and try to increase a notch or two the involvement of those already somewhat active. Calls may be placed to those identified through a variety of means: those noting a willingness to do more on their initial joining or renewal forms, those who send Common Cause congressional responses to their letters (something members are encouraged to do), or those identified as writing letters to the editor at their local newspapers, to name a few examples. In addition, cold calls are sometimes placed to the members at random.

This description suggests that there are actually two subclasses of temporal activists in Common Cause. *Core activists* are the 4 percent of members who are leaders of local congressional or state organizations; these are the

members whom Common Cause designates as activists and who are overrepresented in the stratified sample. *Occasional activists* are the 11 percent who are not part of the leadership group but engage in what would be considered activist behavior. They may be involved in their congressional district or state organizations or may perform a variety of other tasks. The rank and file, as defined here, constitute the remaining 85 percent of the membership; they contribute their dues (and 56 percent have given something more financially) and may be the objects of mobilization efforts (for example, 27 percent of those defined here as being in the rank and file reported that they had been contacted through Common Cause in the previous year to write to their senators or congressmen).[7]

ALTERNATIVE SCENARIOS

What, then, motivates core and occasional activists, and does it reflect a search process? While some comments have already been made on how activism ought to differ from other organizational decisions, a more general discussion about the types of motivations that might precipitate contributors to move up the associational hierarchy is in order.

Essentially, there are two logical scenarios for why members might make such a commitment, both of which can be consistent with experiential search. One is that activists are true believers who are passionately devoted to the group's ideals. This is certainly the popular image of activists in public-regarding groups like Common Cause. In their study of party activists, Abramowitz and Stone (1984) label this the *purist model*. An alternative view, more in the spirit of narrower, utility-maximizing models such as Olson's (1965) and Moe's (1980a), is that benefits accruing exclusively to activists drive some to participate. Intuitively, it would seem that activists in traditional economic interest groups, and not those in a group such as Common Cause, should conform to this *utility-maximizing model*.

Once again, the expectations that stem from the experiential search framework differ markedly from those implied by alternative frameworks. When extended to the activist choice, models based on the alternative informational assumptions previously discussed imply that members will generally be activists or nonactivists from the start. Only exogenous shocks might motivate a change in status during subsequent periods. By contrast, since volunteering is a good deal more expensive than joining, many members following an experiential search strategy would choose to learn about the costs and benefits of activism while remaining in the rank and file and paying the relatively low monetary costs of membership. Although a few contributors will immediately become activists upon signing up, others will join the cadre later on. As before, the impact of experiential learning will reflect diminishing marginal returns. After a certain period, the additional effect of another year is likely to be quite small. If contributors are perfectly informed or are incapable of learning, however, they will not update their beliefs. They will become

activists from the start; no pattern of diminishing marginal returns will be observable.

What specifically will members discover about activism in Common Cause? Clearly, they will find out about the price of volunteering. Contributors will discover that the costs of Common Cause activism are different from those of rank-and-file status. Occasional activists report spending slightly less than four hours per month working for the organization; core activists, more than eight.

As mentioned previously, these costs will be less burdensome for those with low opportunity costs – that is, for those whose time is worth less. While the well-known conventional wisdom suggests that participation and income (or, at least, socioeconomic status) go hand in hand (e.g., Verba and Nie 1972), this logic is turned on its head when applied to the temporal commitments required of activists.[8] Those with higher wages may find devoting time to an unpaid political position less attractive because of the greater absolute sacrifice in income. High-income members are in essence "charged" more than others for being activists.[9]

Volunteers will also discover that Common Cause has some real advantages or disadvantages relative to other groups that might commonly be perceived as substitutes for the type of behavior that is typically encouraged. One of the characteristics that distinguishes Common Cause is the emphasis on telephoning and writing letters. Occasional memos – sometimes sent to all activists, more frequently to just 10 percent or so – and telephone communications with their Connection Volunteer liaison are what an activist can come to expect. "Across the board communication," is the way Jay Hedlund, Common Cause's Director of Grassroots Lobbying puts it. Unlike the League of Women Voters, for example, being a Common Cause volunteer requires few face-to-face interactions. Even when the staff travels out of Washington, D.C., they generally eschew big membership meetings in favor of meetings with small subsets of the activist cadre. This ought to make it appealing to Common Cause members who are relatively isolated and for whom direct contact is difficult and expensive. Friendships, for example, are developed on the other end of a telephone. It will also give the organization a comparative cost advantage vis-à-vis groups that are potential substitutes in attracting activists for whom indirect interactions are more convenient.

What are the benefits of being a Common Cause activist? If these volunteers are the stereotypical do-gooders, then members' passion and devotion to the group's ideals of promoting a procedurally correct and open government should be especially important. This will be reflected in a high valuation either of what are traditionally labeled purposive rewards or of collective returns stemming from what the organization tries to achieve, rather than how effective it is.

By contrast, if volunteers are more interested in selfish rewards, very broadly construed, then the discovery of whether activism has an impact on the organization and its policy success should be more germane. This assessment can be a function of several factors – whether the activists feel efficacious within the larger political system and within the group, for example.[10]

Divisible benefits might also enter a utility maximizer's calculus in deciding whether to volunteer. However, Common Cause's leadership has not geared the organization to offer such rewards for this purpose. No formal perquisites are furnished exclusively to activists (for a short period in the 1970s there was a publication for activists) except for the occasional memo and phone call; everyone receives the same magazine and other materials. Members quickly learn that the leadership has not created a multitiered hierarchy with cor⁀responding benefits for each level.

Some contributors may decide that the by-products of volunteering serve as selective rewards. Most obviously (and as previously mentioned) activism may be a channel for personal advancement (Schlesinger 1966; Eldersveld 1982). Joining and activism probably must go together if membership is going to be a successful means for advancement. While some political aspirants become dissatisfied with Common Cause and quit altogether, others may move up the organizational hierarchy to better themselves. As antithetical to Common Cause's stereotypical image as using the association for personal gain might seem, volunteers are an ambitious lot: 31 percent of core activists and 24 percent of occasional activists report that they would like to hold a political party position, public elective office, or public appointive office, as compared to only 18 percent of the rank and file. Still, divisible rewards ought to be relatively unimportant in the activist calculus.

Rewards garnered by activists because they enjoy the interactions the group offers may also come into play. Especially with respect to solidary benefits, Common Cause would seem to be at a comparative disadvantage relative to organizations that rely heavily on face-to-face interactions. While the lack of direct interactions may lower the costs for some activists, as mentioned above, others may discover that the opportunities for solidary rewards at Common Cause do not match what they are looking for.

Another element that would seem particularly relevant as a factor conditioning members' assessments of the benefits of activism is whether or not contributors judge the group to be oligarchic. Perceptions that the organization is dominated by its leaders may have either of two opposite effects for those remaining in the association: Members may decide that they are unwilling to make the commitment that activism entails for such a group, or they may determine that accomplishing anything within the organizational context requires getting intimately involved in its politics.

Finally, it needs to be reiterated once more that underlying this entire discussion is the supposition that experience is fundamental. Very few

contributors ought to volunteer immediately. Some will join, like what they learn, and eventually become core activists; others will opt to get involved but to a lesser degree; and most will remain in the rank and file. The impact of experience should diminish with time, as rank-and-file or activist status will gradually become less malleable.

AN EMPIRICAL TEST: ACTIVISM AND COMMON CAUSE

The cross-sectional hypotheses that can be tested with the Common Cause data can be classified into three categories: One pertains to premembership intentions toward activism; a second, to the costs and benefits of volunteering; and a third, to organizational experience.[11] Findings for the first two can possibly be reconciled with alternative theoretical frameworks based on differing informational assumptions; the third unambiguously distinguishes the experiential search hypothesis. These results should also identify the incentives that provide the impetus for organizational activism.

An initial hypothesis is that the importance of premembership dispositions ought to be overshadowed by what contributors learn if they update their beliefs. A second set of hypotheses is that (1) the varying costs of volunteering will be important determinants of activism; (2) although divisible benefits exclusive to activism could be germane, they will be unimportant relative to other factors because few will exist, unless the leadership makes a concerted effort to produce them; and (3) purposive benefits will be of overriding importance if members are strongly driven by purist tendencies; otherwise, if contributors are utility maximizers, purposive rewards will be of minimal consequence, solidary benefits will be very germane, and collective rewards will fall somewhere in between.[12] The third group of hypotheses is as follows: (1) Descriptively, activists will take considerable time after joining the association to get involved; (2) organizational experience will be extremely relevant; (3) the impact of experience will exhibit a pattern of diminishing marginal returns; and (4) the overall predictions from the model will display a similar pattern of diminishing marginal returns.

The findings earlier in this analysis suggest that a desire for activism is probably not a principal motivating force for joining in the first place. A reexamination of the self-professed motivations for joining reported in Table 4.1 makes it clear that members exhibit little inclination to be so involved upon signing up. In a stratified sample in which 31 percent of the respondents are either core or occasional activists, only 11 percent claim that the opportunity for participation was a principal reason for joining.[13] Of this 11 percent, only 47 percent are activists (13 percent are occasional activists; 34 percent are core activists). Whether the remaining 53 percent are former activists who returned to the rank and file is unknown (but, as will be discussed shortly, this seems doubtful given the tenure of most activists), but 83 percent of all current activists did give other reasons for initially joining. These data are inconsistent with either the models based on

perfect information or those grounded on assumptions of imperfect information where contributors fail to learn.

Experience is apparently the key: The average volunteer minimally takes three years after becoming a member to progress to activism; only 16 percent move up from the rank and file within one year of joining.[14] Twenty-two percent of the latter claimed that the opportunity for participation was of principal importance in deciding to join Common Cause, compared to only 14 percent of those taking more than a year.

Indeed, a minority of volunteers actually initiated the process by which they became activists (Table 6.2). Only about a quarter of those asked "How did you become a Common Cause activist?" claimed that they personally contacted the organization.[15] Furthermore, those initiating the process themselves actually took a bit longer (less than a year more) to become activists; that is, they were not joining and immediately getting immersed in organizational endeavors.

These findings confirm the descriptive experiential search hypothesis that future activists will take their time getting involved. Many are likely to wait until they are asked to do something. Still, decisive evidence for the importance of experience requires estimation of the structural model.

Measurement and estimation

Activism (conditional upon membership) is measured trichotomously: Rank-and-file members are scored 0; occasional activists, 1; and core activists, 2.

Many of the factors posited to structure a member's decision calculus have already been discussed:

1. The *premembership disposition for activism* is measured by a dummy variable indicating whether members cited the ability to participate as a principal reason for joining in response to the previously discussed, open-ended question.
2. *Costs* are guaged by (a) the opportunity cost of activism, again measured by family income, and (b) the comparative cost of the indirect interactions required of Common Cause activists relative to the direct contacts typical of other public interest groups, as tapped by whether contributors reside in an urban area.[16]
3. *Divisible benefits* are again measured by a dummy variable tapping whether or not members have political aspirations.
4. *Collective benefits* are once more gauged by whether respondents (a) agree with Common Cause's positions on key issues; (b) consider the leadership effective in providing collective goods; and (c) believe they are efficacious within the group. Additionally, whether respondents think that they are efficacious vis-à-vis the larger political system is included as well.
5. *Purposive benefits* are again tapped by whether respondents feel an

Table 6.2. *How contributors became Common Cause activists*

Response	Number (percentage)
Solicited by fellow member	108 (34.0)
Solicited by fellow member/ contacted by Common Cause	20 (6.3)
Solicited by fellow member/ personally contacted Common Cause	6 (1.9)
Solicited by fellow member/ contacted by Common Cause/ personally contacted Common Cause	1 (0.0)
Contacted by Common Cause	101 (31.8)
Contacted by Common Cause/ personally contacted Common Cause	9 (2.8)
Personally contacted Common Cause	73 (23.0)

Source: 1981 Common Cause survey.

obligation as good citizens to participate and whether they care about the group.
6. *Solidary benefits* are again measured by whether members value the interpersonal interactions Common Cause provides.
7. *Learning* is once more measured by organizational experience, as operationalized to capture the hypothesis of diminishing marginal returns with both logarithmic and linear terms.
8. *Perceptions of oligarchy* are indicated by whether contributors believe that most members are given a small role in the group's internal politics.[17]

Examination of the intercorrelations among the explanatory variables reveals no evidence of multicollinearity. With two exceptions, predictions about each factor are straightforward: The impact of costs should be negative; the influence of all types of benefits, the initial disposition for activism, and the logarithmic learning term should be positive. There are no predispositions regarding the linear learning term or perceptions about oligarchy.[18]

As mentioned previously, another expectation is that the premembership disposition for activism, if properly measured, would be a crucial test of any model that does not incorporate learning. However, especially since it is known a priori that only a small fraction of activists actually gave such responses, it might seem that a straw man is being set up; other benefits might also be reflecting initial intentions. (Again, higher costs of initial membership should translate into premembership intentions being more relevant for activism.) It is nonetheless reasonable to expect that if either individuals fail to learn or learning is not important, premembership disposition should be quite important and organizational experience should be inconsequential.

It is also again anticipated that the model's overall predictions should exhibit a pattern of diminishing marginal returns. The predicted probability of being either an occasional or a core activist will increase with experience but at a diminishing rate.

This research is yet another example of a design that cannot be estimated with standard techniques for analyzing limited dependent variables because the sample is endogenous to the choice being studied. A random sample the size of the Common Cause survey would contain, on average, about 1,050 rank-and-file members, 135 occasional activists, and 50 core activists. The stratified design yields a sixfold overrepresentation of core activists and a 20 percent underrepresentation of occasional activists and rank-and-file contributors. Selecting subjects randomly would make the study of core activism an impossibility with a 1,200-person sample; while the stratified sample provides enough such activists to analyze their behavior, it creates sticky methodological problems.

Once again, the WESML technique offers a solution. The cost of utilizing WESML for studying activist behavior is that taking advantage of the ordinal nature of the dependent variable – which would produce a single set

Table 6.3. *Determinants of activism (WESML estimates)*

Variable	Occasional activist	Core activist
Constant	—11.285***	—11.407*
Reason for joining		
Belief in participation	0.543	0.704***
Costs		
Opportunity cost	—0.191***	—0.196*
Urban residence	0.711	—1.485*
Divisible benefits		
Political aspirations	0.621*	0.656***
Collective benefits		
Agreement with group's positions	—0.004	0.008
Assessment of leadership's effectiveness	0.074	—0.047
Feeling of personal efficacy regarding group	0.230***	0.392***
Feeling of personal efficacy regarding political system	0.079	0.126***
Purposive benefits		
Care about group	0.180***	0.118***
Sense of civic duty	0.110	0.008
Solidary benefits		
Value interaction	0.524**	0.842***

Table 6.3 (*continued*)

Variable	Occasional activist	Core activist
Learning		
Organizational experience	—0.209	—0.275***
Natural log of organizational		
experience	1.792**	3.011***
Perceptions of oligarchy		
Internal politics oligarchic	—0.006	0.094
Number of cases	911	
—2xlog-likelihood function	930	

Note: Weights for the WESML estimator are [.8500/.6757], [.1100/.0871], and [.0400/.2372] for rank-and-file members, occasional activists, and core activists, respectively. Each set of coefficients reflects the comparison of that type of activist to the rank and file. All tests are one-tailed except for those relating to the linear organizational experience measure and perceptions of oligarchy, about which there were no a priori predictions.

$*p \leq .10$ $**p \leq .05$ $***p \leq .01$

of estimates – is beyond the available technology. Activism is necessarily treated as if it were measured nominally, and the resulting confusion from estimating two sets of coefficients as well as the loss of information must be tolerated.[19]

Results: What makes an activist?

The results comparing occasional and core activists to the rank and file are shown in Table 6.3, while information about the relative impact of each

factor is displayed in Table 6.4.[20] Findings confirm the experiential search viewpoint, but the relative impacts of costs and alternative types of benefits are, perhaps surprisingly given the case under study, consistent with maximization of utility rather than purist behavior.

The model does a good job of explaining activism. Findings are stronger for core than for occasional activists, which undoubtedly reflects both that more of the former were surveyed and that being a core activist requires a greater commitment. Overall, the results permit the separation of those with high and low probabilities of activism.

The rarity of activism – like the minimal probability of joining in the first place – makes even small increases in its likelihood important. Changes in the probability of volunteering must be seen in this light. Among the population of contributors, there is an 85 percent chance that individuals will be in the rank and file and only a 4 percent probability that they will be core activists. A 1 percent increase in the probability of core activism therefore makes a contributor 25 percent more likely than the average member to be such a volunteer.

The low probability of activism also needs to be taken into account when the model's overall predictions are considered. The probability that a randomly drawn contributor will be either a core activist or an occasional activist is only 15 percent. By contrast, the model predicts that the probability of activism for actual core activists is 28 percent, which is about twice the likelihood for the average contributor; for those who are occasional activists, the probability is 24 percent; and for the rank and file, 13 percent. These are impressive results for such a rare event and for a group as homogeneous as Common Cause.

As expected, because the average activist takes three years to get involved, the initial propensity for participation is a highly imperfect predictor.[21] Although such predispositions are significant for core-activists, there is no evidence that members either join with perfect information or never learn about the value of activism. Group members who were inclined to volunteer initially are 1.5 percent more likely actually to be core activists. This relatively small effect of predispositions provides tentative evidence that members are updating their beliefs over time.

Three may be two types of activists: those who believe that the net benefits of activism are sufficiently high that they volunteer immediately and learn as activists, and those who will volunteer only after acquiring experience in the rank and file. A priori intentions should translate more directly into activism for those falling into the first category. With this in mind, the explanatory factors were rerun on a variable scored 1 if activists chose that option in a year or less (107, or 36 percent of the 298 activists) and 0 if they took more time. The results (not shown) reveal few differences between those becoming activists immediately and those taking more time, but there is an indication that an intention to participate makes more of a difference for the former ($t = 1.9$).

Table 6.4. Probability of activism

	Percentage change in probability of activism	
Variable	Occasional activist	Core activist
Reason for joining		
Belief in participation	0.9	1.5
Costs		
Opportunity cost	—1.5	—1.8
Urban residence	1.0	—1.3
Divisible benefits		
Political aspirations	1.5	1.8
Collective benefits		
Agreement with group's positions	—0.4	0.7
Assessment of leadership's		
effectiveness	0.5	—0.4
Feeling of personal efficacy		
regarding group	1.5	4.4
Feeling of personal efficacy		
regarding political system	0.8	1.7
Purposive benefits		
Care about group	2.0	1.4
Sense of civic duty	1.2	0.0
Solidary benefits		
Value interaction	1.4	3.0

Table 6.4 (*continued*)

	Percentage change in probability of activism	
Variable	Occasional activist	Core activist
Learning		
Organizational experience	—2.7	—3.9
Natural log of organizational experience	6.1	23.1
Perceptions of oligarchy		
Internal politics oligarchic	—0.1	1.2

Note: Percentages are changes in the probability of being an activist assuming (1) an increase of one standard deviation from the mean of the variable in question and (2) all other independent variables are set at their respective means.

The costs of activism are important for all members. Contributors with greater opportunity costs are 1.8 percent and 1.5 percent less likely to be core and occasional activists.[22] Checkbook participation is one thing; temporal activism is another. Common Cause also has a comparative advantage in attracting volunteers from rural areas – the bivariate relationship between activism and rurality reported earlier remains strong even when multivariate techniques are utilized. Isolated individuals find core activism in the group especially attractive. As suggested previously, the obvious reason for this attraction is that those located in rural areas are more likely than those from metropolitan areas to find writing letters and calling people on the phone preferable to getting together with other activists for face-to-face interactions.[23]

Strikingly, the benefits that attract activists reveal that they are not purists: They are utility maximizers who adopt an efficient information-gathering strategy. The cost of activism is apparently so high that only those with relatively narrow goals and precise information will join the fray.

The results regarding broad purposive rewards are far weaker than the purist model would lead one to expect. Monetary contributions apparently

furnish most of the purposive rewards deriving from membership. Civic duty is unimportant for separating out activists and members, although caring about group issues is relevant.

The effect of collective returns on activism reveals a dichotomy that also buttresses the utility-maximizing proposition. Benefits stemming from collective returns, as measured by issue agreement and approval of the leadership, are unimportant. These would be the factors that would drive activists if they were purists.

This finding is not a statistical artifact reflecting group homogeneity. An insignificant result might have been expected, particularly for agreement on issues, since (as will be discussed in more detail shortly) the Common Cause leadership is careful not to choose issues that will offend large numbers of contributors. However, issue evaluations are no more skewed than other factors that are significant determinants of activism, and they demonstrate disagreement and diversity among members – as reflected by the importance of issue agreement for contributors' renewal choices.[24] Indeed, as demonstrated earlier, this same indicator is a significant determinant of the retention choice.

While benefits are not key, the probability of affecting the production of collective goods is germane. Members with higher assessments of their associational and systemic efficacy are 1.5 percent and 0.8 percent more likely to be occasional activists and 4.4 percent and 1.7 percent more likely to be core activists. Results are more important than passion to Common Cause activists; that is, the perception that mobilization is effective separates volunteers from the rank and file. An increase of just one standard deviation in perceptions of group efficacy makes a member more than twice as likely to be a core activist, ceteris paribus. While students of voting participation have debated whether the p in the Downsian decision calculus should be incorporated (e.g., Ferejohn and Fiorina 1974, 1975), for organizational activism it is the inclusion of the b term that must be questioned.[25]

These findings can be contrasted with Hirschman's (1970) supposition that members resort to voice as well as exit in reaction to deteriorating performance by an organization. Voice (that is, activism) is a response not to diminished performance – as evidenced by the unimportance of assessments of leaders' achievements (or, from Hirschman's perspective, lack of achievements) – but to learning about whether a group delivers.

However, these results *do* make sense when the way that the leadership structures activism is considered: As mentioned, activists are asked to play policy and not organizational maintenance roles. Consequently, their actions revolve around trying to be efficacious. In Hedlund's words, "They genuinely believe if you go about things the right way you can be successful because they've done that in their lives."

By contrast, because Common Cause's leadership offers essentially the same benefits to all contributors, the relative importance of divisible rewards for activism is smaller than it might be otherwise. Nevertheless, the one

divisible return, promotion of one's political aspirations, also does stimulate activism. Members with stronger political aspirations are 1.5 percent and 1.8 percent more likely to be occasional and core activists. The fact that aspirations have an impact provides more evidence that even Common Cause activists are motivated by narrow returns.

Despite minimal opportunities for face-to-face interactions at Common Cause, solidary benefits are strongly tied to activism for both occasional and core activists. If solidary rewards are central for promoting Common Cause activism, they should be crucial for any organization offering few divisible rewards exclusively to volunteers. This strong result, again, should reflect a matching process in which those who value indirect interactions are attracted to Common Cause.

Finally, attitudes about organizational oligarchy are relatively unimportant as a conditioning factor. There is some slight evidence that such perceptions precipitate core activism ($t = 1.4$). If this result is valid, it implies that those who believe that Common Cause is oligarchic and that members of the rank and file are inefficacious tend to get involved, while those who consider the association democratic remain on the sidelines, ceteris paribus.[26]

Specific costs and benefits still tell only part of the story: The effect of organizational experience looms large. An increase in organizational experience of one standard deviation, or three and one-half years, increases the probability that the average member (who has been in the group more than seven years) will be an occasional or a core activist by 1.9 percent and 8.5 percent, respectively.[27] Moreover, these numbers in some sense understate the effect of experience because the marginal returns associated with it diminish temporally. Members are more likely to participate over time, but if after a few years they are still in the rank and file, chances are they will remain there.

A similar pattern of positive but diminishing marginal returns is again found if the overall predicted probabilities of being either an occasional or a core activist are broken down by year (Figure 6.1). The likelihood of being either type of volunteer increases with time, but the size of the upward trend decreases. The predicted probabilities of activism during the first year in the organization are minuscule; by the fifth year, the likelihood exceeds the average for the population of group members. After six years, additional time in the organization has almost no impact on the probability of occasional activism, whereas the likelihood of being a core activist continues to creep slightly upward. One possible explanation of this difference is that contributors learn about occasional activism more quickly. An alternative is that this discrepancy may reflect a transitional process in which nearly identical numbers of rank-and-file members become occasional activists as they leave the latter category to step up into the core cadre. Only a panel study, however, could distinguish between these hypotheses.

To summarize: Initial predispositions are poor predictors of activism. Costs and benefits – especially returns that are largely exclusive to activists – are

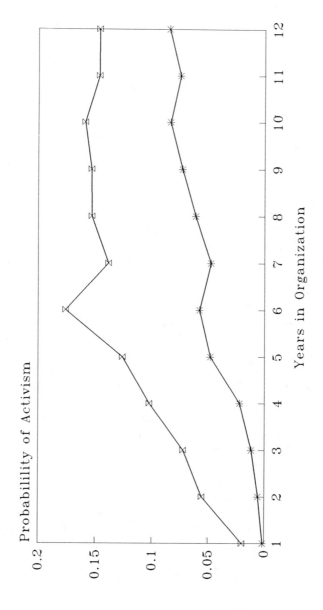

Figure 6.1. Probability of activism and organizational experience.

more important. These findings suggest that informations is accrued and beliefs are updated, but these results are perhaps reconcilable with alternative scenarios of the activist process. What confirms the experiential search framework and falsifies contrasting frameworks are the findings that organizational experience is extremely germane and that it and the overall predictions from the activism model exhibit strong patterns of diminishing marginal returns.

ACTIVISM: A VALIDITY TEST

The four-group survey again provides a validity test for the findings from the Common Cause–specific study. A model analogous to that specified earlier in this chapter, if more limited, can be estimated. The same measures of organizational experience, efficacy, and fit between member and group utilized earlier are again employed as explanatory variables. In addition, a dichotomous measure of whether the respondent entered the association with an initial disposition toward activism is used as a rough analogue to the earlier measure of predispositions toward activism.[28] Similar to the Common Cause–specific measure, only a small percentage of members actually seem to have joined to get actively involved (about 5 percent). Finally, each of the three previously discussed measures of political interest – education, income, and age – are again included in a second model.

Activism is measured dichotomously, with the roughly 20 percent who identified themselves as activists scored 1 and all other respondents scored 0.[29] As expected, the League of Women Voters has far more self-proclaimed activists (43 percent) than the other groups (the Conservative Caucus, 21 percent; the American Civil Liberties Union, 14 percent; and Common Cause, 11 percent). Expectations for each factor in the activism models are straightforward, with one exception. Naturally, those who had a positive initial disposition should be more likely to become activists. Those who made the correct decision to join, who have been in their groups longer, and who discover that the organization is responsive to activist behavior should be more likely to be active because they learn about the organization and find that it is an appropriate match for them. The only uncertainty pertains to how members with no opinion about associational responsiveness should behave. The more politically interested members, that is, educated, older, male contributors, should be more willing to incur the costs of being an activist. It is likely, however, that these measures of political interest will be irrelevant for the conditional activism choice, given the truncated nature of this sample.[30]

These models can be estimated using standard, limited dependent variable methods because this sample is not stratified on the activism choice. Dichotomous probit is therefore employed. Examination of the intercorrelations reveals no problem of multicollinearity, and a pooling test suggests that it is possible to combine the responses of the four groups' members.

The results for both models (Table 6.5) bear out the expectations, and they are consistent with the findings specific to Common Cause. Initial predispositions are significant, but so are a variety of other factors. Most important, the experiential search framework is validated by the finding that individuals selecting the right association are more prone to be activists. Members who learn that their chosen organization is wrong for them are unwilling to incur the higher costs associated with activism.

The effect of experience is once more in the predicted direction and significant at least for those who have belonged to their associations for more than five years. Those believing that contributors can have an impact in their group by getting involved are again more likely to be active. Others with no opinion on how the group operates are actually less prone to get involved than those viewing the organization as dominated by its leadership and staff. This finding underscores the importance of information. Some knowledgeable members presumably believe that only activism can make the leadership and staff respond, and therefore they become active; those without information will simply abstain.

Of the three control variables in model II, none is significant and in the expected direction. Gender is significant but in the wrong direction; that is, women are more likely to be activists. This reflects the propensity of members of the League of Women Voters to rate themselves as activists.

Except for this idiosyncratic finding about gender, these results provide considerable support for the experiential search framework and validate the findings of the Common Cause–specific analysis. As contributors learn, they update their beliefs and act accordingly.

A FINAL NOTE: ACTIVISM AND RETENTION AS A JOINT COMMITMENT DECISION

It has been assumed up to this juncture that activism and retention are sequential choices. At first sight, this specification seems unassailable. Activism is a choice that is continuously made by contributors once they sign up; retention is a decision that is made at prespecified periods, usually annually, after joining. By definition, activism temporally precedes retention.

However, it might be countered that the retention decision – although observable at designated intervals – is also made continuously. Well before the designated time for announcing one's retention choice, contributors may have decided to let their membership lapse when it comes up for renewal. The difference between the retention and activism choices might only be an artifact of an inability to observe the former except at set times. Activism and retention might be conceptualized as a joint decision about commitment level: whether to be active, to form part of the rank and file, or to quit.

To examine what effects this alternative viewpoint might have on the previous findings, the activism models for the four-group survey were rerun

Table 6.5. *Determinants of activism: Four-group study (probit estimates with standard errors in parentheses)*

Variable	Model I	Model II
Constant	—1.391***	—1.221***
	(0.245)	(0.455)
Predisposition toward activism	0.776***	0.724**
	(0.393)	(0.358)
"Correct" choice	0.252**	0.247**
	(0.143)	(0.145)
Organizational responsiveness		
Members decide	0.751***	0.511**
	(0.222)	(0.240)
Interaction with leaders	0.375**	0.297**
	(0.175)	(0.179)
Don't know how operates	—0.919***	—1.074***
	(0.185)	(0.303)
Organizational experience		
Two to five years in group	0.138	0.154
	(0.233)	(0.240)
More than five years in group	0.330*	0.311*
	(0.223)	(0.230)
Political interest		
Gender (male)		—0.355**
		(0.154)
Age		0.033
		(0.048)

Table 6.5 (*continued*)

Variable	Model I	Model II
Education		—0.009
		(0.075)
Number of cases	490	486
—2xlog-likelihood function	423	413

*p ≤ .10   **p ≤ .05   ***p ≤ .01

with a dependent variable measuring the level of commitment.[31] Activists planning to renew were scored a 4, rank-and-file members intending to stay were given a 3, rank-and-file members who were unsure if they would remain were scored a 2, and rank-and-file contributors planning to quit were given a 1. Ordered probit was then employed to estimate these models.

The results (Table 6.6) are strong and generally consistent with the sequential choice results.[32] The only difference is that predispositions toward activism are no longer significant. The findings for making the correct choice, for organizational responsiveness, and for organizational experience all remain strongly significant. Males are again slightly more likely either to stay in the rank and file or to quit altogether.

The joint model in Table 6.6 can be compared to its sequential analogue to determine which depiction of the decision-making process is more accurate. The sequential process is estimated using a conditional specification. Contributors first decide whether or not to be an activist and then, conditional upon being in the rank and file, choose whether or not to stay in the association. A log-likelihood ratio test comparing the sequential and joint specifications demonstrates that the latter is superior (on this test, see Vuong 1989). Activist and retention choices are apparently made simultaneously by contributors who decide upon their commitment level after updating their beliefs.

The more general point to draw from this portion of the analysis is that the overall findings of this study are robust whether these decisions are made jointly or sequentially. The results reveal that decision makers are following an experiential search strategy. Members learn whether they have made the

Table 6.6. *Joint determinants of activism and retention: Four-group study (probit estimates with standard errors in parentheses)*

Variable	Model I	Model II
Constant	0.868***	0.629*
	(0.182)	(0.366)
Predisposition toward activism	0.288	0.263
	(0.329)	(0.331)
"Correct" choice	0.291***	0.280***
	(0.114)	(0.115)
Organizational responsiveness		
Members decide	0.557***	0.417**
	(0.194)	(0.207)
Interaction with leaders	0.348***	0.306**
	(0.145)	(0.147)
Don't know how operates	—0.287*	—0.337**
	(0.160)	(0.166)
Organizational experience		
Two to five years in group	0.500***	0.531***
	(0.167)	(0.172)
More than five years in group	0.820***	0.778***
	(0.164)	(0.170)
Political interest		
Gender (male)		—0.216*
		(0.121)
Age		0.040
		(0.039)

Table 6.6 (continued)

Variable	Model I	Model II
Education		0.065
		(0.061)
Number of cases	431	427
—2×log-likelihood function	801	788

$*p \leq .10$ $**p \leq .05$ $***p \leq .01$

right choice, whether the group is responsive, and whether the association matches their preferences, and then act accordingly.

CONCLUSIONS: MOVING UP

The key issues of this chapter can be summarized by examining two questions: Is what motivates contributors to move up the organizational hierarchy predictable given the earlier discussion? Is this behavior consistent with the idea of an integrated perspective on organizations generally and the experiential search framework for conceptualizing citizens' decisions in organizations specifically? By and large, the answer to both of these questions is affirmative.

The brief analysis of checkbook activism generally conforms to expectations. Contributors behave in much the same way as they do with respect to retention. Experience along with a number of specific factors are key; income, somewhat surprisingly in this instance, is not germane.

As for activism more conventionally defined, while the archetypal image of such a person in a public-regarding group such as Common Cause is of an idealist, the findings in this study dispute this belief. A "perfect" match between member and group will not precipitate activism; devotees to stated group goals, for example, are frequently willing to remain in the rank and file. Rather, benefits that are broadly construed as exclusive to activism and organizational experience – conditioned by opportunity and comparative costs – are fundamental. Career aspirations, the feeling that it is possible to have a large impact, either personally or through the organization, on the

provision of collective goods; and solidary returns outstrip in importance devotion to the cause. Beyond these costs and benefits lies organizational experience, which diminishes the uncertainty surrounding activism. Few enter the group or others like it (or check the box on the original Common Cause membership form) intent on becoming activists, as different informational assumptions would lead one to expect.

Thus, this activism calculus can be characterized as an experiential search process that is conditioned by earlier choices and by leadership decisions. Observed behavior bears out the theoretical expectation that imperfectly informed contributors initially separate themselves into two groups: those who become activists and then learn about the costs and benefits of activism, and the vast majority who wait and decide whether activism is worthwhile after updating their beliefs.

More generally, these findings illustrate the benefits of an integrated perspective. They are more understandable because of the previous analyses and provide intuitions about what the formation of group goals, should look like.

Specifically, these results both make far more sense when joining and retention are understood and provide considerable intuition for what the goal formation process – the next topic to be investigated – ought to look like. With respect to the former, only by understanding how the leadership structures the organization so that individuals join the group with high political interest and then learn more with time can the activism process be fully appreciated. It is then understandable why newer members tend to pay the annual dues, and perhaps a bit in addition, but are inclined to learn about the net benefits of activism on the sideline – generally a superior information-gathering strategy to incurring the high costs from the start. It is also then comprehensible. why if contributors decide to stay in the group but remain in the rank and file for more than a few years, they are likely to stay there.

As for goal formation (and at the risk of foreshadowing some of the discussion to follow) the results in this analysis of activism suggest, most important, that the utility-maximizing incentives that motivate activists will constrain leaders in their choice of political issues and give the latter some discretion. While activists also derive some of their satisfaction from other rewards, they care about the group and whether they perceive it as efficacious – indeed the activist experience is structured by design to foster such feelings. Consequently, leaders will have some room for maneuver but will not be able to decide blithely upon group goals without at least selling them to the activist cadre.

7

The internal politics of organizations III: Leadership behavior and the determinants of group goals

> For most students of politics, the major value of a theory of interest groups derives from what it can say about group goals and, in particular, how they are formulated as a function of member goals.
>
> Terry M. Moe, *The Organization of Interests* (1980a, p. 73)

MOVING FROM THE "DEMAND" TO THE "SUPPLY" SIDE

To this point in the investigation of organizational dynamics, both the empirical and the theoretical spotlights have been squarely directed on the "demand" side of the process. The key issues under investigation have revolved around ascertaining those factors that determine the requests made upon collectivities by their patrons. This entailed scrutiny of the characteristics of individuals and the determinants of their choice behavior: citizens' resolutions whether to join, contributors' choices whether to remain in the organization, and members' calculations whether to be active.

The reasons for concentrating on this series of choices should, by this juncture, be evident. These decisions determine the flow of organizational resources that are needed for group maintenance and the demands to which leaders must respond; as discussed initially, understanding them constitutes a crucial prerequisite for ascertaining how groups actually function and whether they have any impact on the political system's ultimate public policy outputs.

Yet, if the analysis were to cease now, it could be justifiably criticized as grossly one-sided. The corresponding responses by organizational and political leaders to the citizen requests that they at least implicitly receive have garnered comparatively scant attention. However, now that the content and determinants of contributor demands are presumably well understood, redirecting attention primarily from the followers and toward the leaders is analytically feasible and intellectually essential.

Specifically, two more steps are required before broad conclusions can be drawn about organizational politics. Both concern the "supply" side of group dynamics. One is to examine *organizational supply*: assessing whether, and through what processes, contributor preferences get incorporated by

organizational leaders into goals. Goals, in turn, are defined as *"conceptions of desired ends* – conditions that participants attempt to effect through their performance of task activities" (Scott 1987, p. 18, italics in original).[1] Does the membership, or some subset within it, have an impact on the formulation of group objectives? The other is to examine *systemic supply*: investigating if and how policymakers respond, given a previously defined set of associational goals, to organizational mobilization. Does the collectivity ultimately exercise any influence over the outputs produced by formal political institutions?

In other words, assessing the ultimate impact of member demands constitutes a two-stage process. The first involves determining whether contributor preferences are incorporated into group goals; the second, if organizational objectives are translated into policy outcomes.

Why the latter stage – understanding the yields garnered from an association's policy initiatives – is relevant requires little elaboration. What might be less obvious is why there is a need to take a step back and examine the source of organizational aspirations.

Moe's comment cited at the beginning of this chapter is a strong statement in defense of studying the formation of such objectives. He argues persuasively that studying goals is an issue of paramount importance that strikes at the heart of why scholars ought to investigate organizations. They should wish to understand how group objectives are specified and to what extent an association's goals emerge as a product of the will of its leaders, the desires of members as a collectivity, or the preferences of a subset of contributors.

Moreover, explanations for why goals are of widespread interest can be furnished from either a positivist or normativist perspective. For the positivist who aspires to comprehend how interest groups actually function, it is critical to assess just how significant, if at all, contributors are in determining how the association operates and which members actually wield influence. For the normativist, who wishes to evaluate whether organizations are to be viewed as augmenting or hindering the process of democratic representation, it is essential to ascertain whether collectivities are run democratically, rather than as the exclusive domains of insulated, unresponsive leaders.

However, the obvious logical inference to be derived from statements about how relevant goals are – that a voluminous, detailed literature exists that analyzes the importance of the internal operations of interest groups in goal formation – is incorrect. Consistent with the earlier discussions about the paucity of studies of internal politics generally, there is a dearth of empirical investigations, and only a modicum of theoretical work, inquiring into the crucial linkage between members and goals. Some of the reasons for this lack of understanding have been discussed; a few additional factors that help account for this absence of systematic research will be touched upon shortly.

The shortfall between current knowledge about goal development and its

importance in the larger scheme of things makes understanding the means by which an organization's purposes are conceived all the more crucial. Thus, the determination of objectives and group leadership behavior is the subject of the current chapter, while the political system's response to key associational initiatives is the concern of the next two.

In a broad sense, this chapter's investigation of leadership behavior and organizational goals has two basic components. One is to ascertain how members' perceptions of the governing process correspond with both what contributors are told about how the organization allegedly operates and how it actually functions. The other is to investigate theoretically and empirically how group objectives are actually chosen by focusing on an instance where Common Cause's issue agenda shifted dramatically. With both of these tasks completed, inferences can be drawn about how goals are determined, who has a say in their development, the relationship between contributor perceptions about organizational management and the actual goal formation process, and how all of this might be aided by seeing organizations from an integrated perspective.

Specifically, this analysis begins with an evaluation of formal democratic processes at Common Cause in order to determine whether the association approximates a classic, representative democracy. At the same time, emphasis will be placed on generating a case for how understanding goal formation at Common Cause can furnish insights into the general questions of interest such as whether, and by what mechanisms, individual contributions translate into changes in public policy.

DEMOCRATIC PROCESSES AT COMMON CAUSE

If Common Cause is a democratically operated organization comprising like-minded individuals dedicated to common goals, investigating the structure by which associational objectives are determined will constitute a mundane and unilluminating exercise. Before proceeding further in the examination of goal formation, therefore, it is essential to determine whether Common Cause in fact functions as a representative democracy. As an ideal type, an organization that operates as a representative democracy can be defined as an associational body in which members are uniformly well informed, contributors are accorded an equal say in the group's governing process, and leaders are loyal agents who accede to the wishes of their constituents. How closely does Common Cause conform to this depiction in terms of both the processes that the association follows and the goals that are chosen?

Although a number of previous results might immediately produce a certain degree of skepticism about how closely the group approaches this exemplar, Common Cause does appear to have many of the necessary accoutrements to be termed an organizational democracy. The association is often trumpeted as being unique among even public interest groups for its dedication to

democratic processes (e.g., Hayes 1983); indeed, it relies heavily on its commitment to representative devices in its efforts to recruit new members. By contrast, many public interest groups are pronounced as being little more than staff organizations (e.g., Hayes 1986).

Unlike those belonging to other collectivities that might complement or substitute for membership in Common Cause, contributors have two formal vehicles through which they allegedly exercise control over the leadership. One is that members elect the organization's governing board, which is charged with determining policy for the association. The board is composed of 60 persons elected by the membership to three-year terms – after two terms one must rotate off – plus the chairman and the president of Common Cause (currently Ned Cabot and Fred Wertheimer). The second mechanism is that, at the same time that they are voting, contributors are asked to fill out a questionnaire known as the Membership Issue Poll, which is supposed to furnish the leadership with the information they require to represent their contributors as faithful delegates. Members are queried what they think about various issues and which concerns Common Cause ought to be involved in politically. Theoretically, assuming a unidimensional world, Euclidean preferences, and majority rule, it might be posited that the election outcomes and poll data would ensure that the preferences of the organization's median voter would prevail (on the median voter theorem, see Black 1958).

However, for a variety of reasons, this idyllic depiction of representative democracy in action crumbles when subject to close scrutiny. A number of empirical regularities exist that, when considered jointly, might shake the confidence of even an advocate claiming that Common Cause functions in a manner consistent with the ideal of egalitarian, representative democracy.

For one thing, the proposition that elections are likely to be effective devices for contributors to maintain control would seem to be called into question by the analysis of members' behavior in previous chapters. Most obviously, the characteristics of individual contributors fail to live up to the picture of an informed electorate capable of making learned choices and of effectively monitoring the group leaders charged with functioning as their agents.

As an example, it has already been demonstrated that a considerable number of contributors lack the requisite knowledge about the association to be able to furnish detailed advice on the policies the group should be advancing. Remember that the 1981 Common Cause survey revealed that many members (24 percent of the rank and file, although only 8 percent of activists) do not even *know* that the governing board is elected, no less anything about the board members, what they stand for, or how well they would perform once in office. Although it might be countered that the membership is sufficiently homogeneous that it is irrelevant that only a subset of patrons have the capacity to respond adequately, the findings of previous chapters reveal that contrasts in preferences among contributors do exist for quite

explicable reasons and that they are of substantial relevance for behavior such as retention and activism. The mere subtlety of differences among individuals fails to negate the reality that these are behaviorally germane distinctions.

Indeed, as McFarland (1984) points out, elections to the governing board are low-information contests in which members know little about the alternative candidates, only 20 to 25 percent of the membership even bothers to vote (fewer actually fill out the poll), and the vast majority of those elected are chosen as candidates by the leadership. Although McFarland bases his conclusions primarily on qualitative information, the results of the current, quantitative analysis about the lack of contributor knowledge add considerable fuel to his argument.[2]

For another thing, careful analysis of the issue poll does nothing to buttress the confidence of proponents of representative democracy. Besides the obvious problems that plague this survey, such as the same response rate deficiencies that characterize governing board elections (a full 27.2 percent of all respondents to the Common Cause survey said they had never heard of the Membership Issue Poll)[3] and members' lack of knowledge, yet another reason exists to doubt its general utility: the wording of questions. Specifically, the inquiries are phrased in a manner that ensures that the information accrued is relatively unilluminating given the nature of those being sampled. The basic problem is that the survey research techniques are inappropriate for discerning the germane, yet subtle, differences that exist in members' preferences, because they do not force respondents to prioritize the issues they want the organization to pursue. The results cannot provide organizational leaders with the clear instructions they would need if they sought to use the resulting data as their principal guide for faithfully representing their constituents' wishes.

To illustrate, consider the data reproduced in Table 7.1 from the 1987–1991 issue polls. Every year, respondents are probed about whether the organization should get involved in specific issue areas such as those displayed in the table. In all five years the alternatives included campaign finance reform, ethics and conflict of interest issues (sometimes linked with whether lobbyists should be subject to increased regulation), civil rights controversies, and nuclear arms control debates.[4] In 1987 and 1988 concerns about federal budget issues – such as the possibility of a Balanced Budget Amendment – were also incorporated into the questionnaire.

Minute differences across issues and over years are overwhelmed by the one-sided, skewed distribution of members' responses. Lumping the two negative categories, strongly disagree and disagree, together reveals that the level of opposition never exceeds 11 percent (which pertains to nuclear arms control in 1989). That any number of other issues, such as environmental concerns, gun control, or worries about the selection of judicial appointments, might also be presented to the membership and receive similar levels of

Table 7.1. *Results of issue polls on the appropriate role of Common Cause:*
1987–1991

Issue/response	Strongly agree	Agree	Strongly disagree	Disagree
Campaign finance				
1987	79.3	17.4	0.8	0.7
1988	79.5	19.6	0.7	0.2
1989	89.2	10.2	0.5	0.1
1990	89.7	9.9	0.3	0.1
1991	89.8	8.9	0.2	0.1
Ethics, conflict of interest, and lobbying reform				
1987	78.7	19.1	0.3	0.1
1988	80.9	18.5	0.4	0.1
1989	89.7	10.1	0.2	0.0
1990	88.4	9.9	0.3	0.0
1991	87.8	11.0	0.2	0.0
Civil rights				
1987	59.3	32.6	4.9	0.9
1988	59.1	35.2	4.7	1.0
1989	57.4	35.1	6.0	1.5
1990	52.3	39.8	6.5	1.9
1991	49.6	41.0	6.2	1.5
Nuclear arms control				
1987	68.8	20.1	5.8	2.3
1988	67.6	24.1	6.2	2.2

Table 7.1 (*continued*)

Issue/response	Strongly agree	Agree	Strongly disagree	Disagree
1989	66.1	22.8	8.1	3.0
1990	54.4	36.8	6.9	1.9
1991	53.7	35.5	6.9	1.9
Federal budget				
1987	62.9	30.8	3.3	0.6
1988	66.8	30.3	2.4	0.5

Source: Common Cause Magazine.

support can also be imagined.[5] Remember that in the 1981 Common Cause survey, only 10.5 percent of the membership disagreed with a statement supporting abortion rights and that 81 percent of the group's members favored the ERA.[6] In short, creative group leaders might conceivably use the results to justify a plethora of major organizational initiatives.

Unfortunately, this posits the existence of a type of Wonderland that bears little resemblance to the universe that the vast preponderance of organizational decision makers inhabit. In the real world, the fundamental dilemma that regularly faces leaders, who are subject to resource constraints, is how to winnow down the host of issues that members will look upon favorably. Indeed, from the early years of John Gardner, this has been a primary leadership concern. The need to "focus" is how Fred Wertheimer puts it. Thus, devising means to expand the collection of matters that members will view in a positive light is, at best, a secondary problem – although sometimes ascertaining whether contributors truly perceive a given initiative favorably is a genuine concern. Organizational entrepreneurs universally lack the time, money, and resources to accomplish everything that might be part of their associational agenda.

In other words, a realistic interpretation of the issue poll data is that it reflects a population that sincerely believes that, in a perfect world that imposes no constraints, Common Cause should be involved in a broad array

of worthwhile causes. This is not tantamount to inferring that contributors are willing to pay the price, particularly given collective action problems, that it would cost to mobilize around all of these issues. To reiterate, only 40 percent of members reply that they would stay in the group if dues were, hypothetically, doubled to avoid cutting back on activities. This finding is indicative of many contributors' unwillingness to dig deeper into their pockets and of the dilemma that leaders face in setting organizational agendas.[7]

As long as members responding to the questionnaire are not compelled through precise question wording either to make explicit trade-offs or to order their priorities, few of them will express opposition to the notion that Common Cause should be immersed in a wide variety of procedural and substantive issues. Implicitly, the organization has recognized this fact by establishing a policy of rejecting an issue in the rare instance where even 20 percent of the membership responding to the questionnaire states their opposition (McFarland 1984).[8]

Interestingly, in principle, the membership disagrees with this policy: When questioned, "Sometimes all members do not agree with a position Common Cause is considering taking on an issue. Disagreement by what percentage of the membership do you think should be enough to prevent Common Cause from taking a position on an issue?," the 50 percent threshold was the one that received the most support. The mean percentage advocated by members was 45 percent, with no discernible difference between those designated by Common Cause as rank and file or as activists. A full 30 percent of the sample named either 50 or 51 percent as the appropriate level of disagreement for the membership not to take a position – 25, 33, 35, 40, and 75 percent were the other principal responses. Clearly, Common Cause is undemocratic if a defining characteristic of a representative system is either majority rule or the adoption by group leaders of processes that members advocate (which, in this case, is essentially majority rule or small oversized majorities).

Provided that the world is an imperfect place and that Common Cause's resources are circumscribed, the issue poll provides only very crude and imprecise guidance. The resulting data are of insufficient quality to form the bases for the inferences that organizational leaders might need to draw in responding to members' demands and in formulating goals for the association. Decision makers at Common Cause will certainly have to look elsewhere (and as will be seen, do so) if they want to discover what is best for the membership and the association. While it is unfair to infer that the information derived from the survey is useless, it is far from ideal and results in the collectivity functioning via processes explicitly disapproved by members. In reality, the survey seems to serve a number of purposes besides providing a modicum of usable data, notably legitimating the organization by demonstrating both to members and the outside world that a mechanism for member input is available and that a high degree of solidarity exists.

In summary, a critical look into the functioning of Common Cause's official mechanisms of democratic elections and member feedback make them appear, after closer examination, to be considerably less than initially meets the eye. Election results only serve to select from a group of handpicked candidates; the issue poll provides little more than affirmation for any number of policy alternatives that the group might pursue. Like the proverbial drunk and the lamppost, the electoral and polling results jointly provide mainly support, rather than illumination, for the development of group goals. While these findings are insufficient to infer that the association fails to advocate policies and dedicate resources in a manner that would be produced in a representative democracy, certainly one of the reasons why Common Cause might be thought of as atypical – its adherence to formal democratic processes – appears a less distinguishing feature after closer inspection.

MEMBERS' ATTITUDES TOWARD REPRESENTATION

The obvious rejoinder to the findings in the preceding section is to pose two follow-up questions: Does the membership understand this state of affairs? If so, do they feel that the process of representation has resulted in a serious mismatch between the group's goals and their preferences?

With respect to the first query, the answer seems to be that at least to some degree (taking into account members' incomplete information), contributors appear to comprehend. Feelings of confusion and ambivalence about the governing process – if not unhappiness about the extent of actual representation – come through when the data from the 1981 Common Cause survey are examined (Table 7.2). Those contacted were asked to agree or disagree with five statements made regarding internal organizational politics and representation.[9] The responses to the first three remarks displayed in Table 7.2 can be construed as evaluations of organizational process, while the answers to the latter two assertions can be interpreted as reflections of perceptions about the association's actual extent of representation, that is, results.[10]

If only the findings regarding process are considered, the consequence might be profound concern about how members feel toward the association. Certainly the inference would be made that the group is not the paragon of democracy that it claims to be. Little more than 40 percent of all members (using the correct population weightings) concur with the statement that "Members of Common Cause are given a large role in determining its policies." Even fewer dissent from the contention that "Only a small minority of members take part in Common Cause decision making." And although almost nobody agrees, more than 60 percent of the contributor population are simply unsure when asked if "Sometimes a small minority of members prevents Common Cause taking a position supported by the majority," although, as mentioned before, very few believe that minority vetoes are appropriate.[11]

Table 7.2. *Members' attitudes about internal politics*

Question	Response (percentage)		
	Agree	Not sure	Disagree
Members given a large role			
in determining policy			
Activists	147	88	50
	(51.6)	(30.9)	(17.5)
Rank and file	377	434	107
	(41.1)	(47.3)	(11.7)
Only a small minority take part			
in decision making			
Activists	126	72	84
	(29.8)	(25.5)	(44.7)
Rank and file	352	369	198
	(38.3)	(40.2)	(21.5)
Sometimes a small minority prevents			
a position preferred by majority			
Activists	10	150	121
	(3.6)	(53.4)	(43.1)
Rank and file	21	567	327
	(2.3)	(62.0)	(35.7)
Most members agree with positions			
Activists	214	66	7
	(74.6)	(23.0)	(2.4)
Rank and file	677	242	11
	(72.8)	(26.0)	(1.2)

Table 7.2 (*continued*)

Question	Response (percentage)		
	Agree	Not sure	Disagree
Leaders care what members think			
Activists	253	24	5
	(89.7)	(8.5)	(1.8)
Rank and file	804	116	6
	(86.8)	(12.5)	(0.6)

Note: Activists are those so designated by Common Cause. For specific

wording of statements, see text.

However, assessments might be moderated considerably when statements dealing with feelings about outcomes rather than about the underlying process are taken into account. More respondents have an opinion and that belief tends to be favorable. Thus, roughly three-quarters of all contributors assent when confronted with the statement that "Most members agree with Common Cause positions," and better than 85 percent respond affirmatively when it is asserted that "The leaders of Common Cause care about what members think."[12]

Attitudes about the fit between personal preferences and group positions corroborate these assessments of the relationship between aggregate membership preferences and leadership behavior. When asked "In general, how frequently would you say you agree or disagree with Common Cause positions?" 8 percent said they always agree, 82 percent replied that they usually agree, 10 percent answered that they sometimes agree/sometimes disagree, 0.3 percent (3 members) responded they usually disagree, and not a single member said that they always disagree.[13]

As a whole, despite some obvious flaws in their understanding of group governance, the membership comes across as having a fairly good sense of the reality of the association. (Consistent with previous discussions, those who have been in the group a shorter time are more likely to be unsure.) At

least they are not convinced that the group functions quite as the leadership advertises. For example, of the almost 90 percent of members who said that they always or usually agree with Common Cause positions, less than 12 percent (1) agreed that members of Common Cause are given a large role in determining its policies, (2) disagreed that only a small minority of members take part in Common Cause decision making, *and* (3) disagreed that sometimes a small minority of members prevents the group from taking a majority-supported position. While this is a severe test, it serves to highlight just how few members who applaud the group's political stands see it as purely democratic. Yet, while the large majority of contributors are, at least, uncertain about whether the association measures up to the representative democratic ideal, they maintain that Common Cause continues to stand for what they believe.

The larger point to be emphasized is that the goals that Common Cause pursues, and the processes by which they are chosen, clearly require further, careful analysis. Only then can the implicit tensions contained in the finding that a substantial proportion of members are unsure about the association governing process but nonetheless feel represented be reconciled.

SHIFTING THE ISSUE AGENDA

Thus far in the analysis, only hints of how these results can be meaningfully integrated have been furnished. It is obvious that something beyond a system of elections and polling where members determine organizational goals as a part of a "one person, one vote" scheme must be functioning at Common Cause. For contributors to be satisfied with the ends of goals formation, if not necessarily knowing or approving of the means, some governing mechanisms must exist that reconcile contributors' preferences in a satisfactory manner.

With this empirically driven (but, as will be seen in more detail shortly, theoretically sensible) set of expectations as guidance, the next step is obviously to fill in the remaining gaps. In particular, it is necessary to ascertain what processes actually underlie goal formation at Common Cause, whether they correspond to, and are illuminated by, the findings of the first part of this analysis, and whether they are theoretically sensible.

However, devising a compelling research strategy might appear to be problematic. Despite the case made earlier in this chapter for analyzing the development of goals at Common Cause, had this research been written in the early 1980s, it might still have been necessary to respond that disentangling the subtle processes operating in the organization would be close to impossible. In other words, even if the previous discussion convinced skeptics that goal formation at Common Cause is a valid concern, they might have subsequently replied that the combination of two factors – the relative homogeneity of the membership regarding good government structure and process

issues (despite the fact that existing differences do have an impact on contributor behavior) and the organization's seemingly unflagging commitment to these concerns – makes separating out who in the group is most relevant for goal formation impractical. Only if members' preferences somehow became more heterogeneous (which is highly unlikely) or the association's issue agenda dramatically changed would it be feasible to examine the issue of goal formation in a satisfactory manner.

Luckily for the purposes of research, Common Cause's political goals did shift dramatically during the early 1980s. Until then, the group's political agenda had remained rather stable and seemed to be a matter of considerable consensus. Although there were some relatively minor disputes within the organization over specific issues, the organization remained fundamentally dedicated to its traditional structure and process projects (McFarland 1984). While Common Cause did become involved in several substantive debates in the late 1970s, such as the B-1 bomber and trucking deregulation, its efforts were limited. Indeed, even staff members who were interviewed admitted that many potential allies had become skeptical about the organization's commitment to substantive causes. There is little dispute that Common Cause's principal raison d'être and its public identity continued to revolve around its longstanding good government concerns.

However, late 1982 marked a period of profound change. During a six-month period, the group decided to veer away from its established structure and process focus and concentrate on a qualitatively different issue. This process officially began in July of 1982, when the governing board committed the organization to joining the battle to end the nuclear arms race. Then, in November, the official culmination of this process took place when the governing board met and decided that the association would center its energies and resources on preventing the production and deployment of the Air Force's MX missile.

The commitment to lead the anti-MX initiative did not mean that if a traditional Common Cause issue, such as campaign finance reform, came to the fore it would be ignored. The feeling was that at least in the short term, people would perform double duty. Rather, the group's guarantee meant that barring unexpected exogenous events such as the reemergence of campaign finance on the congressional agenda, the organization's energies would be principally devoted to fighting what everybody understood would be a major legislative battle to stop the missile.

The question then arises, why did Common Cause make this dramatic switch? Explaining such a deviation in group objectives is just the sort of opportunity that promises to provide new insights into leadership behavior, organizational goals, and the role that contributors perform.

Consequently, rather than continuing a broad, sweeping survey of Common Cause's internal politics, the remainder of this chapter will focus

on understanding the events that led to the adoption of a campaign against the missile as the group's major effort. Doing so promises to be the most illuminating means of understanding the process by which associational objectives are defined. This task is really a three-step process: (1) understanding what the MX missile debate was about and why it was such an intuitively strange match for Common Cause; (2) developing a theoretical model of goal formation consistent with the general guiding principle of utilizing an integrated perspective, which will provide some expectations and insights about what might trigger a move to an issue such as opposition toward the MX; and (3) applying this approach to the events underlying Common Cause's decision to become embroiled in the anti-MX movement.

THE MX MISSILE DEBATE

An obvious prerequisite for comprehending the decisions of Common Cause leaders in 1982 is to place the issue that they settled on in its proper context. It is important to underline just how crucial the MX missile was as an element of the Reagan administration's push to modernize the American military (the new president and his staff were absolutely committed to the program for both symbolic and strategic reasons, and they made the missile a top priority) and just how divided the country was politically over its production and deployment.

The MX, which stands for Missile Experimental, is a land-based intercontinental ballistic missile (ICBM) designed to replace the Minuteman II and III as they allegedly approached technological obsolescence. Advocates trumpeted the MX as having a variety of advantages over its predecessors: size, accuracy, the ability to carry more warheads, and less vulnerability to attack. The new missile rose to prominence in the 1970s, especially with the Carter administration's decision in early 1979 to move beyond research and development to full-scale engineering development for 200 MXs. The government awarded $7.4 billion in prime contracts to a network of associate prime contractors between FY77 and FY82.

Although the MX was never without its critics, the flap over the missile escalated during the first Reagan administration, when the MX emerged as the most controversial element of the president's "strategic modernization program" (e.g., Hartung 1984). Two interrelated factors, in particular, seemed to galvanize attention on the missile that Reagan affectionately reminded the citizenry was officially designated Peacekeeper by the air force.

One difficulty was that the basing needs of the MX embroiled the program more deeply in domestic politics than probably any other Reagan arms proposal. Proponents originally argued that the Peacekeeper should be mobile; they called for constructing twenty-three silos for each MX and shuffling the missile among them in a shell game that would necessitate the

destruction of 4,600 shelters to disable the entire force. Besides its being an extraordinarily expensive basing mode, representatives of each state considered as a shelter site vehemently opposed the plan. Even many congressional hawks were unprepared to endorse a strategy that would entail having to explain to their constituents why it was necessary to have 200 of the ICBMs wandering over thousands of miles in their states. Ronald Reagan himself pledged during his 1980 election campaign to search for an alternative basing solution. But the president's willingness to scrap the shell game only precipitated a stream of unsuccessful and frequently derided proposals – the implications of abandoning the multiple shelters alternative were of "almost theological proportions" said one interviewee. By the early 1980s, a total of thirty-four different basing plans had been considered and rejected. Among the more notorious were a presidential proposal that the MXs remain in existing silos and the last unsuccessful administration plan that the missile sites be densely packed together so that early arriving Soviet warheads would commit "fratricide" by striking later arriving ones.

A second factor, related to the basing problem, was real concern over the nation's nuclear deterrent; this worry was voiced even by certain members of the military establishment. (The missile was opposed by three former secretaries of defense and two former Central Intelligence Agency directors.) Many were unsure what the Peacekeeper's technical capabilities would ultimately be. It was unclear whether an immobile MX could survive a Soviet first strike. The missile could conceivably be deployed by the United States for a first strike of its own, but many of its supporters (for example, Reagan in trying to reassure vacillators) argued vigorously that the MX was not designed for the purpose of launching such an attack. The Peacekeeper suffered from the potential problem of being best suited for an unsavory "use it or lose it" strategy that would probably be destabilizing as well.[14]

By late 1982 the entire program seemed in jeopardy. The debacle over basing in general and the dense-pack option in particular and the implications of the lack of a basing mode for the MX's utility – not to mention the growing nuclear freeze movement and the budget deficit – appeared ominous for the missile's future. The project's precarious state was driven home by the successful passage of a congressional directive that the president submit a recommendation for a basing scheme by the following spring, at which time the legislature would have a forty-five-day window in which to decide upon further funding. In the meantime, the nearly $1 billion that the Reagan administration requested for production of the first five missiles was deleted from the budget.[15] While opponents of the MX lamented that these provisions permitted continuation of ongoing research and development, it was widely believed that the program was at death's door. However, the Reagan administration was absolutely committed to the program for reasons that seemed both symbolic and strategic, and insisted on making the missile a top priority.

A STRANGE MATCH: COMMON CAUSE VERSUS MX

Why would a substantive foreign policy issue with heavy support from the incumbent presidential administration be a good match for an organization that had spent more than a decade building a reputation around progressive concerns? Tautologically, the answer must be that the issue in question was considered what was best for the association – that is, where it would get the most in return for its efforts. These benefits might be private, such as favorable publicity, or collective, such as actually changing the course of public policy. Presumably, in organizations such as Common Cause, where members are interested in collective goods, both factors could be relevant.

What makes the selection of the MX so curious is that, at first blush, it appears to fall short on éach count. The reasons why investing in stopping a missile system like the MX would intuitively appear to have been a strange choice all emanate from the same source: the organization's investment in structure and process issues such as campaign financing. It would have seemed that Common Cause was forgoing its inherent advantages in terms of its reputation and its credibility by deciding to focus on the MX missile. Consequently, what the organization would receive and what it could provide might both have appeared problematic.

It was quite obvious that Common Cause would not receive very much popular recognition for its efforts with respect to the MX; the nation's popular media would have a strong tendency to gravitate toward individuals and organizations with more credibility on defense issues. The association's popular image continues to be as an organization that seeks "to reform the political system, to make it more responsive to the nation's citizens" (Hrebenar and Scott 1990, p. 284), rather than as a group with substantive goals and expertise. Compared to acts that cost few tangible resources and garner realms of free publicity, such as calling for an investigation of Speaker of the House Jim Wright – which the group did in 1989 – stopping the MX represented an expensive commitment that was certain to generate far less attention not just proportionally but absolutely. This could be quite detrimental, given that 72 percent of members responding to the 1981 survey claimed that news coverage of Common Cause was an important mechanism by which they heard about the group *before* they joined. This only seems to buttress Godwin's (1988) contention that citizen groups heavily dependent on direct mail must be highly visible.

Such expectations that the association's activities regarding the MX would be ignored by the mass media were certainly borne out. The nation's general news organizations never anointed Common Cause a "spokesgroup" on MX the way it has been throughout the years on campaign finance reform or on ethical transgressions.

For example, an analysis of ten years' worth of the *New York Times*, using the *Times Index* (1978–87), reveals the following:

1. Forty-three out of the fifty times Common Cause was mentioned (86 percent) the content of the article involved traditional Common Cause issues – campaign finance, the role of PACs, ethics in government, maintenance of an open political process, and the like.
2. Three times (6 percent) stories were about Common Cause itself.
3. Three times (also 6 percent) the subjects were somewhat peripheral issues.[16]
4. One time (2 percent) the decision by Common Cause in November 1982 to commit itself to an end to the nuclear arms race was noted.
5. *Never* was Common Cause listed in the *Index* in connection with any of the 162 stories written specifically on the MX missile between 1983 and 1985.[17]

The reliability of the results derived from the *Times* are buttressed by analysis of the nightly news broadcasts of the three major television networks, using the *Vanderbilt Television News Abstracts*. The results are quite comparable to those for the *Times*, revealing that Common Cause's anti-MX activities were uniformly ignored by the major television networks. Thus, they reinforce the finding that the group received little free publicity for its efforts. Not a single nightly news broadcast reported in the *Abstracts* mentioned Common Cause in any of their stories on the MX.

To reiterate, the group made a pronounced effort with respect to the MX. It is unnecessary to look any further than the specialized media publications written for Washington insiders such as the *Congressional Quarterly Weekly Report* or the *National Journal* for objective confirmation that the organization was at the forefront of an extensive effort to defeat the missile. Its exertions just went unheralded by the general media.

The upshot is that Common Cause's efforts could not plausibly have resulted in the realization via the mass media by even well-informed citizens, those diligently reading nationally prominent newspapers and regularly watching network news broadcasts, that the organization was heavily involved in this issue. The group's traditional, white, upper middle class, liberal constituency was virtually shut out from the possibility of learning from other sources about the organization's activities. Unlike so many of the group's other initiatives, the crusade to stop the missile did not (and was not expected to) yield a batch of free publicity through the national news media. Indeed, the group was aware that trying to get such attention would likely provoke tensions among the arms control coalition. Common Cause's efforts to capture new members through its defense initiatives came via the considerably more expensive mechanism of networking by direct mail through the arms control community.[18]

Another reason for thinking that the MX was a bad fit for the organization relates to the match between its routinely attributed political strengths and the political characteristics of the battle against MX. At first glance, Common Cause simply appears to have had less to contribute to the anti-MX effort

than to its traditional good government causes. This would have presumably provided the organization with a disincentive to get involved in the MX debate, ceteris paribus. Given the earlier findings that members can learn and that contributions (joining, retention, and activism) are partially contingent on collective goods and associational efficacy, the association's leaders would seem to have had good reason to shy away from an issue that did not fit the group's strong suits.

Consider both elements of the organization's insider–outsider lobbying strategy – the joint application of staff expertise in Washington and the mobilization of grassroots pressure – when it is applied to the procurement and deployment of missile systems. With respect to the former, Common Cause was at an obvious disadvantage when it came to lobbying in Washington about the missile system since, as noted above, it lacked any particular credibility when the subject was the procurement of military hardware. Yet, as will be discussed in more depth in the analysis of the group's impact, technical expertise is one of the primary tools of insider lobbying; it could be an especially valuable asset when it comes to an issue like the MX, involving considerable uncertainty. Common Cause staff members could not be expected to have (and did not possess) the requisite technical know-how regarding missile systems that could be the basis for persuading policymakers.

The organization seemed to face an equivalent challenge in using its vaunted grassroots' networks to apply constituent pressure on legislators. Just as Common Cause faced an obstacle in credibly mobilizing in Washington, the group would have seemed to confront comparable barriers in efficiently organizing at the grassroots level. These local units presumably consisted of members who joined, to the extent that they signed up for political reasons at all, because of Common Cause's efforts on structure and process issues. This would be a clear handicap in terms of both energizing this constituency and achieving the all important credibility for any mobilization effort that did occur.

In short, there is a puzzle: What made the MX missile a reasonable match for Common Cause that would prompt its leaders to change the group's political agenda? Presumably, two pieces are needed to complete this puzzle. One is an explanation of what the organization gained, given that its public identity is so caught up in structure and process issues. Another is what the association might contribute to the larger cause when it lacked credibility on defense issues and its grassroots organizations would seem unsuited to the cause. Solving this puzzle should shed substantial light on the formation of organizational goals and the behavior of group leaders. Accomplishing this task requires a more explicit model of internal politics than has been furnished to date. Consequently, it is necessary first to investigate in greater depth the available theoretical approaches toward the internal politics of organizational goal formation.

THEORETICAL PERSPECTIVES ON ORGANIZATIONAL GOALS

At the risk of being redundant, an important point to understand is that until the recent development of theories that assume incomplete information and allow for a variety of incentives, the available theoretical approaches all seemed to imply that goal formation is a rather straightforward process. For example, if the pluralist assumption that members share a common interest is valid, it is logical to deduce that goal formation is immaterial because members' opinions should not vary; there is no reason to presume that any subgroup will advance its own concerns at another's expense. Similarly, if Olson is correct in severing the linkage between members' preferences and group goals, organizational objectives reflect the will of the association's leaders or of the few large members who can influence how much collective goods the group can produce. Assuming this logic can be expanded to public interest groups, determining political objectives at a collectivity that lacks large members such as Common Cause should be the province of the leadership.[19]

Finally, thoughts about group goals have also been strongly influenced by the perspective on political parties developed by Michels (1958 [1915]). He argued that Western European socialist parties quickly lost their zest for transforming the political landscape, and their leaders became exclusively interested in their own self-perpetuation. Party heads used their specialized skills and control over the party structure to maintain themselves. Soon after, scholars transported this perspective to the analysis of organizations. Even when pluralism was the conventional wisdom, a separate orthodoxy developed about the role of leadership in organizations, concerning the so-called iron law of oligarchy.

However, as mentioned earlier, the ideas of an iron law of oligarchy and of membership based on shared interests are contradictory – the Michelian view of the world is much more consistent with the Olsonian viewpoint. Yet, as a number of so-called antipluralists have pointed out (e.g., Kariel 1961 and McConnell 1966; see also Moe 1980a), beliefs in pluralism and the iron law coexisted for a long time. To reiterate, the only explanation for this combination is that theorists who reflected on why groups exist did not attempt to link in logical fashion this conceptualization to internal politics. Ironically, once scholars began thinking of organizations in more economic terms, the belief in the iron law – at least as characterizing one ideal type of association – began to make more sense.

Nevertheless, in the wake of revisions regarding incentives and information to the Olson approach, there are also ample reasons to believe that organizational goals cannot be taken as the product of a dictatorship by group leaders, no less member harmony. Once it is accepted that collective goods, purposive rewards, and member learning can play important roles in decision making, the likelihood that objectives are the result of an interactive process between members and leaders increases dramatically.

This could seem an odd statement given some of the conclusions drawn earlier about how the democratic process operates at Common Cause. However, although it might initially appear paradoxical, leaders both possess an incentive to pay attention to their constituency and lack any inducement to operate a truly representative democracy.

Representative democracy cannot constitute the answer to the dilemma of how to select organizational objectives. Strict adherence to democratic processes could result in unraveling of the association as one stratum after another of disgruntled contributors departs (Johnson 1987, 1990). For example, if the group selects goals by advocating all the positions preferred by the median member, then those whose interests are most poorly represented – at least among those who care about collective goods – will tend to exit or otherwise diminish their contributions. Of course, all of this depends on the premise that members are able to learn and react to change occurring in the association.

What would make a strategy of "one person, one vote" especially damaging if it were religiously followed is that, as the results of the earlier chapters have already foreshadowed, members are not equal. In fact, at Common Cause, at least, contributors differ dramatically in terms of the information at their disposal, their attentiveness to the group's activities, and the level of monetary and in-kind aid that they are willing to furnish the group. As will be discussed in more depth shortly, from an organizational maintenance standpoint, members who are more involved in the association should be accorded more attention, ceteris paribus.

Thus, the earlier empirical findings about how Common Cause's governing processes do not ensure formal democratic representation are reinforced by the theoretical logic of member behavior. A strategy of egalitarian representation would heighten the possibility of organizational instability. Although the association leadership's advertising of its democratic processes might seem callous and calculating – maintaining that the existence of the Membership Issue Poll and governing board elections means that the organization is run democratically is certainly misleading – it is also true that the very nature of collective decision making dictates that they could not practice representative democracy even if they wanted to do so. The reality is that adopting a civics class approach to group governance has too high a price.

If formal, representative democracy is out of the question, what, then, might group leaders fall back on? Interestingly, the answer flows in a straightforward manner from the theoretical and empirical depiction of unified citizens' decision making presented thus far. Remember that the portrait developed in analyzing individual behavior is of incompletely informed persons who deal with complicated decisions in an efficient manner. Remember also that in all instances individuals were assumed to be deciding whether a fixed package of organizational benefits was worth a given (monetary and temporal) contribution level.

However, it was also mentioned that exogenous shocks might prompt

members to leave; presumably, such disruptions could also force an organization to reevaluate its goals. If such a shock occurs, the issue then becomes ascertaining which factors determine how the leadership alters the group's set of political objectives.[20]

The answer is that, quite obviously, leaders – assuming that they care at least minimally about maintaining the organization – should be concerned about those members who offer the largest contributions that are contingent upon the organization's political goals. It should also be evident, from the previous discussions, that both the *importance* members attach to political goals and their *ability to learn* about changes in organizational objectives should funnel into determining whether their contributions are contingent.

Thus, leaders possess an incentive to determine who "relevant members" are, to find out what they are thinking, and to incorporate this information into their calculi about which goals the association should pursue. In turn, relevant members are defined by three criteria:

1. the weight they place on the political goals that the group pursues,
2. their value to the association as measured by contribution levels (both monetary and in-kind), and
3. their ability to learn.

When applying this approach to Common Cause, these criteria position the spotlight squarely on the activist cadre upon whom the group depends for grassroots mobilization. It has already been demonstrated that these activists care about purposive/collective returns and particularly whether they perceive the group to be effective. Also, remember that these activists make substantial contributions of time as well as frequently donating additional cash to the organization. The value of the total contributions that such activists make is inordinately large relative to what a rank-and-file member who exclusively contributes annual dues offers. Furthermore, these activists learn more not only because of their involvement but because they tend to have been in the group a long time as well. Their immersion in its activities makes it easy for them to learn about the organization and the direction that its goals are taking – in fact, they almost cannot avoid learning since they are called upon to mobilize other members. Thus, activists satisfy all three of the key prerequisites elaborated above for exercising intra-organizational influence.

Does the fact that Common Cause leaders possess an incentive to pay special attention to activists imply the converse: that it is in their interest to ignore the rank and file completely? Not at all. Consider four already established facts: (1) Activists are more consistently liberal than the rank and file. (2) Many rank-and-file members give more than the bare minimum dues (or are, using the term employed earlier, checkbook activists) and do so to a considerable degree because of the group's political activities. (3) Even those who give only small amounts are valuable since their contributions jointly constitute a considerable portion of the budget, and many of them factor

political goals as one element in their decision calculus. And (4) even if they are not as well informed as activists, the rank and file have also exhibited a capability for learning about what goes on in the organization – indeed, this learning might propel them to become activists in the future. In other words, members generally are interested in, and capable of learning about, purposive and collective returns when they make their contribution choices.

Thus, any leadership strategy focusing exclusively on activists would involve a strong element of risk that could threaten survival of the organization. Adopting an activist proposal without double-checking that others in the group do not object in large numbers could prove quite disastrous. The logic of leadership behavior and goal formation dictates that at Common Cause the rank and file must be accorded a significant, even if a secondary, role.

In short: When activists talk, the leadership should listen. Put another way, when the logic of contributor behavior is linked with that of organizational politics, the implication is that Common Cause leaders must place activists on a pedestal. However, this joint consideration of individual and organizational behavior dictates that the group's rank-and-file members should also be germane for the formation of associational objectives. Since these members make their contributions partially contingent on their assessments of the group's adopted goals, are capable of learning about changes in the organization's agenda, and tend to have systematically different preferences than activists, they too must be consulted.

Obviously, this viewpoint reflects a different view of goal formation than that derived from the pluralist nirvana of shared interests, the standard "one person, one vote" conception of direct democracy, or the oligarchic, Olsonian portrayal of leadership dominance net of large members. Instead, in the organizational world depicted, the unequal distribution of members' willingness to contribute and the variance in their knowledge and the intensity of their preferences accords each stratum in the group differing levels of influence.

This portrayal of what to expect from goal formation also meshes well with previous discussion of how Common Cause's formal democratic processes operate. Group leaders' utilization of a system that is not, in practice, actually democratic makes sense. Leaders possess a motivation both to avoid being chained to formal decision processes and to listen to their members' views on organizational goals – although in a more discriminating fashion than a believer in egalitarian representation might advocate.

However, the ultimate test for ascertaining whether this viewpoint on goal formation is more consistent with reality than pluralism, pure representative democracy, or oligarchy depends upon how well each predicts events. Thus, for example, pluralism would suggest that shared interests would have made military issues a rather natural choice for the organization; pure representative democracy would imply that the MX initiative flowed from members' preferences, with each contributor being accorded roughly equal weight; the oligarchic, Olsonian viewpoint would imply that this was a leadership

initiative in which contributors passively went along; and the viewpoint developed in the current analysis would indicate leaders chose this strategy with strong input from activists and a lesser role accorded to other members as well. At this point, it is essential to turn to the events at Common Cause and the world around it that led to the leadership's decision to become involved with the MX.

COMMON CAUSE, GOAL FORMATION, AND THE MX MISSILE

Common Cause's external environment changed dramatically in the early 1980s. While through the second half of the 1970s the group was fundamentally tied to its structure-and-process concerns, particularly reforming the campaign finance system, the early 1980s proved a time of considerable stress when it came to the association's goals. These difficulties were epitomized, more than anything else, by one event: the election of Ronald Reagan as president in November 1980.

For if the 1970s were kind to Common Cause in terms of keeping its structure-and-process issues in the public eye, the 1980s found the group's issue agenda diametrically opposed in emphasis from that adopted by the Reagan administration. The scandals of the Nixon administration and the good government pledges of the Carter years were replaced with the laissez-faire rhetoric of Reagan. Campaign finance reform suddenly faded from political view in the early 1980s, despite a dramatic increase in the level of campaign spending and a proliferation in the number of PACs. As will be discussed in more depth subsequently, the late 1970s had witnessed a series of unsuccessful efforts, despite support from Carter, to break a partisan deadlock over electoral reform.[21] With a lack of presidential encouragement once Reagan assumed office and no obvious means of arranging a legislative accord, campaign finance was placed on the back burner. Common Cause's other core issues met similar fates and fell from public view as well.

While the so-called Reagan revolution could be termed just the sort of exogenous shock that might cause a readjustment in group goals, and one of the new administration's primary initiatives was to increase military spending in a dramatic fashion, why Common Cause selected defense issues is still not self-evident. Indeed, at first the organization's leaders held firm to their basic issue agenda. However, they did not stake out daring new structure-and-process initiatives either. For example, Common Cause could have redirected its energies toward concerns such as battles over congressional redistricting in the wake of the 1980 census or efforts to facilitate voter registration, including the fight over renewal of the Voting Rights Act of 1965, which took place in the early 1980s. Although Common Cause was somewhat involved in each of these, the organization did not allocate major levels of resources in either instance. Then, in 1982, the group made its dramatic commitment to stopping the MX.

Why did the group react this way to the exogenous events surrounding it? The explanation corresponds very neatly to what would be expected from the prior theoretical discussion. The impetus behind the change in group goals came from a process in which member input flowed through informal channels and reflected the disproportionate attention that some contributors should be given compared to others.

As mentioned earlier in passing, Common Cause routinely sends its organizational staffers from Washington around the country to maintain contact with their activists. Not only do such interactions with the folks from the home office help coordinate grassroots operations and make activists feel that their efforts are appreciated, but these trips also provide the organization with an informal means of sampling the feelings of its most valued members. Most of the time the feedback should be positive, since contributors are rather homogeneous and the group's monitoring of opinion is fairly continuous. When the feedback is negative, however, it raises a red flag for the leadership that there is something wrong with the goals they are pursuing.

Just such a warning went up in the early 1980s. Staffers, as they traversed the country in their grassroots travels, noted a flurry of unsolicited pleas that Common Cause get involved in the blossoming arms control movement and brought this information back to Washington. "The Reagan rhetoric and the ... real fear that this nuclear stuff was out of control affected our organization the way it affected the rest of the country," is Wertheimer's characterization.

Thus, while Common Cause is a good government organization rather than an arms control group – and it would be expected that its activists, more than anybody else in the membership, would comprehend this – activists wanted to do more. These feelings undoubtedly reflected the fact that the supply of structure-and-process issues had run dangerously low in the early 1980s. ("The opportunity on the campaign finance issue was not particularly there," is the way Wertheimer sums it up.) Meanwhile, on the demand side, issues of war and peace had gained an intensity that harkened back to the height of the Cold War. U.S. politics was consumed with the implications of the Reagan "revolution" military buildup. The backlash to this massive escalation in defense spending and its associated tensions was the almost overnight development of a widespread peace movement, much of it tied to the idea of implementing a nuclear freeze. So Common Cause included a large grassroots contingent that was predisposed to being mobilized and that was being kept on the political sidelines.

Importantly, while these contributors could have fallen on either side of the nuclear freeze debate, virtually every signal that the leadership received was in opposition to militarization. There is no doubt that had the direction of activist opinion been split, the defense issue would have remained a latent issue on the Common Cause agenda with little fanfare. However, even though

Common Cause is avowedly nonpartisan – as epitomized by the group's petition for the investigation of Speaker Wright – consistent with their general liberalism, the association's activists at the time were nearly uniformly opposed to the Reagan buildup and troubled by the images of nuclear holocaust that it conjured.

This consensus is reflected in the data produced by the 1981 Common Cause survey. For example, when asked to agree or disagree in response to the question, "Defense spending should be greatly increased," only 14.5 percent of Common Cause activists agreed even before the full effects of the Reagan buildup began to be felt (Table 7.3). (The rank and file was slightly more hawkish, with 18.6 percent responding affirmatively; $\chi^2 = 9.36$, $df = 4$, $.05 < p < .10$.) Given that any affirmative response bias would have led respondents to favor higher levels of defense spending, these numbers are quite impressive.[22]

So staff members uncovered a profound concern in the activist cadre through their normal temperature taking. While these contributors may have always been against defense buildups, the key difference had to do with the intensity of their opposition. Especially given the larger context – that the supply of structure-and-process issues was low as a result of the Reagan revolution – the leadership had an incentive to take these opinions seriously.

However, this did not mean that the organization proceeded full steam ahead. Rather, another question required consideration: How would the rank and file react to a change in course? No organization wants to witness an exodus such as that experienced by the ACLU (30,000 members, although many were quickly recovered; see Gibson and Bingham 1985) after its support of the rights of neo-Nazis to march in Skokie, Illinois. Given that this was a dramatically new initiative and that there are differences between preferences of the rank and file and those of activists, the group commissioned a private poll of members to assess whether the preferences of the activist cadre were in lockstep with the bulk of contributors. This poll confirmed that there was considerable accord throughout the membership over defense issues.

Finally, the governing board was confronted with the evidence that Common Cause should make a commitment to the arms control movement. This was a fairly simple task in that a large proportion of the board – who, like the activists, were generally involved in politics – were anxious to see the group move in a more substantive direction. As John Gardner puts it, Common Cause's structure-and-process focus has always proven to be "a somewhat austere approach for a lively, politically sensitive board" (pers. commun., 1990).[23] Although some, including Gardner, were opposed to the departure from the organization's bread-and-butter issues, the initiative was easily endorsed.

Political scientist Thomas Cronin, who was also on the Common Cause governing board and who opposed the move to the MX along with Gardner,

Table 7.3. *Members' attitudes toward increased defense spending*

	Category (percentage)		
Response	Rank and file	Activist	All members
Strongly agree	43	6	49
	(4.6)	(2.1)	(4.0)
Agree somewhat	130	35	165
	(14.0)	(12.4)	(13.6)
Not sure	70	19	89
	(7.5)	(6.7)	(7.3)
Disagree somewhat	181	43	224
	(19.5)	(15.2)	(18.5)
Strongly disagree	506	180	686
	(54.4)	(63.6)	(56.6)
Total	930	283	1,213

Note: Activists are those so designated by Common Cause. The specific statement to which respondents were asked to agree or disagree was worded, "Defense spending should be greatly increased."

sums up the events that transpired as follows:

I felt, as I believe he [Gardner] did, that the organization would weaken its focus or its mission if it got involved in a variety of other issues outside the explicitly structure and process issues the organization was formed to address. It was very hard, however, to contain or dissuade the antiwar activists on this set of issues. I believe that to some extent here is an example of where the citizen activists and constituents "led" the leadership in the organization. (pers. commun., 1990)

Activists, with the blessing of the rank and file, did not simply take hold of the organization with the leadership sheepishly going along. Rather, the top echelon at Common Cause had considerable room for maneuver. Typical of mandates, whether presidential, congressional, or organizational, the direction given is broad in scope and short on details. Other personal and institutional objectives can then come into play.

For Common Cause, assuming that the leadership wished to be effective, ceteris paribus, the MX was a logical selection when it came to deciding upon how its antiwar activities should be manifested. In relative terms compared to other arms control issues, the MX could be dealt with using the group's insider–outsider strategy (despite the caveats made earlier about the organization's ability to affect peace issues generally). It was also high on the congressional agenda – "Common Cause thinks in legislative terms ... it fights specific battles" notes David Cohen – potentially winnable, of strong interest to both members and nonmembers at the grassroots level, and was being pursued by a coalition to which the group could make a contribution.[24] It fit the organization's needs and abilities much more than an idealistic concern such as the nuclear freeze, which seemed to have little hope of long-term success. So the organization went from the previously discussed general declaration in mid-July to the specific announcement in November that it would concentrate on the MX. It also remained the province of the Common Cause could, and did, furnish its inexperienced allies was its general the group would employ in constructing the roadblocks required to stop the MX.

However, while this discussion provides an answer as to where pressure for getting involved in the MX came from, it does not speak to another issue raised previously: What could Common Cause provide to the effort? Earlier it was maintained that Common Cause had no obvious comparative advantage on defense matters. Although this was true, it was not the case that the organization had nothing to offer the anti-MX coalition. Rather, what Common Cause could, and did, furnish its inexperienced allies was its general expertise about how to go about influencing public policy; that is, its professional staff had experience with conducting political mobilization efforts. Or as Jay Hedlund, Common Cause's Director of Grassroots Lobbying, put it,

The two things we added were nationwide, broad-based, membership, which a lot of the other groups didn't have, and more Hill experience than anybody else had. When we started lobbying ... there were twenty or thirty groups that all had lobbyists ... and we would go up to the floor and nobody would be there ... Everybody would be down there [in a basement boiler room] watching the debate on the floor [on TV]. ... This tremendous grassroots kind of pressure didn't know what to do when it got to the Capitol, didn't know how to work the inside of the Capitol. Well, Fred Wertheimer does. (interview)

A fundamental problem that plagued the arms control community was that it was populated with many small actors who were novices to the

Washington game and neither had the wherewithal nor the expertise that it takes to get things accomplished politically. Many were also politically extreme when it came to defense issues and risked being tagged radicals who were incapable of compromise and whose positions were so immoderate that what they said lacked credibility.

It became Common Cause's role to mold these forces into a mature political movement, to teach those in the peace community how to lobby in Washington and through grassroots mobilization. In the capital, the arms control groups would furnish the requisite technical know-how about military issues that Common Cause lobbyists lacked. One advantage that those trying to have an influence over the MX faced was that this was an issue around which there was great technical uncertainty; while Common Cause could not fill in the technical gaps plaguing policymakers, it could act as a conduit for those who might have the credibility to do so.

At the grassroots level, the coalition would add citizens engaged in the arms control movement to those in Common Cause's congressional district organizations caught up in the groundswell of the peace movement. While using Common Cause's grassroots organizations to mobilize against the MX missile might have seemed ludicrous at first blush, it turns out that the organization had several advantages. For one thing, compared to virtually any other potential Common Cause issue, the MX was a concern that voters outside the organization genuinely cared about – a point that will be examined in detail when the impact of Common Cause lobbying is analyzed in the next chapter. As will be discussed in more depth, when an issue such as campaign finance is addressed by Common Cause, the organization faces the problem of convincing policymakers that there exists a sizable constituency outside the association that also feels passionately about it. With the MX, by contrast, many legislators already believed that how they voted on the issue could have direct electoral consequences. For another thing, as already discussed, while Common Cause members certainly did not join the organization to be arms control activists, many of those who played vital roles in the group's grassroots organizations felt strongly about the Reagan military buildup. Thus, the association's obvious disadvantage in mobilizing its constituency was somewhat mitigated.

While other groups might have stepped forward to fill this niche of a generalist organization with political savvy, Common Cause was the only one willing to commit the resources. Interestingly, being at the heart of a widespread coalition was a rather novel experience for those in the group: The organization had traditionally been a lone wolf with few committed allies rather than at the center of a coalition. Even staffers admitted that integrating Common Cause activities in a highly coordinated effort was far from typical coming from a Fred Wertheimer.

Consequently, for two and a half years Common Cause was at the forefront of the anti-MX coalition led by David Cohen.[25] Joining Cohen and Common

Cause as the lead organization in the coalition was the peace group SANE (A Citizen's Organization for a SANE World). (John Isaac of the Council for a Livable World is another individual actor who played an especially prominent role.) The MX proved to be Common Cause's principal issue for this entire period. The small inner circle around Cohen plotted the allies' strategies and worked at keeping a unified front, especially in light of the aforementioned tendencies of some of the more extreme members (including some in SANE) to oppose anything in the way of compromise.

In its newfound role as an arms control organization, Common Cause quickly found itself embroiled in a series of highly visible, bruising congressional fights, with both the president and the Pentagon strongly mobilized in opposition. Eventually, after a number of dramatic twists and turns (which will be detailed shortly), a compromise was hammered out in 1985 stipulating that fifty MX missiles should be deployed in existing silos. This accord furnished the air force considerably fewer missiles than it wanted but nonetheless represented a concession by program opponents who wanted the MX scrapped altogether. With this, the missile designated Peacekeeper faded from the congressional agenda until the end of the Reagan administration, when the matter of building additional missiles to be placed on railroad cars brought the program back into public view.

Ironically, almost as soon as the MX faded from the nation's political consciousness in 1985, the traditional Common Cause issue agenda swung back to electoral reform. In late 1985 Senator David Boren of Oklahoma began a frontal assault on the campaign finance system, the idea of enacting more restrictive regulation consequently regained some prominence, and Common Cause began mobilizing its forces. In addition, the nation's attention began to be directed again toward ethical issues as the Iran–Contra scandal commenced unraveling. Although maintaining a modest interest in military matters, Common Cause has refocused its attentions where it might seem they more naturally belonged in the first place.[26]

MAKING SENSE OF IT ALL: THE POLITICS OF ORGANIZATIONAL GOALS

Clearly, then, the recitation of the events of the early 1980s at Common Cause meshes nicely with the general theoretical propositions outlined previously. Leaders did not arbitrarily make decisions by themselves, shared interests were not taken for granted, and pure representative democracy was not practiced. Rather, activists' opinions were given special weight, credence was given to the views of other contributors, and leaders exercised discretion as well. More concretely, it is possible to characterize activists, rank-and-file members, and the leadership as possessing three types of authority with respect to the MX: *agenda setting, veto,* and *discretionary.*

By agenda-setting authority, it is meant that Common Cause activists have the opportunity to define the general issues that the organization considers.

To reiterate, instances where activists feel compelled to open new fronts will not occur very frequently at a group such as Common Cause, where there is considerable harmony among contributors about what organizational objectives should look like, where the leadership should be able to anticipate what its more valued participants desire, and where dramatic exogenous events occur infrequently. As is familiar to anyone who studies congressional decision making, considerable authority is associated with the right to set the agenda of what issues will be deliberated (e.g., Romer and Rosenthal 1978). The ability to advance a proposal that at least in broad terms can be either accepted or rejected yields significant influence.

Similarly, in giving its opinion regarding a new policy initiative, the rank and file might be conceptualized as fulfilling a comparable role to that of Congress as a whole when it must consider the proposed legislation. Organizational contributors, like members of Congress, have the authority to reject the proposition and retain the status quo or to accept it and see the group's policy change. This veto authority, it should be stressed, is a function of the contingent nature of member contributions to group goals. When it came to the MX, the rank and file was in accord, while in other instances tests of member opinion have been a deathblow for initiatives such as desires to get involved in certain international issues (McFarland 1984).

Much like the bureaucracy that is delegated authority after a vague piece of legislation is passed, once a broad initiative has been agreed upon the organizational leadership has the discretionary authority to decide upon implementation (e.g., Bardach 1977). However, just as the bureaucracy is limited by the possibility of congressional oversight (e.g., Miller and Moe 1983), the leadership's latitude is constrained by the potential reaction of its rank and file and, especially, its activists, as well as by the need to attract new members. If members learn that the leadership has strayed off the beaten path, they may react by withholding support. This delegation of what was described by interviewees as "management issues" is significant nonetheless: It allows leaders to winnow out some issues, to narrow broad objectives into specific goals, and to decide upon the means ("resource allocation") to realize these ends.[27] The leadership may also possess agenda-setting authority by proposing an initiative that it will then have to present to the activists and rank and file, paying particular attention to the veto authority of the former. So even while there may be times that leaders seem to be taking a policy initiative, they will still anticipate the reaction of their contributors, particularly the activists.

CONCLUSIONS: LEADERSHIP BEHAVIOR AND GOAL FORMATION

The sum total of what has been uncovered weaves a multifaceted portrait of leadership behavior and goal formation at Common Cause that illustrates nicely the utility of developing an integrated perspective. This depiction can

be summarized succinctly in six steps:

1. Common Cause is not governed in a formally democratic manner despite the organization's advertisements to that effect.
2. A large proportion of contributors either recognize this failure of the representative process or are at least unsure whether the association is managed in such a fashion.
3. A considerable majority of members advocate a governing process that is far closer to majority rule than currently exists.
4. Despite the first three statements, an overwhelming majority of contributors feel that they are well represented.
5. The explanation for (4) rests with leadership incentives and citizens' decision making: Organizational decision makers possess an incentive to listen to members, but not to all equally. Instead, they need to design a system that finesses the idea of "one person, one vote." While individuals in the group might rightfully feel that this process is inconsistent with their preferences, they may – and apparently do – also believe that the end result matches their desires rather well. Of course, as was seen earlier, many of those who feel inadequately represented will exit.
6. The upshot is that the leadership, the activists, and the rank-and-file contributors all play different roles that are explicable because of the incentives and processes that drive organizational maintenance and prosperity. This is extremely well illustrated in the move to adopt the MX missile as the organization's principal issue from 1983 to 1985, when campaign finance reemerged on the nation's political agenda.

These findings have a myriad of interesting implications for organizational democracy. They demonstrate that the formation of group goals at Common Cause corresponds to none of the classic conceptions of associational democracy or oligarchy that routinely spring to mind. Rather, deciding upon objectives for the organization (and the resulting positive and normative evaluations of group politics) is a subtler process. Goal formation is intimately tied to the way the logic of citizens' decision making – and its implications about member information, incentives, and preferences – interacts with that of group governance.

This logic implies that leaders may set up organizations that attract individuals willing to contribute different amounts for a variety of reasons with varying levels of information. The former need to satisfy contributors giving larger, politically contingent gifts.

Thus, by necessity, in an organizational context like that found at Common Cause, members' rights are not equivalent. In addition, given contributors' level of information, there is considerable slack between members' sentiments and the leadership's execution. Whether this is thought of as democracy in action, an aberration of democratic principles, or something in between depends upon one's normative stance.

Although this substantive analysis is specific to Common Cause, the lessons that can be taken away are more general. Organizational goals are fundamentally important to the understanding of groups, and the presence or absence of formal democratic processes should be far less important empirically than the nature and extent of members' contributions and knowledge. Only an integrated approach that matches the contribution process to goal formation is likely to provide a comprehensive perspective on associational objectives and organizational democracy that, ultimately, provides a key link in discerning whether and how individual behavior is tied to public policy.

Does group activity make a difference?
The case of the MX missile

THE POLICY LINKAGE

To this point, the analytical focus has been upon the relationships that develop between organizations and their members and how they produce a set of political goals for the leadership to implement. At Common Cause, the result has been a focus on two principal goals: prevention of the construction and deployment of the MX missile and reform of the campaign finance system to foster political accountability. Limiting the Reagan defense buildup and overhauling the election system were the two issues in the 1980s (and for campaign finance into the 1990s) that satisfied all the requirements for being incorporated as a primary feature of the group's political agenda and soaked up most of the group's scarce political resources: At this point, it is imperative to turn to the *policy linkage*: whether, or to what extent, the organization has been effective in pursuing its goals in the political system. Ultimately, it is understanding this linkage comprehensively that makes organizations of concern to political scientists.

Common Cause's realization of its political goals, like its group influence generally, seems open to question. Actual, rather than perceived, effectiveness is a tricky concept to gauge. It is possible that members, even leaders, may have difficulty discerning whether they are being influential. As will be discussed in greater depth shortly, social scientists certainly find judging effectiveness problematic. Thus, this chapter and the next focus directly on organizational effectiveness by examining whether, or under what conditions, Common Cause has had an impact on congressional decision making.[1]

Interestingly, when the subject is organizational influence, there are two extreme scenarios that might be plausible. On the one hand, associations may be politically ineffectual. If this were the case, groups would represent nothing more than a political sideshow. Leaders become better off and the returns to members are purely private, divisible goods, although members may feel more positively about themselves because they think that they are making a difference in the outside world. Normative arguments about groups dominating the political scene generally, and of public interest groups somehow bringing the general population's concerns into the political arena

specifically, would then fall flat. As mentioned initially, a belief that associations are not potent is one of the reasons frequently given for the atrophy of research on organizations; indeed, if Common Cause is found to be ineffectual, much of the previous discussion would appear rather vacuous.

On the other hand, associations may have a large impact. Leaders are able to take group demands, mold them in a politically practical manner, and direct them effectually. If this is the case, the findings of the rest of this analysis are seen in a different light: They then answer the question, what are the precursors to organizational influence? In other words, if groups matter, then organizations furnish something that political decision makers value, and symbolic groups are not merely public relations outfits that sell a feeling of well-being and some private rewards to a naive constituency. What makes these organizations tick – how they get their money, motivate their activists, and decide upon their goals – become key issues because they are crucial precursors to understanding policy outcomes.

As discussed to some extent already, scholars have not been able to decide between these two scenarios. There is no agreement on whether groups have much of an influence on congressional policymaking. Whether interest groups have an impact on Congress's public policy choices has been debated. An initial flurry of research portrayed associations as virtually omnipotent (see Bentley 1908, Truman 1951, and Latham 1952 on interest groups generally and Schattschneider 1935 on lobbying specifically); this was replaced for several decades by a revisionist viewpoint that depicted groups and lobbying as ineffectual (see especially Bauer et al. 1963).

The belief in organizational impotence has itself come under attack in the last decade by a new generation of counterrevisionists who maintain that associations play a significant role in legislative decision making. Hayes reflects that "legislators and lobbyists are interdependent; their relationship is genuinely transactional, inasmuch as both parties benefit" (1981, p. 162). Smith (1984; see also 1989) finds that the National Educational Association has an impact on the level of support for the issues they target. Fowler and Shaiko (1987) discover that lobbying is of value, albeit modest, in their empirical examination of environmental organizations' influence on a number of Senate votes – on shale oil development, park expansion, preservation of the outer continental shelf, protection of endangered species, and energy tax credits. Wright (1990) concludes that lobbying is extremely relevant in his examinations of three Superfund amendments considered by the House Ways and Means Committee.

Given this long, if sporadic, history of studying the relationship between lobbyists and legislators, why has the issue of group influence remained unresolved? Three not mutually contradictory reasons seem to stand out.

One is that effectiveness is difficult to measure; teasing out exactly the degree to which behavior is a function of group efforts as compared to other features in the political environment is a considerable challenge. Conducting

detailed, qualitative examinations of given issue areas to determine influence is a considerable task. Utilizing quantitative techniques also has its pitfalls. Minimally, an econometrically correct analysis requires data on lobbying activities, the strength of an organization net of mobilization efforts, and legislators' predicted votes if no efforts were made. Thus, even the recent counterrevisionist analyses (all of which are quantitative), while making important contributions, have not completely satisfied the criteria and thus have left unsettled the issue of whether groups and their lobbying make a difference. For example, Smith (1984) estimates equations with fewer than thirty cases; Fowler and Shaiko (1987) have no evidence about whether legislators were actually lobbied on the issues in question or whether their aggregation of state information prejudices their results; Wright (1990) openly bases his analysis on some strong assumptions that, even if they hold, are not necessarily generalizable.

A second reason why group influence has been difficult to assess is that it has often been unclear what exactly organizations have to furnish to political decision makers in order to have an impact. While not without important precursors, in recent years scholars have begun to develop much more explicit frameworks for understanding the nature of group influence (Mitchell 1990; Mitchell and Munger 1991).

Finally, a third reason why settling the issue of whether groups are influential is difficult is that scholars have not tended to focus on citizens' decision making and internal politics (but see Wright 1985 on PACs). Put another way, it is conceivable that under some conditions organizational processes result in group goals that are ripe for activity and in other instances they produce objectives that are difficult to attain. Differences in scholarly findings may reflect real differences in organizational politics.

Having already determined why Common Cause became active with respect to the MX, the analysis in this chapter attempts to investigate whether the group and its allies had an impact as they sought to block the production and deployment of the MX missile in 1984 and 1985. Given that the examination is largely quantitative, although such data are supplemented with contextual information provided by Washington interviews, an effort is made to circumvent as many as possible of the empirical problems that plague such work. In addition, a general framework explicitly suggesting how interest groups should fit into the voting and lobbying process is presented to motivate both this chapter's analysis of the MX and the next chapter's examination of campaign finance.

When it comes to the MX, a large sample is generated that includes specific information on who gets contacted and is then analyzed using the general framework. Of particular importance, Common Cause generously furnished (upon a pledge of anonymity) a list of the legislators whom they actually lobbied, as well as data about the group's strength in each congressional district in the form of information about the geographic distribution of

membership. Such clean, objective measures of lobbying and organizational capacity should make it feasible to ascertain whether Common Cause was able to move representatives.

A number of other interrelated factors make the MX stand out. One is the crucial nature of the issue. The missile was a major concern of citizens, groups, legislators, and the presidential administration; and the votes over its appropriation and authorization were consistently close and hotly debated. There has "really never been another issue like MX" comments one veteran congressional staffer.

Efficacy in swaying outcomes vis-à-vis the MX at least seems possible since there is reason to believe that representatives' preferences were potentially malleable. Journalistic accounts depicted legislators as wavering back and forth in support and opposition of missile production and deployment. In four House votes in 1984 that will be studied in this analysis, twenty-three legislators cast at least one pro- and one anti-MX vote; in the four 1985 votes analyzed the number jumped to fifty-one.[2] This does not necessarily prove that preferences were fluctuating, since each vote involved choices over somewhat different alternatives. Still, the widely reported waxing and waning of legislative sentiment coupled with the observed reversals by a nontrivial percentage of those casting ballots – in numbers sufficiently large to sway the outcome – makes it conceivable that group mobilization could make a difference for the MX.

However, very much corresponding to the common disagreements stemming from the difficulty of assessing lobbying, it needs to be emphasized that the evidence on whether lobbying mattered is murky. The situation was so complex and the identification of winners and losers sufficiently difficult that firsthand observers have made reasonable prima facie cases about both the efficacy and impotence of lobbying.

Some who watched events unfold claim that associational efforts were key to the near demise of the MX. They point out that the fight over production and deployment was the closest any Congress had ever come to killing a major weapons system that a president desired and that production and deployment levels were scaled back despite opposition from congressional hawks, the air force, and the Reagan administration. Illustrative of this point of view is Michael Pertschuk, a colleague of David Cohen's, who goes so far as to call the MX battle the "Thermopylae of citizen lobbying campaigns," as the foes of the missile fought back against great odds (Pertschuk 1986, p. 29). The resulting victory, according to Wertheimer, was that few enough missiles were agreed to so that "a first strike weapons system was not built."

Others who viewed the same legislative fracas at least implicitly belittle the role of interest group mobilization. They cite reasons for the MX's difficulties and cutbacks that are orthogonal to organizational lobbying. According to this logic, it is dismaying that extensive group efforts could not defeat a weapons system whose effectiveness (if it ever existed) both as a military tool

and as a bargaining chip with the Soviet Union was badly hamstrung by the basing mode dictated by other domestic political concerns. In this vein, Elizabeth Drew has written that the approval of MX deployment is a puzzle:

> At some future time, historians may look back and wonder how it was that politicians and policymakers made a decision to proceed with the development of a weapon that they knew had lost its original rationale, might escalate the arms race, and could put their own country's military forces at greater risk...given the MX's bizarre history, the convoluted reasoning that went into its most recent justification, the serious misgivings of those who were most responsible for helping the weapon win congressional approval, and the potential consequences of their action, the story is an unusual one. (1983, p. 39)

To distinguish between these two scenarios, the first part of this analysis will lay out a theoretical framework for analyzing lobbyists and legislators, which will also guide the discussion of campaign finance in the next chapter. This is followed by a chronicle of the events from late 1983 through 1985 surrounding development, procurement, and deployment of the MX missile and a detailing of the lobbying efforts surrounding the controversy. Once the stage has been set, attention is then directed to distinguishing the factors that structured legislative decision making through an analysis of key congressional roll call votes on the MX and Common Cause's decisions on whom to lobby.

LOBBYING STRATEGY AND VOTING BEHAVIOR

An organization's internal processes bring an issue to the forefront of its political agenda. Those making politically contingent decisions combine with leaders to determine what goals the group will pursue. But is this enough to ensure political success? What determines whether lobbying makes a difference?

Any theoretical framework designed to answer these questions must contain two elements: an outline of the determinants of voting behavior in Congress and, embedded within it, a perspective on which legislators groups lobby. The two, as will be shown, are inherently intertwined.

Four basic assumptions underlie this analysis:

1. Legislative decision makers are motivated by reelection incentives (Mayhew 1974).
2. Members of Congress are imperfectly informed about both district preferences and the results that will stem from the adoption of a given proposal. Imperfect information is a sine qua non for interest group influence according to Denzau and Munger (1986).
3. Group leaders are motivated by a desire to influence legislative outcomes, subject to a constraint on the amount of effort organizations can expend. (At various points, however, the implications of other motivations will be discussed.)
4. Associational lobbying is designed (a) to furnish representatives with

information about the preferences of their constituents and thus about the electoral ramifications of their actions (this is the primary purpose behind grassroots lobbying; see Austen-Smith and Wright 1991) and (b) to provide information on the value of a given program to a legislator's coalition – broadly construed to include the provision of factual information about the operations of programs and their importance to the nation as a whole – which is akin to what Smith (1984, 1989) labels "interpretation" (this is a principal function of lobbying in Washington).

Consider first the question Who gets lobbied? Stated more broadly, what cost/benefit calculation do group leaders employ in deciding how to have an impact on policy? Since organizational leaders want to influence legislative outcomes, they will utilize their available resources to change unfavorable votes and maintain favorable ones so as to maximize the number of favorable ballots cast. After assessing the benefits and the costs of contacting each representative, leaders will lobby those congressional decision makers for whom the expected payoff is greatest, subject to the budget constraint. Given the assumptions stated, four factors stand out as potentially significant; three condition the benefits accruing to group leaders, and the fourth structures their costs.

In considering what the benefit stream looks like, the organizational decision maker will tend to lobby the following legislators: (1) those whose preferences make how they will vote questionable; (2) those who are most likely to adjust their preferences over the course of a legislative decision process; and (3) those whose support is most likely to sway the choices of other representatives or to structure their decisions.

Of these three factors, it is likely that the most important influence on a group's cost/benefit lobbying calculus is whether the legislator is perceived to be a fence straddler.[3] Ceteris paribus, interest groups should approach those representatives whose expected probability of voting one way or the other is approximately one-half (Smith 1984; Fowler and Shaiko 1987); that is, associations should concentrate on those most likely to be at the margin.[4]

A subsidiary consideration likely to enter group leaders' decision calculus is the potential variability of legislators' preferences: Members of Congress who are especially uncertain about what policy positions to adopt should be most malleable. This will also be reflected in leaders' greater uncertainty about their voting expectations. In the spirit of the work by Gilligan and Krehbiel (1987, 1989), uncertainty is likely to be most prevalent when issues are technically complex and unfamiliar to members of Congress.

Another consideration of group leaders is the value of a given legislator's support. Attracting leading congressional decision makers to one's cause is vital. This generally entails wooing key committee members, who may serve as agenda setters (e.g., Romer and Rosenthal 1978) or as cue givers funneling information to other uncertain legislators (Matthews and Stimson 1975).

The price of lobbying any legislator should also vary: Differential costs

will be contingent on local organizations' level of development (Wright 1987). Creating a new organization from scratch is clearly much more expensive and difficult than melding current efforts onto existing structures. Thus, it should be cheaper to mobilize support in a representative's district if the group already has an institutionalized presence there. This, quite obviously, applies primarily to making grassroots contacts.

Having specified whom groups might lobby, the next question that must be considered is what are the determinants of the vote? Not only is it important to provide a baseline model against which to measure the effect of lobbying, but as was spelled out previously, the expected vote is potentially crucial for the mobilization decision itself.

While there are many well-known problems with formulating models of member voting (e.g., Fiorina 1975; Achen 1978; Snyder forthcoming), a straightforward framework can be profitably applied. Following, among others, Shepsle and Weingast (e.g., 1984), it is assumed that the geographic incidence of benefits and costs induces legislator preferences among electorally motivated decision makers. Specifically, three key components of the voting decision must be measured: (1) the benefits accruing to the voting district; (2) the money (or "costs") earmarked to be spent in the district; and (3) any negative externalities or tax costs borne by the constituency. If the expected value of the benefits exceeds the negative externalities and tax costs, the expenditure policy is adopted.

This model as initially formulated does not extensively incorporate groups, but it can be readily modified to do so (Shepsle and Weingast 1984). Given the framework for lobbying suggested here, voting may simply be conceptualized as a function of the factors listed and (linearly or perhaps interactively) lobbying.

In summary, legislative balloting is posited to be a function of the costs and benefits accruing to the decision maker's constituency (see Figure 8.1). Such assessments may be conditioned by the information furnished through the lobbying process. This, in turn, is presumed to be a function of expectations about the vote, the potential variability in members' preferences, the importance of a given legislator for an issue domain, and the costs of grassroots mobilization. The task that confronts the researcher is to disentangle the intertwined system of relationships to see which factors are key for determining legislative outcomes. Before trying to do this econometrically, it is necessary to provide some basic information about the events under consideration.

SETTING THE STAGE: THE BATTLE FOR THE PEACEKEEPER

The MX is the right missile at the right time.
     Ronald Reagan, November 22, 1982

As discussed earlier, at the end of 1982 the Reagan administration's efforts on behalf of the MX appeared to have been largely defeated and the whole

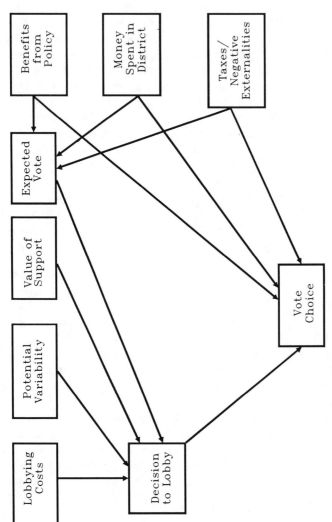

Figure 8.1. Determinants of congressional vote choice.

program was in jeopardy. But the missile made a remarkable recovery and climbed off the critical list. To half the anti-MX tide, the Reagan administration created a bipartisan commission, known as the Scowcroft Commission (Presidential Commission on Strategic Force 1983), with an appointed mission to review nuclear strategy generally and the Peacekeeper specifically. The commission's mandate was explicitly to build a politically winning compromise that would appeal to vacillating legislators, the most notable of whom was future House Armed Services Committee Chairman Les Aspin, widely acknowledged to be the key House moderate on defense issues.

The commission's blueprint for salvaging the MX had three elements. The first was to maintain that the MX was needed as a transitional weapon until the smaller Midgetman missiles supported by many moderate Democrats (most prominently, then Representative Albert Gore) could be developed. Because the MX was a transitional weapon, it was argued that only 100 Peacekeepers were needed to match the Soviet's ICBM capability. Finally, despite the negativity that had greeted Reagan's original suggestion, the commission advocated that these 100 missiles be placed in existing Minuteman silos (there was some talk of "superhardening" these silos). This package was heartily endorsed by the Reagan administration.

At least in the short term, the Scowcroft proposals did the trick. In May 1983 – amid Reagan's assurances that he would reorient his administration's long-term nuclear weapons and arms control policies – Congress voted with relatively large majorities compared to the previous MX votes (first 239–186 and then 223–167 in the House; 59–39 in the Senate) to release funds to build and deploy 21 MX missiles. Those opponents who thought in late 1982 that the MX would be unable to overcome the roadblocks they had created had their hopes dashed as key moderates, for example, Aspin, Gore, Norman Dirks, and Thomas Foley in the House, and William Cohen, Sam Nunn, and Charles Percy in the Senate, came into the fold.

However, the deployment issue remained far from settled: In fact, the controversy surrounding the MX became even more heated in the ensuing months. Whether this reflected the efforts of the anti-MX forces or other causes such as the administration's turbulent relations with the Soviet Union, criticisms of the MX from sources such as the GAO (1984), the escalating budget deficit, or growing popular sentiment for a nuclear freeze, House votes in the second half of 1983 revealed diminishing support for the program from the highwater mark immediately after the Scowcroft Commission reported its findings. The 50-plus vote margins in favor of the Peacekeeper in May 1983 dissipated to 13 (207–220) in July and dwindled to just 9 in November (208–217).[5] Declining support did not, however, prevent continued funding and production of the missile; opponents worried that if production were not stopped shortly, political support for the MX would snowball as more jobs were created.

The controversy reached its zenith in the appropriation and authorization battles of 1984 and 1985. The Reagan administration requested $2.9 billion

to be a battleground with both sides alternately winning and losing on key issues. To begin with, the anti-MX forces – led in the House by Charles Bennett (second-ranking Democrat on the House Armed Services Committee) and Nicholas Mavroules (a strong prodefense representative) – lost their gambit to restrict the degree of the amendment to make production an all (down to 30 missiles) or nothing decision.[6] In rejecting this proposal, the House Rules Committee ensured that a series of votes would take place as moderates, led notably by Les Aspin, tried to forge a middle ground. These moderates settled on a proposal to approve the production of 15 missiles at a cost of $1.8 billion dollars, with the caveat that money be spent only after April 1, 1985, and only if the president judged that the Soviets were unwilling to negotiate for ICBM reductions.

MX opponents lost another strategic battle when the rules on amendments prevented those favoring a halt to production from forcing an initial vote on the choice of 0 versus 30 Peacekeeper missiles; they had hoped that it would make it difficult for those voting that they preferred no MXs to the status quo of 30 to turn around and support the production of 15 missiles. Aspin, despite a lack of seniority, was able to control the agenda through an alliance with Melvin Price, chairman of the House Armed Services Committee. The Price proposal for 15 rather than 30 missiles was approved initially via voice vote.[7] It was followed first by a vote on the anti-MX amendment (no procurement in FY85), which failed by a mere 6 votes (212–218), and then by an amendment to substitute the Price proposal, which passed by 30 votes (229–199).[8] There was considerable flip-flopping among legislators. Eleven Peacekeeper supporters (8 Democrats, 3 Republicans) from 1983 switched to oppose the program, most notably Majority Whip Tom Foley, the last member of the Democratic leadership to support the MX, who gave up his hope that support for the missile could be used to jump start arms control negotiations. On the other side, 10 previous opponents (8 Democrats, 2 Republicans) came out in favor. Converts included four tobacco state legislators widely rumored to have opted for sidepayments. Nevertheless, it seemed that the anti-MX forces had lost.

However, just two weeks later, these opponents came back and won what seemed to be a stunning victory. Rather than trying to kill production altogether, the project's foes opted to shift the issue to whether it should be the president or Congress that could release funds. After a first, restricted amendment restating the status quo was again approved (203–182), Bennett introduced an amendment that would give Congress responsibility for releasing funds. This measure was widely perceived as undercutting whatever negotiating leverage the president had gained from the previous status quo. With the backing of Speaker O'Neill (who cast a rare vote) and his organization, the amendment squeaked through with a two-vote margin (199–197).[9] Eight representatives who had voted for the previous status quo chose to support the new plan, while not a single opponent of the prior

status quo voted against Bennett's amendment; this overcame an asymmetry among the many absentees on Memorial Day weekend (23 previous opponents did not vote as compared to only 13 supporters). Opponents to the MX had succeeded in preventing production of the missile, at least temporarily, and had given themselves another shot at ending the program during the next legislative session. An analogous vote later that evening was virtually unchanged, with the speaker's vote providing the margin of victory (198–197).

Meanwhile the Senate Armed Services Committee had unconditionally approved 21 missiles for production in mid-May 1984. But support dissipated in the upper body as well in the days following the House action. Opponents of the Peacekeeper program, notably Patrick Leahy, Dale Bumpers, and Carl Levin, tried to eliminate the program's $2.6 billion allocation altogether but failed by a considerable margin (55–41). However, the vote on an amendment spearheaded by Lawton Chiles, which allowed the program to continue and kept production lines ready but without any actual production, ended in a tie that had to be broken by the vice president in favor of the status quo. The same amendment was to be offered again in August, but this effort was dropped once Lowell Weicker made himself scarce (reportedly in return for the award of a submarine contract to General Dynamics' Groton, Connecticut, facility).

The House and Senate positions took over three months to reconcile, holding up the entire defense budget in the process. Amid uncertainty on both sides about what would happen if a compromise were not forged and adhered to, Speaker O'Neill and Majority Leader Baker finally fashioned an agreement between the House and Senate positions: $2.5 billion was appropriated for the purchase of 21 Peacekeeper missiles, but only $1 billion could be spent before April 1, 1985, and none of the money could be used to complete any MXs other than those approved for FY84. Funds could also be used for spare parts and to make sure that no project contracts were canceled. To release the remaining $1.5 billion, both houses of Congress had to vote twice via joint resolutions rather than once (a victory for the anti-MX forces that came at the price of a slightly higher defense spending total).[10] It was also agreed that no more votes on the MX would take place until the next session convened after the election. The accord limped through, with worries about its survival every step of the way.

President Reagan strategically waited to request the remaining $1.5 billion until March, just two days after arms control talks with the Soviets were resumed, and he used the talks as the primary reason for supporting the missile. Against this backdrop, project opponents had to search for a majority in either the Senate or the House. Success would all but completely kill the MX program.

The Senate was the first of the two houses where the battle was fought. But with Reagan lobbying the senators directly – capped by a rare presi-

dential visit to Capitol Hill – and the administration threatening to punish defecting Republicans, the MX's proponents enjoyed identical (55–45) victories on both votes. The going was also tough in the House: There was strong opposition in the House Appropriations Committee and declining support from reelected incumbents.[11] But the administration was able to receive sufficient assistance from House freshmen (who voted 30 to 13 in favor of the MX) to fashion a narrow victory (219–213) for funding the missile. The second mandated vote was no more successful for opponents of the missile (217–210).

With the larger issue of the proposed Strategic Defense Initiative looming in the wings, opponents virtually admitted defeat on the MX. They were joined by many moderates, such as Sam Nunn, who were determined to put an end to what had become twice yearly bloodlettings. As John Isaac characterizes the situation, Nunn "wanted to settle the fight, he didn't want this thing to continue forever, each year having one or two tough votes on the MX."

In the Senate, Nunn and other moderates took charge and negotiated a compromise with the Reagan administration. Although the president requested $3.2 billion dollars and 48 MXs for FY86, the Nunn agreement mandated 12 new missiles for FY86 and 12 to 21 for FY87 and incorporated a statement that it was the "sense" of the Senate that the number of missiles should remain at 50. It passed easily (78–20).

The MX's foes in the House tried to hold out for a more stringent final settlement in which production would be subject to a permanent cap of 40. After procedural jockeying, a series of crucial votes took place. Bennett made one last futile (185–230) attempt to kill the program with a proposal to allow no more missiles. This was followed first by a victory (233–184) for an amendment proposed by Dave McCurdy of Oklahoma, which placed a permanent cap of 50 on MX deployment, then by an unsuccessful amendment offered by William Dickinson of Alabama stipulating a temporary cap (analogous to the Senate position), and finally by a reaffirmation by voice vote of support for the permanent cap.

The two houses' positions were reconciled through a compromise that called for 12 new MX missiles in FY86 and a permanent cap of 50 on the number of missiles that could be deployed (which could be repealed with a majority vote). Without lifting the ceiling of 50, 12 additional Peacekeepers would be produced in subsequent years for testing and training purposes and to keep the production lines open. This compromise served to produce at least a temporary truce to one of the prominent political battles of the Reagan administration.[12]

The end result was that the MX missile was produced despite some obvious shortcomings. In an era of enormous budget deficits and antinuclear movements, the go-ahead was obtained to produce a missile for which a politically determined basing decision surely reduced, and perhaps eliminated, its

usefulness as a strategic weapon. The MX was successfully steered through a quintessential example of the legislative labyrinth.

Nonetheless, the outcome does not prove that lobbying by the opposition was ineffective. It can easily be argued that without the opposition's efforts, the votes would have been more lopsided or that more missiles would have been produced. Indeed, the essence of the coalition's victory, according to Wertheimer, was that few enough missiles were agreed to so that "a first strike weapons system was not built." Thus, evaluating the evidence on whether lobbying counts will be the subject of the next sections.

THE ROLE OF THE MX'S OPPONENTS

There had always been outside opposition to the missile, much of it over-lapping with the more general nuclear freeze movement. But it was not until 1983 that a strong, institutionalized coalition (anchored by Common Cause) began to form that was designed to lobby against production and deployment of the MX (Pertschuk 1986). To an extent, this reflected a general change in the nature of the opposition to military spending offered by the arms control community: "There is a vast difference in the [heightened] skill and [increased] maturity of the arms control network. That's one of the pluses of the eighties" notes David Cohen.[13]

Interestingly, there does not seem to have been much of a conservative counterpart to the anti-MX forces (McDougall, forthcoming). The major proponents of the MX were the Reagan administration, the air force, and the contractors involved. According to those interviewed, the contractors played a decidedly secondary role, only occasionally reminding those members of Congress whose districts would receive work from the missile. While one explanation given in interviews for contractor inactivity was that they had very little to contribute, this must be viewed in the context that Reagan and his advisors had made a decision that the MX would not be the first strategic weapon system that an administration heavily valued to be defeated. According to Michael Mawby, a SANE lobbyist now at Common Cause, "The adminis-tration lobbyists were always there and they were the opposition. ... The administration was carrying the water for the contractors and anybody out there who wanted this thing." The lack of contractor presence is well illustrated by the following description of the vote of May 16, 1984:

Twenty-two anti-MX lobbyists clogged the corridor leading to the House floor. Two administration lobbyists stood among them, all but engulfed in a sea of bright red "Stop MX" lapel buttons.

But the number of votes on the floor is not decided by the number of lobbyists waiting in the wings. And when the 15-minute roll call was completed the night of May 16 and the MX survived by a slender six votes, it was the two White House lobbyists who clapped each other on the back in victory. The ones wearing the buttons were left to brood their voting lists and try to figure out what went wrong.

With the seconds in the 15-minute roll call ticking away, the mini-army of lobbyists watched anxiously, knowing a cliffhanger was in the works. "It ain't over 'till it's over," Rep. Mike Synar, D-Okla, told disheartened anti-MX partisans as the vote began to slip away. But moments later it was over. One lobbyist took cold comfort in the fact that MX foes had picked up votes since November. "The way I look at it, in all that time, we picked up three votes and they only picked up one," said Jay Hedlund of Common Cause. That means we were three times more effective than they were, right?"

(Pressman 1984, p. 1156).

The strategy of the opponents to the MX was quite thoroughly designed. Common Cause plotted a month-by-month timetable that was based on its standard insider–outsider lobbying technique. District activists were given a timetable as to when to utilize the plethora of alternative techniques to influence the legislators. The methods included networking with other community groups, coordinating meetings with representatives when they came home for recess, infiltrating the member of Congress's district gatherings to bring up the MX issue, attending local meetings to hand out literature on the MX and encourage individuals to contact the representative, being guest speakers at local meetings, holding coffee klatsches, canvassing door to door, generating petitions, manning community phone banks to contact persons within the district and to call the representative, sending mailgrams and public opinion messages, and organizing letter-writing campaigns.

Nationally, there were efforts to coordinate the coalition's activities in Washington, attempts to generate publicity on the MX issue through news conferences and studies, and naturally, personal contacts with legislators and their staffs. To aid with lobbying, representatives were surveyed regarding their voting intentions. However, it is important to emphasize that opponents of the MX felt that taking advantage of the intensity of citizens' preferences through grassroots lobbying was of paramount importance. Indeed, not only did Washington volunteers help coordinate the grassroots efforts, but lobbyists were also sent to the hinterlands.

Slightly under 30 percent of legislators in 1984 and more than 20 percent in 1985 were actually lobbied by the anti-MX coalition.[14] Members of Congress were broken up into finer categories (at least in 1984): those who were the best prospects, those who were longer shots, those who needed reinforcement, etc. In short, a sustained, coordinated effort was undertaken to sway roughly 100 legislative votes in each of the two years during which the fight over the MX was at its zenith.

DOES LOBBYING MAKE A DIFFERENCE?

In the theoretical discussion, it was posited that three factors besides lobbying are key for the congressional decision-making calculus: (1) benefits accruing to the voting district; (2) money spent in the district; and (3) the negative externalities or costs that the district bears.

Assessing the benefits of a missile program is clearly far more subjective than making such judgments for a stereotypical pork barrel project. The major reward accruing to most districts from a defense project will be the collective benefits associated with the incremental change in the nation's level of defense. The questions that legislators must answer about a system such as the Peace-keeper are far more complex than those associated with constructing a post office or a dam. Does the MX bolster or undermine the national defense? Are the benefits worth the opportunity costs of forgoing an alternative weapon system, such as the Midgetman, or other governmental services? Members of Congress will answer these questions based on their own under-standing of military technology and defense strategy and their perceptions of district preferences on such issues. Not surprisingly, ideology – presumably acting as a summary measure of legislative and district preferences toward defense as a collective good – has virtually always proven to be the key predictor of congressional roll calls on defense initiatives (e.g., Bernstein and Anthony 1974; Fleisher 1985; McCormick 1985; Wayman 1985; Nelson and Silberberg 1987). Conservative representatives, and the coalitions that keep them in office, believe that there are large benefits to be derived from major defense initiatives; liberals, and their supporters, are far more skeptical.

Legislators may temper their assessments, however, according to the level of divisible benefits flowing to their constituencies. Where will the money on the MX be spent? Even if a missile lacks military utility, it might deserve support if it creates jobs. One caveat is required, however: While there is plenty of anecdotal evidence supporting this proposition, empirical analysis has uncovered little validation. Feldman and Jondrow (1984), for example, maintain that spending has no impact on House reelection possibilities – breaking the crucial link necessary to establish that such benefits are important. Wayman (1985; see also McCormick 1985) discovers that arms voting in the Senate is at best weakly related to a state's economic base. Arnold (1979) similarly asserts that there is no relationship between constituency benefits and voting on defense issues. The implication is that the importance of the collective good being provided overwhelms the relevance of where the dollars are flowing domestically. Nevertheless, one does not want to assume a priori that where the billions will be spent makes no difference in congressional calculations, although it is true that once hardened silos were settled on, the costs of the MX program were modest by the standards of most major weapons systems. About 10 percent of all congressional districts (principally in California, Florida, Massachusetts, Missouri, Pennsylvania, Utah, and Washington) contained MX associate contractors and received a chunk of the several billion dollars spent annually on the program.[15]

While advances in national defense are different for the representative to assess and the rewards of military contracts are potentially unimportant, it should be relatively easy for legislators to identify who is footing the bill. Those states or districts that have the largest tax share ought to pick up a

disproportionate share of the costs for any governmental program (Wayman 1985). The real issue here, it would seem, is whether legislators, at least in the House of Representatives, are sensitive to these discrepancies across districts given that each represents only one of 435 districts. Do legislators actually bother to take into account whether their constituents are paying 1/435th, 1/335th, or 1/535th of a project's cost?

Having applied the voting framework to the case of the MX missile, attention turns to the issue of lobbying itself. Recall that three factors besides the expected vote were posited to be possibly influential – the importance of a given legislator, the potential variability of a member's decision, and the differential costs of lobbying.

Clearly, bringing an Albert Gore or a Les Aspin on board in the House or winning over a Sam Nunn in the Senate would be considered a major coup for either side, far more of a victory than garnering the support of a nonspecialist who had exactly the same expected vote. The backing of noted legislative authorities on military issues would provide an important informational signal about the proposal under consideration. More generally, winning the support of legislators sitting on either the House Appropriations Committee's Subcommittee on Defense or the House Armed Services Committee would be a major victory for those fighting over the MX.

With respect to potential variability, two groups that clearly stand out are freshmen and those who are electorally vulnerable. With regard to the former, especially when it comes to military issues, most new legislators will have little experience; even if they have held other elective positions, for example, nothing analogous to the purchase of a missile system is likely to have been on the agenda. Rather than suffering from lack of experience, those who are electorally vulnerable may simply have to be much more sensitive to their perceptions about which way the wind is blowing.

Finally, the differential costs of lobbying should reflect the varying levels of organizational strength in each district. It would be very costly and difficult for the anti-MX coalition to implement Common Cause's insider–outsider strategy without having a good base in a given district.

Measurement and estimation

Having identified the likely determinants of decision making by both organizational leaders and congressional decision makers, it is possible to operationalize and estimate the relationship between lobbying and voting. Two *lobbying* variables are defined: A dummy variable is scored 1 if a legislator was subject to mobilization efforts by the Common Cause–led anti-MX coalition in 1984 and 0 otherwise; and an analogous variable is created employing 1985 data.[16] Similarly, dummy variables for each of eight previously discussed key *House* votes on the Peacekeeper (which are

summarized in Table 8.1) are utilized; a pro-MX vote was scored 0, and an anti-MX vote, 1.[17]

The factors alleged to influence both lobbying and voting can also be operationalized using the available data. The following measures of the determinants of voting are employed:

1. *Collective district benefits*, for lack of a better term, from perceived improvements in national defense are measured using three indicators: (a) legislative ideology, measured with *Congressional Quarterly* Conservative Coalition scores (following Fowler and Shaiko 1987) adjusted by removing both the effect of abstentions and the influence of votes on the MX[18]; (b) contributions received from defense PACs in the previous election cycle, on the presumption that larger contributions will be given to those legislators who believe that high levels of military spending strengthen the national defense; and (c) a dummy variable scored one for Democrats and zero for Republicans.
2. *Divisible district benefits* accruing from resources flowing to the constituency are measured by the amount of money received for the MX by associate contractors in each legislator's district during the preceding fiscal year.[19]
3. *District costs* for the MX are measured by the mean income level of a district. The higher the district's income, the larger the tax bill for the MX.
4. *Lobbying* is gauged with an instrumentalized measure of lobbying (to be discussed shortly) as well as with the dummy variables mentioned above. Also, since direct measures of MX contractor activity are unavailable, their political action committee contributions during the past election are employed as a surrogate.[20]

In turn, the following measures of the determinants of lobbying are employed:

1. *Fence straddling* is measured as the following:

$$-1 * |E(p) - .5|,$$

   where $E(p)$ is the expected probability of voting (which will be defined more precisely soon). Scores range from -1 (certain to vote one way or another) to 0 (no directional vote expectation).
2. *Key legislators* are defined with dummy variables scored 1 for representatives sitting on either the House Appropriations Committee's Subcommittee on Defense or the House Armed Services Committee and 0 otherwise.
3. *Potential variability* is measured by a dummy variable scored 1 if a legislator is a freshman and 0 otherwise and the degree of members' electoral marginality.[21]
4. [Low] *lobbying costs* are tapped by the number of Common Cause members in the congressional district.[22]

Table 8.1. *MX House votes analyzed*

Vote	Date	Outcome (Pro—Anti MX)	Description
1.HR5167	5/16/84	218—212	Amendment to amendment to bar procurement of MX missiles in FY85
2.HR5167	5/16/84	229—199	Amendment to substitute to amendment to allow the production of 15 MX missiles subject to certain conditions
3.HR5167	5/31/84	203—182	Amendment to amendment to authorize the production of 15 MX missiles subject to certain conditions
4.HR5167[a]	5/31/84	197—199	Amendment to amendment to authorize the production of 15 MX missiles but prohibit the obligation of funds appropriated for that purpose unless Congress had given its approval by passing a joint resolution after 4/1/85
5.SJRes71[a]	3/26/85	219—213	Passage of the joint resolution to approve authorization of $1.5 billion to produce 21 MX missiles in FY85
6.HR1872	6/18/85	230—185	Amendment to substitute for amendment to deny all funds for production of MX missiles
7.HR1872	6/18/85	184—233	Amendment to amendment to express the

Table 8.1 (*continued*)

Vote	Date	Outcome (Pro—Anti MX)	Description
			sense of Congress that no more than 40 MX missiles should be deployed
8.HR1872	6/18/85	182—234	Amendment to substitute for amendment to express the sense of Congress that no more than 50 MX missiles should be deployed in existing missile silos and to authorize the production of 12 MX missiles in FY86

[a]A virtually identical vote that immediately followed is excluded.

In all cases, expectations are straightforward. In other words, representatives who are conservative, Republican, recipients of large contributions from defense political action committees generally and the MX contractors' PACs specifically, whose constituencies will benefit directly from MX spending, who are not lobbied, and whose constituents will foot a small share of the tax bill should favor the MX, ceteris paribus. Members of Congress who are fence straddlers, who are key actors in the legislative process, whose positions appear movable, and whose constituencies are easy to mobilize should be the most likely to be lobbied.

The obvious problem with the specification as it now stands is that both the possibility of being lobbied and voting for or against the MX are potentially endogenous to each other. The acknowledgment that lobbying is partially a function of the expected vote – something that has not been explicitly incorporated into past research – highlights this possibility.

Coping with this dilemma requires a three-step estimation procedure.[23] First, the lobbying equation is estimated using the variability, key legislator, and cost measures specified above and a variety of other factors exogenous to the vote.[24] From these results an instrument for lobbying is derived. This instrument is then included in the voting equation along with the dummy variable for lobbying in accordance with procedures on how to deal with

endogeneity in a probit analysis (e.g., Newey 1987; Rivers and Vuong 1988). If the instrument is significant it is utilized as the measure of the concept in question; if not, the original measure (the dummy variable) is employed. From the voting equation an expected probability of voting is estimated that can be inserted into the lobbying equation – after being transformed in the specified manner to measure fence straddling – and the proper structural equation can be estimated.

Results: The influence of lobbying

In accordance with the methods discussed, the 1984 and 1985 lobbying instruments are initially placed in the roll call equations for each respective year (results not shown). Interestingly enough, lobbying is endogenously determined by the vote in 1984, but it is exogenous to the 1985 roll calls.[25] The final vote equations are consequently estimated with an instrument for 1984 votes and the dichotomous lobbying measure for 1985.

The results from the structural equations (Tables 8.2 and 8.3) successfully explain most MX voting: Over 90 percent of votes are correctly predicted for all but one ballot, despite the very even split between pro- and anti-MX forces. The findings have several key points in common – both across years and between votes in given years – as well as a few differences. They are largely in line with expectations.

In all instances, collective district benefits, particularly as measured by congressional ideology, are extremely germane. This finding is unsurprising since it is consistent with prior analyses of voting on military issues, although it may reflect some of the Reagan administration's lobbying efforts as well. The strength of this relationship is perhaps best illustrated by considering what would happen if the world were made up of either pure liberals (0 on the Conservative Coalition scale) or pure conservatives (a tally of 100 on the scale), with everything else remaining the same. In a pure liberal world, the pro-MX side would garner only two votes (both on vote 6 in 1985) on all eight roll calls combined. In a conservative nirvana the liberals would get three votes (one on vote 7 and two on vote 8).

Of the other indicators of collective rewards, defense PAC contributions are irrelevant, while party is insignificant in 1984 and important in 1985 for all but the roll call on Bennett's attempt to kill off the MX program altogether (almost one-third of anti-MX Democrats defected to the other side). This change in the partisan nature of the debate was subsequently confirmed in interviews and was primarily attributed to leadership behavior: Only late in the game did the Democratic leadership (notably O'Neill, Foley, Tony Coehlo, and Richard Gephardt) come to believe that the MX was a winnable issue and mobilize in a strong, unified fashion.

The impact of party, even when it is significant, pales in comparison to ideology.[26] In a world consisting only of Republicans, for example, the

Table 8.2. *Determinants of anti-MX voting (HR5167), 1984 (probit estimates with standard errors in parentheses)*

Variable	Vote 1	Vote 2	Vote 3	Vote 4
Constant	3.876***	2.625***	2.418***	3.577***
	(1.160)	(0.924)	(0.955)	(1.222)
Collective district benefits				
Ideology	—6.467***	—5.869***	—5.641***	—6.307***
	(0.701)	(0.587)	(0.593)	(0.728)
Defense PAC	0.014	0.068	—0.049	—0.026
giving ($10,000s)	(0.191)	(0.170)	(0.186)	(0.202)
Democrat	—0.089	—0.147	—0.053	0.187
	(0.316)	(0.302)	(0.317)	(0.323)
Divisible district benefits				
MX spending	—0.059**	—0.038*	—0.036*	—0.058**
($10,000s)	(0.028)	(0.027)	(0.027)	(0.029)
District costs				
Income	—0.168	0.049	—0.009	—0.197
($10,000s)	(0.360)	(0.318)	(0.337)	(0.394)
Lobbying				
Anti-MX lobbying	0.794	1.199**	1.487**	1.405**
(instrument)	(0.740)	(0.637)	(0.706)	(0.835)

Table 8.2 (*continued*)

Variable	Vote 1	Vote 2	Vote 3	Vote 4
MX PAC giving	0.045	0.127	0.020	—0.098
($10,000s)	(0.816)	(0.732)	(0.797)	(0.837)
Number of cases	430	428	385	395
—2xlog-likelihood	153	183	157	134
Percentage predicted	92.1	90.4	91.7	91.9

$*p \leq .10$ $**p \leq .05$ $***p \leq .01$

Table 8.3. *Determinants of anti-MX voting (SJRES71 & HR1872), 1985 (probit estimates with standard errors in parentheses)*

Variable	Vote 5	Vote 6	Vote 7	Vote 8
Constant	2.855***	3.253***	4.331***	4.661***
	(0.854)	(0.904)	(0.962)	(0.990)
Collective district benefits				
Ideology	—5.331***	—5.555***	—5.931***	—5.924***
	(0.567)	(0.605)	(0.682)	(0.690)
Defense PAC	0.066	0.011	—0.091	—0.189
giving ($10,000s)	(0.139)	(0.149)	(0.149)	(0.160)

Table 8.3 (continued)

Variable	Vote 5	Vote 6	Vote 7	Vote 8
Democrat	0.384*	—0.147	0.392*	0.381*
	(0.268)	(0.299)	(0.260)	(0.261)
Divisible district benefits				
MX spending	0.002	—0.038	—0.037	—0.044
($10,000s)	(0.038)	(0.048)	(0.053)	(0.053)
District costs				
Income	—0.114	0.066	—0.246	—0.338
($10,000s)	(0.291)	(0.295)	(0.308)	(0.316)
Lobbying				
Anti-MX lobbying	0.280*	0.256	0.638***	0.678**
	(0.206)	(0.213)	(0.214)	(0.218)
MX PAC giving	—1.088**	—1.622***	0.082	-0.030
($10,000s)	(0.604)	(0.681)	(0.620)	(0.064)
Number of cases	432	428	417	416
—2×log-likelihood	201	197	186	181
Percentage predicted	90.0	88.9	91.8	92.1

*$p \le .10$ **$p \le .05$ ***$p \le .01$

anti-MX forces would win only 14 votes less on vote 5, 7 fewer on vote 7, and 5 less on vote 8.

Nevertheless, whatever the variations, it is clear that collective benefits are a crucial factor for all MX votes. Only once such elements are controlled can the effects of lobbying be discussed.

Divisible benefits play a significant role for MX voting only in 1984. One plausible explanation for this difference is that the 1984 votes dealt directly with funding levels. Thus, jobs were at stake. According to Common Cause's Jay Hedlund, "We absolutely lost people who we could have had who had jobs in the district." In 1985, in contrast, the number of MX missiles to be produced was not much at issue (it was clear almost immediately that the number would not exceed 12); rather, the debate centered around how many missiles ought to be deployed.

Would higher funding levels have made a difference in 1984? To get a feeling for what effects funding increases might have had, assume that every legislator in 1984 received $100,000 more in MX spending; that is, suppose that just another $40 million or so was put into the pot and distributed with absolute equity. According to the estimates, this would lead to an extra two votes in favor of the MX on vote 1, one more on vote 2, none on vote 3, and three on vote 4. Considering that prime contract and not subcontract data are being used, that the amount of money being discussed is small relative to the costs of defense contracts generally, that the effects of money flowing to neighboring districts is impossible to measure, and that it is difficult to find linkages between divisible benefits stemming from military programs and voting, this sensitivity to spending is impressive.[27]

While the missile's benefits – collective or divisible – have significant impacts that are in the expected direction, the role of income is uncertain and, if anything, in the wrong direction. However, this finding is weak and only begins to approach a level of significance for the 1985 votes.

But even after costs and benefits are taken into account, lobbying matters.[28] Anti-MX efforts are consistently important for votes on modifications to the missile program; these forces have a weaker impact on proposals designed to ban production altogether (vote 1 in 1984, vote 6 and, to an extent, vote 5 in 1985; see Table 8.1 for the exact details). Perhaps one reason for this difference is that legislators may fear being termed antimilitary or anti–arms control (the Reagan administration's argument) for voting against the MX program altogether; therefore, the impact of lobbying is dissipated. Lobbying is more effective around the margins where the ordinary voter's ability to monitor congressional behavior is severely diminished. There is little evidence that lobbyists simply reserved their efforts for those Peacekeeper votes on which mobilization is statistically significant.

Ironically, in 1985 lobbying was especially important when the anti-MX forces were losing badly during the last two votes. They were able to hold supporters who otherwise would have defected when a groundswell of opinion in favor of an MX compromise emerged.

Table 8.4. *Effects of anti-MX lobbying on vote outcomes (estimates of number of anti-MX votes for those lobbied)*

Vote	With lobbying	Without lobbying	Difference
1984			
Vote 1	45	30	15
Vote 2	41	31	10
Vote 3	38	29	9
Vote 4	45	36	9
1985			
Vote 5	39	32	7
Vote 6	33	27	6
Vote 7	54	39	15
Vote 8	54	39	15

Does anti-MX lobbying influence the outcomes? To check this, predictions are derived on how legislators who were lobbied would have voted if they had been left alone; these findings can then be compared with the predictions derived from the model with lobbying included.

The results (Table 8.4) demonstrate that the predicted impact of lobbying in 1984 produces a shift of 9 to 15 votes, ceteris paribus. Lobbying only

helps close the gap on the first three votes (also, remember that the estimate for lobbying on vote 1 does not quite reach statistical significance). However, not surprisingly given the realized margin, it is absolutely essential for the crucial victory on vote 4. Ironically, in 1985 the anti-MX movement had its largest impacts at the wrong time: It could have much better utilized the 15 representatives it swayed on votes 7 and 8 for vote 5, although the loss of all 15 would have made the last two roll calls uncomfortably close. The inability to sway three or four more votes (depending upon whether the speaker was willing to cast a ballot) on SJRes71 represents a barely perceptible turning point in the evolution of the MX missile. The anti-MX movement's shortfalls are all the more poignant when one considers the higher "batting average" of votes swayed to legislators lobbied in 1985.

The finding that the anti-MX lobby had a significant but moderate effect on vote outcomes was also echoed in interviews. As one key congressional staffer puts it, the arms control lobby was "a factor in the debate [but] probably not the critical factor in the resolution of the issue."

However, regardless of the limitations of the anti-MX side, their results are much more impressive than the efforts by the other side. The surrogate indicator for pro-MX lobbying, campaign contributions by those receiving contracts, are important only in 1985. Interestingly, the impact of contributions is the mirror opposite of anti-MX lobbying. On the votes barring production (vote 5 and, especially, vote 6) money matters; on the votes expressing the sense of the Congress about how many missiles should be deployed (with production levels not a major issue, it should be noted), the effect of the pro-MX forces evaporates. While such weak findings may reflect imperfections associated with the measure employed, they are also consistent with the earlier observation that there was no group counterpart to the anti-MX side.

In summary, voting on the MX is heavily determined by the collective benefits involved, notably ideology and party. To reiterate, to some extent, these factors may pick up the lobbying efforts of MX proponents in the Reagan administration and the Defense Department. There is also evidence that divisible benefits are important, while district costs seem irrelevant (or they work in the wrong direction). Finally, lobbying is a force, particularly the behavior of the anti-MX coalition. The interests opposed to the missile were able to sway legislators on the details of the issue even if they could not convince them to take the risk of abandoning the program altogether.

THE STRUCTURAL DETERMINANTS OF LOBBYING

Once voting probabilities are estimated, it is possible to turn back to lobbying. When the estimates of voting probabilities are transformed to measure fence straddling and the structural determinants of lobbying are identified, the results are quite impressive (Tables 8.5 and 8.6). (Note that there are four

Table 8.5. *Determinants of anti-MX lobbying (HR5167), 1984 (probit estimates with standard errors in parentheses)*

Variable	Vote 1	Vote 2	Vote 3	Vote 4
Constant	0.700***	0.265	0.201	0.700***
	(0.249)	(0.240)	(0.257)	(0.269)
Fence straddling				
Expected vote	2.140***	1.202***	1.189**	2.194***
	(0.484)	(0.484)	(0.516)	(0.521)
Key legislators				
Defense	0.566*	0.569*	0.809**	0.704**
appropriations	(0.383)	(0.379)	(0.415)	(0.399)
Armed services	—0.238	—0.200	—0.204	—0.279
	(0.175)	(0.226)	(0.236)	(0.237)
Potential variability				
Freshman	—0.217	—0.195	—0.180	—0.224
	(0.175)	(0.172)	(0.179)	(0.180)
Marginality	0.006***	0.006**	0.005**	—0.006***
	(0.002)	(0.002)	(0.003)	(0.003)

Table 8.5 (*continued*)

Variable	Vote 1	Vote 2	Vote 3	Vote 4
Costs of lobbying				
Common Cause membership (1,000s)	—0.130 (0.105)	—0.113 (0.105)	—0.084 (0.104)	—0.084 (0.105)
Number of cases	430	428	385	395
—2xlog-likelihood	489	500	443	446
Percentage predicted	70.2	71.0	72.2	70.9

*p ≤ .10   **p ≤ .05   ***p ≤ .01

Table 8.6. *Determinants of anti-MX lobbying (SJRES71 & HR1872), 1985 (probit estimates with standard errors in parentheses)*

Variable	Vote 5	Vote 6	Vote 7	Vote 8
Constant	0.685*** (0.262)	0.500* (0.257)	1.161*** (0.295)	1.095*** (0.295)
Fence straddling				
Expected vote	3.556*** (0.537)	3.189*** (0.535)	4.607*** (0.601)	4.544*** (0.599)
Key legislators				
Defense appropriations	—0.017 (0.414)	0.360 (0.418)	0.157 (0.409)	0.221 (0.409)

Table 8.6 (*continued*)

Variable	Vote 5	Vote 6	Vote 7	Vote 8
Armed services	—0.110	0.023	—0.322	—0.359
	(0.244)	(0.240)	(0.259)	(0.267)
Potential variability				
Freshman	0.455**	0.506**	0.531**	0.577***
	(0.237)	(0.238)	(0.243)	(0.244)
Marginality	0.002	0.001	0.002	0.001
	(0.003)	(0.002)	(0.003)	(0.003)
Costs of lobbying				
Common Cause membership (1,000s)	—0.157	—0.197	—0.240	—0.226
	(0.128)	(0.132)	(0.142)	(0.142)
Number of cases	432	415	417	416
—2×log-likelihood	385	380	352	347
Percentage predicted	78.5	80.2	80.8	80.8

$*p \leq .10$ $**p \leq .05$ $***p \leq .01$

measures of expected vote per year; each is utilized separately in the lobbying equation for that year.) Two factors stand out in particular: (1) Fence straddling is crucial for determining lobbying in both years and (2) anti-MX forces vary their lobbying strategies across years in intuitive ways.

These results unequivocally demonstrate that expected vote is of overwhelming importance for who gets lobbied in Congress. The greater the likelihood of being crucial, the more prone one is to feel anti-MX pressure.

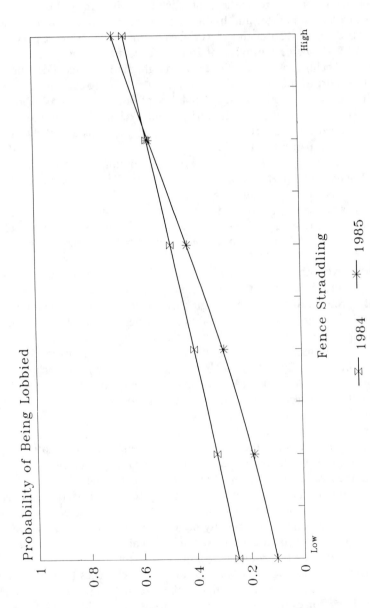

Figure 8.2. Lobbying and fence straddling.

The strength of this relationship between fence straddling and the probability of being lobbied for the average legislator are illustrated, using the estimates from the vote 1 and vote 5 lobbying equations, in Figure 8.2. (The basic relationship remains roughly the same no matter which equation results are employed.) For an average legislator who is neither a freshman nor a member of a key committee and has an average number of Common Cause members back in the district and an average margin of victory in the previous election, each 10 percent movement toward fence straddling increases the probability of being lobbied anywhere from roughly 8 to 13 percent depending upon which part of the normal distribution curve is being considered. True fence straddlers, members whose probability of voting each way prior to lobbying is equal, have a better than 65 percent likelihood of being lobbied; members judged to be absolutely certain of their positions are likely to be lobbied 10 or 15 percent of the time.

These findings serve to highlight how the pinpointing of fence straddlers was considered to be part and parcel of the maturation of the arms control community. As Common Cause's Hedlund puts it, "Typically [in the early years] the arms control groups would go to the same 10 or 15 liberal Democrats. ... Literally, they couldn't talk to Republicans. ... We literally held training sessions for some of the new lobbyists [on whom and how to lobby]."

In 1984 two other factors matter for lobbying: being on the House Appropriation's Subcommittee on Defense, although that result is not especially strong,[29] and electoral marginality. In 1985, with the election over and a new Congress in place, the coalition switches its strategy. Freshmen, whose support was key to determining outcomes, become a focus of attention rather than committee members. There is an intuitive logic to concentrating on the freshman. By 1985 all other legislators have a strong track record reducing the overall level of uncertainty in the system. Exploiting marginality is likely to be less effective since the next elections are well over a year away. Therefore, except for the fence straddlers, the strategy is to target those about whom there is the greatest uncertainty.

On the cost side, Common Cause district membership has no relationship to who is lobbied. While feeling heavily constrained by the absolute costs of mounting their campaign, the anti-MX leaders felt that the relative costs of mobilizing grassroots movements were roughly equal across congressional districts. Swing members could be defined first and the cost of mobilizing against them considered subsequently because the very nature of the grassroots coalition helped equalize costs: Where the local Common Cause organization was insufficiently strong, the coalition was able to tap into the local memberships of other organizations and even local churches to pick up the slack. Efforts were also made to utilize other techniques (demographically based mailings, for example) to mobilize citizens when additional support was needed.

Do these findings prove that the conventional wisdom – that interest groups lobby their friends – can be rejected? To examine this further, the lobbying equations were rerun with the absolute expected probability of voting for or against MX (as compared to the absolute difference from 0.5) substituted for fence straddling. For 1984 friendship is statistically significant, although the explanatory power of the models, as measured by the log-likelihood functions, is worse than for the fence straddling model.[30] For 1985 friendship, at least as measured by expected vote, is relevant for only votes 7 and 8; that is, once again, votes 5 and 6 differ from the other two. Also, the differences in the explanatory power of the alternative models are even more dramatic in favor of the fence straddling specification, even when friendship is significant. This result – that the anti-MX forces were less solicitous of their friends in 1985 and concentrated on those most likely to be malleable – might explain why the lobbying activities of those who opposed the missile were more effective the second time around. Regardless, the results suggest that while there may be a bias to go after friends, presumably because they are easier to lobby, lobbyists' primary focus is on pivotal representatives.

In short, lobbying is largely, although not exclusively, a function of expected vote. Member variability and importance may also come into play. Fence straddlers are the major object of lobbying, although the ease of soliciting support from friends as compared to enemies may be germane.

CONCLUSIONS: VOTING, LOBBYING, AND PUBLIC POLICY

The analysis in this chapter may be assessed at two levels. Most obviously, it may be conceived as an attempt to overcome the difficulties of evaluating the nexus between associations and representatives. In addition, it can be conceptualized as an effort to demonstrate, along with previous analyses, whether and how member preferences may be translated into public policy outcomes.

In other words, one means of assessing the results of this chapter is to what degree it casts new light on the basic processes that underlie the linkage between the efforts of organized interests and the outcomes of the political system. At this level, the basic finding is that even public interest groups may possess a significant, if moderate, influence through their lobbying on the decisions of elected officials. Mobilization involves more than symbolic displays for public relations.

Given the long, if sporadic, research tradition that questions whether any organization has much of an impact, the finding that associations have an influence is of interest in and of itself. Indeed, investigation of lobbying activity is inherently difficult, and rigorous examinations are few and far between.[31] Moreover, there are some crucial differences in the findings that make the current effort stand out.

1. Lobbying is sometimes endogenous to roll call voting itself. Empirical estimates of the role of lobbying in the political process may be distorted if this is ignored.
2. The effects of lobbying may vary, just as theory would suggest, with the ability of voters to monitor the situation. When representatives find themselves vulnerable – for example, to the charge of being antimilitary – the impact of lobbying may be reduced.
3. Mobilization strategies may change over time (generally for quite intuitive reasons as the political context evolves), and such variations may produce different outcomes.
4. Expectations about voting, particularly who is likely to be pivotal, feed back into the lobbying choice. Models and estimates of who gets lobbied that do not build in assumptions about expectations will be seriously in error.

However, for the purposes of the larger project, what perhaps makes the analysis in this chapter most compelling is that it illustrates the linking of citizen, organizational, and systemic support. Contributors' preferences can be translated in some modest way into public policy outcomes. Given a membership that is capable of learning and that takes political goals into account in their decisions about retention and activism, rumblings from the grassroots can guide an organizational agenda which, in turn, may provide elected officials with cues regarding how to behave. The very same membership sensitivity to political factors that helps determine goals may also feed back into a group's ability to have an impact on policy. Thus, public interest groups are not necessarily impotent, symbolic vehicles that lack political influence; their actions may even be prompted and facilitated by organizational contributors.

Nevertheless, the discovery that members *can* influence group leaders who, in turn, may sway political decision makers leaves open the issue of whether the effective functioning of this process is *necessary* for group maintenance. As discussed previously, there are a number of factors that might affect how influential an association may expect to be: Do issues that lack the characteristics facilitating group influence still get the attention of associations and, if so, for what reasons?

Although completely answering this question is beyond the scope of the current endeavor, the remaining substantive analysis may at least provide some insights. For after Common Cause was finished expending its energies on the MX, it returned to a very different sort of concern – changing the nature of the campaign finance system. As will become clear shortly, campaign finance differs from the MX rather dramatically; how a single group got intimately involved in both in the same decade may provide some important intuitions about the larger process of representation.

9

Does group activity make a difference?
The politics of campaign finance

While the MX grabbed the attention of Common Cause decision makers for a few years, the association found itself quickly shifting gears in the second half of the 1980s. Almost inevitably (or so it seemed), the attention of Common Cause reverted in late 1985 to the enduring issue that galvanizes the organization's membership and defines its popular image: the financing of elections. Virtually as soon as the MX issue faded from the agenda, campaign finance burst back upon it. As one staffer put it, "If we had planned it, we couldn't have planned it any better." By February 1986 the governing board had officially declared that campaign finance reform would be the group's top priority.

Of course, this was an easy, indeed essential, thing to do given that electoral reform was prominently reemerging on the national agenda. As mentioned, members seconded their leaders' commitment about the general need to reform the campaign system and tended to feel intensely about it and to make decisions about whether to stay in the organization based on it. In short, given the nature of citizens' decision making, the Common Cause leadership would have little choice not to reorient the group toward campaign finance – despite some desire on their part to expand the political agenda.

In the succeeding years, Common Cause has almost totally refocused its political efforts toward legislating and implementing an overarching reform of the campaign finance system. In its singleminded pursuit to revamp the finance system, it has increasingly garnered a reputation as a one-issue group. Particular emphasis has been placed on instituting limits on the role that money plays in congressional elections.

To examine whether this is another instance of citizens' preferences being translated into public policy (or, if not, why not), this chapter examines electoral reform and Common Cause's efforts to shape it from late 1985 to mid-1991. The method used is (1) to provide an outline of what, given the theoretical framework set up in the last chapter, it should take for Common Cause to influence campaign finance reform, and how this compares to the situation encountered in the struggle over the MX missile; (2) to develop this

understanding further by detailing the broad differences that separate political decision makers and illustrating where the organization's preferred outcome both coincides and conflicts with the preferences of the former; (3) to review the events from 1985 to 1991, recounting first the efforts of the two Senate entrepreneurs who spearheaded the charge for reform and then charting what happened once their initiatives failed; and (4) to evaluate Common Cause's efforts.

Before proceeding, a note of caution is in order about the methods employed in this chapter: The mix of data utilized are, by necessity, somewhat different than those employed in the MX study. Relying principally on a quantitative approach is not feasible because events amenable to such testing (such as key votes) have not occurred to the same extent as they did with the MX. (Most of those that have occurred have been party line votes and, therefore, the resulting roll calls are not conducive to determining the impact of factors besides party.) Consequently, more of the data are culled from interviews and from other qualitative source materials. Because of the reliance upon such information, some of the inferences and conclusions drawn are necessarily more speculative than those made in the preceding chapter. Nevertheless, it is believed that the data uncovered are illuminating and that insights can be derived regarding organizational influence.

CAMPAIGN FINANCE, THE MX, AND COMMON CAUSE

Despite the evidence demonstrating that Common Cause had an impact on representatives' behavior regarding the MX missile, it is by no means a logical certainty that this influence reflects a general phenomenon that cuts across all issues. In other words, the mere fact that the group and its allies had a significant impact on the MX controversy does not automatically dictate that it possesses analogous clout over campaign finance.

Plausible scenarios can be envisioned which suggest that the organization should be a more important player on this issue or, on the contrary, that it should have no role whatsoever. On the one hand, the association's superior expertise and the previously illustrated membership commitment to campaign reform relative to the MX might seem to dictate that Common Cause would be far more dominant with respect to the former. On the other hand, there are a number of factors, which will be discussed in more depth shortly, such as legislators' own proficiency on this issue, that would appear to undermine the group's potential effectiveness in restructuring the electoral process.

Specifically, Common Cause's impact on regulating elections might logically be judged by one of two standards.[1] The more rigorous is, Does the group have an impact on the functioning of the electoral process? However, given the fact that there have been no major changes to the finance system in a decade and a half, this might be construed as setting up a straw man.

A more reasonable criterion for assessing the efficacy of Common Cause might be the following: Has the organization been able to affect the level of support for campaign finance reform, even if it has been unsuccessful to date in bringing about statutory change? In other words, has the group at least demonstrated the potential to change the status quo?

Answering these questions dictates understanding campaign finance reform and its potential determinants and how it relates to the common framework developed in the preceding chapter about what is takes to be politically influential. This, in turn, requires recognizing the characteristics that make reform stand apart from an issue such as the MX. It is fair to say that these two controversies, which took up so much of Common Cause's time in the 1980s, are qualitatively different from one another. Such a contrast is only partly a function of the substantive versus structure-and-process issue dichotomy typically referred to during discussions of the group. Rather, at least four broad distinctions might be drawn; they can be labeled political, economic, procedural, and technical.

Politically, opposition to the MX in the interest group community was broad in scope, while support of campaign finance reform is narrowly based. Common Cause, as discussed, was placed in an uncharacteristic position of being the leader of a large coalition opposing work on the missile. By contrast, the organization stands largely alone when it comes to campaign finance. It has a few allies such as Congress Watch (the lobbying arm of the Nader public interest groups) and an ad hoc group called Lobbyists and Lawyers for Campaign Finance Reform. However, there is no coordinated union of the type that organized around the MX debate. Again, there are any number of organizations that sign on as part of the coalition but do not expend significant resources. Within the Washington community, the perception is that there is Common Cause and little else. Common Cause staff acknowledge that the coalition they put together on campaign finance does not measure up to the arms control network.

The group's political isolation is also reflected in citizen attitudes. While many did care intensely about Reagan's defense policy, relatively few feel strongly about campaign finance. Survey results consistently discover that electoral reform is low on people's list of priorities. "It would be hard to find five persons to put campaign reform as a top priority," says one key staffer about his member's (admittedly conservative) congressional district. To keep the public eye on the issue and to try to stir up passion among the citizenry, the association often resorts to slash-and-burn techniques such as conducting grassroots campaigns in a muckraking tradition against members of Congress perceived to be in the hands of monied interests – alienating many of these representatives (some of whom have made their objections quite public) in the process.[2]

Economically, billions of dollars were at risk with the MX missile (or many other substantive programs); the direct cost of campaign finance, presuming

this includes some form of public financing, is no more than a couple of hundred million dollars annually. Of course, foes of the status quo would argue that the indirect costs of the present system exceed this amount by a large multiplier, since it is a principal mechanism by which politicians are corrupted. The irony, given the small direct expenditures required for campaign finance, is that opponents of changing the system typically employ resistance to taxes as a rhetorical device to buttress their position.

Procedurally, there were actually three differences between the MX and the regulation of campaign finance. One was that the greater urgency to deal with the MX created by exogenous events (and strong presidential pressure) produced a different context than that surrounding campaign reform; events of the day virtually dictated that the missile's production and deployment be placed on the political agenda. Decisions had to be made whether to authorize the missile and appropriate the necessary monies. By contrast, elections will continue to function whether or not there is reform of the campaign finance system.

A second procedural difference was what the reversion point – the resulting policy if no action is taken – looked like for those championing the progressive position if no changes in the status quo were mandated. When it came to the MX, reversion to the status quo (no additional production or deployment) meant that Common Cause and its allies had achieved their goals. In comparison, Common Cause must shift the status quo to meet its stated targets on electoral reform. As will be illustrated later, the ability of opponents to employ procedural machinations that end up maintaining the status quo has played an extremely prominent role in the recent battles over reform.

A third procedural difference (in a broad sense) is more subtle. Employing procedural maneuvers when it comes to campaign finance may be complicated by the additional factor that legislators may be constrained in their strategic behavior in much the manner discussed by Denzau et al. (1985; but see Krehbiel and Rivers 1988, 1990).[3] On a straight up and down vote, there is a possibility that a "killer amendment" will be offered, against which proponents of reform are unwilling to cast a recorded ballot because it would appear to signal opposition to clean government. While to some extent fears of appearing antidefense may have played a role in the MX debates, the constraint on strategic behavior was clearly weaker (for instance, most opponents cited support of Midgetman as an alternative missile).

Another quite important difference between the MX and campaign finance is technical uncertainty. While such uncertainty about the MX helped make preferences quite malleable, legislators are highly confident that they understand the interaction between money and elections. Therefore, there is strong reason to believe that members of Congress have relatively fixed views about which financing system they would like to see in place. Indeed, this response was echoed time after time in interviews. As one congressional

staffer put it, "The United States Congress is composed of 535 experts on campaign finance." The Common Cause response to such statements is that members of the legislature are myopic, understanding only the interaction of money and elections on their own campaigns.[4] Consequently, they assert, if the organization can provide members with a broader vision, it can influence their behavior. Yet few outsiders believe that such education is Common Cause's strong suit. Alternatively, Fred Wertheimer notes that the group may be able to provide information about what legislators from other parties and in the other chamber are willing to accept as a deal; others claim that the group is ill equipped for this role, particularly since its own point of view makes it difficult to operate as an arbitrator.

The implications of these differences for the ability of Common Cause to influence campaign reform, ceteris paribus, are fourfold:

1. *The absence of a broad group coalition may restrict the organization's ability to have an impact.* In Washington the lack of manpower and contacts restricts the accessibility to key decision makers (although the group's own contacts are probably more effective than they were for the MX, this is counterbalanced by a loss of access associated with not having coalition partners). At the grassroots level, it may be far more difficult to mobilize a legislator's constituents (those not in Common Cause) with respect to campaign finance. In other words, the fact that Common Cause must act alone can only hurt the political appeal that electoral reform might have for representatives.

   This was reflected in interviews in Washington. The idea that nobody outside Common Cause cares (except perhaps about a tangential issue like honoraria or, more recently, term limits) was frequently voiced. The organization's staffers dispute this claim and go on to maintain that incumbent members of Congress have increasingly learned the salience of campaign finance issues for themselves.

2. *Consistent with the idea that those in the grassroots lack interest, the dearth of concentrated economic benefits should provide an advantage for those wishing to amend the campaign finance status quo in comparison to cutting a program like the MX that generates district spending.* (Conversely, this lack of spending puts reform proponents at a disadvantage relative to advocating a program that creates particularistic benefits.) While most entrenched organized interests favor preservation of the current system (or at least specific provisions of it), legislators need not worry about the direct adverse effects that change might have on their districts; for example, there is no obvious linkage between votes for campaign reform and lost jobs among their constituents. This political edge will be reinforced by the fact that the majority of opinion in almost any district or state will be against the status quo in a broad sense. Advocating clean politics is a mother's milk issue, and no member of Congress will have to

worry about explaining to constituents why he or she supported a program that can be interpreted as making politics less corrupt. Given the lack of economic importance and the clear direction of popular opinion, an organization such as Common Cause's chief concern is to influence the *intensity* of district opinion. Even if nobody favors special interests, does anybody really care about their role when the costs are not directly observable?

3. *Campaign finance reform will be more difficult to achieve because of the viability of ignoring the issue altogether and the likelihood that opponents will manipulate the process so that reversion to the status quo is the outcome.* The constraints imposed by the problems of explaining oneself to the home district might either hurt proponents of reform by causing votes for a killer amendment or help them in garnering support for a viable program depending upon who is effectively manipulating the voting agenda.

Interviewees particularly stressed the first of these three procedural obstacles: that there is no driving force dictating that campaign finance reform gets on the legislative agenda. A budget crisis, the Persian Gulf, and any of a number of other issues were cited as reasons for delay. Changing the campaign finance system was often referred to as a luxury that might be afforded if other necessary measures slated for the political agenda moved expeditiously and nothing came up unexpectedly; alternatively, election reform could be ignored and pushed to some other session if things went slowly or more pressing concerns required remedial attention.

4. *Using informational advantages to influence congressional representatives' opinions about campaign finance will be difficult.* Perhaps the principal informational asymmetry concerning reform that its organizational proponents might exploit is electoral. By alerting legislators' grassroots constituency about how the financing system functions and about their representatives' own involvement with monied interests, groups such as Common Cause may have an impact. But the difficulty is that voters just do not appear to be very concerned about such data.

As for technical information, to reiterate, efforts to demonstrate to members of Congress how money functions in the electoral process are unlikely to be a very successful means of changing their opinions. One exception would be to help show members of Congress with varying interests how they might be reconciled in a mutually agreeable manner.

Thus, Common Cause takes upon itself the role of trying to turn the heat up in members' districts or states. This involves both mobilizing individual voters and using the group's credibility to generate publicity through the media, particularly with reports issued through its Campaign Monitoring Project exposing the perceived corruption of the connection between legislators and PACs, and by initiating editorial opinions in local

papers through press releases and other forms of contact. It also sometimes involves using paid media to publicize the unsavory behavior of legislators (by detailing PAC contributions to their campaigns, for example) as a means of embarrassing the member and creating the fear of bad publicity. All in all, however, the lack of informational leverage on this issue as compared to one like the MX should make exerting influence more difficult.

Taken jointly, these four implications have a broader ramification. For Common Cause to have an impact on campaign finance reform, it must almost singlehandedly (without support from other groups) help to forge a coalition of representatives. These members must support a program that the association's leaders find preferable to the status quo and simultaneously be sufficiently strong and cohesive that the proposed changes cannot be derailed by procedural maneuvers. The organization has to accomplish this without being able to rely a great deal upon its technical expertise to persuade members of Congress – although Common Cause may try to play on its credibility in mobilizing district opinion either directly or through the media.

How difficult is it to form such a winning legislative coalition? To make this assessment, it is first necessary to understand where the divisions regarding campaign finance lie.

CHARTING THE DIVISIONS

As mentioned previously, campaign finance reform is an issue about which, in the abstract, there is little diversity of opinion. Most Americans believe that campaigns are too expensive and that "special interests" play too large a role (Sabato 1985); a majority has even been consistently willing to commit federal dollars to public financing of congressional campaigns if it means that private contributions will be prohibited ("Federal Funding of Campaigns" 1987).[5] (Admittedly, given the lack of salience of such issues for most citizens, results can be sensitive to changes in question wording.) Few politicians dare speak out in favor of having well-heeled individuals and groups contribute millions of dollars to campaigns for positions that only pay a fraction of that amount to the officeholder. Members of Congress hate the idea of casting a vote in full public view that represents a clear choice between a reform that is anathema to them and maintenance of the status quo they prefer. To guard against it, they have gone to great lengths to prevent such occurrences or to devise rhetorical counterattacks.

Public protestations condemning the present system notwithstanding, there is no consensus (and a great deal of interest) among politicians on how the campaign finance system should be governed (e.g., Magleby and Nelson 1990). Rather, there are deep divisions regarding its reform that arise because

reconstituting the system has electoral consequences: Changes designed to improve how Congress functions may determine who gets elected.

Essential to comprehending the dynamics of campaign finance reform is recognizing that members' preferences are intimately related to the effects of changes on electoral outcomes. One's perspective on finance reform depends crucially upon two features: *incumbency* and *partisanship*. The desire of politicians to get elected and to be part of a majority party has structured the debate on this issue.

It is by now well understood that the key for incumbents to maximize their probability of winning reelection is to make it difficult for their challengers to raise money (e.g., Jacobson 1980.) While sitting representatives believe (as evidenced by their observed behavior) that they need to raise funds for themselves, members of Congress – particularly those in the House – have a tremendous built-in electoral advantage, and they are well served if few resources are spent on elections.[6] It is more important to keep the amount of money a challenger can raise down than to outspend the challenger by a wide margin.

Of course, all sitting legislators are incumbents. While incumbency, coupled with high reelection rates, might help explain why officeholders are reluctant to change the status quo, it cannot per se account for differences in preferences among members of Congress.[7] This is where partisanship enters the picture. For one thing, there are benefits accruing to members of Congress that are attached to being part of the majority party; for another, there is an interaction between partisanship and the protection afforded by incumbency in which certain elements of the finance system are more beneficial to one party's incumbents than to the other's.

With respect to the first point, Democrats, who have enjoyed virtually a permanent legislative majority since the advent of the New Deal, find that the goal of protecting sitting members meshes nicely with that of maintaining the party's majority status.[8] Measures reinforcing protection for incumbents buttress their control of committee posts and other leadership positions, not to mention the advantages that greater numbers give in realizing their policy objectives, which, in turn, should further strengthen their status as incumbents. Republicans confront a more delicate problem: They want to protect their own status as incumbents, but they also want to set the stage for their party finally capturing the Congress of the United States. They face the tension of trading off their probability of reelection against the likelihood that they will remain in the legislative minority.

Over time, the nature of partisan conflict has evolved. In the early 1970s there appeared to be more homogeneity among incumbent representatives regarding campaign finance; the original legislation was often referred to as an "incumbent protection act."[9] While Republicans were concerned that this would help sustain the Democrats as the majority party, the commonality of interests that link incumbents, along with the need to do something in

light of the burgeoning Watergate crisis, served to override the partisan differences. In contrast, by the 1980s, preferences that are a function of partisanship had become *the* prominent distinguishing feature in the campaign finance debate.[10]

Why the change? Of course, whatever the level of political scandal that marked the second half of the 1980s, the lack of a crisis of Watergate proportions pressuring members of Congress to do something is probably one cause. Another reason may simply be that another decade and a half of minority status in the House (and for nine of the fifteen years in the Senate) has worn on the Republicans and made them less risk averse.

However, a third driving force is that members of each party, especially the GOP, have developed fund-raising advantages that have altered the nature of the relationship between incumbent protection and party aggrandizement. Each party's representatives can propose changes that hurt the other's incumbents far more than their own.

To illustrate this latter point: Republicans are more adept than Democrats at raising small amounts of money from individuals both directly and through their party.[11] Their incumbents possess a clear superiority over Democrats, net of political action committee contributions. This reflects Republicans' more efficient application of modern technology (e.g., direct mail techniques), coupled with the generally higher sociodemographic status of their supporters (Godwin 1988). Republicans are also expert at obtaining money from nonconnected PACs, also known as single-issue and ideological PACs (which give somewhat less than one-third of all PAC dollars). By contrast, Democrats receive the lion's share of business PAC money as a function of having more incumbents and enjoying majority party status; they garner virtually all of the labor PAC money because of unions' traditional alliance with the Democratic party.[12] The Democratic leadership, especially in the House, also channels some of the funds it receives as a function of being the majority party to Democratic challengers through its own so-called leadership PACs (about $5 million per election).

Each party seeks to employ its comparative advantages to protect its own incumbents and solidify its overall position (that is, Democrats try to maintain, and Republicans to attain, majority status without threatening their incumbents). This dictates advocating means of reform that disproportionately lower sources of contributions to opposition party candidates. Both parties publicly take the moral high road and go on record claiming that they want reform. Often those perceived as most hostile to change (such as Mitch McConnell of Kentucky or, until his death, John Heinz of Pennsylvania) are the proposers of (nonviable) reform legislation.

Democrats demand reductions in spending through expenditure limitations on total campaign spending, while they seek to protect business and labor PACs.[13] This routinely involves some form of public financing, since the ruling in *Buckley v. Valeo* stipulated that spending ceilings can only be

enforced when candidates accept funding.[14] Such support might involve raising money through tax credits or tax check-offs or by dipping into general revenues. Another method, which would surely be the subject of judicial scrutiny, would grant discount mailing and broadcast-advertising rates as a means of circumventing the restrictions on limiting first amendment rights. A final possibility, as suggested by a number of interviewees (see also Cox 1982), is to make a compelling case for limiting speech through expenditure limitations without public financing so that they could survive review by the courts where the 1974 legislation could not.

Republicans inevitably retort that the American people are opposed to any more taxes. (Although, to reiterate, the aggregate cost, somewhere between $100 and $200 million annually, is a trivial public expenditure – consider that the agricultural subsidy for mohair in 1990 was $60 million.) As for broadcast discounts, hostile Republicans generally led by McConnell retort that this only creates Food Stamps for politicians. Members of the GOP argue instead for attacking business, labor, and leadership PACs by restricting how much, if any, they can give, while protecting small individual contributions, non-connected PACs, and party organization expenditures. Lowering PAC contribution limits would hurt Democrats especially because their labor allies tend to give larger contributions than their business counterparts; for example, cutting PAC levels in half would injure only those PACs that tend to give more than $2,500.

Thus, while supporting reform, each party's rhetoric differs. Democrats call for reducing the role of money in elections by limiting spending levels and, out of necessity, relying on public funds or subsidies. Republicans advocate bolstering political parties, turning away from "special interests" (PACs) toward the common person by encouraging small individual contributions, and ensuring that the taxpayers are not picking up the tab.

Common Cause advocates many of the elements in each party's program. The organization's position is that it is troubled by at least three changes in the system that have occurred over the past decade and a half: the widespread growth of PACs after the 1974 legislation; the increase in the amount of money spent on campaigns; and the development of forms of spending – independent expenditures, soft money, bundling, political party intervention, etc. – that circumvent the rules promulgated during the mid-1970s.[15]

The sheer number of PACs, which barely exceeded 100 before 1974, quickly increased to about 1,000, and now exceeds 4,000 (Mahood 1990). While many social scientists are unperturbed and point out that their growth is simply reflective of a new vehicle by which monied interests funnel their dollars, Common Cause views this vast increase in PACs with considerable alarm.

Campaign costs have also spiraled. In the House, for example, the total money raised for elections went from $65.7 million in 1976 to $277.4 million in 1988 – a better than 400 percent increase in absolute dollars. In the Senate the increase was fivefold, from $39.1 million to $199.1 million. Again, many

social scientists worry less about the level of monies spent on campaigns than the amount that challengers have to lay out. However, while Common Cause increasingly voices concerns about ensuring challengers funding and increasing turnover, their bottom line is putting a lid on spending.

Finally, the group views with dismay many of the means developed to evade the statutory limitations initiated in the mid-1970s. Many of these consequences were unintended and unforeseen by those drafting the legislation; others were facilitated by the *Buckley v. Valeo* decision; and, one, soft money, was the inadvertent result of the FECA Amendments of 1979. There tends to be less academic dissension on these issues, except perhaps when it comes to the role of political parties.

As a result of its interpretations of the status quo, Common Cause's ideal bill would (1) reduce the role of PACs (a Republican preference); (2) fix limits on campaign spending (a Democratic preference); (3) provide alternative resources such as public financing or subsidized mail and television access (a Democratic preference at least to the extent that it is necessary to implement spending limits); and (4) eliminate soft money, contributions used for party building (by and large a Republican preference because it would hurt large contributors such as unions).[16]

Given the preference distribution within both parties, Common Cause would appear to possess ample room for political maneuver. In other words, the organization and its leaders could have what it would consider a desirable influence on the electoral process by helping to forge a bipartisan coalition (net of a sufficient Democratic majority to override a presidential veto or the election of a Democratic president). There are two key requirements, it would seem. The first is to come up with a scheme that is sufficiently balanced in its electoral consequences that enough members of both parties to form an oversized majority would prefer it to the current campaign finance system. The second is to use whatever means are at the group's disposal to get legislators (and especially party leaders) to commit to the coalition so that it is sufficiently cohesive to prevent opponents from using tactics that would ultimately maintain the status quo. For any change that would aid Democrats (such as expenditure limits), there would need to be a compensating provision that would benefit Republicans (such as limitations on the contributions of business and labor PACs). While there would not be substantial changes in either turnover rates or partisan composition, the result would nevertheless reduce the absolute amounts of money expended on elections.

The beauty of such a compromise would be that both Democrats and Republicans would be better off in at least three related senses:

1. *Claiming credit.* Each side could take credit for helping to purge the political system of corrupt influences.
2. *Institutional.* Legislators would have to spend less of their time raising funds, not to mention considering campaign finance reform. Senate

members especially complain about the rigors and the degrading nature of raising funds for reelection. Reform would allow both houses of Congress to operate more smoothly and efficiently as institutions (particularly the Senate, where the norm of senatorial courtesy operates) and would make the quality of life on the Hill far more pleasant.

3. *Political.* Substantial reform could be employed to get the pesky issue of campaign finance removed from the political agenda, if not once and for all, then at least for a substantial period until the consequences of the mandated changes have been realized. Even though campaign finance is not a great concern of the average voter, getting rid of the electoral reform issue would undoubtedly please most members of Congress.

Indeed, it is possible to illustrate in very simple fashion how there are numerous possible compromises on campaign finance (Figure 9.1). Assume, reasonably, that there are two basic keys to arriving at a compromise on campaign reform: PAC limits and spending ceilings.[17] For presentational purposes, also assume that there are only two members of the legislature, X_D and X_R, the first a Democrat and the second a Republican (one might think of each of these members as actually constituting a political party) and a status quo, X_{SQ}. The Democrat wants low spending and high PAC limits as represented by his or her ideal point; the Republican prefers no spending limits but severe restrictions on PAC contributions as demonstrated by his or her point; and the status quo is high PAC contribution levels and no spending ceilings. In Figure 9.1, both the Democrat and Republican are indifferent among the large number of alternatives represented by the 45 degree line drawn through the status quo; this line is interpreted as the set of alternatives that are those mixes of limitations that are electorally neutral. Democrats (Republicans) would be better off relative to the status quo if any of the alternatives to the right (left) of the line were chosen.

Particularly given the fact that legislators' preferences would support at least a short-term solution to the problem, the question one might ask is, Why have efforts to reform the campaign finance system by designing a politically balanced solution that exploited these gains from trade failed? More germane in the context of the larger research project presented here, why has Common Cause been unable to broker a compromise, and is this due to some failure on the organization's part?

Answering these questions requires an understanding of what has happened over the last half decade. Given this background information, it will be possible to turn back to the task of assessing Common Cause's role in the entire process.

EVENTS OF 1985–1991

Despite the dramatic rise in the number of PACs, the spiral in the amount of money spent on congressional elections, and a blizzard of Common Cause

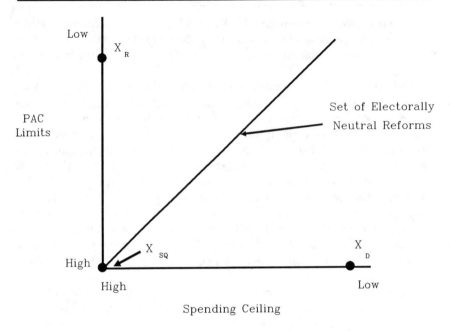

Figure 9.1. Possible campaign finance reform strategies.

press releases on the subject, the issue of campaign finance remained largely absent from the congressional agenda for a decade after the events of 1974. The system created by the FECA Amendments of that year, as modified in *Buckley v. Valeo*, continued to function uninterrupted. Only one serious legislative attempt was made to modify the status quo, and it resulted in only the most limited reforms.[18]

Given a decade-long history of failure, what, then, accounts for the resurgence of electoral reform on the congressional agenda in the mid-1980s? When all is said and done, the principal explanation is the decision of two men, neither a typical Common Cause proponent, sitting in the U.S. Senate.

THE ENTREPRENEURS: BOREN AND BYRD

By virtually everyone's account, the immediate impetus for reform was the efforts of two entrepreneurs: Boren, the Oklahoma Democrat elected in 1978, and Senator Robert Byrd, a Democrat from West Virginia who led his party in the Senate from 1977 to 1988 (1981 to 1986 as minority leader; the rest as majority leader). As instigators for campaign reform, not to mention collaborators, each of these men might have seemed like strange candidates.

Generally, Oklahoma Democrats are not associated with campaign reform. Yet, Boren combined being called "the most popular politician in recent

Oklahoma history" (Barone and Ujifusa 1987, p. 982) with acting as a leader of the reform process. His dedication to reconstituting the finance system appears genuine, stemming from a neat confluence of true conviction and political experience.

Elected to the state legislature at the ripe age of twenty-six, Boren quickly developed a reputation as an advocate of clean government. In 1974, now all of thirty-three, with the Watergate scandal fresh in the voters' minds and an incumbent (David Hall) embroiled in a scandal for which he would eventually be jailed, Boren ran for governor. He pledged to reinstitute clean government (his campaign symbol was a broom), and he was elected the state's chief executive. Four years later, when Senator Dewey Bartlett announced his retirement, the governor decided to run for the vacated seat. In the election, he chose not to accept PAC money and to make his primary challenger's acceptance of such funds a matter of contention, although Boren's primary issue was support of the Kemp–Roth tax cut proposal. He won the primary by a 3 to 2 margin over this competitor and the general election with a 2 to 1 majority.

In this first term, Boren kept fairly quiet on the issue of electoral reform. He proposed a modest PAC reform bill, but it died without a hearing in the Rules and Administration Committee, of which he was not even a member. The senator garnered a reputation as one of the most conservative of Democrats in the upper chamber and as a strong supporter of his state's parochial interests (oil, for one). Boren again renounced contributions from PACs when he ran for reelection in 1984, which obviously put him at a fund-raising disadvantage, but given that he faced a weak challenger, this burden was only marginally onerous at most.[19]

As his second term commenced, Boren, much to the shock of many both inside and outside of the Senate, began more actively employing finance reform to make his mark in the Senate.[20] ("Boren came out of left field. ... it wasn't like we were working Boren," notes Common Cause's Hedlund.) As a Democrat opposed to PACs, he seemed perfect as a middle-of-the-road, bipartisan coalition leader. His efforts (and, interestingly, not really Common Cause's) in the mid-1980s breathed new life into the movement for campaign reform.

Boren's entrepreneurial activities might have quickly faded from the political agenda had it not been for Byrd's own lack of affection for fund raising, not just from PACs but generally (a position that was also more in tune with the interests of the Democratic party). The majority leader possessed the authority to keep the issue of campaign reform on the front burner in 1987 and 1988 for almost as long as he wished; he chose for it to remain there for a sustained period when others wished that it would disappear.

Byrd's antipathy for the status quo (he analogized the current finance system to a political version of AIDS) flowed not from any special moral

repugnancy about money per se but, rather, from a desire to make the Senate function efficiently as an institution, as well as his own disgruntlement with the demeaning nature of fund raising. By all accounts Byrd really does possess a strong reverence for the Senate. His frustration with his colleagues' constant preoccupation with raising money for their reelection bids, which caused them to ask him and other senatorial leaders to postpone the work of the upper chamber, prompted him to make campaign reform a major priority. As campaigns for seats in the upper chamber became increasingly costly (for example, in 1984 Jesse Helms of North Carolina spent $17 million dollars to maintain his Senate seat, the first time that any senator spent more than $10 million, and two years later Alan Cranston expended more than $11 million), the toll that fund raising takes on the Senate became increasingly palpable.[21]

Byrd himself had faced a well-financed incumbent in 1982, against whom he spent $1.8 million to win 387,000 votes. Raising such resources in a small, poor state was no easy feat, and Byrd was forced to appeal to interests outside of his state. Even in 1988, when he faced a weaker challenger, Byrd spent over $1 million. Thus, as will be discussed shortly, Byrd was unwilling to let Boren's initiative fade away; rather, he committed precious floor time and considerable goodwill in an attempt to break the deadlock.

THE FIRST OFFENSIVE: THE PUSH FOR PAC REFORM

In 1985, coincidentally just months after the final MX missile votes had taken place, Boren spearheaded the fight to reform the campaign finance system. With Barry Goldwater, the maverick Republican who had become a biting critic of PACs in his twilight years in the Senate, he proposed to limit the amount that PACs could give to congressional candidates. Specifically, their bill would have lowered the maximum PAC gift to $3,000, raised the amount of individual contributions to $1,500, capped aggregated PAC contributions (no more than $125,000 in the House, up to $750,000 in the largest states in the Senate), offset independent expenditures with free media time, and restricted bundling.

This proposal was not merely a thinly veiled effort by Democrats to capture the moral high ground by proposing a one-sided partisan program. It reflected an effort to build a true coalition in favor of campaign reform – albeit, to many of those dedicated to change, in a limited form. Most notably, there were elements in their legislation that were potentially appealing to members of both parties. Limits on PAC contributions would hurt the Democrats. The lack of overall campaign ceilings would appeal to Republicans. In doing so, the bill also successfully avoided the thorny question of public financing of elections, which opponents of campaign finance reform are so quick to make an issue. By contrast, limitations on independent expenditures and bundling would generally hurt the Republicans, and the increase in individual

contributions was less than Republicans would have preferred, although it was still better than the current $1,000.[22]

As for Common Cause, while Boren's exclusion of public financing and spending ceilings meant that his measure was more modest than the organization's leaders would have liked, the bill was far better than the status quo. And the group was "starved for a legislative victory" (Jackson 1988, p. 242). Its official position, according to Fred Wertheimer, was:

> To see the Boren–Goldwater PAC limit amendment passed in the Senate and a companion bill ... passed in the House. Our long term campaign finance goal continues to be a comprehensive new system for financing congressional races similar to the presidential one.
> It may take another election or even two to set the stage for convincing Congress that it must undertake this kind of fundamental reform for its own campaigns. And the Boren–Goldwater fight provides us with an important bridge in moving from our present congressional system to a comprehensive new one. (Wertheimer 1986)[23]

Consequently, the organization came on board as the principal association supporting the legislation. The group mounted the first of numerous full-scale mobilizations of its membership, characterized by telephone network alerts and pleas for members to contact members of Congress, designed to bring grassroots pressure. As in the campaign against the MX, it relied heavily upon such grassroots initiatives, while employing Washington lobbying as well. Again, special attention was paid to senators who were seen as potentially movable; these, for example, were the objects of the group's negative media campaigns.

Also, similar to the anti-MX campaign, Common Cause's opposition stemmed less from opposing groups than from other political actors. "It's really Common Cause versus the members of Congress," remarks Ellen Miller of the Center for Responsive Politics. Although those operating on the other side included lobbying groups who operate PACs, the primary resistance emanated from members of Congress themselves. Nor was President Reagan a big advocate of reform.

The initial problem that faced Boren and his allies was how to maneuver the bill onto the Senate's agenda. Of course, this is simpler in the Senate than in the House, since in the former germaneness is not a criterion for amendments. At first, the senator threatened to offer his reforms as an amendment to a pact with Micronesia that was vital to the defense establishment because the Kwajalein Missile Range was (ironically) the key test site for the MX missile. The potential havoc that this could generate for the Pentagon gave Boren a certain degree of leverage. He agreed to withdraw his amendment in return for a promise that it would be debated and voted on in early December. In anticipation, Common Cause launched an all-out lobbying blitz with special emphasis on grassroots mobilization and cultivation of the media.

When December rolled around, however, Boren's colleagues – supporters

and critics alike – reneged on this agreement. First, they voted 7 to 84 against killing the PAC amendment, which had been attached to a bill dealing with low-level radioactive waste, so that they could say that they had voted for reform. However, as previously arranged, they then pulled the Boren plan from further consideration and referred it back to the Senate Rules and Administration Committee for hearings.[24]

What accounts for this turn of events? The explanation given for public consumption was "a lack of desire on the part of many members to declare themselves one way or the other on the touchy political issue of 'special interest' campaign contributions" (Pressman 1985b, p. 2567). What this actually meant was that there was insufficient support to pass the bill on its merits. However, opponents, particularly those in the Republican leadership such as Heinz, head of the National Republican Senatorial Committee (who introduced his own partisan proposal), and then Majority Leader Robert Dole, did not want to vote against campaign finance in a "vote of conscience." Boren made the best of the situation and claimed that getting the Senate on record as advocating campaign finance reform was a major victory. "That left only frustrated officials of Common Cause" (Pressman 1985b, p. 2568), who were planning to employ the Senate vote to launch a major campaign.

Come 1986, Boren was back as promised. This time he managed to get the Senate to vote for reform, only to have his efforts again derailed by a classic case of agenda manipulation.

In August, on a 69 to 30 bipartisan vote (Democrats voted 43–3, Republicans, 26–27), the Senate passed Boren's proposal. As Figure 9.2 shows, Boren was able to carry virtually all liberals and moderates, with conservatives splitting more evenly in their support and opposition. However, it should be cautioned that some who backed Boren's effort may have been behaving strategically because they knew what was to come.

Immediately after passage, Senator Rudy Boschwitz of Minnesota, the designated Republican point man on campaign finance, made a blatantly partisan counterproposal. He suggested including in the legislation a prohibition on PAC contributions to national political parties – a change that would have considerably exacerbated the already huge gap between the Democratic and Republican parties' fund-raising capacities (on this gap and the role of various campaign committees, see Herrnson 1988, Sabato 1988) – a prohibition on leadership PACs (an attack on House Democratic leaders), and a requirement to disclose the sources of soft money from corporations, unions, and other donors. On a 58 to 42 vote, the Boschwitz proposal passed on an almost strictly Republican basis (51–2 Republican, 7–40 Democrat). (Reports were that the handful of Democrats who voted with the Republicans on the amendment to the amendment did so once they knew what the outcome would be; that is, given that the final result was known, they chose not to vote "against" campaign finance.) Members of both parties and Common Cause understood that House Democrats would reject the Boren–

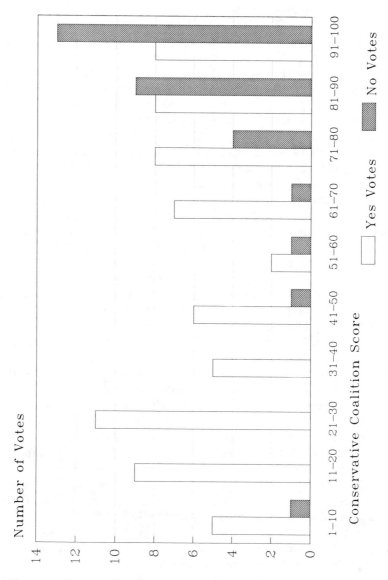

Figure 9.2. Support for the Boren initiative.

Boschwitz bill out of hand while finding some means of not appearing to be against campaign finance themselves if it were reported to the lower chamber.[25]

The campaign finance initiative of 1986 was dead. After a variety of machinations, both sides agreed to forgo the final vote needed to send it to the lower chamber. Boren contented himself with having the Senate on record in support of reform; Common Cause leaders remained chagrined.

Indeed, some did interpret the events of 1986 as a potential breakthrough. For the first time, there was a bipartisan majority on public record in favor of campaign reform although, in political science jargon, the support of certain Republicans may have reflected strategic factors rather than sincere preferences. Nonetheless, it was clear that there was a fairly large proportion of GOP members who favored something along the lines of the Boren legislation (for example, Goldwater and John Stennis), even if they were unwilling to break ranks with the other members of their party when it came to voting on the Boschwitz legislation. Supporters of PACs, certainly, took the threat that future reforms might be successful seriously. This concern was exacerbated when the 1986 elections reconstituted a Democratic majority and party leader Byrd indicated a strong willingness to throw his full weight behind campaign reform. The PAC supporters mobilized to advance changes that would not heavily affect them.[26]

THE SECOND OFFENSIVE: BYRD JOINS THE FRAY

In 1987 the quest to enact campaign finance reform in the Senate heated up as Byrd took center stage. Byrd's more sweeping legislation was, by and large, what Common Cause was looking for and the group was consistently active in promoting change. Yet, the irony of the situation is just as the 1986 election results changed the Senate's makeup so that a bill along the lines of Boren–Goldwater might have become viable, he led campaign finance in a more partisan, divisive direction. Boren himself was forced to endorse the new package if he wished to remain a Democratic leader on electoral reform. ("They said to Boren ... we're taking over, but we're more than pleased to have you still be our spokesman," is how Steven Stockmayer, head of the National Association of Business Political Action Committees, characterizes the situation.) The tone, however faint, of bipartisanship heard during the previous session was replaced with that of vehement partisanship.

One of Byrd's first actions after being reinstalled as majority leader was to endorse a campaign finance bill with 44, all Democratic, cosponsors, give it the prominent designation of S.2, and promise to make its passage a priority for the upcoming session. While this proposal contained the major provisions of the earlier Boren legislation, it added stipulations for spending ceilings (to which Byrd was strongly committed) and for complete public financing of campaigns through an expanded tax check-off. (Obviously complete

funding was needed to meet Byrd's institutional goals.) From the perspective of Common Cause, of course, this was a big improvement over the Boren–Goldwater bill. Republicans, not to be seen as opponents of campaign reform, proposed two bills of their own, each of which focused on restricting PACs.

Thus, while virtually every senator was on record as favoring campaign finance reform of some sort, Byrd's insistence on spending ceilings transformed the battle into even more of a partisan dogfight. Much of whatever Republican support Boren stood to pick up from the previous sessions vanished in light of attempts to cap aggregate spending.

The majority leader and his allies had created a monumental task for themselves. As mentioned before, with the reconstituted Democratic majority, there was probably sufficient partisan support for reform with spending ceilings to produce (at least with some coaxing) a Senate majority. (Indeed, Byrd allowed some changes in his proposal to placate skeptical, largely Southern, Democrats.) However, Republicans could conceivably employ a filibuster, which would require a supermajority of 60 to break; that is, GOP solidarity could stop Byrd in his tracks without a direct public ballot on the proposed legislation.[27] Republicans could structure the voting process so that ballots would be held on procedural motions, which presumably, are more readily ignored by constituents.

Evidence of the partisan divisions were quickly uncovered in the Rules and Administration Committee when an effort in markup by Senator Ted Stevens of Alaska to cut allowable PAC contributions in half and raise permissible individual contributions to $2,500 was rejected on a straight 3–8 party vote. The committee then voted the amended bill to the floor by an 8–3 party line vote.

An early test of Senator Byrd's ability to break a potential filibuster by securing Republican support while keeping his party in line was also discouraging for reform advocates: A budget amendment by Frank Murkowski, the junior Republican Senator from Alaska, calling for the $100 million that Democrats wanted put aside for public financing of congressional campaigns to be shifted to veterans' programs was only defeated 50 to 48. Not a single GOP member broke ranks while three Democrats defected.

Despite this, Byrd – and those at Common Cause mobilized in support – were undeterred. On June 3, he brought the legislation that had been voted out of committee to the Senate floor. A first attempt to break cloture on June 9 failed 52 to 47 with only two Republicans (Chafee of Rhode Island and Stafford of Vermont) and three Southern Democrats (Heflin and Shelby of Alabama and Hollings of South Carolina) deviating.[28] Although both sides expressed a desire to reach a compromise, none was immediately forthcoming. Dole and other Republican leaders seemed to have little desire to cut a deal. On June 11, Byrd and Boren did introduce a substitute amendment that was designed to pacify some Republicans; it halved the amount of public monies available to senators by instituting a matching

funds alternative. Nevertheless, subsequent votes to invoke cloture on four consecutive days beginning on June 16 failed by 49–46, 51–47, 50–47, and 45–43; only the number of abstentions changed.

Even though there was no movement on either side, Byrd vowed to continue the battle, although he did permit the Senate to begin to consider other legislation as well. Rumors of a bipartisan compromise went unrealized; the majority leader's position was that an agreement was possible as long as spending limits were included. Byrd's insistence on aggregate ceilings allowed hostile Republicans to focus their rhetorical opposition on the public funding provision that was the sine qua non for the imposition of legal spending limits. In July the Senate Democrats proposed to employ discounted mail and broadcast advertising rates as the principal public funding mechanism. Reformers did pick up two votes – Hollings and Nancy Kassebaum of Kansas – on the next cloture vote, which took place September 10 (the vote was now 53–42), but received no more five days later on the seventh and final vote of the year. Byrd resolved to come back in 1988, when he hoped election year pressures might sway the few additional votes he was lacking.

However, that February, after a memorable record-setting eighth cloture vote, Byrd gave up. Prior to the vote, Byrd pulled out all the stops. Instead of the usually gentle filibusters in which members are not forced to talk throughout the day and night, the majority leader opted for two nonstop sessions before a truce was reached. The true highlight was when Byrd instructed the sergeant-at-arms to summon Packwood to the Senate under a rarely used provision that gives the majority leader the right to demand the presence of absent legislators; this resulted in the senator from Oregon being dragged feet first into the chamber. Common Cause praised Byrd's tactics.

Ultimately, though, after not gaining a single vote, Byrd admitted defeat and pulled the bill. While Republican operatives admit that Byrd embarrassed them by making them employ a filibuster (and Republicans have eschewed this strategy subsequently), and while the majority leader had come within seven votes of breaking the deadlock, there was no more support to be had. Republican hints that a compromise was possible (an eight-senator bipartisan committee had been formed) did not come close to reaching fruition. Minority Leader Dole (no friend of campaign finance) held firm, even though he was running for president and supporters of change hoped that the embarrassment that could be created from being perceived as antireform would cause him to soften. For example, a Common Cause tactic termed the "Dole watch" was to infiltrate the candidate's presidential campaign rallies and events with people who would question the candidate about campaign reform. Subsequent efforts to reach a solution also failed to galvanize support; for example, Boren proposed that historical dominance by one party (as by the Democratic party in the South) be taken into account in setting spending limits as a means of appeasing Republicans.

Thus, after three years of debate, culminating in the grueling battle of February 1988, the embittered members of the Senate had not even gotten to the point of sending a bill to the House. Perhaps the only lesson learned was that campaign reform was an issue that senators would be happy to ignore for a while. By 1989, with Byrd stepping aside, this seemed quite possible. Although the new majority leader, George Mitchell, was not adverse to reform, and while with Boren and Byrd he had introduced yet another piece of legislation with many of the same features as the previous Boren–Byrd bills, it was believed at the time that little would happen without initial House movement.

LIFE AFTER BYRD

In many ways, the situation looked bleak for proponents of reform as 1989 rolled around and attention switched to the House. Except for the true believers, pessimism was the watchword of the day.

It was not that the House lacked advocates of campaign reform. Al Swift, the chairman of the House Administration Committee Election Subcommittee and co-chairman of the bipartisan task force studying campaign finance laws, was willing to try to form a coalition. He had in the past offered legislation similar to the proposed Senate compromises of 1987. Swift had generally tried to avoid direct public financing, preferring the use of discounted media and mail rates instead. However, except for some hearings, efforts to advance such a program in the House have never gone very far.

There are a variety of explanations for the lack of progress in the House relative to the Senate. One conveyed in interviews is that Swift lacked the devotion to the cause of either a Byrd or a Boren. He had other issues, such as voter registration (so-called Motor Voter bills), on his plate and was not interested in making a big splash on campaign finance that did not produce legislation.[29] Another is simply that the nature of the House means that the ability of one person to get an initiative like campaign reform on the agenda is considerably more limited than in the Senate. In addition, election financing is even a touchier issue for representatives than it is for senators: At least in the upper chamber Republicans have been able to assume control in recent years, it can be argued that the supply of available cash for challengers is already there, and, therefore, incumbents of neither party are considered invulnerable. In the House, where current members are reelected at the rate of 98 percent, the role of money and PACs and the potentially stultifying effect of additional campaign limits is an even more sensitive issue. Given these considerable obstacles, Speaker Wright had in earlier years publicly announced that the Senate would have to move first.

As for Common Cause, its position remained relatively stable and its leadership ever hopeful. The group preferred bill (Synar–Leach) included, among other provisions, limits on the aggregate amount of PAC money a candidate can receive, elimination of leadership PACs, a relatively tight

spending ceiling of $400,000 ($550,000 if there is a runoff), and the institution of public financing in the form of matching funds for gifts of less than $250 (the major difference from Swift's plan). Yet many felt that there was little reason for hope.

However, just when it appeared that all interest in legislation was disappearing, the continuing saga of electoral reform took several, largely unexpected, turns. One was that after eight years of passivity from the Reagan administration, in June 1989 George Bush proposed his own plan to reform the campaign finance system.

The Bush proposal was a mixed blessing. On the one hand, it promised to focus the sort of attention on the finance system that Wertheimer and others craved (Alston and Craney 1989). The president had provided what Kingdon (1984) would characterize as a "policy window," and groups like Common Cause were ready with their own solutions now that a problem had been defined.[30] It also seemed (at the time) to lessen the likelihood that the president would be able to veto a reasonable looking package if one were voted out of Congress and increased the probability that the administration might assist if legislation seemed imminent.

On the other hand, Bush's plan was less dramatic than that favored by progressives such as those leading Common Cause, and even a cursory glance made it abundantly evident that the proposal was overwhelmingly partisan. For example, it called for eliminating all PACs *except* those that give disproportionately to Republicans, it attacked incumbents from all directions, and it tried to bolster party organizations. Even certain Republicans, worried about their own incumbent status, were reportedly concerned about some of the incumbent-bashing provisions. Indeed, the Republican leadership, while agreeing to introduce the president's legislation, came out with its own package.

In short, compared to the early Boren programs or even to the modified Byrd proposals, the Bush program was extreme in its partisanship. In the form it was introduced, it was dead on arrival and had the potential of further galvanizing partisan divisions. Indeed, a number of Democrats and even some Republicans were perturbed by what they felt was a lack of consultation and cooperation on the part of the White House.[31]

While to many the Bush initiative was a surprise (including, allegedly, some in the White House), another even more unexpected event began to rock Washington in late 1989. Increasingly, attention began to be directed toward the large soft money contributions given by Charles Keating, head of the failed Lincoln Savings and Loan, and his relationship to five senators (known around Washington as the Gang of Five) – Alan Cranston, Dennis DeConcini, John Glenn, John McCain, and Donald Riegle. In addition scandals were rapidly engulfing Alfonse D'Amato (which precipitated "Senator Pothole" himself to embrace public financing of elections) and David Durenberger.[32]

Indeed, in late 1989 evidence began to surface that the deadlock might

suddenly be breaking. The most notable event was the public pledge at the National Press Club of House Minority Leader Robert Michel that spending limits, in principle, were open to negotiation, which represented a crucial step beyond the GOP proposal issued just months earlier.[33] There was talk of an imminent bipartisan agreement and of movement on campaign finance by the spring of 1990.

However, as the months wore on, such optimism was not realized in the House. While over forty meetings were held, little progress was made. Wertheimer's efforts to broker an agreement proved unsuccessful. Much to the delight of many Republicans, the recalcitrant group in the House turned out to be Thomas Foley and the Democratic leadership. In a world where both parties' leaderships must simultaneously be disposed to agree to compromise and sell the accord over the cries of dissident elements within each party, such recalcitrance is deadly. Thus, while Michel seemed willing to move – and was willing to rebuke Minority Whip Newt Gingrich and others who opposed this inclination – the Democratic leadership was not.

Given the difficulties in the House, attention again turned to the Senate. Embattled by the savings and loan and Durenberger–D'Amato scandals, members of the upper chamber abandoned their previous decision to remain on the sidelines until the House acted first.

Ultimately, however, bipartisan attempts again failed. In the Senate, Dole and his fellow Republicans appeared generally unexcited about the idea of actually brokering an agreement. Interestingly, in August first the Senate and then the House did indeed pass finance reform legislation. But the basic strategic problem of implementing reform remained untackled: its partisan nature. Thus, after a series of partisan roll calls in the Senate, legislation widely applauded by Common Cause was passed with only one Democrat in opposition and only five Republicans in favor (the final vote was 59–40). Buttressed by antitax rhetoric and their own nonviable alternatives that went down to defeat, Republicans proved willing to step up and vote against reform. In the House, a predictably weaker, but again partisan, bill followed with only 3 Democrats and 15 Republicans deviating from the dominant party position (the final vote was 255–155). Predictably, Common Cause was far less happy with the House legislation; a group-endorsed amendment (Synar–Obey) went down to defeat in a trail of procedural maneuverings.

Nevertheless, Common Cause hailed the Senate bill's passage as a "milestone." The organization had expended considerable efforts, including its usual slash-and-burn tactics, to get what it called a "Keating Five Campaign Reform Bill" passed. The group's efforts, in particular, to link members of Congress other than the Keating Five with the savings and loan scandal created some strong animosity from traditional supporters.

However, with a Bush veto looming in the background – despite the chief executive's previous proposal he has made clear that he will not accept public spending and spending ceilings – efforts to forge a consensus in con-

ference failed. (Indeed, this gave the Democrats the opportunity to pass legislation *knowing* it would not become law.) While Democrats presumably could have agreed upon a bill and gotten involved in a war of words with Republicans over whether the legislation represented clean government or profligate spending, forging the two-thirds majority for a veto override was out of the question.

As of this writing, campaign finance has again passed in the Senate in a partisan context with Common Cause, unlike many others (particularly its opponents), remaining optimistic about its prospects. In the House, the leadership has taken a back seat compared to the previous years, although any successful legislation is sure to have the leadership's stamp. Democrats and Republicans find themselves in a rhetorical chess game: Democrats open with charges of corruption, Republicans counter with cries of no new taxes, Democrats reply with no taxes and media discounts, Republicans (showing that their antagonism has little to do with taxes per se) counter with charges of creating Food Stamp politicians. The president is largely sitting out the battle, except for pledging publicly to veto unacceptable legislation.

Interestingly, even the popular press has become increasingly unimpressed with the passage of legislation in one house of Congress or the other, seemingly recognizing that without a bipartisan consensus, reform efforts will probably continue to flounder. For example, a recent *New York Times* article after the Senate action was titled "A Revival: The Campaign Finance Show, The Senate Passes an Overhaul, but Nothing Really Changes" (Berke 1991). The Rochester *Democrat and Chronicle* lamented in its editorial after the same action that "Once More, Election Reform Is Doomed" (1991).

Yet, Wertheimer's and Common Cause's reaction is that progress is being made: Moving from Boren–Goldwater to the Senate legislation is progress, and the media simply are slow to recognize it. To others, the policy window is slowly closing as the memories of past scandals become more distant.

COMMON CAUSE AND CAMPAIGN FINANCE REFORM

Where does Common Cause fit into all of this? Whether legislation passes or not says little about whether Common Cause is making a difference. Given the group's media clout, a popular interpretation might be that Common Cause is highly influential when it comes to campaign finance. The group's public pronouncements trumpet this interpretation. Do the events of 1985 to 1991 provide such evidence given the theoretical outline of what it takes to exercise legislative influence? The answer advanced here is that, contrary to what may be popular wisdom, Common Cause can only claim, at best, to be marginally effective.

Perhaps the most useful and fairest means of characterizing the group's influence involves breaking the process of altering the status quo into its two crucial stages: the emergence of campaign finance on the congressional agenda

and the subsequent construction of an agreement that from the organization's perspective is an improvement over the status quo. Making use of this dichotomy is especially sensible in the present instance because, while the statutory regulations governing the financing of elections have remained generally stable for a decade and a half, the issue of campaign finance has been elevated from virtual oblivion to a prominent place on the agenda. Put another way, while the necessary condition for campaign reform was successfully met, the sufficient condition for actually changing the status quo went unsatisfied.

Proponents of Common Cause who were interviewed argued that the matter of finance reform would have simply disappeared had it not been for the group's diligent efforts, notably in publicizing the issue through the media. "To me the genius has been to keep the issue alive," asserts David Cohen. There is an intuitive appeal to such a perspective. After all, no one disputes that Common Cause has developed a credibility that allows it to promote the issue of campaign finance in the nation's media. The group can regularly produce laundry lists of newspapers ("an uncanny ability," as one congressional staffer puts it) from around the nation that advocate changes akin to what Common Cause supports. The argument in favor of Common Cause might focus on the stochastic nature of politics (and political scandal): Anytime a proposal finds its way onto the congressional agenda, there is a possibility that something will happen and that, therefore, the organization's contribution is crucial if only for keeping campaign reform alive.

However, when the actual events of 1985 to 1991 are closely scrutinized, evidence that Common Cause actually got the issue on the agenda in the first place seems slim. From what has been recounted above, it is difficult to maintain that the group and its leadership were the principal determinants of getting a reform initiative in front of the Congress. Neither Boren nor Byrd became advocates of reform because Common Cause told them they should or because they came from states with strong constituencies that were particularly easy for the organization to mobilize. Indeed, neither man is the stereotypical liberal do-gooder with whom one would have expected the group's leadership to be especially comfortable. Nor did Common Cause create the Keating scandal, although to some rather small extent it might have succeeded in directing attention toward what had happened.

Is the contention here that Common Cause played no role in getting reform on the agenda? No. But in light of the events of 1985 to 1991, coupled with the lack of any clear mechanism to accomplish this goal except for generating media publicity (since the electorate is generally disinterested and politicians believe they know how money and politics work), an affirmative argument is reduced to a subtler level than proponents of the organization might like. The strongest propositions that might be made for the contention that Common Cause kept the issue of finance reform alive are (1) that the organization's work provides the likes of Boren and Byrd with a strong public relations

weapon to use against their colleagues and (2) that Common Cause's existence as a potential ally makes adopting the issue of reform more inviting to incumbents. However, given that most citizens would probably think, even without Common Cause's effort, that the role of money in elections is one bordering on corruption, the former assertion is not terribly convincing.

What, then, can be said about Common Cause's effectiveness once the issue of campaign finance got on the congressional agenda from 1985 onward? Much of the answer offered to this question has already been foreshadowed. Fundamentally, the nature of the campaign finance issue in the latter half of the 1980s and into the 1990s did not seem particularly amenable to Common Cause's guidance and the various elements of its insider–outsider lobbying strategy. What should have become clear in the earlier discussion is that the absolute bottom line when it comes to electoral reform is *building a viable coalition*. It is not irreconcilable preferences that are preventing reform; it is the lack of leadership to commit political capital when the obvious solution is to draft changes that will not alter the balance of power between the parties. In all likelihood, without a Democratic president or a Republican legislative majority in both houses of Congress, this coalition has to be bipartisan and strong enough so that the almost inevitable attempts to pick it apart will fail. Otherwise it will almost surely collapse of its own weight.

While Common Cause is, in reality (although many Republicans would beg to differ) as well as in theory, bipartisan in its orientation, it is not traditionally a builder of coalitions.[34] But for many, the group is too pollyannish, too much the "National Scold," to serve in this role. Indeed, even staff members admit that the group's ability to maintain cohesiveness among groups – no less legislators – with respect to the MX was rather atypical.

Moreover, Common Cause would appear particularly ill suited to construct a coalition among members of Congress given how much it works through the media to highlight campaign finance issues. Recall that the group's role vis-à-vis the MX was by and large unknown in the popular press. But when it comes to campaign finance, Common Cause is *the* group. As mentioned, in utilizing its status the organization feels compelled to employ slash-and-burn techniques even against those who would, at first blush, appear to be its friends (the organization's motto, "no permanent enemies, no permanent friends," is never more appropriate than when it comes to campaign reform). These tactics are explicitly designed to embarrass members of Congress before their constituents. "Being tough is very important," is the way Susan Manes, the group's Director of Issue Development sums up the group's attitude. Tactics usually involve trying to exploit the media through paid and free publicity to stress the ties between the incumbent and special interests. In the Senate battles, any number of legislators were absolutely furious that Common Cause had impugned their honor. ("Effective, yet counterproductive," is the way one Senate staffer put it.) Similarly, the

group found itself condemned by the House speaker after its 1990 attacks on Democratic legislators. While Common Cause claims that this elicits respect – and that they would continue to focus public attention on campaign abuses even if it did not – others on Capitol Hill beg, sometimes passionately, to differ and assert that it only encourages the proposal and passage of legislation that is bound to fail.

It might be argued, and some individuals did in interviews, that coalition building is simply not a role for groups to play. If this is true, it suggests that Common Cause got involved in the wrong issue. Others asserted that too many members were hostile to, and lacked respect for, Common Cause for it to play such a conciliatory role.[35] Interestingly, as mentioned, Wertheimer did try to insert himself as a broker in the 1989–90 negotiations to form a bipartisan consensus; while some claimed that he was valuable and others maintained that he was biased and unwelcome, it is nevertheless interesting that the group has recognized a special need to play a coalition-building role.

As for the organization's major assets for lobbying inside the Capital Beltway – its expertise and credibility – while those in Common Cause profess that its expertise matters, few on Capitol Hill, including a number of group supporters, echo the sentiment. Perhaps in the early 1970s there was uncertainty about the role of money in elections; this is certainly not the case today when the campaign process has been so professionalized, and rather robust academic findings about money and elections are widely cited within the Washington community.[36] As suggested before, members believe that they are expert on this issue and that they do not need Common Cause's help. In many situations an organization's expertise undoubtedly helps to form coalitions, such as that developed around the MX, because members of Congress depend upon the association for guidance; but when it comes to campaign reform, other factors must provide the glue that holds a coalition together.

Does Common Cause have other strengths that can help offset this deficiency? While Common Cause's ability to mobilize at the grassroots is often cited as the group's principal comparative advantage when it comes to political activities generally, it is of limited effectiveness for reforming elections. Again, as mentioned earlier, legislators believe that there is no strong constituency, net of a dramatic scandal, that can be credibly mobilized. "If you really want to appeal to a wider grassroots interest, you've got to have Brokaw, Rather, and Jennings talking about it, David Letterman talking about it, Carson talking about it," notes one congressional staffer. Given the absence of such pressure, members of Congress have largely come to believe that there are a few Common Cause types in their district, and that even they are being directed to contact them rather than getting in touch with their representatives on their own initiative. Interviewees made clear that this mitigates the effectiveness of the group's success at getting its view into

local editorial pages and of its local campaigns designed to impugn incumbent legislators.[37] Minimally, therefore, the organization's ability to have an impact through its grassroots efforts is mediated by external events. Even when these external events seem to arise, the group has trouble making a strong case that its constituency matters.

Finally, there is one more possible group strength that was suggested in interviews: Common Cause's right to give or withhold its blessing from any piece of legislation coming out of Congress. In other words, Common Cause may use its media clout to renounce a reform bill, mitigating many of the political advantages for legislators of claiming credit for it that should go along with supporting it. However, this veto power is probably rather weak unless one party gains the upper hand (if a Democrat is elected president, for example), because the group would have little incentive to exercise it against any bill in the foreseeable set of legislative solutions that a Republican president would sign. Any statute coming out of Congress would almost surely be preferable to the status quo from Common Cause's perspective, and the organization would only be cutting its throat to spite itself if it then denounced it; many believe that, to the contrary, the organization is desperate for a bill. ("The question is whether they need to declare victory," remarks Ellen Miller of the Center for Responsive Politics.) Indeed, the group would face the possibility of a publicity backlash that could transform its image from being at the cutting edge of progressive change to constituting an impediment to reform.

The obvious question then becomes: Why, if Common Cause has such difficulty in having an impact on campaign finance, does it stick with this issue? Essentially, much of the answer flows from the earlier analysis. Organizational maintenance and self-selection processes reinforce the group's commitment to campaign finance.

Clearly, given the group's previous investment in the issue of campaign finance and the membership's attitude toward the issue, continuing the fight fits the organization's maintenance needs. Common Cause is a niche marketer – campaign finance and ethics are the goods that it sells better than anybody else. "No one else has that as their issue," comments David Cohen. Net of exceptional circumstances that lead the organization to pursue an issue like the MX (including campaign finance falling off the political agenda), the organization would be taking a tremendous risk in even seeming to renounce its commitment.

One response to the preceding statement might be that this only pushes the relevant question back one step to why, if members are capable of learning about campaign finance (e.g., Table 5.3a), do they support the group when it has such difficulty having an influence? This is where the process of self-selection comes to the fore. As illustrated in this analysis, evaluating group effectiveness is difficult and complex compared to learning about other types of costs and benefits pertaining to being in a political group. Or, to make

the comparison to private organizations, there is no profit statement or stock quote analogous to what those investing in, or working for, a corporation receive. A considerable subset of those joining the organization will come to believe that the group is capable of solving the morass over campaign finance and that it has a significant impact on keeping the issue alive. Even though certain promises might not be realized (promises such as Wertheimer's 1986 claim quoted earlier from *Common Cause Magazine* that after one or two more elections there would be public financing of congressional elections), many of the small number who might make such links come to the conclusion that the group has kept the issue alive and that the timing of these promises was just a little off. As shown, others who disagree with the group or think it ineffective will tend to quit or reduce or end their commitment.

This, in turn, will be reinforced by the staff's own perceptions. Those involved with Common Cause are not callous individuals selling a defective good to procure donations. Rather, the association's staff is made up of believers, although they do admit to being optimists. Hired guns are not attracted to working for a public interest group. This does not mean that some operating the group would not like to expand its scope; indeed some would. But there is a generally held belief that what the association is doing is worthwhile and effective. Wertheimer sums up the situation: "When you're in the period we've been in the past couple of years it's easier. There's a common recognition [within the group] that we are making progress." Anyone who becomes disillusioned will, presumably, get up and leave.

In short, organizational maintenance is provided through a selection process. Members and staff who do not believe may depart. Those who remain are dedicated to the campaign finance fight. It is not that such people are incapable of learning, but that learning accurately about organizational effectiveness is sufficiently difficult that people come to different opinions. The organization is locked into the issue of campaign finance because both those contributing resources and those directing their allocation want it to be. There appears no evidence to support the suggestions by some interviewees, usually Republicans, for the baser, Michelian proposition that the last thing the group's leadership wants to do is be effective and see their raison d'être disappear.

CONCLUSIONS: COALITION FORMATION AND GROUP INFLUENCE

Just as the analysis of the MX could be evaluated at two levels – what it illuminated generally about the relationship between associations and legislators and what it implied specifically about the linkage of citizen preferences to public policy – so too can this analysis of campaign finance. In fact, the two might be seen as flip sides of the same coin.

What this analysis demonstrates probably more clearly than anything else

is that lobbying must be able to provide something meaningful, particularly in terms of information, to representatives. In instances where this is not the case, it is likely to be ineffective no matter how much effort is expended.

A fairly convincing case can be made that the time had arrived for campaign finance reform during the second half of the 1980s. The political costs of maintaining the status quo for those who occupy office seemed to be rising. The litany of reasons to reform the system was long: There was continuing bad press about escalating campaign costs, as about explosion in the number of political action committees; the boom in soft money and the negative advertising that went along with it were the cause of much media attention; increases in congressional reelection rates had led to widespread condemnations of the lack of electoral competition; and a myriad of scandals that suggested that government was corrupt had led to discussion of the "sleaze factor." There was also the simple fact that in a budgetary climate that made major expenditure programs increasingly conflictual, if not impossible, campaign finance reform was a cheap, even potentially costless initiative depending upon the specifics of the program. ("Democrats will pass some form of campaign legislation because they will realize it doesn't cost anything," says one Republican staffer.) Its passage would make those year-end assessments of legislative and executive achievements a bit more respectable.

Also, there was an obvious, seemingly Pareto-efficient compromise (that is, both sides would be better off) that could be cut between the members of the two parties. Time after time, those interviewed outlined roughly the same solution: Some reduction in spending in return for more restrictions on PACs. Legislators would have more time to spend on other duties rather than on raising funds, the institution of Congress could function more efficiently, and there would be plenty of credit to be claimed on all sides.

The major obstacle involved putting the requisite coalition together given the desires of incumbents and the problems of partisanship. Democratic and Republican leaders in both chambers had to all be willing to deal and to put down dissidents in their own parties at the same time. Yet, it turned out that Common Cause could do very little to help solve this problem. Given the nature of legislative opinions, the organization had little ability to put together a winning legislative combination. There were few intensely interested citizens to mobilize beyond the Common Cause membership and minimal opportunities for the group to employ its ample expertise to sway members' opinions and help form a coalition.

Again, these findings do not suggest that Common Cause has had no impact whatsoever on campaign finance. Certainly, the Common Cause leadership believes that substantial progress is being made and that the organization is playing a major role. However, these results do imply that to the extent that the group has been influential, it has been on a subtle level that is rather difficult to identify. And the reason for this is that electoral reform is simply not an issue that is very amenable to lobbying.

From the larger perspective, this analysis demonstrates that effectiveness is not necessary for group involvement. Analogous individual and organizational processes that got Common Cause involved with the MX kept it involved over the years with campaign finance. The Common Cause staff and membership both believe in, indeed feel intensely about, the group's efforts. The fact that scholars have tended to debate how important lobbying is might not be because one person is right and the other is wrong but, rather, that *influence is conditional*: on which preferences of citizens, if any, are translated via organizational processes into goals and are then implemented by leaders.

Nonetheless, if the conclusions of this chapter and the preceding one are accepted, the results appear supremely ironic. The issue that seemed inconsistent with the group's agenda was the concern that was most amenable to the exercise of influence. The concern that the group has remained dedicated to, and is nearly synonymous with, is one where there seems little room for making much additional impact. The key linkage between the two lies with the processes that define Common Cause as an organization.

10

Conclusions: Citizens' preferences, internal politics, and public policy

INTEREST GROUPS AND REPRESENTATION

What can the study of interest groups reveal about the nature and process of representation? From the time of Madison to the present day, it is the empirical or normative implications of how interest groups operate in the larger system that ultimately make associations relevant to students of politics.[1]

Of course, it is now well understood that most individuals functioning through associations have, at the very most, a quite limited impact on public policy. Nonetheless, this is not tantamount to stating that there is a consensus regarding the representational role that groups do (or do not) play.

In fact, as discussed at the beginning of this analysis, any number of alternative propositions about groups continue to exist. Some contend that organizations function in the aggregate to link citizens' preferences to the political system even if given individuals lack the clout needed to have a significant impact by themselves. Others maintain that these collectivities act as a means of representing individuals symbolically but that they lack what it takes to have a substantive impact. Still others adopt a bit cruder perspective, maintaining that political organizations operate to aggrandize leaders' interests at the expense of their followers. Naturally, each of these possibilities has very different implications for assessments about representation.

It would be entirely presumptuous and certainly incorrect to claim that the current analysis provides the key for unlocking all the mysteries of associations and politics. Rather, the more modest purposes of this research, as spelled out in the initial chapter of the project, are (1) to examine the process of group influence from the "ground up" and (2) in conjunction with this effort, to make some headway in the process of conceptualizing organizations both as they operate internally and as they relate to the larger political system. Tackling these dual objectives has involved examining what is surely the most widely recognized public interest group in the United States, Common Cause, from a vantage point that is somewhat different from that commonly employed in investigating organizational processes. Modesty aside, it is believed that the results garnered should be relevant to scholars engaged in understanding how organized interests fit into the larger political system.

In practice, the questions posed in this analysis have been at three discrete levels in terms of their generality: a precise microlevel that can be tested directly with the information available (for example, do years in the organization increase the probability of retention?); an intermediate level that necessitates taking a step back from the list of specific questions and hypotheses but can still be assessed relatively straightforwardly with the available data and results; and a macrolevel that requires the assembly and interpretation of a wide range of more specific findings in order to draw broad-gauged inferences. Given the detailed analysis of previous chapters, the microlevel need not be addressed in the present discussion – the intermediate and macrolevels are of relevance here.

When attention is directed toward the intermediate level, the plethora of possible considerations can essentially be boiled down to three queries:

- How do individual citizens make their choices vis-à-vis interest groups?
- What is the nature of the internal organizational processes that determine group goals and influence associational effectiveness?
- When all is said and done, do associations actually have an impact on public policy?

Satisfactorily answering these three inquiries would be an interesting and valuable exercise in and of itself. However, as implied above, it is also hoped that responses to them that will be proposed in this analysis will help illuminate the macrolevel questions of concern to scholars. These overarching questions essentially mirror the two goals of the research spelled out earlier:

- Do group members' preferences, as mediated by their translation into contributors' behavior and by internal organizational processes, get transformed into public policy?
- How should the process by which individuals are represented by groups within the political system be conceptualized?

Thus, the motivation for this concluding section of the analysis is to mass together the litany of findings from the larger investigation to examine what light they shed on relevant intermediate- and macrolevel concerns.[2] The remainder of this chapter is oriented toward accomplishing this task.

INDIVIDUAL CHOICE, INTERNAL POLITICS, AND SYSTEMIC INFLUENCE

In reviewing what has been uncovered over the course of the research enterprise about its three principal empirical foci – individual choice behavior, internal political governance, and systemic political processes – two regularities stand out that are really quite striking. One is just how well the vast preponderance of these results fit together. There are not assorted findings that need to be explained away or cavalierly dismissed as simply

idiosyncratic. The other is the generic nature of many of the behavioral patterns observed; they are quite analogous to those observed in private life. While public and private choices are not identical, they mirror one another in systematic, intuitive ways.

Individual choice behavior

There have been a host of quite specific findings about who members of Common Cause are, why they join the group, why they remain in it, and how they select their level of commitment. It is possible to paint a rather precise picture concerning the nature of individual choice behavior utilizing this set of findings.

The defining features of the image that can be sketched from the previous analysis are twofold. One involves *process*: By what method do citizens go about making decisions? The other concerns *benefits* and *costs*: What returns from and price of participating do individuals incorporate into their calculations?

With respect to the former, one of the nicer examples of how well the results fit together into a larger whole can be illustrated with the findings regarding citizens' behavior. They quite neatly highlight the decision processes by which members make their choices. A few basic assumptions – that the world in which citizens operate is complex, that it is far too much to expect that they will approximate perfectly informed decision makers before they join organizations or early in their associational careers, and that individual decision makers will at some rough level recognize their shortfalls and act accordingly – go a considerable distance in tying together a string of choices by members that might be thought to be quite distinct from one another.

Indeed, the portrait of a Common Cause member laid out by this research jibes quite well with predictions stemming from these assumptions. A citizen, who will be assumed here to be female for the sake of convenience, is interested in politics. She is contacted by Common Cause (a group about which she may be dimly aware) and decides, for the rather modest fee that has been set, to join. Only in the rarest of circumstances will she suggest to the organization that she would like to contribute much in the way of additional time (especially) or money. After a year of receiving *Common Cause Magazine* and other assorted materials and learning about the organization, she has about a 75 percent probability of agreeing to stay on. With each additional year the probability of leaving after that given year declines; if she decides to stay for a few years, she will probably remain for a considerable period thereafter.

As time goes on and she become increasingly knowledgeable, her attitude toward additional contributions may change. She may consent to give additional monies to the organization depending upon a number of factors, such as how good a job she believes the group's leaders are doing. In addition,

now that she presumably is more psychologically attached to the organization and is better versed about the group's activities and has a stronger belief about whether it is effective, she may be contacted and agree to become more committed by contributing time to the group. Her commitment decision will hinge fairly crucially on what she has learned, her perceptions of efficacy, and whether the temporal costs are too great.

Thus, the results of the analysis of choice behavior – that individuals learn, that they decide whether to stay or leave in their first few years in the group, that they initially adopt a low level of commitment and subsequently decide whether or not to increase their contribution – all buttress the point that citizens decide how to deal with organizations in a rational way in a world where incomplete information prevails. Joining, retention, and commitment are not distinct decisions arrived at in a vacuum but rather are a series of interrelated choices structured, in turn, by leadership decisions.

Additionally, this process of decision making where learning is fundamental conditions how organizational benefits and costs enter into citizen and member decision calculi. This is highlighted by two findings in the Common Cause study: one regarding the nature of political rewards and the other concerning the general irrelevance of membership costs.

None of the findings uncovered during the examination of individual decision making refutes the possibility that political rewards matter for members of the group. However, the manner in which benefits enter into decision calculi is patterned in a very particular fashion that is consistent with the experiential search process by which individuals are postulated to make their choices. Given the leadership's decisions to keep costs low and recruit heavily, political interest and broad feelings regarding politics are key for joining; when it comes to staying in the group these attitudes become more crystallized as members learn more; and when the choice is whether to establish a higher temporal commitment level, assessments concerning political efficacy take on a greater weight than judgments about the match between organizational and personal preferences.

In turn, the structured pattern by which political rewards help drive the individual decision process is conditioned by the nature of the costs of participation. For example, one of the more counterintuitive results that consistently arises from the analyses of choice behavior is that the ability to pay financially (read income) fails to have a positive impact on participation, despite the descriptive finding that Common Cause members are wealthy relative to the rest of society. Why correlation is not translated into causation is a function of the linkage between how leaders structure an association and members' evaluations of the benefits the group provides.

Specifically, in developing an organization that offers a specific set of benefits to members at a given price (Salisbury 1969), entrepreneurs will take into account the nature of individual choice behavior in how they set prices, try to recruit, and attempt to increase members' donations to the association.

Costs that are considerably more difficult to control – such as the comparative price of being an activist – are more likely to be relevant for explaining contributors' decisions than those that are manipulated relatively easily.

At the risk of being too heavy-handed, an analogy can be drawn between interest groups and private firms on the one hand, and group contributors and consumers on the other. Individual firms need not only to produce a quality product but to structure its pricing, marketing, and distribution network in an efficient manner. Similarly, enterpreneurs who put together an attractive group but fail to construct a proper pricing, marketing, and distribution system so that the right individuals are introduced to the organization at the correct cost and continue to be cultivated in a sensitive fashion are bound to fail. While social scientists have had a great deal of quite useful things to say about the initial package of benefits, they have had less to offer about the other related aspects of successful entrepreneurial behavior.

Internal politics and goal formation

The preceding comments focusing on leadership activities direct attention rather straightforwardly to the analysis of internal politics and goal formation. After those running the group structure the process so that members agree to try out the organization, how is the association arranged to encourage contributors to remain in the group and to increase their level of commitment? Of special relevance, what do those charged with operating the organization do to make members who care actually believe that they agree with the group's policies and that the collectivity is effective?

As discussed earlier, internal interest group politics themselves operate on both formal and informal levels. There is a formal veneer of democracy where the organization is made to appear as if it functions like a classic representative government. Common Cause is operated through a governing board chosen by the membership, for which about one-sixth of all group contributors actually cast ballots; those elected are, in turn, enlightened by Membership Issue Polls, which attract responses from perhaps one-fifth of those who are involved in the group.

Yet, when one scrapes through the veneer, it becomes abundantly clear that this democracy is less than meets the eye and that group leaders lack incentives to let a voluntary organization function according to formal democratic principles. The purposes of such democratic institutions are, presumably, to furnish the group with an air of legitimacy, to make a subset of those in the organization feel that they are being listened to, and to provide the staff with some feedback from the membership. Nonetheless, it is evident that there is more to governing the association than just these formal processes. Indeed, the survey results presented in the present research illustrate

vividly that even the Common Cause membership exhibits confusion and ambivalence about how effectively the formal governing mechanisms operate.

Rather, much of the real material of internal politics and goal formation is found beneath the surface. To reiterate, there is nothing insidious about organizations being run through less formal means. Indeed, it demonstrates competent leadership since the logic of associational governance dictates that informal mechanisms must prevail. The previously demonstrated findings that for some, joining, retention, and activism are a function of political evaluations makes it clear that a subset of members do care about what the group stands for in deciding upon their level of support. Leaders would be neglecting their jobs if they failed to structure the organization to take into account this process. Even the membership appears to recognize the legitimacy of this means of doing business, given their wholehearted approval of how representative the group is in terms of its outcomes.

Once again, an analogy to the behavior of those operating firms can be drawn. For the executive guiding a private firm to take into account the interests of all workers in making policy would be suicidal; rather, the employees who are most valuable and who are most likely to exit if those conditions at the firm that they care about deteriorate should be accorded the most attention.[3]

Consequently, as the analysis of the decision to focus on the MX missile illustrates, those members who proffer large, politically contingent contributions to the group are accorded the most attention. It was the activist cadre who led the group into the struggle for arms control. However, the rank and file's opinions are also taken into account, given the fact that political factors may matter even for them and activists' contributions are not so great as to trivialize the former's importance. Furthermore, the internal politics of organizations are still characterized by incomplete information – precise definition of the group's issue agenda and the allocation of resources both constitute management decisions that are influenced by the leadership's superior information. Just as those studying firms discuss how factors such as organizational slack and the principal–agent relationship permit managers room for maneuver, so too do group leaders possess areas for discretion and contributor education.

Systemic impact

Given the formation of organizational goals, the final intermediate issue to be addressed in the empirical analysis was whether all of the individual decisions and group machinations over goals amounted to anything in the world of public policy. To examine this, the two issues to which Common Cause allocated the bulk of its political resources in the past decade – the MX missile and campaign finance reform – were analyzed from a common

theoretical perspective. These matters differed with respect to key political, economic, procedural, and technical characteristics. In more practical terms, on one issue Common Cause was part of a large coalition dealing with a concern surrounded by uncertainty that stimulated emotional responses pro and con from elected officials, group representatives, and members of the general public and that virtually had to be addressed; on the other, the organization was largely acting alone and dealing with an issue that elected officials believed to involve little uncertainty, about which these officials were dearly concerned but others cared little, if at all, and that could be easily ignored by the legislature.

The great irony of the comparison between the MX and campaign finance is in the inferences drawn about group effectiveness. Despite the fact that Common Cause's public reputation is almost synonymous with campaign finance, the group appears to have been considerably more successful in swaying members of Congress when it come to the MX issue, although Common Cause is rarely associated with defense issues. Again, to reiterate, claiming that Common Cause is powerless with respect to campaign finance is certainly going too far, yet its influence appears more subtle than the organization would like one to believe. The reasons for this difference in group effectiveness are grounded in what Common Cause had to offer elected representatives that might sway their opinions, given the differing contexts surrounding each issue and the nature of legislators' decision calculi.

When it came to the MX, Common Cause could influence members of Congress by leading an arms control coalition that possessed technical expertise and the ability to sway votes on the grassroots level. This one-two combination made this network of organizations a player, although probably not the key determinant of the outcome, in the debates surrounding an issue that was of fundamental importance in defining America's defense policy in the 1980s.

By contrast, when the issue was campaign finance, Common Cause could generate publicity, but it nevertheless had difficulty making a credible case that the public at large was aroused. This stumbling block constituted a considerable obstacle for having influence on an issue where technical expertise about the role of money in elections (which Common Cause has in spades) is unlikely to be of crucial importance. The leadership often feels forced to resort to sensationalistic tactics that may garner it and campaign finance publicity but which risk alienating the very political decision makers they hope to put together in a coalition. Given this state of affairs, and the association's inability to be the orchestrator of the necessary bipartisan coalition of members of Congress, the association's influence appears circumscribed. This does not mean that campaign finance reform is inherently doomed, but only that Common Cause will probably not be the driving force that decides whether an accord is eventually reached.

Perhaps the most interesting aspect of this entire dichotomy between the

MX and campaign finance is that it suggests that while groups can be effective, they do not have to be to maintain themselves. While both leaders and members may factor in their own assessments of whether the association will be a positive force, there is nevertheless an element of chance whether issues will be selected that match a group's ability to have an impact. With respect to both the production and deployment of the MX and electoral reform, key organizational contributors and those directing the association supported Common Cause's efforts and believed that the group was influential. Both contributors and leaders considered the group to be effective not as a consequence of their incapacity to learn, but rather because such impacts are difficult to measure accurately and there is a process of self-selection through which nonbelievers will remove themselves from the fray.

To draw the analogy between interest groups and private firms one more time, the product that organizational contributors, like investors, are buying is essentially equity in an organization. However, just as investors dispute the value of a firm and whether to sink capital into it, those who might be involved with an organization will debate its worth (without the aid of the balance sheet or stock quotation to which investors have access). Those running the organization firmly believe that the investment will pan out; some contributors will decide otherwise and cut their losses, while others will agree and increase their stake.

THE BIG PICTURE

Having reviewed the findings stemming from the hypotheses tested in previous chapters, what then can be said generally about the macrolevel questions enumerated previously? Thankfully, the inferences drawn in the preceding section also fit together well when aggregated to say something about the larger whole. Member decisions are neatly integrated with the goal selection process, which in turn is reflected in the association's grassroots efforts to influence policy. Consequently, without making too grandiose a claim, the results in this analysis shed light on the macrolevel questions of interest.

Linking citizens to policy

At the risk of boiling down a host of results from this research into a single finding, the overall judgment about whether groups can link citizens to public policy can be summed up succinctly:

While it is possible for citizen preferences to be productively linked to public policy, there are a series of conditioning factors – which might alternatively be termed obstacles to representation – that must fall into place for effective representation to occur. Such obstacles are particularly great when a key representational linkage involves grassroots mobilization.

The conditioning factors, in turn, can be classified into three categories: (1) motivational, (2) informational, and (3) resource-based. Given the previous review in this chapter, these obstacles need only be mentioned briefly.[4]

Motivational factors. Individual obstacles to representation stemming from motivations have been well-documented in this analysis. The representational linkage might be severed because those joining, staying, and being active in the group may simply not care. In the extreme case, associated with Olson's by-product theory, members may lack any political interests whatsoever. Leaders then have no incentive to incorporate members' preferences in forming group goals and cannot make a credible claim to government officials about the grassroots fervor of their membership.

Alternatively, such as in the instance studied here, political factors may matter, but so might other considerations. Only those who care sufficiently so that their contributions are likely to be contingent on political activities will have the motivational leverage to have their interests represented in a group whose leaders must worry about organizational maintenance. Naturally, the impact of having only a subset of members making politically contingent choices will have a minimal effect on organizational goals if participants are homogeneous in terms of the direction and intensity of their preferences (that is, the same objectives will be pursued regardless); but even in a group like Common Cause there is substantial heterogeneity among contributors. In addition, the ability to mobilize effectively at the grassroots will be greater, ceteris paribus, the more that political passion motivates contributions and commitment.

Informational factors. Another factor that can attenuate the representational linkage has to do with information. Even if members are driven by political concerns, the representation process can get thrown off track if they possess only limited ideas about what a group stands for, the nature of the issues at hand, or the possibilities for success. As demonstrated in this analysis, such ignorance at Common Cause (and presumably at most organizations that are inexpensive to join) principally applies to newcomers rather than to veteran members. However, for all involved in an organization the difficulty of measuring impacts on the production of collective goods may also help to attenuate the transformation of personal preferences into public policy.

More specifically, lack of information may again work in two ways: It may interact with how objectives are decided upon or with the feasibility of being politically effective. For goals, ignorance of the group or issues may make it quite difficult to have interests articulated in associational objectives and will delegate to leaders ever greater room for maneuver. In addition, lack of political, acuity about what is feasible to accomplish given political constraints may result in the adoption of goals for reasons of group maintenance that have little chance of success. Leaders who care about having

an influence (and in organizations that fail to offer lucrative private rewards they probably do) may try to mitigate this deleterious effect via the management and resource allocation decisions through which they funnel member preferences into associational objectives.

Naturally, an ill-informed membership will also make having a policy impact more problematic by hampering the possibility of grassroots mobilization, which is inherently difficult enough to begin with. Not only will poorly informed members not be able to make convincing claims to officials that there is fervent grassroots feeling on an issue, but the organizational resources that leaders will be required to pour in to educate and mobilize those in the hinterlands will have opportunity costs in preventing funds from being allocated for other purposes.

Resource-based factors. The last statement highlights another fact of group life: Collectivities are continually strapped for cash. It is a matter of faith that associations receive a suboptimal level of contributions because of the difficulties endemic to collective action. Thus, one obvious resource-based obstacle to the representational linkage is the simple acknowledgment that so much money must go into getting individuals to sign up (especially) and to continue their contributions – and membership costs must be kept at such a low level – that once maintenance needs are met there is relatively little left over for political efforts, even given a well-meaning leadership. There simply is not a great deal of money available for the development of technical expertise or mobilization at the grassroots on a wide range of issues.

However, there are other resource-based obstacles beyond the suboptimality of contribution levels. Such barriers come into play because those who make the largest contributions have the greatest influence in determining what goals will be adopted. This feature, interacting with the contingent nature of such contributions, can again lead an association in directions that do not square with those advocated by the rest of a membership. While a response to inequities created by differentials in ability and willingness to pay might simply be to suggest that the representation process is not tantamount to a one person, one vote democracy, it ignores the likelihood that these internal governing processes can also mitigate the ability of an organization to have an impact. Most notably, if only a small portion of a membership, even if the wealthiest fraction, is behind an initiative, making credible grassroots claims will be difficult at best.

Not surprisingly, in groups such as Common Cause where donations tend to be small relative to the overall budget and there are really no exceptionally large contributors, an emphasis is kept on selecting initiatives supported by large majorities of the membership. However, a very different story would be expected with an association that relied on a few patrons for the bulk of its resources.

Summary. In short, the process of group representation is a treacherous one marked by myriad potential hazards. Given the considerable number of obstacles just enumerated and the emphasis of Common Cause on the type of grassroots activities that appear most susceptible to getting derailed, it might be considered a wonder that the group transforms the interests of its contributors into public policy even some of the time. This is in no small part a reflection of group leaders' skill in structuring the organization, as it is their job to do, in a manner that minimizes the aggregate impact of these obstacles, given the necessities of organizational maintenance. Indeed, behind all these possible pitfalls lie leadership decisions. These choices fundamentally influence who gets recruited and what their motivations are, how much information they possess, what resource level they contribute, what goals are chosen, and whether an association has a political impact.

Viewing organizations

As discussed earlier, there was one other purpose of this study: to investigate whether viewing organizations from the ground up would yield inferences and insights not common to studies that focus on specific microlevel questions. For this reason, efforts have been made to look at Common Cause from an integrated perspective in which the variety of subjects were viewed as inherently linked.

It is believed that this analysis demonstrates the advantage of considering organizations from an integrated perspective. The illustrations of this point are numerous: Membership, retention, and activism are explicable only if they are conceived as a series of interrelated choices conditioned by leadership decisions; the goal formation process and the kind of internal governing mechanisms a group employs can be understood only if the means by which contributors make choices are integrated into the analysis of these leadership decisions; the ability of a collectivity to have an influence, and why an organization might choose to get involved with an issue on which it might have little impact, can be thoroughly comprehended only if citizen motivations and the internal governing processes that lead to the formation of goals are consolidated into the examination.

Thus, one general finding of this research is that studies that focus on one individual facet of organizations – joining, goal formation, policy influence, what have you – will tell incomplete, and frequently incorrect, stories about the processes being observed. Without taking into account the larger context in which members, leaders, and the organizations to which they belong operate, inferences will be advanced that are simply off the mark. For example, one cannot understand how Common Cause had an impact on the MX without knowing why it suddenly shifted its agenda; one cannot understand why the group shifted its agenda without knowing why people are active and stay in the group; and one cannot understand why people are active or stay

without understanding why (and which) citizens join. Finally, one cannot understand how Common Cause had an impact on the MX without having an idea of how leadership influences citizens' decision making, goal formation, and public policy activities.

Of course, these assertions are not tantamount to claiming that the specific perspective adopted here about how to put the whole system together is absolutely correct or sufficiently comprehensive. Rather, the more general point to be stressed is that some form of a larger, more integrated framework is required to put things in proper order.

SOME FINAL THOUGHTS

It is difficult to end a lengthy exercise like the one here without falling prey to the temptation to make a few comments that are perhaps best classified as purely speculative. Essentially, several final thoughts stick in the mind. One has to do with cynicism (or the lack of it); the other, with skepticism.

Quite frankly, it is difficult to be cynical about a group such as Common Cause. Close observation only engenders a healthy respect for the honest efforts of those in the public interest community to have an influence over public policy. It is difficult to walk away from conducting an analysis such as this with a cynical belief that either these groups' leaders or their followers are in any respect not serious about the task they see at hand, despite the efforts of some of the groups' enemies to suggest such motivations.[5]

Yet, conversely, it is possible to develop a healthy dose of skepticism about the abilities of public interest groups to provide a true representation of even their conception of the public good. Grandiose claims that public interest groups, in the aggregate, have transformed the very soul of the political system are hard to swallow. The sheer difficulties of inducing individuals to join and to be involved and the subsequent pitfalls in trying to channel the resulting energies into political influence sometimes seem staggering.[6] The fact that Common Cause is able sporadically to have political influence is far more a tribute than a condemnation. Nonetheless, the final word here is one of caution. The claim that there exists a brave new world of organizations that constitutes a strong, countervailing representation of the public will must be viewed with considerable hesitancy.

Notes

CHAPTER 1

1. Those interested in further discussions and applications of this approach are urged to consult two journals: *Public Choice* and (especially) the *Journal of Law and Economics*.
2. The general problem is how to discern influence when the more one side contributes, the more the other side does as well.
3. The following might be more aptly termed an "integrated *membership* perspective," recognizing that the focus of this analysis is on membership organizations. As a number of prominent scholars have noted (e.g., Salisbury 1984; Walker 1990), there are many nonmembership groups in the political world that function as staff organizations and are dependent on corporate support or foundation grants and the like. Future research should contrast membership groups with non-membership institutions.
4. The survey, conducted by the political science department of Stanford University, was funded by grant SES-8105708 from the National Science Foundation to Professor Heinz Eulau in support of research by Jonathon Siegel.
5. Activists – who responded to the mail survey at a 75 percent rate compared to 59 percent for rank-and-file contributors – constitute 23 percent of the sample, while they are only 4 percent of the population of contributors (McFarland 1984). Although this stratification does cause some problems, these difficulties can be dealt with given the application of proper econometric techniques.
6. There is a good book on Common Cause written by Andrew McFarland (1984). The present analysis is considerably different from McFarland's in both technique and purpose. McFarland employs a qualitative case study methodology in analyzing Common Cause. While the present study also entails a certain amount of qualitative research, standard hypothesis testing, particularly using quantitative methods, is more central to the current research. Also, the current investigation is principally oriented toward exploiting the group as an instance of a more general phenomenon, while McFarland focuses primarily on trying to understand Common Cause itself. In addition, changes in events at the group (as McFarland's book was being completed) have made analysis of the goal formation process, and therefore the investigation of the linkage between citizens' preferences and public policy, much easier. Thus, the research produced by this study should complement rather than duplicate the earlier work.
7. There was, for a brief period (1968–70), a predecessor organization known as the Urban Coalition.
8. To the extent that Common Cause is currently a one-issue group (the organization currently recognizes its core issues as being campaign finance reform, ethics reform, and promoting political accountability and openness in government, with

other concerns, such as civil rights and arms control, as secondary priorities), it is fairly unique among public interest groups. Others, for instance, Americans for Democratic Action, have a much more varied agenda.

9. Some of this increase is a function of changes associated with the development of family memberships in the mid-1980s.

10. Because of the objectives and limitations of the current study, relatively little attention is given to the organization's state-level affiliates and their activities.

11. These data were made available by the Inter-University Consortium for Political and Social Research (ICPSR) and were originally collected by Constance E. Cook of Albion College. Neither the collector of the original data nor the ICPSR bear any responsibility for the analysis presented here. The data were collected through a mail questionnaire sent to 250 members of each organization in the state of Michigan.

12. Interviewees included Common Cause employees, leaders of other public interest groups, Washington-based consultants, and congressional staffers. Some interviews were conducted for attribution, while a good number of others were, at the request of the interviewees, exclusively for background.

CHAPTER 2

1. In many ways, this situation is also analogous to the issue of whether decision makers such as legislators behave in a sincere or a sophisticated manner when given a complicated agenda.

2. This is not to say that the authors of these approaches *believe* that individuals are incapable of learning or lack foresight, only that given the assumptions of the models that they propose, learning is not possible either because decision makers know everything to start with or because they simply are assumed to be incapable of updating their beliefs. The resulting predictions are at variance with an alternative that allows new information to be taken into account. The nature of modeling is to develop a stylized framework for understanding the world by making specific assumptions and then seeing if the resulting predictions make sense.

3. Both the viewpoint taken in this analysis and the tradition of research in which it is written are decision theoretic (which, to reiterate, is equivalent to a game against nature). Among other things, this excludes game theoretic approaches in which a small number of participants compete against one another. Despite the importance of the latter for studying collective action (e.g., Hardin 1982; Axelrod 1984) – and despite the fact that it furnishes many insights into how actors behave strategically in small number situations – it is inappropriate for explaining why individuals contribute (and keep contributing) to large groups. Not only is the assumption that individuals are playing against nature more suitable for understanding the choices to be studied in this analysis, but it has implicitly dominated research on these issues to date.

4. This discussion refers to Downs's assumption that citizens participate if

$$R = PB - C,$$

where R is the citizen's action (voting, joining, activism), B is the potential benefit from the action, P is the probability that benefits will accrue if the action is taken, and C is the cost of the action.

5. Although the traditional distinction between purposive and collective benefits is employed at this point in the analysis, a different perspective on this dichotomy will be introduced later.

6. The phrase "imperfect information" is used in an intuitive manner rather than in the specific way in which it is employed in modern game theory, where the proper term would be incomplete information (the two terms are used interchangeably in this book).

7. Moe (1980a) takes the imperfect information assumption somewhat further, but almost strictly from the perspective of group leaders (particularly, how to structure an organization to encourage donations) rather than from the contributors' viewpoint.

8. An interesting implication that remains for future research is that fewer members will learn experientially in groups with expensive membership charges. Instead, potential contributors will use their resources to search from outside of the organization. Membership in interest groups with relatively high dues should therefore be less volatile than in comparatively "cheap" organizations.

9. This makes experiential search somewhat distinct from, although not inconsistent with, models of Bayesian updating.

10. Indeed, experimental work in economics often finds that a subset of contributors continue to make donations at some level for reasons that can only be termed altruistic (e.g., Palfrey and Rosenthal 1988).

11. A quintessential example of exogenous forces is found in Wilson's (1962) observation that "amateur Democrats" lose their enthusiasm to spend endless hours working for the cause once an election is over.

12. The actual group percentage is about 60 percent: 77 percent of activists gave more than the minimum compared to 58 percent of rank-and-file members.

13. The magazine also has the other subsidiary purpose of helping to coordinate policy efforts by, for example, telling individuals whom to contact when an issue is coming to a head.

14. To reiterate, this should not be construed as an effort to create a series of straw men based on previous approaches. The point to recognize is that theorizing requires making simplifying assumptions that are recognized as being abstractions from reality and that the utility of what is produced is in the ability to make sense of the empirical world.

CHAPTER 3

1. Although these are probably the most germane contrasts, other potential comparisons may be important. For example, interorganizational differences – between those subscribing to one group and those belonging to other associations – may also be of some interest. Restricting the analysis to discrepancies with the national population and to intra-associational differences is done solely for reasons of parsimony.

2. As mentioned, about 11 percent of those defined as rank-and-file members actually partake in activist–like behaviors. However, for the purpose of this descriptive portrait, the simple dichotomy that the group employs will be utilized.

3. In addition, data furnished by Common Cause on the distribution of members by state and congressional district in 1987 and data from the *Congressional District Data Book* are used in measuring the geographical distribution of members. Although the former data are not circa 1981, staffers assured me that while the group's aggregate numbers fluctuate over time, the geographic distribution of members has remained steady over the years.

4. All differences discussed are statistically significant unless noted otherwise. It should be remembered that the Common Cause sample is stratified rather than

random. Although these data could be adjusted, the raw figures are employed. No substantive changes in interpretation would result from such weighting.

5. As will be discussed shortly, the membership is not especially progressive with respect to economic issues.

6. These are the categories (which were also used in the Common Cause survey) and the terminology employed by the NES.

7. This assertion stems from an analysis of the categorical age data adjusted for the year that members report having initially joined. These data indicate that the average new member of Common Cause has traditionally been in his or her mid-50s.

8. Also, as will be discussed later, some of the reasons for the differences between members and nonmembers might have to do with the group's recruitment strategies.

9. The wording of these questions and those on participation can be found in Appendix 3.1.

10. Data about Common Cause contributors' beliefs in procedurally open government will be presented shortly.

11. This assessment might have changed somewhat for Common Cause members in the interim as the Court took a conservative turn during the Reagan era and as a perception emerged that nominations – notably that of Robert Bork, which Common Cause explicitly opposed (see, e.g., Pertschuk and Schaetzel 1989) – were becoming more partisan and political.

12. Gibson and Bingham (1985), in an analysis that focuses on issues of tolerance and the American Civil Liberties Union (ACLU) but includes data on Common Cause members as well, find that Common Cause members are also more tolerant than the mass public although less than those in the ACLU.

13. For example, only 64 of 1,446 respondents to the 1987 GSS reported belonging to political clubs.

   In addition, in their study Gibson and Bingham (1985) find that roughly 17 percent of Common Cause members belong to the National Association for the Advancement of Colored Persons and approximately 33 percent are in the ACLU.

14. This is not to disparage the quality of this literature, because it is principally designed to distinguish participants from nonparticipants and not to differentiate among classes of those who, in the larger scheme of things, are quite active.

15. Nor is there any difference when it comes to income (although the data fall just short of statistical significance), which is usually considered a correlate of participation but not a determinant of it net of education. Interestingly, any differences that may exist show an inverse relation between activism and family income – a relation that is explored in more depth later in the analysis. This is also reflected in the greater tendency of activists to be blue collar employees.

16. Measures of institutional performance such as those discussed in the past section are excluded here for reasons of parsimony; when analyzed they uncover no systematic differences.

17. It is somewhat difficult to characterize Common Cause's structure and process issues as liberal or conservative. Thus, when contributors are maintained to be more liberal with respect to such concerns, this should be interpreted as the equivalent of asserting that they are more in line with the extreme version of the group issue position.

18. This may come as a surprise, since the two measures are relatively highly correlated (.59). Apparently, the greater propensity of activists to be strong Democrats and their smaller likelihood to be leaning Republicans differentiate

them from the rank and file. By contrast, observed differences between the two membership types in identifying as liberals or extreme conservatives were not great enough for statistical significance.

19. The phrase "at the time" is employed because, as will be discussed in greater depth later, defense issues came to the fore at Common Cause soon after the 1981 survey was completed.

20. Conversely, it could be maintained that there are substitution effects by which Common Cause activism replaces alternative forms of political participation. However, this seems rather farfetched.

21. This measure was probably somewhat confusing to respondents because of taxpayers' ability to utilize an income tax check-off to contribute money. Some may answer affirmatively to the question about contribution because of this essentially costless form of participation.

CHAPTER 4

1. As mentioned earlier, the policy impact of membership will be investigated in more detail later.

2. Kau and Rubin's work on Common Cause and on Ralph Nader's Public Citizen leads them to concede that the reason why people contribute is unknown (their study is examined in more depth and compared to the approach advanced in the present analysis in Appendix 4.1). In his innovative paper, Hansen tries to measure subtle concepts derived from prospect theory to explain membership levels using aggregate-level data. Given the inevitable measurement slippage produced by this type of exercise, his results must be dealt with cautiously.

3. Even for voting there has not always been a constant cost for participating: Witness the application of literacy tests and other means to exclude blacks from taking part in the electoral process. In addition, to the extent that candidates, groups, or parties systematically go out of their way to recruit some individuals to vote (e.g., Uhlaner 1989a) – by calling them on the phone, registering them to vote, driving them to the polls, etc. – turnout becomes analogous to the membership joining process and most analyses of why people vote are misspecified.

4. An alternative method would be to estimate first the probability of being solicited (rather than to use data on whether or not an individual has actually been contacted) and subsequently incorporate the estimated likelihood into a joining equation. Such an estimate would be based on how closely a person fits the profile of the type of individual that a group such as Common Cause targets with respect to characteristics that clearly do not function as citizen attributes. (For example, do prospective members belong to other groups whose contribution lists are employed by Common Cause?) However, such information is not available in the present case for individuals not in the organization, although conceivably it would be easier to build into a survey than whether or not an individual has definitely been contacted by a group.

5. A reduced-form equation is an equation that expresses endogenous variables exclusively in terms of predetermined variables and the stochastic disturbances.

6. Specifically, respondents were asked, "There are many ways in which people first hear about political organizations. *Before* you actually decided to join Common Cause, how important to you were each of the following sources of *information about Common Cause?*" (emphasis in the original). In a statistical sense, the rank and file were actually somewhat more likely to claim that mail was very or somewhat important (almost 67 percent). Indeed, if one adjusts for the oversampling of activists and examines only those with an opinion (dropping those who are

not sure), over 73 percent of Common Cause members claim that the mail was important.

Although none of the interpretations of Table 4.2 need to be altered, the stratified nature of the sample also marginally (but significantly in a statistical sense) overemphasizes the numbers of those in the group for whom both advertisements and conversations with a Common Cause member were very important.

7. The alternative to a normal good is a Giffen good, whose consumption rises as income falls. The latter are empirically quite rare. Of course, it is also possible that consumption levels are insensitive to income.

8. When it comes to politics, lowering the costs of participation to eliminate income effects is not a strategy exclusive to group leaders either. For example, it also motivates those politicians and academics who favor electoral reforms such as same-day registration or registration by mail for those who change their residence.

9. Actually, the models estimated in this and subsequent chapters dealing with citizens' decision making were completed *before* the earlier descriptive analysis was undertaken as a means of preserving the integrity of the hypothesis tests that were performed.

10. Given that the general population study had more detailed categories than those in the Common Cause survey, the NES data had to be truncated to fit the broader categories. In the few instances where the NES category was not completely subsumed by that employed in the Common Cause survey, the rule adopted was to utilize the category that incorporated the largest proportion of the category in question. Tests to see whether alternative codings made any difference were negative.

11. While, as mentioned, party identification is routinely characterized as a running tally of retrospective evaluations and has been used as a general measure of policy preferences in the past (e.g., Shanks and Miller 1990), there is, however, no particular harm done if one prefers to think of the underlying concept being measured simply as partisanship. Race is *not* a statistically significant determinant of interest, ceteris paribus. Rather, it should be conceptualized as a summary measure of preferences.

12. Because the results are based on specific assumptions about probabilities, data on changes in these likelihoods must always be seen as suggestive rather than definitive.

13. There is about a fifty times greater likelihood that a white leaning Democrat will be a member than a black strong Republican, but the latter group is empirically almost nonexistent and therefore rather unimportant.

14. One might argue that family income is not the correct factor to measure; total wealth or discretionary income might be more appropriate for assessing the role of money for joining. While the results presented in this analysis are probably robust, alternative measures of the ability to pay are not available and the proposition that the wrong indicator is being employed cannot be refuted.

15. The SVD is a well-known diagnostic for multicollinearity. In simplest terms, it involves an orthogonal decomposition of a matrix to identify rank deficiency; that is, it is a means of making sure that least-squares estimation is identified. A technical discussion can be found in Belsley, Kuh, and Welsch (1980).

16. Given that Northeasterners (and to a lesser extent residents of Alaska and Hawaii) were so much more likely than others to be Common Cause members, a pooling test was conducted to see the implications of combining these high- and low-member states. The results for either model I or model II do show that the assumption that the unrestricted model is no better than the explanatory model is violated ($F = 6.60$ and 7.65, respectively). However, the substantive results are largely

unchanged, and the changes in the explained variance are minuscule (the addition of six additional parameters raises the adjusted R^2 by 0.004 and 0.003 for models I and II, respectively). For the sake of simplicity, therefore, the pooled results are presented here.

17. This estimate is based on the fact that

$$P_{ic} \approx \Delta X [P_{ic}(1 - P_{ic})],$$

where P_{ic} is the probability that an individual i is a member of the group in a congressional district c at a given time and X is any independent variable.

18. In her published analysis of these data, Cook (1984) employs a series of frequency distributions to examine members' motivations for joining and their satisfaction with the associations. She subsequently uses cross tabulations to investigate the bivariate relationship between satisfaction and renewal, and then to examine the bivariate relationships between activism and (1) joining, (2) political interest, (3) satisfaction with the group, and (4) length of membership. She did not conduct any multivariate hypothesis tests.

19. These four groups have several similarities. They offer publications as divisible rewards for membership, and they keep the monetary cost of joining relatively low. But they differ on a number of potentially key dimensions: the issues they address, the positions they adopt, and the way the groups are structured and operate. These organizations, along with other public interest groups, provide real alternatives for individuals who want to join an association devoted to issues regarding the public.

20. However, the questionnaire was designed to take only five minutes to complete and is lacking many desirable features. Among the more notable omissions is the absence of even a rudimentary measure of political preferences, e.g., party identification or liberalism versus conservatism, or any factors that might structure costs (except perhaps education).

21. Respondents were asked (*yes or no*) whether they joined the organization to (1) make a difference in the political process; (2) become involved in the political process because of a sense of responsibility and feeling of civic duty; (3) work on issues that [they] believe in; (4) receive the information that is sent to members; (5) gain political experience; (6) be with people who share [their] interests; and (7) for another reason. They were then asked, "What was the one single reason that was most important to you when you joined this organization?" Possible responses corresponded to the seven benefits just listed.

22. Only twenty-three persons chose either experience or interactions as their principal motivation, so the standard errors tend to be enormous.

23. Given the findings in Tables 4.5 and 4.6 and the distribution of the motivations for joining across each group, respondents were considered to have made the right choice if (1) they chose the League and claimed it was because of duty, information, or experience/interactions returns; (2) they selected the Conservative Caucus to be efficacious; (3) they chose the ACLU for reasons of ideology; or (4) they selected Common Cause to be efficacious. To reiterate, this is a crude classification.

24. This analysis also demonstrates the broader utility of choice-based models to answer questions that have been beyond the realm of more conventional research designs. Although the model specified in the present analysis is admittedly a bit crude, the results have shed light on an important problem that researchers have been unable to examine in depth on the individual level. There are undoubtedly other research questions to which choice-based techniques can be profitably applied.

CHAPTER 5

1. One notable exception to the absence of discussion of internal politics is David Truman's (1951) extensive commentary. However, given its social-psychological framework, his analysis focuses heavily on the moderating impact of overlapping group memberships and how they, along with the leadership, foster stability and thus is not particularly relevant for the present analysis.

2. In practice, this dichotomy between pluralism and a restricted economic approach is a bit muddled. The reason for this obfuscation is that those subscribing to the pluralist doctrine frequently believe that the internal politics of organizations are really subject to the "iron law of oligarchy" (Michels 1958, originally published in 1915), by which it is assumed that leaders dominate the organization (Moe 1980a). Yet, as can be inferred from the preceding discussion, this is much more consistent with the Olsonian viewpoint. Regardless, both the idea of pluralist harmony and the concept of complete domination by the leadership have probably tended to discourage serious investigation of internal organizational politics.

3. The one difference that exists pertains to age: For obvious reasons, veterans are older than newcomers.

4. A strong caveat is in order: Cross-sectional evidence is being used to draw temporal conclusions. It is nevertheless hard to tell a compelling story about how employing this cross-sectional information would confound this part of the analysis. Thus, it is worthwhile to try to uncover evidence of contributors' learning with these data, especially because the data are probably the best currently available.

5. Although it works well empirically, this question might be considered somewhat suspect because the national organization had to give its consent for state organizations to pursue unusual issues.

6. The numbers of those who gave incorrect answers might also be underestimates because they derive from a mail survey. Respondents who wanted to appear knowledgeable and were willing to expend the energy could have looked up the answers.

7. The one exception dealt with constitutional amendments limiting government spending. This issue was relatively new on the Common Cause agenda, and long-time members themselves might not have had time to learn about it. More than 40 percent of the entire membership had no opinion on Common Cause's position on it, compared to a maximum of 18 percent on the other four items.

8. Although comparable data are unavailable from the Common Cause survey on the issue of reapportionment, respondents were asked whether they supported reapportionment by the state legislature or a bipartisan commission (Common Cause's preferred alternative). They also were allowed to respond that they thought it made no difference how reapportionment was done or that they couldn't say or were not sure. Analogous to the findings stated, the likelihood of selecting the Common Cause position (bipartisan commission) was related to years in the organization in a statistically significant way. However, those selecting the *can't say/not sure* option had no less group seniority than those who had an opinion. The inference that can be drawn from these findings is rather similar to that deduced from the data displayed in Tables 5.2a and b: The fact that more junior members have an opinion, just not the "right" one from a Common Cause perspective, suggests that learning is taking place.

9. Building a core membership is extremely important for ensuring long-term survival of an organization. Even these associations that receive foundation grants and support from other organizations often find that those sources of income

are unreliable, particularly because they frequently come in the form of seed money rather than pledges of long-term sustenance.

10. This is a generic problem that all organizational leaders face. Employers, for instance, also deal with the problem of holding onto valuable workers, as well as attracting capable replacements. What sharply distinguishes interest groups from other organizations is that nonparticipation in the public arena is a far more viable alternative.

11. As was mentioned earlier, the ideal means of studying membership would include a panel study. This is particularly important for examining the topics discussed in this chapter. The analysis presented here is a second-best alternative.

12. Unfortunately, efforts to have Common Cause follow up on the actual membership decisions that those interviewed made in future years were unsuccessful. Nonetheless, there is strong reason to believe that the prospective question employed here is valid and reliable (such questions are widely utilized in social scientific research).

13. The family income measure (a scale of 8, representing eight income ranges) used in the Common Cause study (see Table 3.4) is employed here. Cost sensitivity is gauged with two dummy variables coded from a question in which members were asked if they would remain in the organization (yes, can't say, no) if Common Cause raised its annual dues from $20 to $40.

14. Members were asked to answer two questions about the importance to them personally of (a) magazines and other Common Cause publications and (b) the political information the association provides. Answers were on a five-point scale. They were also given a question parallel to the one on cost sensitivity in which they were queried whether they would stop contributing if publications were halted.

15. Position agreement is measured as

$$ -1\left[\sum_{i=1}^{5} (X_{ip} - X_{ic})^2 \right], $$

where X_{ip} and X_{ic} are, respectively, contributors' personal preferences and views of where Common Cause stands on the following issues: an amendment limiting government spending, sunset legislation, campaign finance laws, the ERA, and lobby disclosure laws. Of course, only those respondents with personal preferences and estimates of Common Cause positions are included. Contributors without opinions on issues (see Tables 5.2a and 5.2b) are excluded. Leadership assessment is an additive index combining responses on a scale of 5 to questions about the legislative success of Common Cause and an explicit rating of how well the leadership and staff do their jobs. Activity is tapped by counting whether a person has (a) written or talked to Common Cause staff or leaders about a group policy or position; (b) attempted to attract new contributors; (c) attended a local Common Cause meeting in the last year; (d) voted in the 1981 governing board elections; or (e) completed the 1981 membership poll. Finally, the personal efficacy measure combines the responses to two parallel questions on how important to the success of Common Cause individuals think their own contributions and their own political activities are.

16. The former is an additive index of the importance assigned to membership in Common Cause as a means of fulfilling the responsibilities of citizenship, supporting leaders like group founder John Gardner and then Chairman Archibald Cox, and helping to ensure good government. Caring is an additive scale of member interest in each of the five issues used to construct the position agreement scale.

17. The measure of solidary benefits is derived from a fivefold response to a question

on the importance contributors attribute to meeting interesting people and making new friends.

18. It might be maintained, in the spirit of the so-called garbage can theory (Cohen, March, and Olsen 1972; March 1978), that organizational experience is tapping the adaptation of preferences to what Common Cause has to offer; that is, the conventional assumption that preferences are fixed may be incorrect. Admittedly, it is impossible to distinguish definitively between changing preferences and learning, given the lack of panel data. However, the fixed-preference assumption is probably reasonable. It has already been shown in this analysis that individuals do learn about the organization's operations and its positions on issues. It is also hard to believe that Common Cause members suddenly develop a preference for good government, political information, or social interactions once they sign up for the group.

19. See Appendix 5.1 for a discussion of the econometric techniques employed.

20. In other words, comparing model II with model I ($F_{2,1076} = 33.15$; $p < .01$); model III with model II ($F_{4,971} = 42.11$; $p < .01$); and model IV with model III ($F_{4,911} = 7.93$; $p < .05$), clearly identifies model IV as the best specification (see Pindyck and Rubinfeld 1981, for an explication of joint F tests).

21. Unfortunately, no good measure of nonpecuniary costs was available for the whole sample. An indicator that worked for part of it ($N = 395$) was whether or not members responded to attempts to mobilize them. Even after controlling for all other factors, these costs are important determinants of the retention decision. This result provides evidence that those who find these additional organizational demands taxing depart, presumably either to find an association where they can simply write checks (or perhaps, as will be discussed in the subsequent chapter, to discover a group where the opportunities for activism are more enticing) or to leave the world of organizational participation completely.

22. There is a cost to quitting as well: Just as consumers who stop using a service are frequently contacted, former Common Cause members are contacted for quite some time afterward, including initially by phone.

23. The statement that respondents were given read: "Sometimes organizations have to cut back on some activities in order to maintain others or they have to increase their financial resources. Below is a list of ways in which a group like Common Cause might do so. Although none of these events is likely to occur, we would like to know if you would remain a member of Common Cause if Common Cause raised its annual dues from $20.00 to $40.00." Only 41 percent of members said they would definitely remain in the group if dues were doubled ("low sensitivity"), 33 percent responded that they were not sure ("moderate sensitivity"), and 26 percent claimed that they would quit ("high sensitivity"). The percentage stating that they would remain in the group is slightly inflated by the stratified sample (only 38 percent of the rank and file were sure that they would remain).

24. An increase of one standard deviation in a member's score on each of the collective benefit indicators would result in a jump of 0.71 on the retention scale. This change is slightly greater than the impact of membership costs (.63), followed by divisible benefits (.23), purposive returns (.21), organizational experience (.18), and solidary rewards (.17). The strength of membership costs might be a bit of a surprise. However, the measures of cost sensitivity – the willingness to quit in response to a $20 increase in dues – are also tapping estimates of the value of benefits.

25. These findings are based on a regression analysis using model IV, where the sums of the squared differences for each issue are substituted separately instead of cumulatively. The two relatively new issues on the Common Cause agenda – ERA and placing limits on government spending – are not relevant. These concerns

represent a departure from the issues upon which the organization gained its reputation and apparently had not become a prime reason for remaining in the organization (or for joining, in all likelihood).

26. Even a simple bivariate analysis makes this relationship clear. For example, if one assumes that departures are equiprobable with each year, the likelihood of a member making it to a twelfth year in the organization is roughly 6.5 percent. By contrast, the revealed probability in Common Cause is about 15.3 percent (15 percent for rank and file and 23 percent for designated activists). Clearly, departures cannot be assumed to be the product of a simple random process.

27. The logarithmic term for learning is now unnecessary, since the sample is split according to how many years a contributor has been in the group. The definitive means of testing whether coefficients vary between newcomers and veterans is to employ interaction terms with the full sample. However, multicollinearity makes such estimates unfeasible in this instance.

28. The larger impact of cost sensitivity on newcomers than veterans probably reflects the former's greater uncertainty about the value of membership.

29. This 80 percent figure for Common Cause is again consistent with the previously reported organizational retention rate of 78 percent.

30. Given strong expectations, one-tailed significance tests are employed for all indicators except for the dummy variable measuring whether individuals respond that they do not know how the organization operates.

31. Once this specification was decided upon, both ordinary least squares (OLS) and probit estimation were employed. The results are identical for all intents and purposes; the OLS results are reported here because of their ease of interpretation.

CHAPTER 6

1. These two categories are not mutually exclusive; in fact, they are positively correlated. The average checkbook activist is about 35 percent more likely to be a temporal activist, and these temporal activists are twice as prone to be checkbook activists. (How these two forms of activism are measured is presented shortly.)

2. An analogy might be drawn to research on the economics on transportation costs, which shows that less well-to-do workers tend to spend more time traveling to and from work than those who earn higher wages or salaries; that is, poorer people commit more of their time to activities that do not yield direct monetary compensation.

3. Recently Knoke (1990) has argued that income is a positive determinant of money contributed using data on members belonging to a wide variety of organizations. However, a number of notes of caution regarding his results are in order: Knoke's model does a generally quite poor job of prediction and would seem to be plagued by a variety of specification problems associated with endogeneity (e.g., he claims that organizations with a complex bureaucratic structure are better at soliciting contributions, without acknowledging the [quite strong] possibility that contributions also create the diversified structure in the first place) and the omission of factors, such as purposive and collective rewards, that would seem to be essential controls for judging the role of income.

4. For purposes of brevity, temporal activism is referred to as activism or volunteerism in this section. Also the phrase *rank and file* is employed to include all those who are not temporal activists.

5. Clearly, maintenance and policy tasks are not mutually exclusive. However, some organizational actions are clearly policy-centered (e.g., trying to get a bill passed) even though they may have implications for maintenance (e.g., they may preci-

pitate contributions). Similarly, other group activities may be principally for maintenance (e.g., soliciting contributions) even if keeping the association going and healthy is essential to have policy success.

6. Almost every state also has a lobbying organization; however, to reiterate, they are not discussed here in much detail.

7. To reiterate, for purposes of the analysis of temporal activists, those checkbook activists who do nothing more than contribute additional money were classified as part of the rank and file.

    McFarland (1984) also distinguishes between activists and the occasionally active, but his beliefs about the latter group are based on conjecture. In the present research, occasional activists are defined as any respondent who was not a Common Cause–designated activist but who claimed to be active (1) in a Common Cause state organization, (2) as a steering committee coordinator in a congressional district, (3) as a telephone network coordinator or activator, (4) as a telephone caller, (5) as a speaker before other groups, or (6) in other activist activities. Rank-and-file members formed 69 percent of the stratified sample; occasional activists, 8 percent; and core activists, 23 percent.

8. To reiterate, this is a ceteris paribus argument. While both members generally and activists specifically have higher income levels relative to the population, the question being asked here is, conditional upon being a member and controlling for other factors, what effect does income have on activism?

9. It is conceivable that even though those with lower incomes are "charged" less to be activists, they may sacrifice more in utility because they attach a greater value to each dollar charged than individuals with higher income do; but this seems unlikely.

    Also, the hypothesis that at the very least, income will not facilitate participation involving a commitment of time is supported by the finding that it has no impact on as minimal an act as voting in elections (Wolfinger and Rosenstone 1980).

10. To reiterate a point made in the last chapter, contributors' responses to questions that tap their perceptions about having an impact on the production of collective goods probably reflect their perceptions of the group's, and not their personal, impact on the provision of such benefits. This is why the caveat "very broadly construed" is used when discussing selfish motivations. The distinction is being made between individuals who – along with a preference for divisible and solidary benefits – believe that they are efficacious and those who are involved in the association for the more pristine reason of believing in the statement that the group makes and the collective goods it pursues whether the individual makes a viable contribution to their achievement.

11. As will be discussed in more detail, the ideal means of studying activism, like membership behavior generally, would be through a panel study.

12. With respect to collective rewards, the key test of whether contributors are utility maximizers should be whether they perceive themselves to be efficacious or not. The belief that the group is actually producing something should be what distinguishes collective from purposive rewards.

13. To reiterate, as long as one response was broadly participatory, the contributors were considered to have an initial predisposition toward activism. Nevertheless, only 11 percent met even this minimal threshold.

14. Rather than asking how many years they have been activists, members were requested to choose one of the five categories: (1) 8–10 years, (2) 6–7 years, (3) 4–5 years, (4) 2–3 years, and (5) 1 year or less. The three-year estimate is conservative; it is based on the most years possible – 10, 7, 5, 3, or 1 – that participants might have been involved relative to the number of years they have been in the group. If the means of these categories were substituted for the upper

bounds, less than 9 percent of activists would be classified as having become activists within one year of joining.

15. The question was posed to any person engaged in any of the defining activist behaviors. Respondents were to choose from four possible alternatives: (1) a fellow member asked me to help out; (2) I was contacted by the national office of Common Cause and asked to help out; (3) I was contacted by a state office of Common Cause and asked to help out; and (4) I contacted Common Cause and volunteered my services. However, some members chose more than one option – hence the hybrid categories in Table 6.2. (Indeed, the members who solicited other contributors to become activists may have been working as part of the organization's system to recruit new activists.)

    The fact that so many activists were recruited from those within the organization suggests that, to some extent, the process of how members become activists may be somewhat analogous to the two-step process by which citizens become members; that is, first somebody is contacted and subsequently they decide to join. While this is likely to be a less severe problem than it is for joining and will consequently not be highlighted in the remainder of this chapter, it should be kept in mind that to some extent the determinants of activism may reflect the decision by others to recruit a member to the activist cadre.

16. The latter is measured with a fourfold indicator based on the measure of urbanization employed in Table 3.4, with those who live in suburbs and those who live in small cities classified as equivalent.

17. Perceptions about oligarchy are tapped by combining contributors' responses about whether (1) members of Common Cause are given a large role in determining its policies; (2) only a small minority of members take part in Common Cause decision making; (3) most members agree with Common Cause positions; (4) sometimes a small minority of members prevents Common Cause from taking a position supported by the majority; and (5) leaders care what members think. (The implications of these assessments regarding organizational democracy are also discussed in the subsequent analysis of goal formation.)

18. One-tailed significance tests are therefore utilized for all of the independent variables except the linear learning term and perceptions of oligarchy.

19. This constraint may also lead to some specification error. To test this, an analogue of the test developed by Hausman (Hausman 1978; Hausman and McFadden 1984) was derived for the WESML estimator to help determine whether contributors to Common Cause really make trichotomous choices with respect to activism. The threefold specification was tested against the alternative of viewing the activist decision as a series of dichotomous choices; i.e., members initially decide whether or not to be active and subsequently choose the degree of commitment (occasional versus core). The results led to the rejection of the hypothesis that the slopes are equal. This finding suggests that the assumption concerning independence of irrelevant alternatives is being violated; the damage this causes to the derived estimates is uncertain.

20. To repeat, data on changes in probabilities like those shown in Table 6.4 must always be seen as suggestive rather than definitive.

21. Obviously, panel data that would permit the identification of those who became activists immediately and then went back to the rank and file would be ideal.

22. This result holds up even if education and age are both incorporated into the model (neither comes close to statistical significance).

23. An alternative way to think about opportunity costs is in terms of time available for public service. Individuals with fewer work and family obligations – who are not in the labor force or who have relatively undemanding jobs and who do not have children living at home – might be more likely to be activists. Unfortunately,

respondents only provide data on marital status and not on family composition; also, they only report job status and type of job rather than hours worked per week. When dummy variables for marital and job status are incorporated into the estimated equation, the results tend to disconfirm this perspective on costs: Married persons are more likely to be activists, and job status is irrelevant.

Common Cause's dependence on telephone calls rather than face-to-face interactions might be less threatening than volunteering elsewhere and therefore might give it a comparative cost advantage in appealing to older persons and women. To test this, the model was again rerun with a series of dummy variables tapping age groups and an additional dummy variable for gender. The results reveal that gender has no impact and that the effect of age is very erratic.

24. The constructed issue agreement scale for the sample runs from -110 to 0, with an average of -13.5. A score of -14 represents many possible configurations. For example, a member might have placed him- or herself two points away (out of the possible six) on a seven-point scale from where he or she perceived Common Cause on three issues and one on the other two issues. Those who were one standard deviation more in disagreement (i.e., -27.8) might be three points away on three issues and one point away on another and might agree on a fifth. Only on lobbying regulation did the average Common Cause member disagree by just one point; on the other four issues, the mean was closer to two.

25. To reiterate, b is the potential benefit from a given action and p is the probability that benefits will accrue if the action is taken.

The results for efficacy are especially impressive in light of Moe's (1980a) argument that group members should be highly skewed toward the extremely efficacious, which might imply that there would not be enough variation to be statistically significant. However, the degree of heterogeneity for both efficacy measures is roughly comparable to that of issue agreement. The findings for efficacy provide further evidence that the insignificance of the b term is not a distributional artifact.

26. For others, perceptions of oligarchy may prompt departure. When the previously specified model of member exit was reestimated with oligarchy included, feelings that the group is oligarchic were found to be positively related to quitting ($t = -1.8$). Membership experience may lead to the same evaluation but result in different reactions: Some exit and others become active in organizations they believe are oligarchic.

27. These numbers are based on changes in the probabilities of activism as a result of simultaneous shifts in the values of the linear and logarithmic measures of organizational experience; they are not shown in Table 6.4.

28. This latter indicator is measured by whether members claim that either political experience or solidary returns were their principal reasons for joining.

29. Respondents were asked, "Are you one of the more active members of this organization who contributes more than the average amount of time and/or money?" Given that the relevant comparison is between the respondent and the average member, it might be conjectured that about half of each group's members should reply affirmatively. Yet, the aggregate numbers are far under 50 percent for each group. Apparently, members were relying upon more conventional definitions of activism in which the vast majority are assumed to be part of the rank and file and activists represent the small percentage who are most strongly committed to the organization; that is, answers to the activism question reflect the skewed distribution of commitment level in the organization.

Another potential problem with this measure of activism is that it may confound time and money commitments. This confuses those giving extra money – perhaps as a consequence of having higher incomes – with those sacrificing their time.

Temporal contributions are probably what is conventionally meant by activism, and it is likely that what determines the cost of this behavior differs considerably from what determines the cost of giving extra money. It is also probable that time commitments are what the respondents have in mind. League of Women Voters contributors are twice as likely to claim that they are activists than contributors in any other organization; this undoubtedly reflects the higher probability that League members give time as well as money.

30. Given these strong expectations, one-tailed significance tests are again employed for all indicators except for the dummy variable measuring whether individuals respond that they do not know how the organization operates.

31. Since it was necessary to employ multinomial logit in the Common Cause–specific analysis, an analogous procedure using only those data is not feasible.

32. To estimate this model, the four activists who were considering quitting were excluded.

CHAPTER 7

1. These ends certainly include furnishing an attractive package of selective and solidary rewards for members as well as the purposive statements that the association makes and the collective goals that it pursues. However, it is the formation of political objectives that is of greatest concern to scholars. Consequently, the principal focus of this chapter is on the assortment of collective and purposive rewards that an organization offers to its contributors that embodies its political goals.

2. McFarland's (1984) research focuses heavily on the relationship between the Common Cause staff and its governing board. Given the theoretical interests driving the current analysis – and the fact that McFarland has covered this other territory – relatively little attention will be paid to this set of interactions here. Rather, the principal emphasis of the present investigation will be squarely on determining how various contributors think that their interests are represented and whether this corresponds to what seems to be going on at Common Cause. Throughout this analysis, it should be remembered that the governing board sets policy at its quarterly meetings, with the staff subsequently charged with implementing its decisions.

3. Respondents were asked, "Did you complete the 1981 Membership Issue Poll?" and were given the option of checking off (1) Yes, (2) No, or (3) Have Not Heard of Poll. Not surprisingly, there was a huge difference in the percentages of rank-and-file members (31 percent) and activists (15 percent) who had not heard of the poll. In addition, the aggregate percentage claiming no knowledge of the poll's existence might be biased downward because the wording of the question made it easy for respondents who were unaware of the poll to imply otherwise by merely answering yes or no rather than replying that they had not heard of it. It might also be speculated that the percentage would also be an underestimate because just the sort of persons who had never heard of the poll also would tend not to respond to an academic questionnaire.

4. One might be surprised at this point to see nuclear arms control included. This will be cleared up shortly.

5. As mentioned earlier, slightly more than half of all members responding to the Common Cause survey reported that they were already members of environmental groups.

6. Remember that 41 percent of female contributors reported being in feminist groups.

7. In addition, and confirming a point made in the previous chapter, while only 19 percent of those who reported giving additional monies to Common Cause in the past said they would quit in response to doubled dues, 39 percent of those paying only dues said they would exit. This makes considerable sense in that those regularly giving additional contributions could simply cut back or eliminate these additional gifts if dues were hiked. (Parenthetically, this also implies that raising dues to expand programs would probably be less financially rewarding than such a move might appear at first glance, as evidenced by the failed experiment with a $25 first-time fee.)

8. Another reason for this decision rule may be to prevent the organization's unraveling, a point that will be expounded in more detail shortly.

9. In all cases except the statement about agreement with Common Cause issue opinions where the two look alike, activists are significantly more positive in their assessment about the association in a statistical sense than rank-and-file members – although sometimes the level of these differences is relatively slight.

10. These questions, it might be remembered, were jointly employed for compiling the indicator regarding perceptions about oligarchy utilized in the last chapter. Also, their ordering in the questionnaire was somewhat different than in Table 7.2.

11. Despite the fact that virtually no one responded affirmatively to the question about whether small minorities prevent the adoption of majority positions, it might be reiterated that there is an objective basis to argue that minority vetos operate. Interestingly, if not surprisingly, activists are somewhat more likely to disagree than rank-and-file members; that is, many activists, who are both highly supportive of the organization and tend to know more about it, continue to assert that no minority veto exists.

12. Consistent with the previous discussions, when the relevant equations are rerun, the impact of the process component of oligarchy appears greater than the results component for activism, while the reverse is true for retention.

13. Not surprisingly given the wildly skewed responses for each type of contributor, there was no difference between rank-and-file and activist answers.

14. There were other complicating issues. Members of the Reagan administration argued that the MX was a crucial bargaining chip in dealing with the Soviets in the stalled strategic arms reduction talks (START). In particular, it was argued, the MX was needed if the Soviet SS-18 and SS-19 missiles were to be reduced or eliminated. (Yet, many actions – the refusal to offer to trade away the MX for the elimination of the SS-18s, for example – made it appear to many that this justification was a smoke screen, since the administration was fundamentally opposed to giving up any weapon in its strategic modernization program, e.g., Talbot 1984.) In addition, some among those in the Reagan White House were concerned that cutting off the MX would give their European allies a rationale for blocking NATO deployment of other weapons. Both points were repeatedly made in efforts to pressure legislators into supporting the MX.

15. The vote was 245 to 176 in the House and 56 to 42 in the Senate with a stronger House amendment that cut, rather than "fenced in," the billion dollars surviving the conference committee deliberations (the House position had originally lost 70 to 28 in the Senate).

16. On one occasion, Wertheimer came out against a school prayer bill; on another Common Cause criticized the Congress and Office of Management and Budget for wasting money by not following the recommendations of the U.S. General Accounting Office (GAO) investigations; and on a third the group denounced the idea of a constitutional convention to deal with the budget deficit on the grounds that other aspects of the Constitution might be changed at the same time.

17. There was one prominent picture that included some Common Cause lobbyists that was not mentioned in the *Index*.

18. Interestingly, Common Cause staffers claim that they neither suffered organizationally from relying on these methods nor did these efforts produce a different type of contributor with respect to their demographic attributes or behavior as members. This suggests, consistent with the earlier discussion of member joining, that those signing up for the group in response to MX appeals had some vague idea of what kind of group it was. As former group President David Cohen puts it, Common Cause should have "appealed to people [who were] not apocalyptic," reflecting Common Cause's more mainstream ways.

19. Moreover, there are a considerable number of scholars who believe that this Olsonian perspective is exportable to public interest groups. As already mentioned, a critique of such organizations, including Common Cause, is that they solely exist to perpetuate themselves very much in the Olsonian tradition.

20. This theoretical question has been addressed first, somewhat peripherally, by Salisbury (1969) and Hirschman (1970), and then more directly by Moe (1980a). Of the three, this analysis comes closest to the latter perspective. Salisbury (1969) argued that leaders act as organizational entrepreneurs who furnish a set of benefits to customers to join an organization. Although the subject of leadership behavior is implicitly related to goal formation, Salisbury's fundamental purpose is not to discern who in the association should have the largest impact on associational goals. Hirschman (1970), as discussed previously, emphasizes what happens when an organization is unable to achieve its ends (rather than how the objectives are chosen) because of unspecified, random causes. Nevertheless, his point that members might resort either to exit or to voice and that leaders must be sensitive to this fact is relevant when the subject is organizational goals.

Moe, by contrast, develops a model of internal politics that attempts to explain the source of organizational goals. His basic contention is that internal politics take place within a bargaining context in which those involved advance claims against the entrepreneur. However, while his analysis heavily guides the present research – and what most distinguishes the current research is that the ideas are developed for a specific, detailed, empirical application – there are several subtle differences between his theory and the approach outlined here.

One such distinction is simply that in certain respects the current investigation simplifies Moe's analysis. Notably, he makes a considerable issue out of the potential for alternative entrepreneurs to arise within an organization. While this is a possibility, it is not a relevant consideration at Common Cause (and, one suspects, it is of minimal importance at most public interest groups where the stakes are relatively low). Generally, leaders employ mechanisms that make it quite difficult for such a coup to occur. For example, at Common Cause it would necessitate taking over a majority of the governing board, a task that would seem to be of gargantuan proportions.

Another difference is that the framework presented here is a more self-conscious attempt to tie models of goal formation to assumptions about individual choice behavior. While Moe's analysis of joining appears to allow for no possibility of learning and exiting, when the subject is internal politics, this implicit assumption seems to slip. The present analysis attempts to build on the overall depiction of individual decision making developed earlier. Thus, the emphasis is on what motivates certain types of contributors and what, given leadership uncertainty about member preferences, the entrepreneurs can do to manage the situation.

In his analysis of Common Cause, McFarland (1984) overviews the internal politics of Common Cause using a variety of theoretical ideas, including those of

Hirschman. Although his theoretical approach is somewhat different from that employed here and his analysis was completed before Common Cause made the dramatic break from its traditional agenda by getting involved in the MX debate, the current research attempts in many respects to build on McFarland's work both theoretically and empirically.

21. The Federal Election Campaign Act Amendments of 1979 enacted only non-controversial reforms after efforts by Common Cause and its legislative allies to achieve more dramatic changes were stalemated; pledges that more far-reaching campaign finance reforms would be taken up in the next legislative session(s) went unfulfilled.

22. Interestingly, when I mentioned to Common Cause staffers that their membership polls indicated that the MX was less popular with their contributors than other issues (Table 7.1), they were quick to point out how little the level of support varies from one issue to another.

23. For example, among the best known of the thirteen new members of the governing board elected in 1990 were former U.S. Representative Richard Bolling, former Wisconsin Governor Anthony Earl, and former Dukakis campaign manager Susan Estrich.

24. The focus on a specific weapons program was actually something that others in the arms control movement were leery about. "You kill off one program and another takes its place," John Isaac, head of Council for a Livable World, noted in an interview. Rather, some preferred more encompassing change such as that represented by efforts to implement a nuclear freeze (Meyer 1990).

25. Cohen operated under the aegis of the Professionals' Coalition for Nuclear Arms Control.

26. In February 1991 the Common Cause governing board officially approved a proposal that explicitly stated: (1) the group's long-time issues such as campaign finance should remain top priority, (2) the group should support congressional efforts to reexamine national security policy and priorities, and (3) in coalition with other groups, the organization would choose a number of very specific objectives, such as the B-2 "stealth" bomber, to which it might make a unique contribution. In other words, arms control issues were explicitly relegated to a very secondary position on the Common Cause agenda.

27. While attention in this analysis has focused heavily on the leadership's shaping of the group's arms control initiatives, it clearly has performed the same role in defining the specifics of Common Cause's position and in allocating resources on other issues, notably campaign reform.

CHAPTER 8

1. Congress is the focus here because this is where Common Cause has principally tried to have an influence. Only to a secondary extent has the organization utilized the courts or tried to move the bureaucracy.

2. While Senate votes will be discussed, they will not be analyzed quantitatively because interviewees claimed that the nature of Senate lobbying, given the small numbers of senators, would make quantitative analysis unilluminating. Interviewees also tend to point to their key success in the upper chamber as getting Senate moderates, such as Sam Nunn of Georgia, to compromise.

3. In his model of "buying" legislatures, Snyder (1991) comes to a similar conclusion.

4. Austen-Smith and Wright (1991) have recently specified a theoretical model in which a boundary condition exists by which legislators who are completely in-different ex ante will be ignored by lobbyists. However, this should probably not

be of great concern for the present analysis because it deals only with the idiosyncratic instance where a legislator has absolutely no prior commitment to vote for a given alternative one way or another.

5. The July vote was on an amendment to the Department of Defense authorization bill, and it would have deleted the $2.6 billion earmarked for the first 27 production line models of the Peacekeeper; the November vote was on a similar amendment to eliminate $2.2 billion for 21 missiles from the appropriations bill. In the Senate, only one vote to delete procurement funds took place and only one senator, Robert Packwood, changed his vote (from pro- to anti-MX).

6. The House Armed Services Committee had cut the administration's now $2.9 billion request for 40 missiles to $2.45 billion for 30 missiles.

7. In another piece of legislative maneuvering, the MX supporters who wanted a roll call on the vote for 15 missiles were outflanked by Mavroules, who surprised them by accepting the voice vote and then turned around and reintroduced his amendment for no production as a second-degree amendment and asked for a roll call on it. Because it was a second-degree amendment, Aspin could not preempt it with his own amendment.

8. The GOP leadership was given considerable credit for getting conservative Republicans to accept only 15 missiles.

9. The proposal for a cap allegedly created considerable tensions among those in the anti-MX coalition. For instance, there was a considerable strain created in trying to convince organizations that were strident about their preference for no MXs (e.g., church groups) that advocating a compromise solution was in their best interest.

10. The compromise placed the two votes so close together temporally that, at least in retrospect, the House victory proved merely symbolic.

11. The committee voted 26 to 28 against MX procurement, but under special procedures the House nevertheless had to act on the resolution.

12. Postscript: As Nunn et al. desired, the Peacekeeper faded from congressional prominence for several years. The Reagan administration, however, continued to push for deployment of more MXs in conjunction with a new basing mode. While Congress resisted pleas for developing superhardened silos, it voted funds to explore the development of a December 1986 Reagan proposal for basing a second group of 50 MXs on railroad cars. The cars would remain on military bases except during national emergencies, when they would travel across the nation's rail system. For all intents and purposes, the administration simultaneously tried – with considerable success – to eliminate the Midgetman missile favored by moderate Democrats and used by the authors of the Scowcroft Report as justification for deploying the MX.

13. The coalition of 89 national organizations included arms control groups (e.g., SANE), citizens' groups other than Common Cause (e.g., Americans for Democratic Action), environmental associations (e.g., Sierra Club), labor unions (e.g., International Association of Machinists and Aerospace Workers), professional groups (e.g., Union of Concerned Scientists), religious organizations (e.g., United Methodist Church), and women's groups (e.g., American Association of University Women). However, as with a large number of such coalitions, many organizations provided little support except for the use of their names.

14. These statements are based on the lobbying lists furnished by Common Cause.

15. To put this in another perspective, an analysis of the FY86 data (provided in EW Communications 1988) reveals that the MX was one of the top five weapons systems in terms of revenues produced for six states (California, Colorado, Pennsylvania, South Dakota, Utah, and Washington) and 21 congressional dis-

tricts (Arizona's 2nd and 3rd; California's 12th, 23rd, 31st, 32nd, 36th, and 39th; Colorado's 5th; Florida's 9th; Maryland's 6th; Massachusetts's 3rd, 7th, 8th, and 9th; New York's 22nd; Pennsylvania's 2nd; South Dakota's lone district; Texas's 20th; Utah's 1st; and Washington's 7th).

16. Pooling the votes taking place during a given year does not change the interpretation of results. Given that it is more intuitive to examine roll calls individually, such findings are presented here.

17. Interestingly, despite the touchy nature of the subject matter, there was little strategic abstention (Cohen and Noll 1990); the only time when there were a great many missing legislators was when the bill was voted on over the Memorial Day holiday.

18. Conservative Coalition scores were originally used rather than military-specific rankings to avoid the risk of endogeneity; that is, there was a fear of using an independent variable that was just a measure of the dependent variable. (For similar reasons, previous MX votes are not used as explanators of present votes being studied.) However, it should also be noted that when National Security Index (NSI) scores were subsequently examined, the correlation with the Conservative Coalition scores exceeded 0.9 even when MX votes were removed from the NSI scale; that is, it makes no substantive difference which are used.

19. This involved obtaining computerized printouts of all MX contracts and aggregating where money was spent to the congressional district level.

20. While some of the groups in the Common Cause coalition give PAC money, the main groups abstain. Particularly given Common Cause's hostility toward the use of PAC contributions, incorporating PAC expenditure data from peripherally allied associations would be very misleading and risky.

21. The latter is measured by -1 times each member's margin of victory in the previous election.

22. In a perfect world, information on the number of district activists would be included. However, analysis of the Common Cause survey data reveals that activists are geographically distributed in almost identical fashion to the overall apportionment of group contributors; that is, there is little measurement error associated with the indicator employed in this analysis.

23. Ideally, one would like to formulate a model along the lines of that proposed by Heckman (1978). However, besides requiring several heroic assumptions, applying such a model to the case at hand would be a major research project in itself. Thus, the instrumental variable probit approach that was developed for continuous endogenous variables is utilized instead (it has not yet been extended to the dichotomous case).

24. These additional measures include (1) mean district education; (2) the percentage urban in the district; (3) the percentage of the district classified as white collar; (4) total weapons spending in the district; (5) the average age of those residing in the district; (6) the percentage of the district that is white; (7) whether the district is in the South; (8) committee membership; (9) freshman status. The first six indicators are transformed to measure the absolute difference of these factors from the national means on the presumption, as stated above, that being pivotal should be crucial.

25. This might be a function of the data, since the lists used for 1985 were created further in advance of the votes than those employed to construct the lobbying measure for 1984, or of less than perfect instruments.

26. This is especially interesting given that party might also be thought to pick up some of the effects of the Reagan administration's lobbying efforts.

27. Not much weight should be placed on the lack of subcontractor data. According

to those contacted, there was little strategic use of subcontracting, unlike that associated most commonly with the B-1. The obvious reason is that compared to other military projects the financial rewards were limited (Smith 1988). Rather, those districts that stood to benefit were principally the homes of the Associate Prime Contractors.

28. It is important to emphasize that lobbying is not exclusively aimed at influencing the vote; as is well understood, there are many preliminary stages that are also relevant but are less easily quantified than a roll call (Hall and Wayman 1990). As mentioned earlier, the nature of the floor agenda for the MX in 1984 was quite important. The anti-MX forces were unsuccessful in making the Peacekeeper an up or down proposition on 30 missiles or none at all and had to settle for an amendment that made members vote for 15 or nothing. Also of importance in 1984 was how the anti-MX coalition and its congressional allies came up with the idea of fencing in the money for missiles. According to Mawby, "We were constantly looking for amendments that put us in that position [of occupying a middle ground that members could support]. ... I don't think fencing had ever been tried seriously before the MX battle." Fencing not only represented a middle position but one that members previously supporting the MX could vote for and not be accused of changing their minds.

Interviewees also mentioned other idiosyncrasies; for instance, one explanation given for the successful passage of the amendment that led to the fencing in of MX money in 1984 was that the vote took place late at night after the president had gone to sleep (and was, therefore, unavailable to place the requisite phone calls) and the House Democrats were around to vote because they were watching the televised broadcast of the Lakers and the Celtics in the cloakroom.

29. Information from interviews also provided confirmation of the fact that members with a great deal of credibility did not receive a vast amount of extra lobbying attention. The leaders of the lobbying coalition wanted firsthand confirmation of a legislator's support and were unwilling to accept assurances from other members of Congress. While this did not mean that one member might not be asked to lobby another, it did dictate that the vacillating representative also had to be contacted directly.

30. Because fence straddling and friendship are algebraic functions of each other, they cannot be included in the same equation.

31. Thus, even though this investigation includes only one issue area, raises methodological questions, and presents data deficiencies – notably lack of information about whom the pro-MX side is lobbying and data on MX subcontractors – it is likely to be of some value to those interested solely in the relationship between lobbying and outcomes.

CHAPTER 9

1. The focus of this analysis is on the organization's legislative efforts rather than on what might be labeled its "watchdog" function. The former concerns Common Cause's drive to amend the structure of the finance system; the latter involves the group's role as a police force in making sure that participants do not abuse the current system (e.g., by asking that the Senate Ethics Committee investigate five senators' acceptance of contributions from Lincoln Savings and Loan kingpin Charles H. Keating, Jr.). While these functions are related to one another – for instance, trying to draw attention to the actions of those senators involved in the Lincoln scandal was partially designed to set a fire under Congress to enact statutory reform – they are not identical.

2. An example in the author's own locale occurred during the group's 1990 drive to get finance reform passed. In conjunction with a program to target key members of Congress, Common Cause ran an advertisement in the Rochester *Democrat and Chronicle* urging Representative Louise Slaughter, a member of the Rules Committee, to vote for campaign reform. The ad went on to emphasize both that the savings and loan industry had made large PAC contributions and that Slaughter had accepted $660,000 in PAC money (although none from the S&L industry). Common Cause subsequently followed this up with a visit to the paper's editorial offices. Tactics like these enraged the targeted members and many playing key leadership roles. Slaughter had not forgotten a year later: "I've lost all respect for them [Common Cause], and I think others up here [on Capitol Hill] have too" (Barnes 1991, p. 1556). Eventually, the group was the subject of an angry public denunciation from House Speaker Thomas Foley.

3. In their study of the famous Powell amendment (providing that federal aid to education would only go to states whose schools did not discriminate on the basis of race), Denzau, Riker, and Shepsle (1985) claim that some members of Congress were loath to vote strategically because of the difficulties of explaining their actions at home; for example, Northern Democrats were unwilling to vote against the Powell amendment even if it meant certain death for the bill under consideration.

4. Even if true, one might argue that it is not myopia but rationality and that incumbents have little incentive to learn anything else.

5. The exact question reads "It has been suggested that the Federal government provide a fixed amount of money for the election campaigns of candidates for Congress and that all private contributions be prohibited. Do you think this is a good idea or a poor idea?"

6. Typically, academic research uncovers scant evidence that incumbent spending matters at all – although very few people, including those making such findings, really believe that members' expenditures are irrelevant (and some recent research, e.g., Green and Krasno 1988 and Ansolabehere 1990, has found a positive linkage). Rather, these results are interpreted as showing that incumbents have a huge institutionalized advantage that makes the marginal impact of their spending far less than that of challengers.

7. However, members' electoral vulnerability might contribute to their attitudes toward reform.

8. Naturally, in all cases using the term Democrat or Republican refers to the modal partisan. As will be discussed, both the Democrats and the GOP have some renegades that make life unpleasant for the leadership in brokering a compromise, but in general preferences are rather homogeneous when broken down by party.

9. The 1974 FECA Amendments restricted individual contributions to $1,000 per candidate and $25,000 per year; limited direct and indirect party spending on candidates; and set a ceiling on PAC contributions of $5,000 per candidate. It also provided for federal matching funds in presidential primaries, complete funding of presidential elections, and disclosure through the FEC. Efforts to limit candidates' contributions to their own campaigns were struck down by the Supreme Court in the case of *Buckley v. Valeo* (424 U.S. 1 (1976)).

10. Interestingly, Common Cause staff continue to attribute incumbent protection as the motivation preventing change – despite the likelihood that if this were the case incumbents should be able to get together and arrive at reform legislation reducing overall spending on elections.

11. For example, House Republicans raised almost $82 million from sources other than PACs in 1987–8 for their 624 candidates – over $44 million for their 165

incumbents. House Democrats, by contrast, picked up about $93 million for their 745 candidates, with slightly under $50 million for their 248 incumbents. In other words, Republican and Democratic challengers (either running against incumbents from the other party or seeking open seats) received roughly the same amount of money in the aggregate from contributors other than PACs, but Republican incumbents were the beneficiaries of close to $100,000 apiece more than their Democratic counterparts. This is all the more impressive when one considers the GOP's status as the perpetual minority party: Republicans do not occupy the key chairmanship and leadership posts that can translate into contributions.

As for the parties themselves, the Republican party's total receipts were over $263 million in 1987–8; the Democrats raised slightly less than $128 million. In the electoral arena, the Republican party outspent the Democratic party nearly 3 to 1 in House campaigns ($34 million to $12 million) and more than 4 to 1 in Senate contests ($66 million to $16 million).

12. In 1988 PACs contributed a total of $67 million to 745 House Democrats, $53 million of it to the party's 248 incumbents; comparable figures for Republicans are $35 million to 624 candidates and $29 million to 165 incumbents, respectively. On a per candidate basis, Democratic incumbents and challengers have about a $38,000 and a $15,000 edge, respectively, on their Republican counterparts.

13. The notable exception, as will be discussed, is David Boren.

14. Another route that others (e.g., Senator Ernest Hollings of South Carolina) propose is to amend the Constitution. While this would solve the legal problems raised in *Buckley*, the time horizon and the obstacles facing passage of an amendment make this rather unappealing to those who see an urgent need to change the status quo.

15. *Independent expenditures* are funds that are used in elections but are not contributed to individual candidates; they have recently become associated with negative advertising as nonaffiliated groups virulently attack those they oppose. While the Republicans have some edge when it comes to such spending, its potential regulation is not charged in a highly partisan manner. As discussed, soft money refers to funds that are used for party building rather than for a particular candidate's campaign. Because it allows wealthy donors to get around the contribution limits set up in 1974 and because Republicans are much better than Democrats at raising small sums, controlling this form of spending is a partisan issue (for the detailed discussions of soft money, see Center for Responsible Politics 1988; Jackson 1988). *Bundling* is the technique by which groups and individuals gather contributions from others as a means of exceeding the contribution limits. Once again, this is a big donor, pro-Democratic issue but lacks a strong partisan edge.

16. Of course, such positions are another example of the group's leaders and staff using their discretion in translating a broad membership preference – do something about money and elections – into concrete action.

17. There is really only one dimension (an electoral one) when it comes to campaign finance, so issues of cycle à la McKelvey (1976) are not a concern.

18. As mentioned, the 1979 FECA Amendments enacted only noncontroversial changes following a failure to come to a bipartisan agreement on any major features such as those of the type that Common Cause advocates (for a brief overview, see Congressional Quarterly 1980). Promises made at the time that a renewed effort would be forthcoming to alter dramatically the campaign finance system were not fulfilled.

Also as noted, one inadvertent consequence of the 1979 legislation was to open the floodgates for soft money: The bill permitted state and local party groups to

purchase, without limit, campaign materials for volunteer activities to promote any federal candidate and to conduct, again without financial limit, certain kinds of voter registration and get-out-the-vote drives on behalf of presidential tickets.

19. Neither Boren nor Common Cause has been very successful at having others follow his lead. For example, of those elected in 1988, only three members of the House, Common Cause's two closest allies (Synar and Leach) and a notorious eccentric (Jacobs) refused PAC money; in the Senate, only a rich challenger (Kohl) who relied on $7 million of his own fortune, something else that reformers tend to disapprove, mimicked his new colleague.

    Even Boren is not without those questioning his ethics: His adversaries often point out that he accepts individual contributions from many of the same sources from which PACs receive their money, largely nullifying the cost of his principled stand. His response is that people who contribute to his campaign must do something to earn an income.

20. Brooks Jackson (1988) of the *Wall Street Journal* places great emphasis on Boren's revulsion with the finance system in 1984 as providing the impetus for his taking the initiative.

21. Even in the House, million dollar campaigns are now commonplace – in 1988, 15 victors (and 5 losers) broke the barrier.

22. Boren's bill originally called for a $2,500 limit on contributions, but it was changed to win Democratic support.

23. Parenthetically, a quote such as this one from *Common Cause Magazine* makes it clear that members, if they make enough of an effort, can use leadership statements to estimate whether a group is being efficacious in meeting specific goals.

24. The committee held two sets of hearings, but Republicans – by simply not attending – were able to kill reform by preventing its markup through lack of a quorum.

25. For, example, the House Democrats could have put out an extremely pro-Democratic bill (e.g., low campaign spending ceilings with little or no increase in individual contribution levels) and then forced the Senate into a series of embarrassing conference committee meetings.

26. Such reforms centered on disclosure and the emptying of campaign stockpiles, the elimination of leadership PACs, tax credits for small contributions, and restrictions on bundling.

27. Unlike passage, which requires a majority of those senators present, invoking cloture necessitates sixty votes regardless of how many members are present.

28. Two days later, the Democrats did rebuff (by a vote of 46 to 42) a move by Phil Gramm of Texas to table the bill on the grounds that it violated certain Gramm–Rudman provisions.

29. This assessment was seconded by Barone and Ujifusa, who write that "Swift has been favorable toward public financing of congressional elections and toward changing the rules on PACs, but he is also a practical politician who is not interested in reporting out a measure that can't pass the floor" (1989, p. 1281).

30. Of course, other events that might have also been policy windows, e.g., the Reagan "sleaze factor," the Iran–*Contra* scandal, and Jim Wright's forced resignation for improprieties, seemed to have had no measurable effect on breaking the campaign finance deadlock. While many of these transgressions involved questions of ethics rather than campaign finance abuses, it is widely perceived on Capitol Hill that in the public eye the two are intimately intertwined.

31. The obvious question that springs to mind is whether the Bush proposal represented an opening gambit from which to bargain, or a public relations ploy to garner some favorable short-term publicity. Interviews on Capitol Hill and

subsequent events suggest that the administration's commitment was neither non-existent nor full fledged. Those looking on the bright side were quick to play up the idea that while the administration might not lead the way, the president's ability to veto had been diminished and that was a plus. However, as will be discussed shortly, Bush has made it quite clear that he is ready to veto unacceptable legislation.

32. This could also be coupled with two other events: (1) Wright's resignation as speaker in the summer of 1989, partially because interest groups were caught buying large numbers of his book (even though, as mentioned, this did not precipitate immediate action); and (2) the failure of the Senate to eliminate honoraria in ethics legislation passed in November 1989.

33. Michel's public comments were allegedly a reaction to his private proposals being rejected by Democrats.

34. Conversely, some Democrats expressed annoyance that Common Cause would support proposals that would put Republicans in office without regard for the consequences in the substance of policy.

35. However, to extend this assertion to argue that all Common Cause needs to do is abandon its slash-and-burn tactics seems almost certainly false. While such an action might reduce antagonisms toward the organization, it would not eliminate perceptions that the group is biased and has little to offer. In other words, while strategy is certainly important, the root explanation for the group's impact is how well the issues it tries to influence mesh with what it might have to offer.

36. Interestingly, while the group was quite active in events leading up to the 1974 FECA Amendments, no one has written a detailed account of the passage of this legislation (McFarland 1984); that is, there is no hard evidence about the organization's role or effectiveness with respect to the key legislation of the 1970s. However, given the decline in legislative uncertainty regarding the functioning of the campaign finance system (for example, in the early 1970s Common Cause was the principal provider of information about who was making campaign contributions to whom), *even* if the group were influential in the first half of the 1970s would not guarantee that it would be effective in the 1980s and 1990s. Indeed, by making staff and contributors feel as if they could be effective, influence in the 1970s could conceivably be a contributing factor to the inefficient allocation of resources in the 1980s and 1990s.

37. For example, in testifying in support of S.2, the group submitted a list of 230 newspapers supporting the bill (U.S. House of Representatives, Subcommittee on Elections of the Committee on House Administration 1987).

CHAPTER 10

1. There are other related reasons that might make organizations worthy of scholarly attention: for example, whether groups make individuals feel represented or whether they enhance social stability. Nevertheless, it is almost certainly the issue of whether groups actually serve as a vehicle for the representation process that is the principal concern for scholars.

2. Clearly, any answers grounded in what is largely a single case study are always somewhat speculative. However, given the numerous caveats that have appeared throughout the larger analysis, such warnings will be mentioned only briefly here. It is obvious that definitive answers about the nature of the representation process will not be provided. Rather, the findings from the present inquiry can furnish insights into what factors are likely to be crucial for understanding citizens' behavior, group governance, and associational influence on policy (and the inter-

relationships between these three factors); into the effectiveness of organizations as representational institutions; and into how such groups ought to be conceptualized.

3. Alternatively, one might draw the analogy to how CEOs try to deal with stockholders by paying greatest attention to those who are most willing and able to support an effort to oust those running the company if they are dissatisfied.

4. This part of the analysis will deal only in passing with the implications for representation of either how much an organization reflects the larger universe of citizens it is supposed to embody or the internal homogeneity of the group.

5. For example, it is hard to believe the suggestions of a number of interviewees that Common Cause leaders do not want a campaign finance bill because the group's main issue would then disappear from the political agenda. Indeed, given Common Cause's Board – which, as mentioned, has quite a variety of political interests they would like pursued – it is undoubtedly the case that those setting the agenda would welcome the opportunity to explore new concerns despite the potential organizational challenges. At present, the group is talking through what such concerns might supplement issues of government accountability and openness (e.g., public disenchantment with politics, the budgetary and financial problems facing government, the role of communications and the media in society, substantive issues such as health policy).

6. Given the findings of this analysis, it is not surprising that scholars (e.g., Vogel 1989) are now trumpeting the corporate political operations of firms (rather than public interest groups) as the new ascendant force in politics. Corporations, while confronting certain obstacles of their own in attempting to make a mark, face few of the difficulties plaguing voluntary groups discussed in these conclusions.

References

Abramowitz, Alan I., and Walter J. Stone. 1984. *Nomination Politics: Party Activists and Presidential Choice*. New York: Praeger.

Achen, Christopher. 1978. "Measuring Representation." *American Journal of Political Science* 22: 475–510.

Akey, Denise. 1983. *Encyclopedia of Associations*. 18th edition. Detroit: Gale Research.

Alston, Chuck, and Glen Craney. 1989. "Bush Campaign Reform Plan Takes Aim at Incumbents." *Congressional Quarterly Weekly Report* 47: 1648–9.

Amemiya, Takeshi. 1985. *Advanced Econometrics*. Cambridge, Mass.: MIT Press.

Ansolabehere, Stephen. 1990. "Winning Is Easy, but It sure Ain't Cheap." Unpublished manuscript, University of California at Los Angeles.

Arnold, R. Douglas. 1979. *Congress and the Bureaucracy: A Theory of Influence*. New Haven, Conn.: Yale University Press.

1982. "Overtilled and Undertilled Fields in American Politics." *Political Science Quarterly* 97: 91–103.

Austen-Smith, David, and John R. Wright. 1991. "Competitive Lobbying for Legislators' Votes." Unpublished manuscript.

Axelrod, Robert. 1984. *The Evolution of Cooperation*. New York: Basic Books.

Bardach, Eugene. 1977. *The Implementation Game: What Happens after a Bill Becomes a Law*. Cambridge, Mass.: MIT Press.

Barnes, James A. 1991. "Reform Roulette." *National Journal*. 23: 1563–5.

Barone, Michael, and Grant Ujifusa. 1987. *The Almanac of American Politics 1988*. Washington, D.C.: National Journal.

1989. *The Almanac of American Politics 1990*. Washington, D.C.: National Journal.

Bauer, Raymond A., Ithiel de Sola Poole, and Lewis Anthony Dexter. 1963. *American Business & Public Policy: The Politics of Foreign Trade*. New York: Atherton.

Becker, Gary. 1983. "A Theory of Competition among Pressure Groups for Political Influence." *Quarterly Journal of Economics* 96: 371–400.

1985. "Public Policies, Pressure Groups, and Deadweight Costs." *Journal of Public Economics* 28: 329–47.

Belsley, David A., Edwin Kuh, and Roy E. Welsch. 1980. *Regression Diagnostics: Identifying Influential Data and Sources of Collinearity*. New York: John Wiley & Sons.

Ben-Akiva, Moshe, and Steven R. Lerman. 1985. *Discrete Choice Analysis: Theory and Application to Travel Demand*. Cambridge, Mass.: MIT Press.

Bennett, Stephen E. 1986. *Apathy in America, 1960–1984: Cause and Consequences of Citizen Political Indifference*. Dobbs Ferry, N.Y.: Transnational Publishers.

Bentley, Arthur F. 1908. *The Process of Government: A Study of Social Pressure*. Chicago: University of Chicago Press.

Berke, Richard L. 1991. "A Revival: The Campaign Finance Show." *The New York Times*, May 26, p. E2.

Bernstein, Robert A., and William W. Anthony. 1974. "The ABM Issue in the Senate, 1968–1970: The Importance of Ideology." *American Political Science Review* 68: 1198–1206.

Berry, Jeffrey M. 1977. *Lobbying for the People: The Political Behavior of Public Interest Groups*. Princeton, N.J.: Princeton University Press.

——— 1989. *The Interest Group Society*. 2nd edition. Glenview, Ill.: Scott, Foresman.

Black, Duncan. 1958. *The Theory of Committees and Elections*. Cambridge: Cambridge University Press.

Brody, Richard A. 1978. "Political Participation." In *The New American Political System*, ed. Anthony King. Washington, D.C.: American Enterprise Institute.

Burdett, Kenneth. 1978. "A Theory of Employee Job Search and Quit Rates." *American Economic Review* 68: 212–20.

Carmines, Edward G., and James A. Stimson. 1989. *Issue Evolution: Race and the Transformation of American Politics*. Princeton, N.J.: Princeton University Press.

Center for Responsive Politics. 1988. *Spending in Congressional Elections: A Never-Ending Spiral*. Washington, D.C.: Center for Responsive Politics.

Chow, Gregory C. 1960. "Tests of Equality between Sets of Coefficients in Two Linear Regressions." *Econometrica* 28: 591–605.

Cigler, Allan J. 1989. "Interest Groups: A Subfield in Search of an Identity." Presented at the Annual Meeting of the Midwest Political Science Association, Chicago.

Clark, Peter B., and James Q. Wilson. 1961. "Incentive Systems: A Theory of Organizations." *Administrative Science Quarterly* 6: 129–66.

Cohen, Linda R., and Roger G. Noll. 1990. "How to Vote, Whether to Vote: Decisions about Voting and Abstaining on Congressional Roll Calls." Hoover Institution Working Paper P-90-2.

Cohen, Michael D., James G. March, and Johan P. Olsen. 1972. "A Garbage Can Theory of Organizational Choice." *Administrative Science Quarterly* 17: 1–25.

Common Cause 1984 Budget. 1983. Washington, D.C.: Common Cause.

Common Cause Expenditure Review. 1984. Washington, D.C.: Common Cause.

Congressional Quarterly. 1980. *Congressional Quarterly Almanac, 1979*. Vol. XXXV. Washington, D.C.: Congressional Quarterly Press.

Cook, Constance E. 1984. "Participation in Public Interest Groups: Membership Motivations." *American Politics Quarterly* 12: 409–30.

Cox, Archibald. 1982. "Constitutional Issues in the Regulation of the Financing of Election Campaigns." *Cleveland State Law Review* 31: 395–418.

Dahl, Robert A. 1961. *Who Governs? Democracy and Power in an American City*. New Haven, Conn.: Yale University Press.

Democrat and Chronicle (Rochester). 1991. "Once More, Election Reform Is Doomed." May 27, p. 6A.

Denzau, Arthur T., and Michael C. Munger. 1986. "Legislators and Interest Groups: How Unorganized Groups Get Represented." *American Political Science Review* 80: 89–106.

Denzau, Arthur, William Riker, and Kenneth Shepsle. 1985. "Farquharson and Fenno: Sophisticated Voting and Home Style." *American Political Science Review* 79: 1117–34.

Donohue, William A. 1985. *The Politics of the American Civil Liberties Union*. New Brunswick, N.J.: Transaction Books.

Downs, Anthony. 1957. *An Economic Theory of Democracy*. New York: Harper & Row.

Drew, Elizabeth. 1983. "A Political Journal." *The New Yorker* 59 (June 20): 39–75.

Eldersveld, Samuel J. 1982. *Political Parties in American Society*. New York: Basic Books.

EW Communications. 1988. *Congress & Defense 1988*. Palo Alto, Calif.: EW Communications.

"Federal Funding of Campaigns." 1987. *The Gallup Report* 258: 26–7.

Feldman, Paul, and James Jondrow. 1984. "Congressional Elections and Local Federal Spending." *American Journal of Political Science* 25: 147–64.

Ferejohn, John A., and Morris P. Fiorina. 1974. "The Paradox of Not Voting: A Decision Theoretic Analysis." *American Political Science Review* 68: 525–36.

1975. "Closeness Only Counts in Horseshoes and Dancing." *American Political Science Review* 69: 920–8.

Fiorina, Morris P. 1975. *Representatives, Roll Calls, and Constituencies*. Lexington, Mass.: Lexington Books.

1981. *Retrospective Voting in American National Elections*. New Haven, Conn.: Yale University Press.

Fleisher, Richard. 1985. "Economic Benefits, Ideology, and Senate Voting on the B-1 Bomber." *American Politics Quarterly* 13: 200–11.

Fowler, Linda L., and Ronald D. Shaiko. 1987. "The Grass Roots Connection: Environmental Activists and Senate Roll Calls." *American Journal of Political Science* 31: 484–510.

Garceau, Oliver. 1941. *The Political Life of the American Medical Association*. Cambridge, Mass.: Harvard University Press.

Gibson, James L., and Richard D. Bingham. 1985. *Civil Liberties and Nazis: The Skokie Free-Speech Controversy*. New York: Praeger.

Gilligan, Thomas, and Keith Krehbiel. 1987. "Collective Decision-Making and Standing Committees: An Informational Rationale for Restrictive Amendment Procedures." *Journal of Law, Economics, and Organization* 3: 287–335.

1989. "Asymmetric Information and Legislative Rules with a Heterogeneous Committee." *American Journal of Political Science* 31: 484–510.

Godwin, R. Kenneth. 1988. *One Billion Dollars of Influence: The Direct Marketing of Politics*. Chatham, N.J.: Chatham House.

Gold, David, Christopher Pain, and Gail Shields. 1981. *Misguided Expenditure: An Analysis of the Proposed MX Missile System*. New York: Council on Economic Priorities.

Gotz, Glenn A., and John J. McCall. 1983. "Sequential Analysis of the Stay/Leave Decision: U.S. Air Force Officers." *Management Science* 29: 335–51.

1984. *A Dynamic Retention Model for Air Force Officers: Theory and Estimates*. RAND Report R-3028-AF. Santa Monica, Calif.: RAND Corporation.

Gray, Colin S. 1981. *The MX ICBM and National Security*. New York: Praeger.

Green, Donald P., and Krasno, Jonathan S. 1988. "Salvation for the Spendthrift Incumbent: Reestimating the Effects of Campaign Spending in House Elections." *American Journal of Political Science* 32: 884–907.

Hall, Richard L., and Frank W. Wayman. 1990. "Buying Time: Moneyed Interests and the Mobilization of Bias in Congressional Committees." *American Political Science Review* 84: 797–820.

Hansen, John Mark. 1985. "The Political Economy of Group Membership." *American Political Science Review* 79: 79–96.

Hanushek, Eric A., John E. Jackson, and John F. Kain. 1974. "Model Specification, Use of Aggregate Data, and the Ecological Correlation Fallacy." *Political Methodology* 1: 89–107.

Hanushek, Eric A., and John E. Jackson. 1977. *Statistical Methods for Social Scientists*. New York: Academic Press.

Hardin, Russell. 1982. *Collective Action*. Baltimore: Resources for the Future.

Hartung, William D. 1984. *The Economic Consequences of a Nuclear Freeze*. New York: Council of Economic Priorities.

Hausman, Jerry A. 1978. "Specification Tests in Econometrics." *Econometrica* 46: 1251–71.

Hausman, Jerry A., and Daniel McFadden. 1984. "Specification Tests for the Multinomial Logit Model." *Econometrica* 52: 1219–40.

Hayes, Michael A. 1981. *Lobbyists and Legislators: A Theory of Political Markets.* New Brunswick, N.J.: Rutgers University Press.

——— 1983. "Interest Groups: Pluralism or Mass Society?" In *Interest Group Politics,* ed. Allan J. Cigler and Burdett A. Loomis. Washington, D.C.: Congressional Quarterly Press.

——— 1986. "The New Group Universe." In *Interest Group Politics,* ed. Allan J. Cigler and Burdett A. Loomis. 2nd edition. Washington, D.C.: Congressional Quarterly Press.

Heckman, James. 1978. "Dummy Endogenous Variables in a Simultaneous Equation System." *Econometrica* 46: 931–59.

Herrnson, Paul S. 1988. *Party Campaigning in the 1980s.* Cambridge, Mass.: Harvard University Press.

Hirschman, Albert O. 1970. *Exit, Voice, and Loyalty: Responses to Declines in Firms, Organizations, and States.* Cambridge, Mass.: Harvard University Press.

Hrebenar, Ronald J., and Ruth K. Scott. 1990. *Interest Group Politics in America.* 2nd edition. Englewood Cliffs, N.J.: Prentice-Hall.

Jackson, Brooks. 1988. *Honest Graft: Big Money and the American Political Process.* New York: Alfred A. Knopf.

Jacobson, Gary S. 1980. *Money in Congressional Elections.* New Haven, Conn.: Yale University Press.

Johnson, Paul E. 1987. "Social Choice in Voluntary Organizations: Myopia, Foresight, and Majority Rule Decision Processes." Presented at the Annual Meeting of the Midwest Political Science Association, Chicago.

——— 1990. "Unraveling in Democratically Governed Groups." *Rationality and Society* 2: 4–34.

Kariel, Henry S. 1961. *The Decline of American Pluralism.* Stanford, Calif.: Stanford University Press.

Kau, James B., and Paul H. Rubin. 1979. "Public Interest Lobbies: Membership and Influence." *Public Choice* 34: 45–54.

——— 1982. *Congressmen, Constituents, and Contributions.* Boston: Martinus Nijhoff.

Kingdon, John W. 1984. *Agendas, Alternatives, and Public Policies.* Boston: Little, Brown.

——— 1989. *Congressmen's Voting Decisions.* 3rd edition. Ann Arbor: University of Michigan Press.

Knoke, David. 1990. *Organizing for Collective Action: The Political Economies of Associations.* Hawthorne, N.Y.: Aldine de Gruyter.

Kramer, Gerald H. 1983. "The Ecological Fallacy Revisited: Aggregate-Versus Individual-Level Findings on Economics and Elections, and Sociotropic Voting." *American Political Science Review* 77: 92–111.

Krehbiel, Keith. 1991. *Information and Legislative Organization.* Ann Arbor: University of Michigan Press.

Krehbiel, Keith, and Douglas Rivers. 1988. "The Analysis of Committee Power: An Application to Senate Voting on the Minimum Wage." *American Journal of Political Science* 32: 1150–74.

——— 1990. "Sophisticated Voting in Congress: A Reconsideration." *Journal of Politics* 52: 548–78.

Latham, Earl. 1952. *The Group Basis of Politics: A Study of Basing-Point Legislation.* Ithaca, N.Y.: Cornell University Press.

Lindblom, Charles E. 1977. *Politics and Markets: The World's Political-Economic Systems*. New York: Basic Books.

Lowi, Theodore J. 1979. *The End of Liberalism: The Second Republic of the United States*. 2nd edition. New York: W. W. Norton.

Madalla, G. S. 1977. *Econometrics*. New York: McGraw-Hill.

1983. *Limited-Dependent and Qualitative Variables in Econometrics*. Cambridge: Cambridge University Press.

Magleby, David B., and Candice J. Nelson. 1990. *The Money Chase: Congressional Campaign Finance Reform*. Washington, D.C.: Brookings Institution.

Mahood, H.R. 1990. *Interest Group Politics in America: A New Intensity*. Englewood Cliffs, N.J.: Prentice-Hall.

Manski, Charles F., and Steven R. Lerman. 1977. "The Estimation of Choice Probabilities from Choice Based Samples." *Econometrica* 45: 1977–88.

March, James G. 1978. "Bounded Rationality, Ambiguity, and the Engineering of Choice." *Bell Journal of Economics* 9: 587–608.

March, James G., and Johan P. Olsen. 1984. "The New Institutionalism: Organizational Factors in Political Life." *American Political Science Review* 78: 734–49.

1989. *Rediscovering Institutions: The Organizational Basis of Politics*. New York: Free Press.

Matthews, Donald R., and James A. Stimson. 1975. *Yeas and Nays: Normal Decision-Making in the U.S. House of Representatives*. New York: John Wiley.

Mayhew, David. 1974. *Congress: The Electoral Connection*. New Haven, Conn.: Yale University Press.

McConnell, Grant. 1953. *The Decline of Agrarian Democracy*. Berkeley: University of California Press.

1966. *Private Power and American Democracy*. New York: Random House.

McCormick, James M. 1985. "Congressional Voting on the Nuclear Freeze Resolutions." *American Politics Quarterly* 13: 122–36.

McDougall, John. forthcoming. "The Freeze Movement, Congress, and the M-X Missile." In *Peace Movements in International Perspective*, ed. Bert Klandermans. Greenwich, Conn.: JAI Press.

McFarland, Andrew S. 1976. *Public Interest Lobbies*. Washington, D.C.: American Enterprise Institute.

1984. *Common Cause: Lobbying in the Public Interest*. Chatham, N.J.: Chatham House.

McKelvey, Richard D. 1976. "Intransiveness in Multidimensional Voting Models and Some Implications for Agenda Control." *Journal of Economic Theory* 12: 472–82.

Meyer, David S. 1990. *A Winter of Discontent: The Nuclear Freeze and American Politics*. New York: Praeger.

Michels, Robert. 1958. *Political Parties*, trans. Eden and Cedar Paul. New York: Free Press. (Originally published in 1915.)

Milbrath, Lester W., and M. L. Goel. 1977. *Political Participation: How and Why Do People Get Involved in Politics?* 2nd edition. New York: Rand McNally.

Miller, Gary J., and Terry M. Moe. 1983. "Bureaucrats, Legislators, and the Size of Government." *American Political Science Review* 77: 297–323.

Miller, Warren E., Arthur H. Miller, and Edward J. Schneider. 1980. *American National Election Studies Data Sourcebook, 1952–1978*. Cambridge, Mass.: Harvard University Press.

Mitchell, William C. 1990. "Interest Groups: Economic Perspectives and Contributions." *Journal of Theoretical Politics* 2: 85–108.

Mitchell, William C., and Michael C. Munger. 1991. "Economic Models of Interest

Groups: An Introductory Survey." *American Journal of Political Science* 35: 512–46.

Mitchell, Robert Cameron. 1979. "National Environmental Lobbies and the Apparent Illogic of Collective Action." In *Collective Decision Making*, ed. Clifford S. Russell. Baltimore: Resources for the Future.

Moe, Terry M. 1980a. *The Organization of Interests: Incentives and the Internal Dynamics of Political Interest Groups.* Chicago: University of Chicago Press.
   1980b. " A Calculus of Group Membership." *American Journal of Political Science* 24: 593–632.
   1981."Toward a Broader View of Interest Groups." *Journal of Politics* 43: 531–43.

Mortensen, Dale T. 1986. "Job Search and Labor Market Analysis." In *Handbook of Labor Economics*, vol. 2, ed. Orley Ashenfelter and Richard Layard. Amsterdam: Elsevier Science.

Mueller, Dennis C. 1979. *Public Choice.* Cambridge: Cambridge University Press.

Nelson, Douglas, and Eugene Silberberg. 1987. "Ideology and Legislative Shirking." *Economic Inquiry* 25: 15–25.

Neuman, William R. 1986. *The Paradox of Mass Politics: Knowledge and Opinion in the American Electorate.* Cambridge, Mass.: Harvard University Press.

Newey, Whitney K. 1987. "Efficient Estimation of Limited Dependent Variable Models with Endogenous Explanatory Variables." *Journal of Econometrics* 36: 231–50.

Olson, Mancur. 1965. *The Logic of Collective Action: Public Goods and the Theory of Groups.* Cambridge, Mass.: Harvard University Press.
   1986. *The Rise and Decline of Nations: Economic Growth, Stagflation, and Social Rigidities.* New Haven, Conn.: Yale University Press.

Ordeshook, Peter C. 1986. *Game Theory and Political Theory: An Introduction.* Cambridge: Cambridge University Press.

Palfrey, Thomas R., and Howard Rosenthal. 1988. "Private Incentives and Social Dilemmas." *Journal of Public Economics* 35: 309–32.

Peltzman, Sam. 1976. "Toward a More General Theory of Regulation." *Journal of Law and Economics* 19: 211–40.
   1984. "Constituent Interest and Congressional Voting." *Journal of Law and Economics* 27: 181–210.

Pertschuk, Michael. 1986. *Giant Killers.* New York: W. W. Norton.

Pertschuk, Michael, and Wendy Schaetzel. 1989. *The People Rising: The Campaign Against the Bork Nomination.* New York: Thunder's Mouth Press.

Pindyck, Robert S., and Daniel L. Rubinfeld. 1981. *Econometric Models and Economic Forecasts.* 2nd edition. New York: McGraw-Hill.

Polsby, Nelson W. 1981–2. "Contemporary Transformations of American Politics: Thoughts on the Research Agenda of Political Scientists." *Political Science Quarterly* 96: 551–70.

Presidential Commission on Strategic Force. 1983. Washington, D.C.: The Commission.

Pressman, Steven. 1984. "The Lobbying: A Hard Fight by Both Sides." *Congressional Quarterly Weekly Report* 42: 1156.
   1985a. "Reagan Gets the Credit for MX Success .... As He Out-Communicated Opponents." *Congressional Quarterly Weekly Report* 43: 516–17.
   1985b. "Senate Sidesteps Decision on PAC Spending." *Congressional Quarterly Weekly Report* 43: 2567–8.

Rivers, Douglas, and Quang H. Vuong. 1988. "Limited Information Estimators and Exogeneity Tests for Simultaneous Probit Models." *Journal of Econometrics* 39: 347–66.

References   299

Robinson, William S. 1950. "Ecological Correlations and the Behavior of Individuals."
American Sociological Review 15: 1183–96.
Romer, Thomas, and Howard Rosenthal. 1978. "Political Resource Allocation,
Controlled Agenda, and the Status Quo." *Public Choice* 33: 27–45.
Rothenberg, Lawrence S. 1991. "The Marketing of Politics: Implications for the
'Heavenly Chorus'." Paper presented at the Annual Meeting of the Public Choice
    Society.
Rothenberg, Lawrence S., and Richard A. Brody. 1988. "Participation in Presidential
Primaries." *Western Political Quarterly* 41: 253–71.
Sabato, Larry. 1985. *PAC Power*. New York: W. W. Norton.
1988. *The Party's Just Begun: Shaping Political Parties for America's Future.*
Glenview, Ill.: Scott, Foresman.
Salisbury, Robert H. 1969. "An Exchange Theory of Interest Groups." *Midwest*
Journal of Political Science 13: 1–32.
1984. "Interest Representation: The Dominance of Institutions." *American Political*
Science Review 78: 64–76.
1990. "The Paradox of Interest Groups in Washington – More Groups, Less
Clout." In *The New American Political System*, ed. Anthony King. 2nd edition.
Washington, D.C.: American Enterprise Institute.
Salisbury, Robert H., John P. Heinz, Edward O. Laumann, and Robert L. Nelson.
1987. "Who Works with Whom? Patterns of Interest Group Alliance and
Opposition." *American Political Science Review* 81: 1217–34.
Schattschneider, E. E. 1935. *Politics, Pressures and the Tariff.* Englewood Cliffs, N.J.:
    Prentice-Hall.
1960. *The Semisovereign People: A Realist's View of Democracy in America.* New
York: Holt, Rinehart and Winston.
Schlesinger, Joseph A. 1966. *Ambition and Political Careers in the United States.*
Chicago: Rand McNally.
Schlozman, Kay Lehman, and John T. Tierney. 1986. *Organized Groups and American*
Democracy. New York: Harper & Row.
Scott, W. Richard. 1987. *Organizations: Rational, Natural, and Open Systems.* 2nd
edition. Englewood Cliffs, N.J.: Prentice-Hall.
Scoville, Herbert J. 1981. *MX: Prescription for Disaster.* Cambridge, Mass.: MIT Press.
Shaiko, Ronald G. 1986. "Interest Group Research: Cultivating an Unsettled Plot."
Polity 18: 720–32.
Shanks, J. Merrill, and Warren E. Miller. 1990. "Policy Direction and Performance
Evaluation: Complementary Explanations of the Reagan Administration." *British*
Journal of Political Science 20: 143–235.
Shepsle, Kenneth A. 1979. "Institutional Arrangements and Equilibrium in Multi-
dimensional Voting Models." *American Journal of Political Science* 23: 27–59.
Shepsle, Kenneth A., and Barry R. Weingast. 1984. "Political Solutions to Market
Problems." *American Political Science Review* 78: 44–63.
Smith, Hedrick. 1988. *The Power Game: Washington Really Works.* New York:
    Random House.
Smith, Richard A. 1984. "Advocacy, Interpretation and Influence in the U.S. Congress."
American Political Science Review 78: 44–63.
1989. "Interpretation, Pressure, and the Stability of Interest Group Influence in
the U.S. Congress." Paper presented at the Annual Meeting of the American
    Political Science Association.
Smith, V. Kerry. 1985. "A Theoretical Analysis of the 'Green Lobby'." *American*
Political Science Review 79: 132–47.

Snyder, James M. forthcoming. "Committee Power, Structure-Induced Equilibrium, and Roll-Call Votes." *American Journal of Political Science.*

1991. "On Buying Legislatures." *Economics & Politics* 3: 93–110.

Stern, Philip M. 1988. *The Best Congress Money Can Buy.* New York: Pantheon Books.

Stigler, George J. 1971. "The Theory of Economic Regulation." *Bell Journal of Economics and Management Science* 1: 3–21.

1974. "Free Riders and Collective Action: An Appendix to Theories of Economic Regulation." *Bell Journal of Economics and Management Science* 5: 359–65.

Talbot, Strobe. 1984. *Deadly Gambits: The Reagan Administration and the Stalemate in Nuclear Arms Control.* New York: Alfred A. Knopf.

Truman, David B. 1951. *The Governmental Process: Political Interests and Public Opinion.* New York: Alfred A. Knopf.

Uhlaner, Carole J. 1986. "Political Participation, Rational Actors, and Rationality." *Political Psychology* 7: 551–73.

1989a. "Rational Turnout: The Neglected Role of Groups." *American Journal of Political Science* 33: 423–39.

1989b. "'Relational Goals' and Participation: Incorporating Sociability into a Theory of Rational Action." *Public Choice* 62: 253–85.

U.S. General Accounting Office. 1984. *Status of the Peacekeeper (MX) Weapons System.* NSIA 84–112. Washington, D.C.: U.S. Government Printing Office.

U.S. House of Representatives, Subcommittee on Elections of the Committee on House Administration. 1987. *Campaign Finance.* Washington, D.C.: U.S. Government Printing Office.

Verba, Sidney, and Norman H. Nie. 1972. *Participation in America: Political Democracy and Social Equality.* New York: Harper & Row.

Vogel, David. 1989. *Fluctuating Fortunes: The Political Power of Business in America.* New York: Basic Books.

Vuong, Quang H. 1989. "Likelihood Ratio Tests for Model Selection and Non-Nested Hypotheses." *Econometrica* 57: 307–33.

Walker, Jack L. 1983. "The Origins and Maintenance of Interest Groups in America." *American Political Science Review* 77: 390–406.

1990. "Political Mobilization in America." In *Institutions in American Society,* ed. John E. Jackson. Ann Arbor: University of Michigan Press.

Wayman, Frank Whelon. 1985. "Arms Control and Arms Voting in the Senate, 1967–1983." *Journal of Conflict Resolution* 29: 225–51.

Wertheimer, Fred. 1986. "1986: A Year of Challenges and Opportunities." *Common Cause Magazine* 12 (March/April): 44–5.

Wilde, Louis L. 1979. "An Information-Theoretic Approach to Job Quits." In *Studies in the Economics of Search,* ed. Steven A. Lippman and John J. McCall. Amsterdam: North-Holland.

Wilson, Graham K. 1981. *Interest Groups in the United States.* Oxford: Clarendon Press.

Wilson, James Q. 1962. *The Amateur Democrat: Club Politics in Three Cities.* Chicago: University of Chicago Press.

1973. *Political Organization.* New York: Basic Books.

Wittenberg, Ernest, and Elisabeth Wittenberg. 1989. *How to Win in Washington: Very Practical Advice about Lobbying, the Grassroots, and the Media.* Oxford: Basil Blackwell.

Wolfinger, Raymond E., and Steven J. Rosenstone. 1980. *Who Votes?* New Haven, Conn.: Yale University Press.

Wright, John R. 1985. "PACs, Contributions, and Roll Calls: An Organizational Perspective." *American Political Science Review* 79: 400–14.

    1987. "The Allocation of Lobbying Effort by Organized Interests." Presented at the Annual Meeting of the Public Choice Society.

    1990. "Contributions, Lobbying, and Voting in the U.S. House of Representatives." *American Political Science Review* 84: 417–38.

Young, Louise M., with the assistance of Ralph A. Young, Jr. 1989. *In the Public Interest: The League of Women Voters, 1920–1970*. Westport, Conn.: Greenwood Press.

Index

activism (*see also* checkbook activism,
    efficacy (personal), experiential search,
    information and citizen decision
    making, lobbying, member learning),
    6–7, 8, 266
  determinants of, 127–57
  experiential search and, 14, 19–20, 26–7,
    28, 268, 269
  goal formation and, 174, 178–88, 259, 285
  integrated perspective and, 265
  leadership choices and, 259
  member learning and, 104, 108, 279
  MX missile and, 191, 203, 222, 286
  rank and file and, 29–30, 43–56, 57, 269, 270
  retention and, 101, 110, 115, 120–1, 125, 276
American Civil Liberties Union (ACLU),
    13, 86–92, 120–3, 151, 182, 268
American Medical Association, 100
antipluralists (*see also* pluralism), 176
arms control (*see also* nuclear freeze), 162,
    184, 186
Aspin, Les, 198–9, 205
Austen-Smith, David, 284

B-1 bomber, 170, 287
B-2 bomber, 284
Baker, Howard, 200
Bartlett, Dewey, 236
Bennett, Charles, 199–200
Bentley, Arthur, 18
Bolling, Richard, 284
Boren, David, 186, 235–42, 244, 289, 290
Boschwitz, Rudy, 240–1
Brokaw, Tom, 250
Buckley v. Valeo, 231–3, 235, 288, 289
Bumpers, Dale, 200
Bush, George, 245
Byrd, Robert, 235–7, 240–4

Cabot, Ned, 161
campaign finance (*see also* lobbying,
    member learning, MX, political action
    committees), 9–10, 39, 52, 104, 115,
    190–2, 194, 222, 223–53

internal politics and, 162, 170, 173–4,
    180–1, 185–6, 188
  systemic impact and, 260–2
Carson, Johnny, 250
Carter, Jimmy, 180
Center for Responsive Politics, 251
Central Intelligence Agency, 172
Chafee, John, 242
checkbook activism (*see also* activism),
    127–36, 147, 156, 278
Chicago school (of economics), 2–4
Chiles, Lawton, 200
Chow (test), 125
citizen attributes, 70
Cohelo, Tony, 209
Cohen, David, 184–5, 193, 202, 248, 251, 283
Cohen, William, 198
Cold War, 181
Common Cause (*see* activism, campaign
    finance, checkbook activism, dues,
    efficacy (group), efficacy (personal),
    governing board, joining, leadership,
    lobbying, member learning, MX, public
    interest groups, retention)
  history of, 9–10
  membership levels and, 10–12
Common Cause Magazine, 10, 26, 74, 138,
    252, 257, 269, 275, 290
Congress Watch, 225
Congressional Quarterly Weekly Report, 174
Conservative Caucus, 13, 86–93, 120–3, 151
Conservative Coalition, 206, 209, 286
Council for a Livable World, 186
Cranston, Alan, 245
Craver, Roger, 73
Cronin, Thomas, 182–3

D'Amato, Alfonse, 245–6
DeConcini, Dennis, 245
Denzau, Arthur, 226
Dickinson, William, 201
Dirks, Norman, 198
Dole, Robert, 239, 246
Downs, Anthony, 18, 70, 148, 268

Downsian (*see* Downs)
Drew, Elizabeth, 194
dues, 24
 activism and, 30, 127–36, 157, 178
 decision making and, 19, 22
 joining and, 65, 70–74, 82
 retention and, 111–13, 165
Durenberger, David, 246

Earl, Anthony, 284
efficacy (group), 116, 148, 175, 193, 229–30
efficacy (personal)
 activism and, 131, 151, 258, 280
 joining and, 20, 39, 59, 74, 87–8
 retention and, 115–16, 117
Estrich, Susan, 284
ethics and conflict of interest, 162
experiential search, 101, 257
 activism and, 128, 129, 131, 136, 139–40,
  142, 144–5, 151, 152, 154, 156–7
 Common Cause and, 24–8
 joining and, 65–6, 73, 81, 86, 94
 member learning and, 102, 108
 retention and, 109, 111, 115–20, 123–4
 theory and, 15, 17, 24–8
 unified framework and, 28

Federal Election Campaign Act
 amendments of 1974, 9, 235, 288, 289, 291
 amendments of 1979, 233, 284
Federal Election Commission (FEC), 10, 288
Feldman, Paul, 204
Foley, Thomas, 198–9, 246
Fowler, Linda, 191–2

Garceau, Oliver, 100
Gardner, John, 9, 26, 164, 182–3
General Accounting Office, U.S., 198, 282
general characteristics, 22
General Dynamics, 200
General Social Survey (GSS), 13, 31, 41
Gephardt, Richard, 209
Gilligan, Thomas, 195
Gingrich, Newt, 246
Glenn, John, 245
Goldwater, Barry, 237, 241
Gore, Albert, 198, 205
governing board, 161–2, 170, 177, 182, 223,
  259, 281, 284
Groton, Ct., 200

Hall, David, 236
Hausman (test), 125
Hayes, Michael, 191
Heckman, James, 286
Hedlund, Jay, 137, 184, 213, 220
Heflin, Howell, 242
Heinz, John, 231, 239
Hirschman, Albert, 148, 283

Hollings, Ernest, 242–3, 289
House Administration Committee, Election
  Subcommittee, 244
House Appropriations Committee, 200
 Subcommittee on Defense, 205
House Armed Services Committee, 198–9, 205
House Rules Committee, 199
Huwa, Randy, 82

information and citizen decision making,
  16, 18–21, 166, 176–8, 188, 257–9,
  263–4, 265, 268, 269
 activism and, 136–7, 139, 145, 147, 148–50,
  152, 157
 experiential search and, 17, 21–8
 joining and, 64–6, 87, 93, 95, 96
 retention and, 108, 109, 111, 113, 115–16,
  117, 120, 121, 123–4
integrated perspective, 4–6, 13, 15, 29, 262,
  266, 267
 internal politics and, 101, 124, 156–7,
  160, 171, 187–9
 joining and, 94
intercontinental ballistic missile (ICBM),
  171–2, 174, 198–9
internal politics (*see* activism, experiential
  search, integrated perspective, joining,
  leadership, member learning, retention,
  unified framework)
Isaac, John, 186, 201, 284

Jackson, Brooks, 290
Jennings, Peter, 250
joining (*see also* dues, efficacy (group),
  efficacy (personal), experiential search,
  integrated perspective, member
  learning, public interest groups, unified
  framework), 63–99, 273
Jondrow, James, 204

Kassebaum, Nancy, 243
Kau, James, 95–9, 271
Keating, Charles, 245
"Keating Five" ("Gang of Five"), 245–6
Kemp–Roth tax cut proposal, 236
Kingdon, John, 63
Krehbiel, Keith, 195
Kwajalein Missile Range, 238

Latham, Earl, 18
leadership (*see also* campaign finance, dues,
  efficacy (group), experiential search,
  lobbying, MX), 158–89
League of Women Voters, 13, 42, 56, 86–93,
  120–3, 137, 151–2
Leahy, Patrick, 200
learning (*see* member learning)
Lerman, Steven, 78
Letterman, David, 250

Levin, Carl, 200
lobbying, 9, 12, 52, 96, 104, 115, 162, 192–3, 276
  activism and, 134–5, 278, 280
  campaign finance and, 237–8, 249, 252–3
  influence of, 1–2, 3, 191–2, 209–15, 221–2
  MX and, 175, 184–5, 192–4, 200, 202
  strategy and determinants of, 194–6,
    203–5, 215–22
Lobbyists and Lawyers for Campaign
  Finance Reform, 225

Madison, James, 255
Manes, Susan, 249
Manski, Charles, 78
Mavroules, Nicholas, 199
Mawby, Michael, 202
McCain, John, 245
McConnell, Mitch, 231
McCurdy, Dave, 201
McFarland, Andrew, 162, 281, 283
member learning, 17, 24–8, 30, 100–8,
    257–8, 262
  activism and, 43, 136, 138–9, 140–2,
    145–9, 151–2, 154, 157, 279
  campaign finance and, 104
  checkbook activism and, 131, 133–4
  experiential search and, 20, 21–4, 28, 269
  group goals and, 176–9, 187, 283
  joining and, 65, 81–2, 87, 93–5
  MX and, 174, 222
  retention and, 108–11, 114–20, 123–4,
    126, 276, 277
Membership Issue Poll, 161–5, 167, 281
Michel, Robert, 245, 290
Michels, Robert, 176, 252, 274
Micronesia, 238
Midgetman missile, 198, 204, 226
Miller, Ellen, 238, 251
Missile Experimental (*see* MX)
Moe, Terry, 20, 136, 158–9, 269, 280, 284
Murkowski, Frank, 242
MX, 14
  campaign finance and, 223–9, 236, 237–9,
    249–54
  internal politics and, 170–5, 179–88, 260
  lobbying and, 190–222
  systemic impact and, 260–2
  viewing organizations and, 265–6

Nader, Ralph, 225
National Association of Business Political
  Action Committees, 241
National Election Study (NES), 13, 31, 34,
    39, 40–1, 270
  membership investigations and, 65, 75,
    77, 82, 96
  questions, wording in, 58–62
National Journal, 174

National Republican Senatorial Committee,
  239
new institutionalism, 6
New York Times, 173–4, 247
Nixon, Richard, 180
nuclear freeze (*see also* arms control), 181
Nunn, Sam, 198, 200–1, 205, 284

oligarchy, 1, 138, 140–2, 149, 176, 179, 188,
    274, 279, 280, 282
Olson, Mancur, 18–19, 26, 95, 100–1, 109,
    114–15, 136, 176, 179
O'Neill, Thomas, 199–200
organizational attributes, 70
organizational supply, 158–9

Packwood, Robert, 243, 285
Peacekeeper (*see* MX)
Percy, Charles, 198
Pertschuk, Michael, 193
pluralism (*see also* antipluralists), 100–1,
    176, 179
political action committees (PACs), 3, 9,
    174, 180, 192
  campaign finance and, 229, 231–41, 242,
    244–5, 253, 288, 290
  MX and, 206, 209, 286
Professionals' Coalition for Nuclear Arms
  Control, 284
Public Citizen, 95
public interest groups, 12–13, 160–1, 176,
    251–2, 266, 268, 283, 292
  activism and, 134, 140
  checkbook activism in, 130–1
  Common Cause as, 7–10, 29–30, 40, 42,
    255, 268
  experiential search and, 21, 24
  joining and, 66, 86–7, 273
  MX and, 190, 231–2
  retention and, 108–9, 114–15

rank and file (*see* activism, checkbook
  activism)
Rather, Dan, 250
Reagan, Ronald, 10, 171–2, 180–1, 186, 190,
    196, 200, 225, 238, 285
retention (*see also* activism, dues, experiential
  search, information and citizen
  decision making, integrated perspective,
  joining, leadership, member learning)
    100–1, 108–26, 276, 277
Riegle, Donald, 245
Rochester Democrat and Chronicle, 247, 288
Rubin, Paul, 95–9, 271

Salisbury, Robert, 283
SANE (A Citizen's Organization for a
  SANE World), 186, 202, 285
Scowcroft Commission, 198

Senate Armed Services Committee, 200
sequential search, 21
Shelby, Richard, 242
Shepsle, Kenneth, 196
singular value decomposition (SVD), 82,
    126, 272
Slaughter, Louise, 288
Smith, Richard, 191–2
soft money, 245
Soviet Union, 198
specific characteristics, 22
Stafford, Robert, 242
Stennis, John, 240
Stevens, Ted, 242
Stockmayer, Steven, 241
Strategic Defense Initiative, 201
sunset legislation, 52, 104
Swift, Al, 244, 290
Synar–Leach (campaign finance proposal),
    244–5
systemic supply, 159

temporal activism (*see* activism)
trucking, deregulation of, 170
Truman, David, 18, 274

unified framework, 13, 15–17, 28, 29, 63,
    124, 127, 177
Urban Coalition, 267

Vanderbilt Television News Abstracts, 13, 174
voter registration ("Motor Voter") bill, 244

Wall Street Journal, 289
Weicker, Lowell, 200
weighted exogenous sampling maximum
    likelihood estimation (WESML), 78–9,
    88, 99, 142, 279
Weingast, Barry, 196
Wertheimer, Fred, 9, 26, 161, 164, 181, 185,
    202, 236, 245, 247, 252
Wright, Jim, 173, 182, 290, 291
Wright, John, 191–2

"To my knowledge this is the first time someone has made the useful distinction between members, activists, and leaders in an interest group and actually produced data about the activists. I believe it is one of the best interest group studies ever done."

Andrew McFarland, University of Illinois at Chicago

The proliferation of interest groups in American politics has spawned heated debate about their role in the formulation of congressional policy and in U.S. government more generally. Important questions about how interest groups operate and particularly about how they arrive at their policy positions and what effects their lobbying efforts have on congressional decision making are in need of examination.

In this book Lawrence Rothenberg examines some of the most elusive aspects of interest group operations through an in-depth study of one of the largest interest groups in Washington, Common Cause. In developing an integrated theory of membership organizations, he asks such questions as: Why do members join a group? Who stays and who leaves and why? What is the nature of the relationships among the activists, the group leaders, and rank-and-file members? How do these relationships shape the lobbying policies of the group? And how is the lobbying impact of a group related to the nature of its membership? In addition, Rothenberg analyzes the impact the lobbying efforts of Common Cause have had, through case studies of the congressional vote on the MX missile system and efforts to enact a campaign finance reform bill.